Syria:
An Outline History

Syria:
An Outline History

John D Grainger

PEN & SWORD
HISTORY

Falkirk Council	
Askews & Holts	2016
956.91	£25.00

First published in Great Britain in 2016 by
Pen & Sword History
an imprint of
Pen & Sword Books Ltd
47 Church Street
Barnsley
South Yorkshire
S70 2AS

Copyright © John D Grainger 2016

ISBN 978 1 47386 081 0

The right of John D Grainger to be identified as the Author of this Work
has been asserted by him in accordance with the Copyright, Designs and
Patents Act 1988.

A CIP catalogue record for this book is available from the British Library

Typeset in Ehrhardt by
Mac Style Ltd, Bridlington, East Yorkshire
Printed and bound in the UK by CPI Group (UK) Ltd,
Croydon, CRO 4YY

Pen & Sword Books Ltd incorporates the imprints of Pen & Sword
Archaeology, Atlas, Aviation, Battleground, Discovery, Family History,
History, Maritime, Military, Naval, Politics, Railways, Select, Transport,
True Crime, and Fiction, Frontline Books, Leo Cooper, Praetorian Press,
Seaforth Publishing and Wharncliffe.

For a complete list of Pen & Sword titles please contact
PEN & SWORD BOOKS LIMITED
47 Church Street, Barnsley, South Yorkshire, S70 2AS, England
E-mail: enquiries@pen-and-sword.co.uk

Contents

Introduction

Syria achieved its name perhaps halfway through its life as an organized political entity (at least so far) when a careless, probably only semi-literate Greek, dropped the initial vowel from 'Assyria'. This must have been in the century and a half during which the Assyrian monarchs ruled 'Syria', between the ninth and the late seventh century BC. The Greeks could sail to the Syrian coast, and evidence of their presence exists in the frequent discovery of their pottery, and even in the names they bestowed on some of the coastal towns and villages of the country.

Thus by historical chance a name was invented for a land which did not have one, but which stuck because no other could be devised. It was applied to the land usually by foreigners like the Greeks (and the Romans and the Arabs and the Turks), but rarely by its inhabitants, who clung to the names of their smaller and distinct localities (Judah, Damascus, Lebanon, and so on) until Syria was adopted (by the foreign French) as the name of a fragment of the whole, and applied to the modern republic of that name by the French in 1919.

So 'Syria' is the most convenient label for the land at the eastern end of the Mediterranean Sea, whose coast was for long – another foreign label – described as the 'Levant'. No other term will serve, despite its modern connotations – and these are only a century old. It is thus a name which floats up and down, at times meaning the whole, at other times a part, but it is the only one which will do. But then we have the problem of what is the whole?

For Syria as a land is as difficult to delimit as it is to label. It is no good using the modern countries to describe it, because they are merely temporary, are constantly changing both in size and in their names and will presumably continue to do so.

It is, for example, very disappointing that some modern accounts dealing with 'Syria' in the ancient world restrict themselves to the boundaries of the modern republic.[1] To be sure, it is a relatively large area, but for any time before 1919 it makes no sense. In terms of the modern states in the region, the term Syria used here certainly includes the modern states of Lebanon, Syria, Israel, Jordan, and the Palestinian fragments. Yet this is still not good enough, for any objective geographical view insists that the boundaries of these states collectively include land which is not Syrian and exclude lands which are Syrian.

So we must resort to geography to discover the bounds of Syria. The western boundary is easy: the coast of the Mediterranean Sea is reassuringly straight. The south is not so difficult either: the Sinai Desert has usually been part of Egypt, so the boundary is somewhere between Gaza (Syrian) and Raphia (probably Egyptian), and the present Israeli-Egyptian border has repeatedly been used in the past. This area has been the scene of more than one battle between lords and rulers of Egypt and Syria, where the future of Syria rather than Egypt was at stake. The northern boundary is only a little more difficult. The complexity of the mountain ranges of the north gives one a series of choices of boundaries. Moving out from land which is certainly Syrian (and so north from Aleppo or Antioch) there are the Amanus, the Taurus, and the Anti-Taurus ranges, all linked and overlapping. The most decisive of these ranges is the Taurus, but using that as the boundary would mean including Kilikia in Syria, which has historically mainly been separate from Syria. It seems best to take a combination of the Amanus and the Taurus as the northern boundary, but bearing in mind that Kilikia and the mountain valleys and other similar parts of the north would often be reckoned as almost-Syria.

The eastern bounds are the most difficult; indeed, it is impossible to draw a line anywhere which is in any way satisfactory. In the northern sector the section of the River Euphrates where it flows more or less due south might be on a superficial view seen as a useful line, were it not that the land on each side of the river is much the same, and the river is fairly easy to cross and forms a zone of its own rather than a line of separation.

This region from the Taurus to Sinai has frequently in the past been treated as a whole; the boundary between Euphrates and Tigris has been the real problem. For the Persians of the Akhaimenid Empire, coming from the east, the Euphrates was the boundary, and Syria was Aber-Nahara, 'Beyond-the-River'; for the Romans, coming from the west, the boundary shifted gradually eastwards from the Euphrates in 60 BC to the Tigris by AD 200. For the Ottomans, coming from the north, the land was 'Suriye', and like the Roman boundary, it extended as far as the Upper Tigris. So the region between the rivers, the true Mesopotamia, was a region where the Syrian boundary fluctuated. It was called, for different reasons 'al-Jazirah' – 'the Frontier' – by the Arabs, and it is best to see it as such. In the event, the region, called indiscriminately Mesopotamia or al-Jazirah, will be taken as just that, an area which may or may not be included as circumstances dictate, though generally the valleys of the Khabour and the Tigris will be excluded.[2]

Southwards lies the desert, first called the 'Syrian' desert, which then becomes the 'Arabian' desert at some indefinable place. Some of the oases, notably Palmyra, are to be called Syrian, even though closer to Iraq. But again it is hopeless to draw a firm line. The desert boundary must be considered as a zone. So the whole eastern boundary of Syria is a variable space, the line, if a line must be drawn, varying with political power and cultural preference.

This is a relatively small land, a country perhaps 200mi. (300km) wide from the coast inland, and about 600mi. (1,000km) from north to south: smaller than any of its more geographically well defined neighbours – Egypt, Iraq, Turkey – smaller than France, about the size of England or Virginia. Yet its people have been most astonishingly productive of ideas and inventions. It was in this area that farming (and pastoral stock raising, and dog-domestication) was invented; it was here that the alphabetical writing system was devised, with letters whose original shapes are recognizable today; it was here that monotheistic religion was invented; it was from here that a small section of the population explored all the Mediterranean from end to end, and ventured into the Atlantic, and sailed around Africa 2,000 years before Vasco da Gama.

These are surely sufficient achievements for one country so that its history needs to be investigated. But when one does a curious pattern emerges. Syria has gone through a strange historical process, alternately subdivided into small states and then united. It was in the periods of the small states, in a version of neo-liberal competitiveness perhaps, that the inventiveness took place; and the periods of unity were always imposed from outside, usually brutally, since the Syrians resented – to the point of effectively committing political suicide – being conquered, in a process which required their political and physical destruction. (They show no willingness to knuckle under even now, as the long Palestinian resistance to Israeli conquest and the bitter fighting in Syria and Lebanon has shown.) Never has Syria been united by its own people, always by foreigners – including the descendants of our semi-literate Greek.

Within the bounds thus set out in all their vagueness, Syria is geographically complex, varied, difficult, and much divided. Left to itself it is a land in which relatively small areas are able to develop in independence; when not left to themselves this multiplication of small sections renders it possible to subdue the whole, as Egyptians, Assyrians, Babylonians, Persians, Macedonians, Romans, Arabs, Turks and British have discovered.

The essential geographical element which determines all else in the interior is the mountain ranges which parallel the Mediterranean coast. These are, from south to north, the Judean Hills, Galilee, Lebanon, the Jebel Ansarieh (or Jebel Alawiyeh) and the Amanus. As this catalogue of names indicates these mountains are not continuous, but are separated by lower areas, sometimes by no more than a narrow pass, though these do permit penetration from the coast to the lands east of the mountains. But, further, the mountains themselves are separated into two parallel ranges by the Great Rift Valley which spreads up from Africa. So the Judean Hills are split from the trans-Jordanian plateaux by the great ditch of the Dead Sea and the Jordan Valley; the Lebanon is separated from its fellow range, the Antilebanon, by the Bekaa Valley; the Jebel Ansarieh is separated from the low plateaux to the east by the hollow of the Ghab (a formerly marsh region, now drained) and the middle course of the Orontes River; the Amanus is separated by the valley of the Aksu from the low plateaux to the east.

In such conditions the courses and actions of the rivers become crucial for communications. Almost all the rivers flow from north to south but the Orontes does the opposite, using the intermontane valleys east of the Lebanon and the Jebel Ansarieh, and then turns due west to break through the mountains to reach the sea; it thus provides a useful route into the northern interior. The Eleutheros and the Litani rivers are relatively short but also provide important routes from the sea into the interior between the Jebel Ansarieh and the Lebanon and through the Lebanon. These are not routes formed by the rivers, but they are geological faults which are exploited by the rivers. The Litani has its source only just south of that of the Orontes, but flows in the opposite direction, southwards, and then also breaks through the mountains to reach the sea near Tyre; a third river originates about the same place as the other two, the Barada, and then flows south and then east, forming a gorge which provides a difficult route from the Bekaa into the great Damascus oasis, the Ghuta.

In the south the Jordan occupies the Rift Valley, but few rivers of any size are in Palestine. There the Galilean and the Judaean Hills are separated by a wider area of lowland, the Vales of Esdraelon and Jezreel, linking the northern Palestinian coast with the Jordan Valley. The Judean Hills gradually lose height to the south, so that it is relatively easy to reach the Rift Valley south of the Dead Sea from the area of Gaza – except that this is a desert route. It will be seen that not only is Syria complex and awkward geographically, but nothing in the land is easy.

The Jordan empties into the Dead Sea, heavily salt. This is the typical fate of many Syrian rivers. The Barada flows into the desert, ending in two small lakes; two rivers in the north, the Quweiq and the Afrin end in salt lakes. The Orontes twice seems to attempt the same end, in the marshes of the Ghab east of the Jebel Ansariyeh and in the Amuq Lake, but achieves its end by way of the mountain gap west of Antioch. The greatest of the southward flowing rivers is the Euphrates, which has the melting snows of Anatolia to give it the strength to reach the sea at the Persian Gulf. It is joined by two other rivers from the Taurus, the Balikh and the Khabour, whose waters help to make parts of the Jazirah liveable.

The basic physical geography has had decisive effects on the climate in many parts of Syria. The line of mountains along the coast intercepts the regular succession of climatic depressions which funnel eastwards along the Mediterranean between the autumn and spring seasons. The Lebanon Mountains are high enough to have a regular snow cover in the winter, and snow is not that uncommon in other highland areas – at Jerusalem in the Judaean Hills, for example. This, however, also means that the land 'behind' – that is, east of – the mountains are in their 'rain-shadow', so the annual precipitation in the inland areas is a fraction of that of the mountains. At the same time, the gaps between the coastal mountain ranges do admit the wetter air into the interior, so that the precipitation tends to penetrate further inland to the east of those gaps. Even fairly narrow mountain gaps, such as that of the Orontes, can have a significant effect. Generally, however, even in those places the annual rainfall is not heavy enough to permit the cultivation of rain-fed crops very far inland.

This clearly has its effects on the lives of the people. Not only is the physical geography of the country thoroughly divided into relatively small and discontinuous regions by the mountains and the Rift Valley and the rivers, but the local climates intensify this divisive effect. Once again, Syria emerges as a much fragmented land, one which in the normal political and economic circumstances forms a set of relatively small regions. These have been, and were, the bases of all the states when the land is independent – or rather composed of independent polities – but are depressingly liable to conquest from outside, being relatively small and so weak.

NB As will have been realized in this introduction, I will use certain geographical terms in particular senses:

'Syria' is the land from the Taurus to Sinai;

'Mesopotamia' is the land between the Euphrates and the Upper Tigris, the Arab Jazirah;

'Babylonia' is the modern Iraq, a term also used;

'Palestine' is the land from the Ladder of Tyre to Sinai.

None of these are to be taken as indicating any present political preference.

Chapter 1

Origins

We may begin in the Ice Age. One of the effects of the accumulation of masses of frozen water in the ice sheets of the northern hemisphere and on the highest mountains was to lower the level of the sea by several tens of metres. As it happens this had only a marginal effect on Syria because the sea bottom plunges steeply at the coast. The coast therefore advanced westwards only a few kilometres or even less. But another effect was to deflect southwards the track of the climatic depressions which now flow from the Atlantic into western and particularly into south-western Europe all the year round, but mainly in spring and autumn. This in fact happens even now in the Mediterranean in the winter, when cyclonic storms funnel along the sea, pushed south by the high pressure which builds over Eurasia in the cold weather. During the Ice Age this high pressure was the norm in all seasons, and so the wet storms came.

Given the flow of these moisture-laden depressions, the cooler temperature generally (perhaps 8 or 10°C lower generally than now), and the high mountains along the Syrian coast, Syria's weather was drastically different than it is today. The Lebanese mountains were permanently snow covered, and housed glaciers, the quantity of rain in the coastlands was much increased, and the penetration of rainstorms inland beyond the mountains was much greater and more effective. The rivers were full and powerful, cutting down the present deep valleys, finding their way through the hills by opening up faults and wearing away at them – the Orontes especially. The snow and ice cover guaranteed year-round water flows. Rains were heavy and happened in all seasons.

This all meant that the deserts were smaller than now. Much of inland Syria was tree-covered, and the steppe lands behind the coastal mountains spread far to the south. The animal life included large beasts up to and including mammoths, which could find enough food because of the increased vegetation. And the animal life included at least two varieties of mankind – *Homo neanderthalis* and *Homo sapiens* – though by the end of the Ice Age, only the latter survived.

The Ice Age ended in a mixture of sudden rises in temperature – sometimes raised only for a time, with the occasional relapse – and a gradual thaw. The effect in Europe was to open up the Arctic margins to colonization by trees as the great ice sheets retreated northwards; in Syria the effect was even more drastic. The water-laden depressions became less frequent, and eventually became solely winter phenomena as now; the summers became dry and hot; the mountain glaciers and snows melted, and the rivers after a time of great power as the snows melted, were less full; and from its refuge in southern Arabia the desert spread north.

The vegetation changed. Deciduous trees retreated northwards and uphill and were replaced by spikier, tougher, Mediterranean trees such as olive and terebinth and carob; the treeline in the mountains climbed to colonize the melting snowfields. Inland, trees were replaced by grasslands. Moving eastwards therefore one would find, as now, a fairly well-watered (except in summer) coastal area populated by a variety of trees, then a region of grasslands, the steppe, and lastly the encroaching and invading desert. Always bearing in mind, of course, that the complex physical geography of the land meant there were areas where changes were either less drastic or more so.

For the human inhabitants, of course, this would have been an incremental disaster. Their customary processes of gathering food, either by hunting or by foraging, became in some areas steadily more difficult and time-consuming. Some of their campsites – they were all nomadic – became uncomfortable, either by a decreasing access to water in a dry landscape, or by the disappearance of the game whose earlier presence had been the purpose of choosing the camping site. Rivers and streams dried up and vanished; lakes disappeared or became intermittent – or salt, as their waters evaporated.

The people had in fact several choices for coping with this period of drying and warming. The obvious one was to leave, following the game, which tended to withdraw northwards, searching for the water, a process which would probably mean leaving the interior for the wetter coastlands. They could resort to violence, driving away other humans whom they would see as competitors for the increasingly scarce resources. Or they could stay (or resist eviction) and make do. It is the last group that was the most important for the future, both for Syria and for other humans.

A final alternative, of course, was that they could simply die, and no doubt starvation accomplished this in places. However, there were obviously relatively few people in the country, and all of them were mobile, and the changes in the climate were relatively slow, so it is unlikely that either violence against others or death by starvation was at all common. Some families, however, certainly moved away, into other nearby lands where the rains were larger, longer, or more persistent. Studies of human remains in Palestine have linked them with remains from Europe, or, alternatively, from Africa – presumably meaning Egypt – emphasizing how mobile these populations were.

It was the people who remained in Syria who devised a new way of life which enabled them to produce enough food to allow them to survive. They resorted to consuming some of the foods which had sustained the animals they had hunted. Most of these animals were herbivores, grass browsers. Grass, of course, is insufficient to sustain humans, but the foragers knew well enough that the seeds of some grasses contained a usable food resource, once broken open. In a series of inventions spread over perhaps a thousand years the practices of agriculture – not eating all the harvest, but keeping some back to plant and grow in the next year, digging and planting, reaping and threshing, grinding the seeds, and the processing of the flour taken from the seed, from milling to baking, were all worked out.

Not only was this all done as a result of a series of bright ideas developed by the erstwhile foragers – probably mainly by the women – but it was a process which occurred almost simultaneously all over Syria and in the hills overlooking the valleys of the Tigris and Euphrates. The several communities of the region remained nomadic for a long time, and their various ideas were passed around between groups when they met. Periodic meetings, feasts, and marriages – exogamy was probably normal – will have produced a wide understanding of the geography of the whole region, of the changes taking place in the climate (even if not why) and of the best means of coping with the problematic times. Because these people were poor in material resources and lived long ago we must not imagine they were slow of understanding or unwilling to adopt changes.

In Syria we know this was happening in Palestine as early as perhaps 10,500 BC, within a thousand years of the beginning of the end of the Ice Age. This comparatively rapid reaction to the change in the climate is a measure of the stress on the local environment produced by these changes. The type site is at Wadi en-Natuf in Palestine, where a small temporary settlement has been excavated, showing a group of huts (or at least the rings of stones laid down as foundations and to pin down the roofs, which were probably of hide). The huts had hearths, and evidence of tools clearly used to harvest grasses was found. The most telling artefact is a knife from Ain Mallaha (Eynan) near the Sea of Galilee, whose blade has the characteristic shiny deposit produced when grass is cut; the knife was of bone; its handle was carved to imitate the head of an animal. These people might have invented agriculture – and if they did not do so then they quickly adopted it from those who had – but they were not about to give up hunting for meat.[1]

This small, and briefly occupied, set of huts is the precursor of the other developments which agriculture produced. The first, of course, was a more stable food supply, combined with the determination and willpower to store food for later use rather than consume it right away. For the supply was not mobile, unlike the animals which the new farmers' ancestors had followed and hunted, and which to a degree they still did. Rather, their stationary food supply – the fields – had to be guarded against those very animals. In a way this was surely a welcome development, since if the animals tried to get at the fields of cultivated grasses, they were that much easier to hunt. But the balance of nutrition now shifted from meat to vegetable foods, and the greater value of the farmers' produce required that the community becomes immobile, and is settled at one place. At first no doubt this was regarded as purely temporary, until the field could be harvested, and a new field would be sown later elsewhere, but it will have quickly become obvious that some places were better than others for producing food – indeed it is likely that it took no more than a moment's thought to appreciate this. The end result was a village, more or less permanent. Many of these probably lie at the bases of the innumerable tells which are so widely distributed throughout Syria.

Natufian sites are found scattered throughout Palestine and Jordan, spread from the Negev northwards, favouring no particular area, though the Jordan Valley and the coast south of the Carmel Ridge seem popular. The accumulation of dots on a map makes it look as though the region was well populated, but this is misleading since none of the settlements was occupied for more than a generation. Perhaps the longest lasting was Jericho, but even that was abandoned. The Damascus oasis, the Ghuta, had been a lake in the wet years and when this was reduced to the two small lakes now remaining several Natufian settlements appeared. On the coast of Palestine at Wadi Fallah/Nahal Oren a village of at least fourteen houses was built – implying a population of perhaps fifty. Similar temporary villages, possibly on sides reoccupied over several growing seasons, are at Ain Mallaha in the Huleh Valley in northern Palestine, at Mureybat in the Euphrates Valley, and at Abu Hureyra nearby. Further east the Upper Khabour, where several streams flow from the hills eventually to unite in the Khabour River, was the area for other sites of the Natufian type. Excavators have detected some differences between the various groups of settlements, occasioning academic disputes, but overall they are very similar; differences are hardly surprising in such a divided land.[2]

The early results of the development of agriculture were an increase in the population, because of the more stable food source and the less dangerous lifestyle compared with hunting, and the permanent or semi-permanent settlement of that population in one place; the two together produced populated villages which in favoured cases grew into settlements large enough to be called towns. Most of these were, however, only permanent in the sense that they lasted several generations. All were eventually abandoned, sometimes after only a single season, no doubt to be replaced by another and similar village not far off, where the people pursued much the same way of life. In the absence of any explicit testimony as to the reasons for the abandonment, soil exhaustion is perhaps best assumed.

Hunting, however, was by no means abandoned. Men continued to search out and take their toll of the herbivores. Cattle, goats, and above all gazelles, were hunted and killed. The gazelles in fact had established a regular migration pattern from south to north and back again, which was the opportunity for them to be attacked by the hunters as they passed. At Abu Hureyra the gazelles contributed overwhelmingly to the meat diet.[3] Some of the smallest Natufian sites, lasting a few days only, and in places not good for farming, are assumed to have been hunters' camps.

The series of developments which shifted the Syrian population from a complete reliance on hunting to a heavy dependence on agriculture, took several millennia to work through. At Abu Hureyra, for example, it was not until the mid-eighth millennium that goats and sheep displaced gazelles as the main meat source – and so that domesticated animals replaced hunted. The expansion of the population was inevitably slow. Amongst hunters the span of life is normally little more than thirty or so years, just long enough to reproduce; few of them ever became old; many of the youngest did not survive. Living an agricultural life at first made little difference, particularly to the women who, in addition to the constant dangers of pregnancy and childbirth, had to do much of the agricultural work; the men were still hunters, and then became the herders, and as pressure on resources developed as the climate became hotter and drier, they had to guard the crops against all enemies, had to build, make tools, plough, herd animals (who were domesticated out of the former hunters' prey) and do much of the heavy harvest work. Agriculture as a way of life may have resulted in a much more dependable food supply, but it came at the cost of a more laborious work style.

The Natufian is one of the earliest agricultural cultures, but it existed at much the same time as other similar cultures spread over the whole region from Sinai to the Zagros Mountains. Archaeologists give several names of these groups based on minute differences in their finds. 'Natufian' tends to be confined as a label to Syria from the Sinai to the Euphrates, but similar cultural developments existed throughout the Middle East. These are also grouped into an overall culture called the 'Pre-Pottery Neolithic' – 'Neolithic' being the usual term for Stone Age farmers. Pottery was invented and developed partway through this cultural sequence, one of the several cumulative changes which took place over several millennia.

The geography of this culture follows the presence of water. The villages are spread across the north Syrian steppeland and along the better-watered coastlands as far south as Sinai. Apart from the better food supply this greater stability also encouraged the development of architecture and the invention of useful tools and products (such as pottery). In fact pottery is a good example of the way innovation occurred.

The earliest pottery was of poor quality, with far too much temper included, usually of chaff, so that the finished product tended to crumble away. Clay, of course, had been used for various purposes in the past (figurines, hooks, plaster) – and even some bowls of plaster ('white ware') had preceded pottery, as had baskets lined with this plaster, or made of hide. There was clearly a demand for containers. Making a hollow pot was now possible, and soon became a necessity. Probably the idea originated in Anatolia; what therefore arrived in Syria was the idea, not the actual pottery. From the start the pots were produced for domestic use, no doubt to hold water and store food. Every settlement at first had its own types, shapes, and decoration of pot – decoration appears from the very beginning. All this strongly suggests that once again it was the women who were the inventors. Fairly quickly improvements resulted in better tempers – grits especially – standard shapes and more robust fabrics, but also a great variety of these. Not only that but the shapes and decoration appears as very similar over wide areas.[4] The development of pottery is a testimony to the inventive interchange of ideas – and no doubt of people – throughout Syria. The preceding attempts to make containers – baskets, white ware, hide bags, also testify to experimentation.

The manufacture of pottery required also the ability to construct kilns (the early pottery was probably baked in the open), to select the most suitable clays, and to shape the clay into predictable forms. When the kilns were invented, the potters developed the ability to control the heat inside the kiln in order to ensure the optimum condition of the finished pots and to ensure that the decoration, when paint was applied, was of the anticipated colour. Thus a whole series of new skills was developed – the use of heat in particular would be crucial in the future manufacture of metal goods. The use of pottery also had its effect on the human users, giving them the ability to store food and water, to cook in more ways than simply in a fire.

The people were thus capable, as their successors have also been, of innovating, and of accepting innovations; they could think big and carry out large-scale projects, such as the recently discovered Gobekli Tepe stone circle in the Jazirah. The society may have had chiefs and certainly had specialists – good potters, for example, and especially skilled hunters – but there are signs that each village was itself a unit of government. Some were no doubt controlled by chiefs, but this was not necessarily the obvious form of government. At Jerf al-Ahmar on the east bank of the Euphrates was found a circular building, sunk 2m into the ground, and the walls lined with stone. Vertical beams inset into the walls supported a roof. A bench a metre wide ran round the building inside the wall; six posts, placed equidistantly supported the roof, which was no doubt of poles and thatch with a central hole for light. The walls were plastered and decorated; the bench was lined by stones which were carved with geometrical decorations.[5]

This building illustrates many aspects of the society of about 8,700 BC. The design is clearly one for a community meeting place – there was no indication of domestic occupation. It was well constructed and must have lasted quite a number of years; it was also elegant and pleasing to the eye; being sunk in the earth and shaded by a roof, it was probably cool in the summer. It had been a communal activity both to build it and was surely used for communal meetings. The design implies all this. What discussions took place is not known; religious ritual is possible, though there was no evidence of this. Much more likely it was the scene of village meetings where communal discussions took place and decisions were made. The form of government implied is, given the small size of the community, democratic; there was enough room in the meeting house to accommodate all the heads of families of the village.

These people were as artistic as they were practical, with painted plaster on their house walls, highly decorated pottery, well made tools of stone (and probably of wood). They carved figurines of animals and people in wood and stone, and moulded them of plaster or clay, models which they no doubt treasured and displayed. They built secure houses, and communal buildings, often with an eye to pleasing form. The people may have had comparatively short lives, but they were also, it seems, comparatively rich in both material things and cultural matters.

The nomadic style of life had thus been changed into one in which the majority of the people stayed in only one place for their whole lives. And yet they could not exist only on what they produced for themselves. Trade was necessary, and had existed in some form or another since the Ice Age, and probably before. (The importation of the idea of pottery from Anatolia is an example.) Some stones, for example, were particularly useful for making tools. Of these one of the easiest to recognize is the smooth, shiny black of obsidian, which holds a sharp edge even better than flint; it is also very attractive to look at, and perhaps this was as strong an attraction as its quality as a cutting tool or an arrow point. It is also relatively easy for archaeologists to detect its origin, and many of the examples found in Syria were carried there from sources in Anatolia.[6] Trade in obsidian carried examples as far as coastal Palestine. Living in one place did not result in a total ignorance of the rest of the world outside Syria, and probably many of the people knew a good deal about Syria itself.

The populations of the farms and villages and towns were stable and even growing slowly in numbers, and they were obviously descended from the original Ice Age hunting population whose successors had invented farming. They instituted an area of notably productive agriculture, but there is no sign of, and no reason to believe that, they were supplemented by migration from outside the country, other than a movement out of the expanding desert areas into the lands where agriculture was possible, and the arrival of occasional adventurous travellers and traders. The population grew by natural reproduction, not by invasion and immigration.

This is not to say that there was no violence. In a population descended from and including hunters, violence is only to be expected, and one of the earliest settlements, at Jericho, had elements of fortification about it. Rectangular building forms quickly replaced the circular huts of the Ice Age and the Natufians, probably because, once dried bricks began to be used for construction, such a building shape was now logical – but circular forms were not forgotten and seem to have been used for particularly important buildings, such as the circular meeting place at Jerf al-Ahmar. Rectangular buildings were often built with common party walls, so that from the outside the village presented the aspect of a blank wall (with entrance to rooms from the roof and by ladders), but this apparent fortification may be merely an accident of the architecture; such places were usually surrounded by workplaces such as pottery kilns and threshing floors outside the walls. Nevertheless, one may assume that fighting took place, and that leaders emerged.

A good deal of anthropological speculation has been undertaken to produce theories of the operation and organization of these Natufian societies. Often this tends to wander off into the wilder reaches of theory, losing touch with the ground reality. For the reality is archaeological findings, and that can only provide some facts – such as the circular meeting place at Jerf al-Ahmar (which, of course, may have been nothing of the sort). Certain assumptions seem reasonable. Once semi-permanent villages were established some sort of local government became necessary. Those circular meeting huts suggest an egalitarian society. If a region succumbed to violence, leaders or chiefs probably emerged.[7] But none of this is in any way apparent in the archaeological remains. Settlements were regularly abandoned after a shorter or a longer time, and whether the whole population transferred as a unit to a new site, or dissolved into family units, each of which went their own way, is not known; in either case it is likely that any earlier political organization was shaken up.

There are some settlements which did last a considerable time. At Tell el-Kerkh near the Orontes in Northeast Syria, the archaeologists have detected fourteen successive villages built one on the other, in total lasting some centuries.[8] In Palestine the introduction of pottery tended to the simultaneous with an increasing dependence on agriculture and a reduction in the practice of hunting – but the settlements were no more permanent than elsewhere.[9] For example at Tell Ramad in the Damascus Ghuta, occupied during three phases and for at least five centuries, a length of time which has to be regarded as 'permanent', the source of food for the inhabitants shifted away from hunting; but in the last phase, the place seems to have become merely a month a hunters' camp. It also seems that much of the Ghuta was abandoned during the sixth millennium.[10]

Despite a series of cultural names being applied to all these villages and village societies, essentially they are all much the same. There is, of course, a good deal of variation within the overall culture, and local differences are to be expected. When pottery was being adopted, almost every village produced its own type, until exchange and experiment sorted out a regular set of shapes, sized, and decoration. The sizes of settlements, dependent as they were on the fertility of the land and the reliability of water supplies, tended to be similar. Everywhere there was a constant need at variable periods to shift the site of the village, for whatever reason, and it would be reasonable to assume a similar variation in government and authority, material possessions and beliefs.

The process of settlement in the well-watered territories separated off those who became farmers from those who continued the wholly nomadic life of hunting and herding in the drier lands. It also emphasizes the localizing forces inherent in the much dissected geography of Syria. This is reflected in the archaeologists' recognition of the different Neolithic cultures, named from typical sites in distinct regions – Jericho, for example, in the Jordan Valley, Mureybat by the Euphrates, and so on.

There is however also some indication of the development of a series of regional centres, each surrounded by smaller settlements. Tell el-Kerkh is one of these, another is at Tell Halula near the Euphrates; further east was a site called Sabi Abyad.[11] In Palestine a group of sites close under Carmel has been suggested as one such. All of these lasted longer than usual and were larger than other contemporary sites. On the other hand, they were also in particularly favourable agricultural areas, and so could be expected to grow larger than most sites; nor does this necessarily mean a great deal so far as society or politics is concerned. It would be possible to assume that each of these larger places exercised some sort of political hegemony over its surrounding villages, but of this there is no evidence. Possibly they were active market centres for the immediate region, but again no such evidence is known. And in the end they faded away and became deserted like all the other sites around them, big or small.

It is possible that their fading away was the result of a change in the climate. About 6,200 BC there began a temporary cold phase which was marked in Syria by a reduction in rainfall. Several areas were abandoned about this time, including much of the Damascus Ghuta and the Amuq Plain in the north; the crisis may have forced the dispersal of the larger sites like that at Tell Halula because of a new shortage of resources.

The climate recovered from about 5,800 BC, and it is after this a type of pottery called, from its first identification, Halaf ware, spread across the north of Syria. This is essentially a type of pottery whose style was adopted over much of the Jazirah in the sixth millennium. Behind this pottery type, however, other elements of life were little different from other regions, at least in the archaeological record. It may be supposed, however, that other elements besides a style of pottery were transferred through the region, and the adoption of the new style indicates that innovation was generally acceptable everywhere. Archaeologists have decided that the whole ensemble merits the name of 'Halaf Culture'. (It is, of course, highly unlikely that Tell Halaf was in fact the place of origin of the culture.)

The people of Syria therefore inhabited a country which promoted the division of the population and enhanced their localism. This was a result of their settlement on permanent sites, but at the same time these local societies were open to influences from elsewhere, perhaps especially since they were often on the move, and so would more likely encounter other groups on their travels. Travel between the several sections of the country, though never precluded or impossible, as the evidence of the movement of goods and cultural traits (and ideas) shows, was generally awkward and slow, and the self-containment of the inhabitants as well as the necessity they were under to work close to home, further restricted their adventurousness. For example, the first beast of burden, the donkey, was not domesticated until much later; until then, transport of goods had to be by human porter, or by boat. When the time came that the political divisions were clear, this geographical division was reflected in it. It also had its effect on the religion professed by the Syrians.

They had inherited from the deep past a set of assumptions by which natural phenomena were assigned a divine origin or purpose, to be enticed or appeased as seemed necessary. The Ice Age hunters were as sensitive to weather as any farmer or sailor, and passed on their beliefs in the spirits of thunder, of rain, of the sun, of wind, of the moon, and so on. The geography of Syria also stimulated the identification of local spirits of place – rivers, water sources, mountains, forests, especially in a time of change, when local conditions might alter drastically – and when such change had become expected. When these spirits became visible in the written record (in the third millennium BC), there were about seventy of them at one place, all of them identified as gods and spirits by this time by the Syrian people. If it can be assumed that the Ice Age had perhaps half a dozen of these deities, the elaboration had taken place in Syria by the farmers.

In this they were really in much the same way as their neighbours in Egypt, in Babylonia, in Anatolia, and probably everywhere else in attributing special powers to the natural phenomena whose actions and effects they could not explain. The names for the gods were different, of course, but the attribution of the spirits to the dominant natural phenomena was very similar. The geographical organization of these neighbouring lands was different, distinct from each other and from Syria, so a different emphasis on particular spirits emerged in each land. In Egypt the sun, the river, and the desert were the predominant local natural forces, and so these became the most important gods – notably the sun, which, for anyone who has felt the heat of an Egyptian summer, is readily understandable; the total reliance for life itself on the Nile's water, and the obvious hostility of the desert is equally clear in an Egyptian context. In Babylonia, the waters of the great rivers, and the thundering mountains to the east and north had their own effects on the local beliefs. But in both lands the generally uniform geography produced a generally uniform hierarchy, though the existence of the early city-states and dynasties in Babylonia meant that each of them – cities and kings – identified themselves with particular gods or goddesses. One result was that the relative importance of individual gods tended to shift with the political balance among the cities: Babylon's Marduk, for example, only became widely important when Babylon itself became important, presumably on the assumption that the city's success was in part due to the power of its particular god.

Syria's set of gods also tended to become attached to localities, with particular gods becoming emphasized as a result of local needs. At the same time the functions of the gods clearly became mixed, and in individual cases they shifted. One example is Athlit who was a goddess of the desert but when she was adopted into the pantheon of the city of Ugarit (Ras Shamra) on the Mediterranean coast she became both the consort of the great god El, the mother of many of the other gods, and the lady who trod the sea. The shift from desert to sea seems startling, but not too much so when it is recognized that both environments were regarded as barren and hostile and dangerous by the people of Ugarit, and that by bringing the lady into their pantheon and elevating her to the highest place, she was symbolically being defused of her hostility (and hence that of the desert and the sea as well). Gods could be emphasized at different times – Baal was a warrior god, though originally a weather god, and became important at Ugarit as the city came under serious threat during the last two centuries of its existence.[12]

The best collection of information about the Syrian gods is in the pantheon of Ugarit, which is listed in an inscribed tablet which dates from about 1500 BC, though there are also earlier records of individual members. Dagon (or Dagan) was a popular god in the middle Euphrates a thousand years earlier, and was brought into the Babylonian pantheon by the great conqueror Sargon (active about 2300 BC). He was also one of the principal gods of Ebla about the same time. And Dagon/Dagan survived as the most important god of the cities of the Philistines in the Iron Age in the first millennium BC; in other words he was a Syrian-wide deity and was eventually the particular choice of god by the Philistines. Even earlier than Sargon, at Ebla Reshep was one of the most senior gods, where he functioned as a patron of the king; later he was both the god who brought pestilence and the healer; the god of the city, however, was Dagan; again the separation implies a particular political choice, not to say enmity.[13]

All this can be confusing, and can easily be made more so with only a little effort, but it only means that the senate of the gods in Syria was as malleable as in Babylonia or elsewhere and was composed of gods who were common to all Syria. The same gods, possibly with differing powers, perhaps in different locations within the general hierarchy, maybe with new or altered attributes, were worshipped (or cursed) throughout Syria from the time we can see them in any sort of record, until the campaigns of Christians to suppress them. They were, that is, the gods who were accepted by the people, a popular religion, even if particular cities and kings picked out and emphasized their own favourites. There were intellectual attempts to formalize their powers, their relationships, and so on, at various times, but only some of this penetrated down to the ordinary population. So at Ugarit at the time of King Niqmaddu, by his order, the myths and histories and stories of the gods were all written down on the tablet mentioned above. He used a script specially invented for the occasion (an alphabetic cuneiform) and the tablets were stored in the house of the priest next to the two temples (of Baal and Dagon) which were built on top of the old tell. But this version of the religion disappeared when the city of Ugarit was destroyed about two centuries later – always supposing that anyone after Niqmaddu could read his special script.[14]

These gods, however, did not disappear, and they continued to be worshipped in the rest of Syria, and it is reasonable to assume that they were the self-same deities that had formed the Syrian pantheon from the beginning of the cultivation of agriculture. From the initial few who were related to natural phenomena, they were elaborated in number and attributes over many millennia, their interrelationships and their positions in the hierarchy of the gods could be changed, but they were essentially the same deities as at the beginning. This was a religion which had lasted at least 10,000 years when it was finally suppressed.

The burial or other disposal of the dead is usually seen as an aspect of religion. The ancient Syrians generally practiced burial by inhumation, often within their communities, and frequently actually inside their houses. The interpretation of the various practices is as speculative as are most archaeological revelations, though the general assumption has been that the dead were regarded in most cases with respect, and in some cases with reverence. It was normal to give them gifts (a boon to archaeologists); this might be merely a matter of sentiment, or it might be a present to see the dead on a journey to another dimension. The existence of a concept of heaven (or hell) is not attested. On the other hand, the number of dead recovered in excavations is nowhere near enough to account for the whole of the inhabitants in Syria over several millennia. Either many graves have not been found, or some of the dead were disposed of negligently.

Research into the language of Ugarit and other early Semitic dialects suggests that the original language of Syrians developed in a time when the speakers knew agriculture, but had no metals. This puts the emergence of the language into the earliest Neolithic period when people were learning to farm, domesticating sheep and cattle, but were still hunters. Since these were the characteristics of the Natufians it is evident that the original language, which was no doubt fully serviceable for a hunting and foraging people, was elaborated and developed under the necessity of describing their new work and society. The Semitic languages were spoken in all Arabia as far north as the Taurus and as far east as the Zagros Mountains. The desert peoples and their farmer neighbours in these lands were the same people and spoke the same language, and there was clearly communication not only between these two, but the length of the Levantine coastal region. The relationship between the languages called Northwest Semitic – those spoken in Syria – is close enough to imply continual interaction for millennia. The other major group of Semitic dialects – East Semitic (Akkadian, for example) in Babylonia, and the early Arabic spoken in southern Arabia – developed somewhat independently, but were clearly from the same original language pool. (They were also related to several North African languages, including Egyptian; the separation clearly took place early, probably before the development of agriculture in both regions; earlier assumptions were that these relationships were the result of population movements in the pre-literate millennia,[15] but this can only be an assumption, and archaeology does not, and probably cannot, confirm it; archaeological fashion, however, is now firmly against any invasion theories.)

Once again, as with the religion and the geography, we are already contemplating a single people spread over the whole of Syria; the divergence of 'Syrian Semitic', Akkadian, and Arabian Arabic eventually produced a series of languages which were not mutually intelligible, but the basic 'Semitic-ness' – the very similar structure and inflection of the languages – of all these (and other) dialects allowed new languages to be adopted throughout Syria, as by Amorite, then Aramaic, then Arabic. (Arabic of course has now fractured in the same way, into several different Arabic dialects, which are, again, unintelligible to each other. And yet in some things, any modern Arab could understand an Akkadian from 3000 BC – in the count from one to ten, for example.)

The influence of external societies was minimal during the Neolithic. If there was any it seems to have been mainly from Anatolia – obsidian in trade, pottery – for neither Egypt nor the Iraqi region was yet wealthy enough to exert much influence. It is likely that there was contact, at least between Palestine and northern Egypt, and much more probably between northern Syria and Iran and southern Iraq (as the wide adoption of Halaf pottery suggests), though precision in locating evidence is absent. This was to change from the fifth millennium onwards.

Chapter 2

Foreign Influence

The Halaf Culture, recognized by its pottery style but showing few other changes in the way of life of Syrian villagers, was succeeded by the slow adoption of a different pottery style, based on a type developed in southern Iraq, and called, from the type site where it was recognized, 'Ubaid'. The style spread over north Syria from about 5200 BC onwards, being accepted at villages with greater or lesser enthusiasm over the next thousand years or so. In the past it had been identified as introduced by invaders, now it is accepted as being merely influential, though associated in some degree with some cultural and technological changes. It had as little, or as much, effect on the local population as the Halaf ware, though the new pottery was produced on a slow potters' wheel, one of the new technological effects.[1]

The Ubaid period was a time of the usual desertion of old settlements, movement of peoples, and foundation or refoundation of new villages, but perhaps less extensively so than in earlier periods. The villages of the late sixth and early fifth millennia were often now on reoccupied sites – though most eligible sites had surely been used already in the past several thousand years, but they appear to have lasted longer than before, and some of them grew to a size to be counted as large towns, if not cities. This would imply a more organized and sympathetic agricultural regime, whereby the local resources were managed more carefully. Some regions, such as around and in the Damascus Ghuta, were effectively abandoned.

In Palestine the introduction of pottery, somewhat later than in the north, coincided with an apparent break in the archaeological record, though it may only be that the introduction of pottery stimulated the archaeologists to recognize a new culture. For a time indeed, it was thought there was a thousand-year 'gap' in the record. But then several new cultures were recognized; Yarmukian, Wadi Raba, and others, none of which were much different, except for the use of pottery, from the earlier Pre-Pottery Neolithic already recognized.[2] But the impulse deriving from both the Halaf and Ubaid Cultures did not reach so far south, at least not directly.

The Pottery Neolithic gave way to the period called by the archaeologists the Chalcolithic ('copper-stone'), used to account for the slow adoption of the use of copper, and the continued employment of stone for many tools and weapons. In many ways this is a better name for the period than Ubaid, since it concentrates on what archaeologists find – the material remains. Copper was in fact a rather less useful development than most until the techniques of alloying it into bronze were developed. It appears to have first been processed into usefulness in Anatolia, where it is comparatively common. It needed to be imported into Syria, where the only local sources are in the Amanus Mountains in the north and in the Negev in the south, where mines and possibly furnaces have been found at Timna in the Wadi Arabah.[3] Copper itself was not of much specific use, though it was attractive in colour, both in its refined state and when it had acquired its green patina; it had been used as jewellery even in the late Neolithic period. But having found a use for one material, other metals, notably gold and silver, zinc and tin, were also used (and eventually, of course, iron).

In addition different ways of processing the new material were developed. It could be hammered cold, if in nugget form; it could be heated to malleability or even into a molten state and then used in moulds; it could, alloyed with arsenic, for example, be made liquid and so poured into hollows, to produce such things as statues and figurines by the 'lost-wax' process. All these techniques were invented or developed in the Chalcolithic in Syria. And, of course, the alloying process eventually developed into the production of bronze.

So copper was a material used to manufacture tools, weapons, and jewellery. Occasional items of copper had appeared, usually found in graves, for some time before 4500 BC, especially in areas such as Anatolia and Iran, where nuggets of the metal could be found and hammered cold into shape. The bright colour made it particularly attractive as jewellery. The use of the metal spread, both geographically and in its uses, but it had only a marginal effect on the society for some time. The former Neolithic lifestyle continued, but with some copper technology added. Since copper was expensive to acquire and needed specialized smithing and forging skills to shape it, its use was restricted, but this did stimulate some economic growth. Since it was expensive its use represented a clear increase in both the wealth of individuals and in the general wealth of the community.

The technology involved first mining the ore, then refining it, and then manufacturing it into whatever was needed. It was the latter process which was the most difficult, and if possible it was kept a secret. One industrial complex has been located in southern Palestine. The ore was mined at Feinan in the Wadi Arabah, and was transported by donkeys to Shiqmim, a site on the Wadi Ghazze south of Beersheba. There it was refined and manufactured into either saleable goods or ingots of pure metal. The market was no doubt largely local to southern Palestine, but some of the goods were exported to Egypt. The laborious process of transporting the ore 100 km before smelting it is explained by the need to keep the smelting process secret; it may also be that it was easier to transport the ore than the other materials needed, such as wood – and the workers, of course.[4]

The connection with Egypt is not surprising. It was no further away than central Palestine, and reflects a series of other connections of Egypt with Syria. Egypt received strong cultural influences originating from Sumer during the fourth millennium. The idea of writing and aspects of architecture and iconography are examples.[5] The intermediary was obviously Syria. It is also known that Egypt was in contact by sea with Phoenicia. As a largely unforested land, wood in Egypt was of considerable value. The main contact port in Syria was Byblos, but this cannot have been the only place. For Sumerian influences to reach Egypt a substantial traffic may be presupposed, though the actual material transferred could in some cases have been carried in a man's mind. Writing, for example, was clearly very different in execution in the two lands, and was obviously an idea rather than a direct transfer; and architectural techniques could easily be the result of an architect's visit. On the whole, however, these ideas seem more likely to have travelled if they had accompanied more material objects.

The Ubaid/Early Chalcolithic period in Syria is the obvious time when the Sumerian influence could begin to spread to Syria and on to Egypt. In fact that is probably somewhat early, but as Sumerian society developed and grew in power and wealth in the late fourth millennium, and Egypt's kingdoms battled for supremacy amongst themselves, the time was ripe in both regions for both expansion and the reception of outside influences.

Syria lay in the middle, geographically between the two richer and more powerful areas. The cold climatic phase at the end of the Neolithic had resulted in a new dispersal of the population, but the old hierarchy of large villages surrounded by small hamlets became re-established. The copper town at Shiqmim on the Wadi Ghazze was one such large village, and there were three others in the same area, at Ze'elin, Safadi, and Gerar. In central Palestine half a dozen more of these large village centres have been recognized, and others are in the Jordan Valley. That at Tuleilat Ghassul in the Moabite plateau east of the Jordan was at least 20ha in size, and was clearly a wealthy place.

In north Syria less archaeological work has been done, but Ubaid period occupation has been detected at a whole series of sites spread from the Khabour region in the east to the Mediterranean coast. Some of the sites in the Jazirah were uncommonly large – Tell Brak in the Upper Khabour, Hammam et-Turkman in the Balikh Valley, are examples. Brak had a built area of 43ha; it is surrounded by other sites, none of them larger than 5ha. In the Euphrates Valley the continuity of Ubaid period occupation from the past is strongly evident, though often the sites of occupation were new.

This is also the pattern in other distinct geographical regions. In the Amuq basin, where the Orontes turns sharply westwards, and is joined by two other rivers, and where a large lake occupies the centre of the basin, a large settlement has been excavated at Tell Kurdu, and the basin contained at least fifteen other villages of the period. Another group was in the Rouj Basin to the south along the Orontes, and more at the southern end of the Ghab; a series of sites have been detected in the Quweiq Valley; the excavations at Hama found a substantial building near the bottom of the deep sounding made in the 1930s. And on the coast there were at least two of these large villages–cum–small towns, at Byblos and at Ras Shamra; at the latter very large quantities of Ubaid style pottery were found, but the buildings were not thought to be of any merit.

This is, as will be appreciated, much the same sort of dispersed, peasant society as in the preceding Neolithic. There is little sign that copper was available to most of the population, and the acceptance of Ubaid pottery was slow. Many of the villages were occupied for a time then abandoned, but there were usually larger settlements which developed in each region. Geographers would regard them as central places, and it is possible that they were market centres for their regions, and quite possibly political centres as well.

The use of copper, its peculiar and difficult technology, and the associated need for organization and administration, are indications of the expansion of all the societies in Syria, in numbers, wealth and complexity. But this was a slow process, and a distinct lack of archaeological evidence for the period following the Ubaid hampers description. What there is implies that the changes which are characterized by the Halaf and Ubaid periods continued to work themselves through, but with the usual dislocations and divisions.

The Chalcolithic was therefore a period of slow growth, but one in which the differentiation grew between most villages and the growing towns, which were thinly scattered over the land. Some of these won included large buildings which can best be seen as 'public' in the sense that they were monumental rather than domestic. Some are regarded as temples, some appear to be 'mansions', even palaces. All this suggests a growth of individual wealth, perhaps the growth of a central authority, and the gathering together of public wealth as a resource for these greater 'public' buildings.

From the middle of the fourth millennium a new influence out of southern Babylonia appeared. Its origin is conventionally ascribed to the Sumerian proto-city of Uruk, which is almost the only Sumerian site to have yielded datable evidence for the period, and which therefore the Syrian remains have been compared with. The actual origin is very likely to have been as wide as Sumer itself, though the name 'Uruk' has become attached to the phenomenon, probably irretrievably.

The basis of the development was the economic expansion of Sumer in the early fourth millennium, which brought Sumerian influence into Iran, as far as Anatolia, and into northern Syria. One of the reasons was a need to acquire copper and other resources. Certain places in north Syria, especially along the Euphrates, have produced substantial quantities of materials manufactured in Sumer, and evidence of buildings which are of Sumerian type, and this has suggested that colonies of Sumerians had been planted there. The aim would seem to have been to establish control over the trade routes from Anatolia which presumably went along the Euphrates, but more seems to have been involved than that.[6] (Other colonies have been traced in Elam, Iran, and northern Iraq.)

The site of Habuba Kabira South was a fortified town of about 10ha. It was founded on previously unoccupied land, and laid out to a clearly predetermined plan. The streets, oriented north–south and east–west, were paved; the city walls were equipped with towers at regular intervals, and there were two fortified gates. The Sumerian origin of the plan and the population is indicated by the size and shape of the bricks used in the walls and the houses, which are of a distinctly Sumerian pattern; the layout of the houses is similarly typically Sumerian.[7]

Not far off, at Jebel Aruda, a smaller site, there were two buildings interpreted as temples, and it has been suggested that this place was the 'administrative centre' of the colonial settlement.[8] The conclusion is that these places were inhabited by Sumerian colonists. They used Sumerian pottery, and employed seals of Sumerian type; written records, a Sumerian specialty and unique to Sumer, were employed.

These two sites were just two of a series of Urukian or partly Urukian sites scattered along this part of the Euphrates as far as Hacinebi north of Birejik and on as far as Samsat. Some were new foundations, like Habuba, some were small posts or villages, some were Urukian sections inserted into existing Syrian villages. A similar group of places has been found in the Balikh Valley, and others are scattered along the trade route as far as the Tigris. To the west two sites on a presumed route to the Amanus Mountains, at Tell ed-Danneh not far from Aleppo and at Tabara el-Akrad in the Amuq Basin, have produced evidence of the implantation of Urukian colonists within existing Syrian villages.

So some of these places were exclusively Urukian, and apparently maintained that exclusivity for two or three centuries. But other Syrian places were evidently also in contact with the Sumerians, though only received Sumerian products as a supplement to their own manufactures. And, of course, the further from the 'colony' the less intense the Sumerian influence. So at Tell Brak in the Upper Khabour Valley, the Sumerian influence was strong, to the extent of the existence of a major temple of Sumerian type and the use of much typically Sumerian everyday material; west of the Euphrates, at several sites in the Amuq Basin near the future site of Antioch, there are hints of that influence, as there are at Hama, further to the south; there is none, however, in Palestine.[9] The period of the Chalcolithic was apparently prosperous in southern Syria, and so the region would have enjoyed an intercourse with a similarly prosperous Sumer had contact been established.

Some of the places of this period were large enough to be regarded as urban settlements. Tell Brak, for example, was completely built up over the whole tell, an area of 53ha; and there were suburbs taking the inhabited area to 100ha; this would imply a population of about 20,000 people. The 10ha site at Habuba Kabira would suggest a population of 2,000. Both of these places can be considered, given their sizes and their fortifications and dense populations, as cities. But Habuba Kabira was heavily fortified; if it was a planted Sumerian colony it might possibly have been locally unwelcome. On the other hand most of the Urukian places were small, and either exclusively Urukian but planted close to an existing Syrian village or town, or were an Urukian insertion into an existing village – in either case such foundations were clearly done by the consent of the local populations.

The precise purpose of this intrusion is not altogether clear. Since the direction of thrust lay towards Anatolia, with 'branches' established as far north as Samsat, it seems reasonable to suppose that metals were one of the objects it was intended to acquire. Anatolia and the Amanus were also sources of wood, and the Euphrates was an obvious means of transporting goods down river. It is also noticeable that some of the main settlements – Habuba, Carchemish, Nineveh, and others – were established at constrictions along the trade routes, such as river crossings; participating in, and perhaps taxing, the trade following these routes is another likely purpose.

These colonies, and other places, were abandoned towards the end of the fourth millennium, in some cases such as Habuba Kabira, very abruptly. The reason does not seem to be local hostility, but is more likely connected with changes in the Sumerian homeland. It seems likely that the colonists were always heavily dependent on their Sumerian market. Many of them, even those planted inside indigenous villages, show continuing contact with Sumer even across several centuries. At the time the colonies collapsed, their home market had collapsed, and this seems to be the cause of the break.

The effect on the Syrian societies amongst whom these colonists had lived may not have been great, in part because of the continuing Urukian exclusiveness. Their characteristic artefacts have been found in only a few other sites in north Syria, only in the Amuq Basin and at Hama. It seems that they did not rely on local labour for their food, but worked the fields themselves. If the suggested trading system is correctly understood, the colonists had little or no contact with the local communities, even though many of them lived in or close to Syrian villages. It is suggested that the most likely export they received from the Sumerian region was textiles, which were presumably intended in part for sale in Syria and Anatolia. These, of course, leave little or no trace in the archaeological record, but it seems most likely that the search for metals and raw materials left little space for local trade with communities manifestly less developed either economically or politically, than themselves. However it is not possible that such colonies existed in the region for several centuries without some effects on the local society. Even if, as it seems, the colonists did much of their own food production, trade with other villages and towns must be presumed, more than likely on the initiative of the Syrians. And their disappearance, which in some cases was abrupt, can only have been highly disruptive to the Syrian society among which they had lived. If nothing else, the ability to live for long periods in comparatively large settlements will have had its effect. It is noticeable that this area in the following period was a centre for intensive settlement, including the development of several towns-cum-cities.

So Syria in all likelihood had become the target for a large-scale foreign intrusion. The Sumerian presence followed on from the influences of Halaf and Ubaid, and came at the same time as Egyptian traders ranged along the Palestinian and Phoenician coasts, and southern Palestinian copper merchants sold their product in Egypt. These three areas, Egypt, Syria, and Sumer were thus connected, however tenuously, above all by trade, but also by the transmission of cultural influences, even if it was only, in the early stages, the transfer of a style of pottery.

Yet their political developments diverged. While the Sumerian enclaves and traders and colonists operated in north Syria, in Egypt there was a period of desiccation and desertification which in the fourth millennium promoted the concentration of human affairs into the constricted Nile Valley; this was one of the main reasons for the relative ease of the political unification, achieved about 3000 BC by a dynasty of warrior kings from the south who became the first pharaohs.

Sumer, affected by the same climatic alteration, had a wider geographical area within which to operate, and the result in political terms was the emergence of a series of independent cities, but also their constant warfare over the control of land, even of individual fields. Food was the essential requirement, and the basic source of wealth, but the productivity of the irrigated land was such that there was sufficient surplus wealth available to engage in widespread trade.

Syria, geographically larger than either of these two regions, was also the most geographically diverse. It shared to some extent in the early urban development of the Sumerians, but not in their concentrated wealth creation, and its geography has also prevented it from unifying on the Egyptian pattern. It was this perhaps which was one of the attractions for the Sumerian colonists. Their project of colonization may have been stimulated by Sumerian demands for foreign products, but it might also have been a response to a stressed population caused by climatic disorientation. No doubt precisely because the land was divided, Syria became one of the more desirable territories. It was already a major centre for trade, for it was not only diverse and curious, it was central to the whole economic and political development of the Middle East. The Sumerians saw an economic opportunity and aimed to seize it, no doubt assuring themselves, as colonists always did, that they were able to manage the system more efficiently than the natives, and that it was also the natives who would benefit.

By the Chalcolithic therefore one of the basic patterns of Syria's future history had already been settled. It was divided, and because of that it was vulnerable to outside pressures; at the same time it was readily receptive of influences from outside, and even of foreign populations. It may at this point be useful to summarize just what had been achieved in the seven or eight millennia which had elapsed between the end of the Ice Age and the revelation of the usefulness of metals.

The evidence is very largely technological and social. That is, there is little or no evidence outside the archaeological record which indicates the means of acquiring food and the arrangements for living. This has, however, been sufficient to enable theorists to extrapolate from the archaeological data into some suggestions as to the social organization of the farmers and to some degree also their political and religious systems – though it has to be emphasized that this is always theory, and not always very convincing ones, and that new discoveries are always liable to upset theories.

Partly this was because of the continuing need to relocate settlements which has made the collection of information a rather chancy process, particularly as archaeologists, like everyone else, tend to concentrate on particular problems, so that other matters are left to one side. This practice of repeatedly moving settlements might be a customary inheritance from the nomadic hunting-and-gathering past, but since some settlements clearly lasted several centuries even in the earliest days, this is hardly convincing. The exhaustion of the soil might be a better explanation, and perhaps climate change could be added in.

What was certainly a necessary inheritance from the past was the practice of living in communities, and over the millennia these became bigger, indicating an increasing ability to accept bigger numbers of people close by. One indication of this archaeologically is the recognition that particular buildings, usually larger or more aberrant than the ordinary house, were set aside for particular communal activities. The assumption is that if such a building shows evidence of domestic occupation it is a sign that the community had a chief; if it does not the building is generally assumed to have had a religious purpose. It is, of course, somewhat speculative: there is no inherent reason why a bigger house should be that of a chief, and it could simply be the house of a man who wanted a bigger house, and had the wealth and energy to build one. On the other hand, there were certainly specialized religious buildings later, and in a few cases that speculation can be traced back archaeologically into the Neolithic.

These developments can be traced originally from the end of the Ice Age onwards. The settlements were, as elsewhere, more or less temporary, particularly at the beginning, but the many tells which dot the Syrian countryside indicate that the settlements, from the Neolithic onwards, were relatively long-lived, and there is enough chronological overlap between places and cultures to make it clear that the population was composed of the descendants of those who inhabited the land in the Natufian.

These were people who readily adopted the new technologies as they were discovered, or invented, or developed, and who accepted the general cultural assumptions and practices of the whole region. The Neolithic settlements in the south are not necessarily identical to those in the Euphrates Valley in the north, but the differences are easily explained by reference to the geography. This must also be the case with the language that the people spoke. It is to be assumed that those living in Mureybat in the Euphrates Valley were able to converse with the people of the el–Ghazal or Beidha in the south.

The domestication of grain crops, beginning with 'primitive' types of wheat, was only the beginning of a wider process whereby many other crops were induced to allow themselves to be cultivated. Once one plant was clearly available, it would be automatic for others to be searched for. Similarly the domestication of cattle and goats stimulated the special breeding to increase meat and milk and wool yields, and so the evolution of sheep from goats. Other animals – pigs, ducks, and geese – were brought into farms; other crops were cultivated. Some of these items are thought to have been domesticated elsewhere, but it is likely that Syria was the scene of two particular successes – olives and vines. In fact, of course, the process of propagating such crops was one of cloning (which is what taking cuttings amounts to) and there were plenty of subsidiary processes which had to be developed before olives became olive oil and vines became wine, but this had certainly been done before the end of the Chalcolithic, which is dated about 3500 BC. Both of these products were traded in exchange for, presumably, such things as metals which Syria did not have. Neither crop would grow in either Egypt or Babylonia, which were expanding politically and economically during the Chalcolithic. One of the regional kings in Egypt was buried with a store of wine for his post-mortality comfort – hence trade with Syria was clearly well-established by the fourth millennium BC.[10]

All the regions of the Middle East were constantly affected by climatic changes. The Chalcolithic saw the development of cities and states in the whole region from the Upper Nile to the mouth of the Tigris and Euphrates in part because this was a period of climate change. From about 5000 BC the monsoon rains of the Indian Ocean moved gradually south and east, so that in Egypt for example the rains failed in the lands to either side of the Nile, so the land slowly dried out and shifted from steppeland to desert, compelling the cattle herders of those regions to move into the valley where there were water supplies. (The water, of course, came from the Central African lakes and the Ethiopian highlands, and is actually still provided, at least in Ethiopia, by the monsoon.)

Syria was affected by this change because the rain belt which had watered the Arabian Peninsula also shifted south; no doubt the same phenomenon of people moving out of the near deserts affected Syria, as in Egypt and Babylonia. It is not easy to spot archaeologically, however, and since the movement out of Arabia could go in several directions over a long period of time it may mean that the pressure was not as powerful as it clearly was in Egypt. Syria's wider and better watered land had room for an influx of refugees.

The effect of the desiccation process in Egypt and in Babylonia was to stimulate the growth of urban settlements. Uruk, close to the desert, was clearly a sizable town by 3500 BC, if not earlier. In Egypt the towns which developed as royal centres in Upper Egypt did so in the centuries after that date, being based on older and smaller settlements. In Syria, on the other hand, perhaps because of the wider spaces and greater available area, the urbanization came somewhat later and less insistently. The size of the land, 100 miles wide and 600 miles long, gave space for people to move. The steppe, a region of grassland, could support a pastoral economy. One of the continuing aspects of Syrian history is the link between the agricultural lands farmed by peasantry (*fellahin*) and the pastoral economy of the steppe where animals, particularly sheep and goats, were herded by mobile herders (*bedouin*).

This seems to have been a decisive period and event which pushed all three regions – Egypt, Syria, Babylonia – into developing new political and social, even new technological, systems. Certainly it seems that the shift from the Chalcolithic into the Bronze Age – though these are very arbitrary archaeological period-terms – took place in Syria about the time that the climate began to worsen. How far this was a true connection is not known. Bronze had been developed elsewhere earlier, but its use, and its technology, did not reach Syria until about 3500 BC, and then only very tentatively. It could be that the pressure of the worsening climate provoked a search for a more efficient material for tools and weapons. One of the results of the pressure was an increase in warfare, at least in Egypt and Mesopotamia, and quite probably therefore also in Syria, and bronze weapons were more efficient than copper or stone.

The political and social changes produced fortifications in towns – a clear indication of the increase in warfare – which in the peculiar geographical conditions in Egypt brought about the unification of all the Nile Valley from the First Cataract to the Delta by about 3000 BC. In Mesopotamia it led to the development of a whole series of independent city states from about 3500 BC; they settled into a relationship of constant if intermittent warfare for 1,000 years, with the fortunes of war swinging back and forth, until Sargon of Akkad brought about their unification, though this condition lasted for only a relatively brief time.

The Syrian land was thus by the beginning of the Bronze Age, an old land. It had been the host of farmers and their villages for more than 7,000 years. The inhabitants knew some of this, for wherever they went there was evidence of their predecessors' lives – tells, graves, ruined villages. No doubt they had stories, developing into legends and myths to account for what they saw around them. And they knew of the other lands adjoining Syria – Sumer, Anatolia, Egypt – and probably of the major changes taking placed there. That they lived in villages and farmed the land does not mean they knew nothing of the rest of the world. Certainly those in southern Palestine knew of Egypt, and those in north Syria knew of Anatolia; the presence for several hundred years of the Urukians from Sumer in north Syria will have sensitized the Syrians to events in that country.

Chapter 3

Cities and Invasions

The withdrawal or collapse of the Sumerian colonies took place round about 3200 BC. This was two centuries or so before the unification of Egypt by the kings of the Theban kingdom, and five centuries before the final clear emergence into the light of history of the congregation of city states in southern Iraq in the 'Early Dynastic' period. During the centuries after the end of the Sumerian intrusion the use of copper gradually developed into the use of bronze, though this was as slow as any other technological change in this time – and the use of the term 'Early Bronze Age' is at the beginning of that period more anticipatory than accurate. But, once again, it was accompanied by a radical development in Syrian society, though how far one was the cause of the other is not at all clear.

Bronze is an alloy of copper with another element, a process which produces a much tougher metal. The best alloy is tin, though other materials can be used – arsenic was one of the earliest. The problem with tin is that it is relatively scarce. There was none in Syria (or Egypt or Sumer) and so it had to be sought elsewhere and imported. The usual source was Anatolia. Yet, rather as with the domestication of plants and animals, once one metal had been shown to be of use, others were quickly found. The Chalcolithic age had also seen the beginning of the use of gold and silver and lead, all of which had varied uses, but all of which might also be the source of wealth for the few; gold and silver were especially prized by the emerging rulers.

There was thus by about 3000 BC, which is well into the Early Bronze Age, a considerable repertoire of skills available to the inhabitants of Syria, several metals, building in stone and wood and brick, the cultivation of numerous plants, the herding of several breeds of animal. This variety necessarily encouraged the growth of both personal and communal wealth and the opportunities for trade. The necessary skills also encouraged, or even required, clear artisanal specialization. There is evidence of this along the Euphrates, where, at Carchemish, a considerable variety of copper tools, weapons, and jewellery, were found in excavations before the Great War.[1] The site of Hajji Ibrajim near Tell es-Sweyhat has produced a ring of store buildings around a house, interpreted as a store of animal feed for pastoralists on the steppeland.[2] At Ziyadeh a workshop was excavated where there was evidence of the whole sequence of operations for the production of pottery from the raw material to the finished product.[3]

The great majority of the population were farmers and herders, and it was upon their surplus production that the elaboration of artisan and other specialization rested. This specialization was the foundation for the increasing agglomeration of population into towns, and eventually cities. In Iraq this happened earlier than in Syria in part because of the greater productivity of the irrigated agriculture of the Tigris-Euphrates alluvial plain, and the dearth of any other resources. But it seems evident that Syria was not really very far behind. There is, as it happens, little evidence of the growth of towns in Syria until about 2700 BC, but there are hints that some places had already by that time developed into sizable places. These would include Tell Sukas and Ugarit on the Mediterranean coast, Hama and Qatna on the middle Orontes, Tell Habuba and Mari on the Euphrates, and Carchemish further north on the same river.

In fact it is along the Euphrates in north Syria that the best evidence for the development of towns seems to lie. The river is enclosed within high banks at some distance from the river itself. The flood plan between these banks was the site of a considerable number of settlements, some inherited from the Chalcolithic and some new, during the third millennium. The variable width of the plain meant that there were areas where the banks precluded settlement and others where there was plenty of space. Most of the places lasted only a relatively brief time though some were continuously inhabited throughout the millennium (the Early Bronze Age is dated about 3200 to 2000 BC).[4]

That is to say the same process of movement, dissolution and resettlement took place than earlier millennia but to have done so within a fairly narrow space, and the number of places which lasted throughout the period suggests that it had become possible to organize affairs in such a way that the need to move was much reduced.

Most of the places which were settled were small, only a few hectares, though it is not always clear that the measurements relate to a well-surveyed area, or a briefly viewed place. Experience has shown that it is only after a detailed survey that a reasonably accurate idea of the size of an ancient settlement can be arrived at. In particular there is a difference between the settled area and the fortified area. Even the smallest places were normally fortified by the end of the millennium, but in most cases the occupied area stretched some distance beyond the walls.

Given the variable sizes of the settlements, it is necessary to discriminate between those of a size which might entitle them to be called a city and the rest. Yet even the largest of the sites were still relatively small, though those whose governmental system is known or hinted at are said to have a king. Each of the wider sections of the flood plain tends to have one of these larger sites: possibly Carchemish in the north, with a suburb across the river at Tiladar Tepe (though the size of the Carchemish site is disputed, with estimates ranging from half a hectare to 44ha); Bedayeh at the southern end of this area, though it is hardly large enough at 10–3ha; Banat, a rich and spectacular site of 30ha in a relatively small embayment; Tell es–Sweyhat in a large embayment, growing from 5–6ha in about 3200 BC to 40ha at the end of the period; Hadidi across the river on the west bank, 56ha; Selankahiye on the same bank, 12–14ha, and Halawa opposite about the same size; in the far south of the area Emar, about 27ha.[5]

Most of these might be counted as 'central places' surrounded as they were by smaller settlements. They were certainly dominant in their small sections of the river plain. They were also generally permanent throughout the Early Bronze Age, that is, they existed as organized and continuous communities for over a thousand years. Some of them can be seen to have grown during that time, and if they did not dominate their small neighbourhoods at the start of the period, they grew into that situation. The source of their growth is not obvious, but it is likely that some of the more temporary smaller villages around them supplied their people to the bigger places.

To the west and east of the Euphrates Valley the same general remarks also apply. In the Balikh Valley Hammam et–Turkman is a medium sized site with solid fortifications. Close to the junction of the Balikh with the Euphrates is Tell Biya, the ancient Tuttul, a large mound of almost 40ha, the same size as, say, Emar. These can be reckoned in the same league as the bigger Euphrates sites, and of the same importance.

To the west there are places of the same rank and size on the Amuq Basin, continuing on from the Chalcolithic. Beyond the Jebel Ansariyeh, Ugarit on the coast eventually grew from a Chalcolithic base to a size of truly city proportions, of about 150ha, though only in its last phase was it so big. It is likely that Hama, on the Orontes to the south was of a considerable size, but the excavations only detected a relatively small area of the place of this period.

There would seem to be gap in evidence south of Hama, until one reaches northern Palestine – the Damascus Ghuta was still not seriously occupied – but there is a clear indication that connections between north and south existed. This is, once again, evidence provided by a species of pottery, called originally 'Khirbet Kerak ware', but now more prosaically called 'Red–Black Burnished Ware'.[6] This is found throughout much of Palestine and Syria, notably on the western parts, and is supposed to have originated among potters in eastern Anatolia. (This is, of course, much the same direction as the Halaf and Ubaid wares originated.) It was attractive in its colouring (achieved by a particular kiln technique), its decoration, and its shapes. Originally assumed to be the mark of an invading people, it is now, more romantically, thought to be the work of travelling potters, then adopted by local potters. Its importance – besides its ready recognizability by archaeologists – is that its existence throughout Syria is clear evidence for the continued contacts which existed from the end of the Ice Age onwards between all parts of Syria and between Syria and its geographical neighbours.

The fact that most of the population was occupied in agriculture means that the practice of moving settlements, dividing communities, and settling new sites (or reoccupying old sites) continued. In Palestine this has been supposed to indicate a crisis at the end of the Chalcolithic, but the changes of settlement were not really more drastic than at any other time (and to suppose that the change from the 'Chalcolithic' to the 'Early Bronze Age' was important in itself is putting mere archaeological terminology on too important a level). It is clear that not a great deal actually changed in everyday life between the two periods.

Palestine has, of course, been much more intensively examined by archaeologists than the rest of Syria, and the Early Bronze Age is one of those periods where the contrast between the evidence from the two regions is most glaring. But it is certain that the former Chalcolithic contacts between southern Palestine and Egypt continued, as did those between north Syria and the Anatolian region. And the spread of the manufacture and use of Red–Black Burnished Ware is a clear sign that internal communications continued as well.

The Chalcolithic connection between Egypt and Palestine had been mainly the export of copper, often in ingot form. The terminus of the trade route was at Maadi in Egypt, a little south of the site of Cairo. This apparently ended and was replaced by new connections (perhaps because sources of copper in Egypt were developed). Several sites in southern Palestine – notably En Besor and Tell Erani, show indications of connections with Egypt, while others in the Nile Delta suggest the reverse connections. At Abydos in southern Egypt there have been found large numbers of 'Canaanite' pottery – that is, pots manufactured in Palestine but transported, presumably as containers of wine and oil, to one of the most economically and politically dynamic centres in Egypt. This connection faded with the establishment of full unitary control soon after 3000 BC, but it is curious to note that it had existed more or less at the same time as the Uruk intrusion in the north.[7]

These connections were clearly important. Trade is a prime means of increasing wealth, and it was this which was at the root of the development of urban centres. This had happened before, of course, both in the time of the Uruk intrusion and earlier, but in neither case had the growth being sustained. The causes of failure were probably an agricultural failure, withdrawing the basis for the towns' growth, or in the case of the Uruk colonies, the collapse of the home society – it did not help that the colonists were not rooted in the Syrian society and so had no independent basis. The same may be said of the Egyptian connection, though its fading had a different cause.

The reasons for the earlier failures are probably as much climatic as anything else, for like every agricultural society, both Sumer and Syria were heavily dependent on a continuing favourable climate to foster their agricultural production. This was less so in Egypt, though the height of the Nile flood was a reflection of the success of the Ethiopian monsoon. But the normal Nile flow came from the Great Lakes in Central Africa, which tended to be constant, so there was always water, even if or not quite so generously supplied as during the floods.

The conditions for the development of a human settlement into a large enough community to be regarded as a city include the craft specializations already noted, a sufficiently wide and fertile territory to provide most of the requisite food for the population (and therefore a large part of that population would live outside the city) and the incentive to bring a large population together in the first place. It is perhaps above all the failure of that incentive which is crucial to explaining the failure of the early cities, since without it for many people there was no real advantage over living in the country. The repeated dissolution of smaller communities, which had been a constant feature of village life in Syria since the end of the Ice Age, operated also in the case of the cities.

The first two elements were clearly in Syria all along. The land is generally fertile, water in the narrow zone between the desert and the sea is normally plentiful, and the specialization of craftsmen into potters, bronze-smiths, woodworkers, artists, architects, and so on, was clearly present from the late Neolithic, and became fully articulated with the advent of copper. The matter which is unusual is therefore that of the incentive to form a large enough community to form a city.

It is striking that the cities which emerged in Syria in the Middle Bronze Age (after about 2000 BC) and some increasingly so in the Early Bronze Age, were generally fortified. This had been one of the characteristics of even earlier cities at times, as far back as Pre-Pottery Jericho, but in the new period, after say 3000 BC, every community in the end required and built walls to enclose itself and separate itself from the surrounding countryside and from other cities. This work presupposes a large degree of public cohesion and participation, and implies that some communities had submitted themselves to a supreme authority with the right to plan, organize the civic workforce, and impose other requirements, including taxation. It was a process which seems to have gradually taken in all possible sizes of settlement: on the Euphrates, even small villages of a few hectares in area were fortified by the end of the period.

How this particular society emerged is not clear, but the widespread practice of fortification is probably the best clue. For this implies a fairly constant threat of war. This, like the cities, was a new condition. There had no doubt been fighting, conquest, and war in Syria before, but it had never yet been so endemic that it was thought necessary to develop fortifications to protect settlements on a wide and systematic scale. The unification of Egypt had been achieved only after a prolonged bout of internal fighting, which imprinted on the aura of the Pharaohs the need to be seen as victorious warriors for ever after. In Sumer the new cities quarrelled constantly. The Egyptian wars spilled over into southern Palestine; the

Sumerian wars did not reach Syria for some time, but the requirement of a city and its king to expand his power and territory was an infectious matter.

The major city in Syria in this period, both in its size and in the quantity of its records, was Ebla. This was a city which came to political supremacy in Syria and exercised control over much of north Syria for a considerable time. It was walled, it had a dynasty, or dynasties, of kings and a dynasty of chief ministers, a literate and assiduous bureaucracy, and an aristocracy of 'elders'. A large palace housed the king and the bureaucracy as well as a large part of the product of taxation. In fact it seems that the king himself 'owned' much of the surrounding land, or perhaps the animals which grazed on it. The principal commercial product of the city seems to have been textiles, woven from the wool of the city's sheep, but the demand for pottery was sufficient that a fast wheel was used to produce a constant supply of virtually identical pots.

Ebla also demonstrates the characteristics which are common to powerful rulers who are barely restrained by their subjects. The king was wealthy, so much so that he was enabled to import large quantities of very expensive lapis lazuli which came from central Asia. It was the tax-take from his subjects which allowed him to do this – as well as, of course, mere gold and silver and bronze in quantity – though those subjects no more shared in that wealth than did the subjects of later kings.

The city was situated in a part of the western region, between the Orontes Valley and the salt marsh-cum-lake of el-Madkh. This is a region only thinly occupied by other sites, is not particularly fertile, but these circumstances gave Ebla plenty of room for expansion and exploitation. Yet it had few geographical advantages, and it would seem that the main motor for its growth to power was the ability of its kings. Without clear guidance and central control it is unlikely to have ever grown beyond a large village. Of course this is an unverifiable proposition, though it is clear from one of the documents recovered from the archives that the former kings were revered, indeed deified, and offerings were made for a list of twenty-one preceding kings in the time of the king who was ruling when the palace burned down. One of the likely factors is that the kings succeeded each other without dispute, probably as a true dynasty, from father to son in most cases. The list of kings presupposes therefore a continuous and undisturbed history covering perhaps four centuries (allowing about twenty years for each king's reign, on average).[8]

The third millennium BC throughout the Middle East was a time of warfare, hence the fortifications, and hence perhaps the concentration of local power in the hands of one man in every city, who might be supposed to have a particular ability to organize the defences, to command soldiers, and to contrive either victory or at least avoid defeat. In Ebla the size and complexity of the community required the rulers to import from Sumer the practice of writing, probably early in the city's development. The bureaucrats who were thereby also required (and supported from general taxation) kept an exhaustive and numerous record of the animals, the

soldiers, the shepherds, the quantities of tax goods, and so on, in the normal mode
of such a system – an early example of the bureaucrats finding ever more subjects
of which they felt the need to have a record. By the time of the records recovered
in the excavations, the bureaucracy was clearly well established and operating in a
routine manner, a situation which suggests a lengthy period of development.

The importance of writing was one of several Sumerian practices which Ebla
adopted from outside. Sumerian influences are clear in the artistic and architectural
work of the city; the citizens adapted other Sumerian influences to their daily
lives, but without being overwhelmed by them. The writing, though, was tailored
to the local language. The clerks used cuneiform, which had been invented
originally to express the Sumerian language, but had already been adapted for the
Semitic language Akkadian, and could be further adapted to the dialect which was
Semitic 'Eblaite', which belonged to a different subdivision of the general Semitic
language. It is clear from these records that Ebla was part of a language region,
called 'Northwest Semitic', which covered all northern Syria.[9] The conclusion,
given the absence of any clear indication of any mass population movements –
as opposed to the relocation of villages, which was constant – must be that the
Semitic language was descended from that of the original Neolithic inhabitants.

The powerful mobilization of resources in the new cities also brought an
increased emphasis on religion. In Sumer it was the temples and their priesthoods
which had been the originators of civic developments; in Syria this was the task of
the kings and elders. One of the necessary developments, in a superstitious society,
was to bring the gods onside. Some of the tax revenues were diverted to religious
uses, a house for the god or gods – or houses for the gods – were built.[10] This is the
first evidence on any serious scale that the Syrians took their religious beliefs and
practices so seriously. In fact, of course, it is not really an indication of the beliefs
or religious practices of the people, but of the perceived requirement of the rulers
to be seen to have divine allies.

The cities which resulted from this new situation therefore contained within
their fortifications a palace for the ruler and his clerks, a temple or temples for the
gods, but it also included large storehouses for the collected taxes, which constituted
the king's store of wealth and the reserve of food for the general population. There
were other storehouses elsewhere in the city, often built up against the inner wall
of the fortifications. The temple, probably the largest building after the palace,
might also house its own storehouses. In the smaller settlements, however, the
walls might just be for the protection of the village population, who would move
into the walled area when danger threatened,

Ebla is almost certainly exceptional in all this. It is, in particular, the only site to
have yielded a large quantity of written material. Others have been located in several
places which have some of the characteristics of Ebla in the third millennium, but
none have produced the same serious quantity of records. They are all generally

smaller in area than Ebla, though they show evidence of local wealth. It is not always easy to decide if these places were cities, though they may certainly be referred to as towns. Hama on the Orontes seems to be one such city, though the excavations did not reveal much of the remains of this period. Alalah in the Amuq region is smaller, though the final report on the excavations will probably never be produced because of the faulty excavation method. On the coast Ras Shamra, later to be Ugarit, shows evidence of some size. Byblos further south was a substantial city, with kings and temples and a profitable trade with Egypt. In the north Syrian interior there are suggestions of towns at Tell Rifaat north of Aleppo, and as noted already there are several places along the Euphrates. Further east in the Jazirah, the Balikh Valley has the substantial site of Hammam et-Turkman, about the size of Ebla. Further east still the Khabour river system has others, though these are more to be considered Iraqi sites than Syrian.

Only a few of these places have produced occasional written texts of the third millennium, but all have similar institutions as Ebla – a palace, a temple, city walls, storehouses, artisan works – and probably had the same internal systems, including a repository of records. All might thus be considered to be cities, though all of them, even Ebla, are in fact quite small in area. The situation was replicated in Palestine, where only a small number of sites can be compared with those in the north.[11] Megiddo is one, and Beth Shean, both in the lowlands between the Judaean and Galilee Hills. It is difficult to decide if Jericho is to be included, and the same may be said for Ay, in the Judaean Hills. Both of these are really quite small places, though walled, with temples and presumably ruling kings.

The tablets from Ebla are mainly, as noted, administrative documents recording taxation receipts and government expenditure. There is, however, also a set of tablets charting the diplomacy of the kings, particularly with regard to a long war with the city of Mari. They cover only events of about a long generation (thirty to forty years), but they show that the city had a longstanding dispute with Mari, on the middle Euphrates, a series of wars in which fortunes fluctuated. They also show that Ebla exercised an imperial domination over much of north Syria for a time.[12]

This is the first occasion in Syria's already long history as a set of organized human communities in which we can see a case of diplomatic disputes, conquest, and imperial domination. It is as certain as anything in human affairs can be that it was not the first such case of conquest in Syria. Every site which has been investigated has been seen to have suffered destruction, usually by fire, and in some cases repeatedly. But archaeology can only in relatively rare cases produce evidence for the causes of these disasters. At Jericho the repeated collapses of the city wall could be ascribed in some cases to earthquakes, but not all. At Ras Shamra a destruction was followed by a two-century period of desertion; the original cause of the destruction cannot be determined; it could be an earthquake but it is normal for people of a city destroyed by an earthquake, or another natural disaster, to return and rebuild. In Palestine several sequences of destruction have been detected, at the end of the first phase of the 'Early Bronze Age', as already noted, and an end of that period, both ascribed to invaders. The destructions certainly took place, and it seems clear that there were probably 'invaders' who were in all likelihood nomads from the desert, but the word 'infiltration' may well be a better description of the process. The second of these episodes, in 'Early Bronze IV', actually covers a period of about three centuries, so the idea of a sudden devastating invasion hardly fits.[13]

Ebla's feud with Mari was one between contemporaries. The origins of both cities lay in the first century or so of the third millennium (in the period after the fall of the Urukian colonist regime to the north), but Mari, on the river, was a much bigger site – over 100ha – than Ebla. The two cities, about 400km apart in a straight line, were commercial partners and rivals, especially for control of the route along the Euphrates from Mari to Carchemish. At one point Mari established a brief control over the Syrian city, but the end result of the wars was a qualified Eblaite victory. Ebla's empire covered much of northern Syria, into the Amuq plain, towards Hama, and along the disputed part of the Euphrates; that of Mari lay along the Euphrates and appears to have spread into the steppe between the two cities.

This war lasted perhaps eighty years, with truces, brief periods of peace, treaties, and the other concomitants of warfare. One result seems to have been that Ebla's empire came under much stricter control than at the start of the fighting. The empire consisted in part of Ebla's own territory, perhaps the settled land within 50km of the city; then there were the existing kingdoms beyond that region. These places tended to remain under their own kings, so long as they paid tribute. As the war surged back and forth along the river the loyalty of these kings and cities was put under serious strain. Some kingdoms were broken up into their individual components, others were placed under direct rule, or had their kings replaced by a commission. It is fascinating to see the essential elements of empire being invented on the hoof, so to speak.

Both of the contending cities, and others, fell victim to a greater power. Sargon of Akkad united the cities of Sumer under his autocratic rule, bringing a sort of peace to a region long distracted by wars; but the energy generated by this unification was discharged in wider conquests. In a campaign which may have reached the Mediterranean coast, he conquered large areas in the Jazirah and in northern Syria. Mari was destroyed, as was Tell Brak. Ebla, whose royal palace had been destroyed some decades before, apparently succumbed, possibly without fighting. Certainly Sargon travelled through Eblaite territory to reach the Cedar Forest (Amanus) and the Silver Mountain (Taurus), but it is unlikely that he established direct control of the city.[14]

The empire Sargon built was repeatedly racked by rebellions, and at least three of his successors were murdered in palace conspiracies. The fourth king, Sargon's grandson Naram-Sin, boasted, like Sargon, of capturing Ebla, which might be merely a recapitulation of Sargon's achievement, or perhaps the quashing of one of the rebellions. The collapse of the empire after was followed by an invasion of Sumer by Gutians, mountain men from the east. The Eblaite Empire, thus freed of its Sumerian overlords, continued.

Sumer revived after a century of barbarian rule, and was reunited by a dynasty of kings out of Ur (the 'Ur III' dynasty). They revived not only the unity of Sumer but Sargon's military ambitions as well. Once again Ebla came under the overlordship of the lords of Sumer for about a century. This time, however, it seems that the empire was not favourably regarded by the Sumerian kings, and it began to fray at the edges, with parts being detached by the Ur III kings into direct dependence on them, rather than on Ebla. One of the earliest detachments was Ursu (the modern Gaziantep), which dominated the route from the Euphrates to 'the land where the cedars are cut', the northern part of the Amanus. Others which became independent, at least of Ebla, were places also on the north and along the Euphrates.[15] When the Ur Empire in turn collapsed it seems to have taken Ebla and many of its former dependents with it.

Ebla suffered a curious fate in the chaos of the Ur III collapse. The city surrounding the palace (which had replaced that destroyed earlier) was now destroyed, largely by fire. But the palace survived, apparently undamaged. This appears to have been the action of a conqueror who regarded the existing inhabitants as hostile, and chose to drive them out, and prevented their return by destroying their homes and works. The city was then surrounded by a new rampart, and a new population (presumably) occupied the lower city.

In other parts of the lands which had been part of the Eblaite Empire, a trail of destruction can be discerned: in the Euphrates region, Tell Ahmar, Tell es-Sweyhat, Tell Banat, Tell Mumbaqat, Selenkahiyeh and Hadidi, all places larger than the average for the area; two places, Gedikli Huyuk and Tilmen Huyuk, east of the Amanus; Hammam et-Turkman and Tell Bia in the Balikh Valley; two sites in the Quweiq Valley; three just east of Ebla; and Hama. These all suffered destruction about the time of the end of Ur III rule; for once it does not seem that this can be attributed to mere changes of site, but of a 'wave of destruction'.[16] A considerable proportion were not reoccupied; at Hama the desertion lasted a century. At Ebla, however, a new community took over the palace and the city resumed its role, under the new rulers, as a local great power.

The Akkadians, Sargon's people, were Semitic speakers who had become Sumerian enemies and then conquerors during the third millennium BC. As already mentioned they adopted that Sumerian invention, writing, and used their writing method, inscribing marks on soft clay tablets, to express their own language. This method was then taken up by the Eblaites, whose own Semitic language was similar to, but not the same as, Akkadian. In other words the Akkadians and Eblaites spoke dialects of the basic Semitic language.

The Akkadians lived in northern Babylonia, the Eblaites in northern Syria. Between them was the land which became the Syrian Desert, inhabited, so far as we can tell, by peoples also of Semitic speech who had developed a way of life dependent on herding animals (and hunting) – nomads, that is. Most of them had been subjects of Mari; others were not attached to any formed state. This had taken a long time to become clear, for as in Egypt the lands which are now desert became so after a long and erratic process of desiccation, and then the water sources had to be detected and tapped by wells. Some of the evidence for early farming, in fact, comes from sites now in the desert, but as the land dried, so the possibility of arable farming in the region decreased, leaving the inhabitants the usual alternatives: to die, to move, or to stay and adapt.

Those who stayed became the pastoral nomads. They had always been nomadic, and the early farmers had retained this propensity to regular movements from their hunting past. They had always herded animals, at least since goats and sheep and eventually cattle had been domesticated. As the desert dried, so they concentrated on the animals, which could survive in this new regime where cultivation was not possible. The evolution into a full lifestyle of pasturing desert nomads took millennia, and in fact was never complete, since the nomads continued to depend to a lesser or larger extent on the products of the agricultural regions, in part for food, and later, as the settled societies developed their manufacturing capabilities, on supplies of manufactured goods.

They also cohabited, in a sense, with the farmers. It was, and is, common enough for nomads to turn their flocks and herds on to the stubble of the farmers' fields. The exchange is food for the animals and manure for the farmers; a further exchange, more commercial, is of animal products for the farmers and food for the nomads. This arrival on their lands is probably part of the process which in times of unrest and violence the farmers might see as a nomad invasion, though in times of peace it would better be seen as an instance of friendly cooperation. And it was these nomads, partly dependent as they were on the farmers' products, who would be most likely to move into the farmlands permanently.

The 'true' nomads, the people who made a living almost entirely in the desert, only developed their style of life from the late second millennium, once the camel had been domesticated. Such a life depends on regular migrations, and that can only be achieved once such an animal as a camel, capable of extensive periods of endurance on little or no sustenance, was available. So eventually there were three groups: the nomads of the desert, the 'semi-nomads' who lived in the steppe and the fringes of the desert, and the peasants who farmed the arable lands, but until the camel was tamed, only the latter two counted.

There was always a degree of enmity between the peasants and the men from the desert fringes. Envy was included, in that the life of movement of the nomads was contrasted with that of the people with a settled home who were tied to the land; if the nomads became very numerous, they were seen as a threat by the farmers, who might find their crops were devoured and their animals stolen. The two groups also competed in the hunting of the wild animals they both coveted. They insulted each other, using terms such as dirty and degenerate and idle about each other. With such contrasting groups, conflict was always likely.

They were also related to each other. Intermarriage occurred and there was a constant seepage of nomads into the farmland where they eventually settled, either as reinforcements to the existing villages, or in new villages of their own foundation. They were, of course, one of the sources of the archaeologists' discovery that Syrian villages tended to be repeatedly deserted, or destroyed, reoccupied, or newly founded in a constant process. This had been going on from the earliest development of farming and pastoralism, and was part of everyday life in Syria. The settlement and resettlement was not necessarily difficult, for both groups could contribute to any new settlement, and they could communicate, for it is clear that both the farmers and the nomads spoke much the same language, though, given their different work and life priorities, their dialects developed differently – it was the nomads who developed the successive Semitic languages of Amorite, Aramaean, and Arabic.

The disturbances which had been detected in the Palestine region in the beginning of the Early Bronze Age, say 3500 to 3300 BC, were presumably one of the occasions when the nomads became especially pressing. The ending of occupation in the earlier Chalcolithic villages began in the north and spread gradually, over a fairly lengthy period, to the south, where it petered out. Many of the villages were abandoned for shorter or longer periods, and a considerable fraction of the original total were never reoccupied. In the north the change of occupants was more or less total; in the south it was minimal.[17]

The same process took place at the end of the Bronze Age, in the period named by the archaeologists as 'Early Bronze IV', between about 2300 and 2000 BC, and this time it is possible to give a name to the infiltrators – Amorites – though this is not wholly accepted. These were people who were known from all around the edges of the Fertile Crescent. They were familiar in Sumer at the time of Sargon, who boasted in his usual way of defeating them with great slaughter, both in and near Sumer itself and in the north, in a region which seems to have been the Jazirah. Naram-Sin also boasted of defeating and massacring them in a great battle in the Jebel Bishri. They are named in Sumerian texts as MAR.TU, a term meaning 'West', implying that they came to Sumer from the west, from the steppelands of the Jazirah and along the Euphrates.[18]

They are also named as Amorites (or Amurru) in some of the Ebla tablets. This city, of course, was in the eastern part of the well-watered lands, not far from the borders of the steppe, and it is hardly a surprise to find the bureaucrats of the city taking note. Coming to live close to a prosperous and powerful city could well be an attraction for the nomads. They could gain protection, in exchange no doubt for paying taxes – and Ebla was noted for its production of textiles. They would also gain access to the city's products: pots made on a mass production scale would be cheaper and better than anything the nomads could produce or buy elsewhere. And they could gain employment; their young men would be ideal mercenary soldier material. It has been theorized that they were mainly part of Mari's state system, and that as life on the steppe became better organized they developed a more independent attitude.[19]

The warfare associated with Sargon provided a clear opportunity for those Amorites who wished to penetrate more deeply into the lands of the farmers, and Sargon's brutal treatment of them no doubt stoked the enmity, while their recruitment into the armies of the surrounding states gave them entry and a taste for civilization. Hostility between the two groups in Babylonia was asserted by the clerks, and in the end when the cities had fought themselves into exhaustion, the Amorites moved in and took them over. By this time, about 2000 BC and after (the end of Syria's Early Bronze Age, and the collapse of the Ur III state) many of them, as mercenaries and traders, were virtually assimilated to the urban society anyway.

It may be the resistance to their infiltration in the east by the militant kings of the Sargonid and Ur III dynasties which encouraged their similar move westwards. It is the Amorites who are believed to be the nomadic groups whose presence in Palestine in 'Early Bronze IV' becomes so very obvious in the archaeological record. Many of the sites of this period are recognized to be temporary nomadic encampments, perhaps returned to repeatedly over a considerable period. It is in this period that even the smallest of the settled communities walled themselves in, which suggests a high level of instability, even hostility, comparable with that in Babylonia. The small size of many of the walled communities, however, suggests that they could hardly resist a determined assault; but then the nomads were scarcely capable of much beyond a raid, against which these walls would probably suffice, just as in the Ottoman period, the virtual barbed wire of the prickly pear barriers defended villages against similar raids. In Palestine there was no great central power, disposing of wealth and arms, to provide organized resistance. Instead the evidence suggests a mixture of peaceful intercourse between the two groups and occasional local warfare. How far the Amorites succeeded in taking control of the towns and villages is unlikely ever to be determined. They were no doubt using the same pottery and burying their dead in the same way as the farmers by the time they took over in any particular places.

The situation in northern Syria was different again. Here there were powerful cities and wide lands, with effective governments throughout the third millennium. The cities could provide resistance; the wide lands provided accommodation for the nomads. The Amorite infiltrations are known to have been taking place in the Ebla lands at the time of Sargon, and it can be assumed that his brutalities for a time prevented their movement eastwards. Being mobile, their infiltration westwards probably intensified. This certainly seems the case in Palestine, and the later Syrian societies included plenty of people – and rulers – with Amorite names.

The violent events round about 2000 BC in the north, with the collapse of both the Ur III Empire and that of the remnants of the Ebla Empire, and the 'wave of destruction' which took out many of the cities, was not, it seems, the doing of the Amorites. It does mark both the end of the archaeologists' Early Bronze IV period and a major setback for urban life in north Syria; in Palestine this was the time of the nomadic infiltration which is associated with the Amorites; in Egypt the earlier dynasties had broken the society they had constructed by their heavy demands; in Sumer the same had happened after the warfare of the last four centuries, and the new period saw the seizure by Amorites of several of the old cities. The result was a fallow period followed by a renewed growth of power, in which the Syrians took a full part and suffered accordingly.

Chapter 4

A Moment of Independence

The dismantling of Ebla's empire, followed by the collapse of the Empire of the Ur III dynasty, left the whole region of Syria composed of relatively minor states. Ebla, as noted, was taken over by a new set of rulers, but without restoring its empire. Mari, having suffered a similar destruction, revived. Ugarit, on the coast, had suffered a destruction some time earlier, and by now had also revived. Qatna, which had played a minor role in the wars between Mari and Ebla, emerged as a newly important city, and was refounded on a much higher site; it had not suffered destruction, and this may have given it added strength and authority. In the Amuq Basin Alalah had also survived, and became the locally important city in the area. On the Euphrates Carchemish developed a similarly local importance. But the main power in the north which emerged was Yamhad, on the site of the later Aleppo, newly important; during the two centuries following the collapse of Ur III it developed to the status of a great power under a line of able kings, in effect replacing the dominance Elba had enjoyed in developing a very similar empire.[1]

One of the lessons for all historians (if not for contemporaries, though it is quite probable that they understood it even better than we can) is that Syria was a land which was repeatedly subjected to the attentions, generally hostile, of outsiders. Two successive Babylonian empires, the Akkadian and the Ur III dynasties, had either raided into Syria or had established their domination over it. In the new age following the Ur III collapse (which archaeologists call the Middle Bronze Age) other new powers attempted to achieve the same domination. In the Upper Tigris region the kingdom of Assyria emerged, one of those originally overshadowed by Ur III, and soon developed imperial ambitions. In Anatolia, long an object of commercial exploitation by southerners from Syria and Babylonia, a new kingdom was developing. And in the south Egypt had gone through the same sort of collapse as had happened in Iraq (the First Intermediate Period, c.2200–c.2000 BC). Once again, it proved easier to unite (or reunite) Egypt than it did Babylonia. The Pharaoh Mentuhotep II (c.2010–c.1960) succeeded in vanquishing his internal enemies, reunited the Nile Valley and established his control over the desert oases, then turned his attention to the Nubian Frontier south along the Nile. His rule was harsh, but his successors were less capable, and in the circumstances Egyptian attention was turned inward.[2]

Many of the new Syrian states were Amorite, by which it is best to assume that the language the people spoke was now Amorite, though in most cases there was no obvious change in the ethnic composition of the population. Even if 'Amorite' should designate the people rather than their language, the fact that the language had developed in Syria implies a continuity among the population. But there was also one more new ethnic group arriving in Syria.

Probably infiltrating from the north-east, presumably out of the eastern parts of Anatolia, this new group were Hurrians. (They seem to have come from the same region, the southern Caucasus and eastern Anatolia, where the Khirbet Kerak/Red-Black Burnished Ware originated.) Like the Amorites rather earlier, they appear in many of the cities of Syria first of all as individuals, recognizable by their names, probably as itinerant labourers or merchants. Since they came from the north-east their densest occupation was in the Khabour area – they were fended off by Assyria further east. One particularly aggressive Assyrian king, Shamsi-Adad (c.1814–c.1782) extended his rule over much of the Jazirah and even conquered Mari. Both Mari under its preceding king, Yahdun-Lim, and Assyria under Shamsi-Adad sent raids to the west, a practice which had become a sort of test of manhood for Babylonian kings since Sargon. But neither kingdom was stable – Yahdun-Lim was assassinated, Shamsi-Adad's kingdom collapsed on his death. Out of the wreckage emerged a smaller Assyrian kingdom, a revived Mari under Zimli-Lim, a son of Yadhun-Lim who had been in exile in Yamhad, and a new state in the Khabour Triangle, the Hurrian kingdom known as Mittani.[3]

For several centuries after the end of the Ur III Empire, however, Syria was left more or less to itself. The kingdoms of Assyria and Mittanni were preoccupied with nomads, and then with developing events in Babylonia where the contest for supremacy finally resulted in the emergence of Babylon to supremacy in the first half of the eighteenth century. By that time also the situation in Anatolia was developing in much the same way, though the great power there did not emerge until late in the seventeenth century, with the unification of several small states under the kings of Hatti.

Yadhun-Lim's expedition to the west involved a good deal of fighting. He fought, either then or later, a group of kings of cities and/or tribes along the Euphrates, and later he conquered Emar at the Euphrates bend. His route to the west took the track from Emar to the Orontes which had been one of the sources of Ebla's prosperity. His contemporary at Yamhad was Sumu-epuh, who may have been the first of that city's kings. At first he was one of several local and independent rulers, but by the end of his reign (around 1780 BC) he had established his supremacy. One of the reasons that this strength lasted was that he founded a dynasty which followed a clear line of hereditary succession through seven generations.[4]

In the southern regions, the reunification of Egypt was followed by the deliberate fortification of the frontier over against Palestine. The trade between the two countries, which had continued since the Chalcolithic, was now directed along the route called by the Egyptians the 'Way of Horus', close to the north coast of Sinai. The Egyptians established a firm control of this route by planting a series of military posts along it. A region called the 'Wall of the Ruler', established by Amenemhat I, in effect a military frontier, covered the western part of Sinai.[5] The trade continued, in both directions, but it is obvious that the Egyptians were very wary of the situation in Palestine from the time of their revival as a united state. They established a central trading city at Tell ed-Daba in the eastern delta as a means of controlling and taxing the traders from Palestine.

The situation in Palestine is the least clear of any part of Syria. The upheavals of the last part of the third millennium had resulted by the early half of the second in a new distribution of habitations. Nomad camps have been located in the Negev and in Sinai, but these were soon abandoned and the nomads probably absorbed into Palestinian society. As in the north some places survived and continued, and some new sites were developed. Gradually the old urban order revived.

The combination of archaeology and Egyptian texts (usually not far from contemporary with events) gives an outline picture of Palestine in the early part of the Middle Bronze Age (c.1900–c.1750 BC). Two groups of 'Execration Texts' name lists of cities in Palestine and further north which the Egyptians held in particular dislike; the archaeology confirms their occupation at the time. The Texts refer to these places and peoples because the Egyptians regarded them as 'rebels' – that is, enemies – though it is a term which also implies that it was assumed, at least in Egypt, that Egypt had some authority in the region. But the lists are not exhaustive, and several other places clearly existed without provoking Egyptian enmity.[6]

The Texts only give names, but by doing so they imply that the places so named are of some power. Ashkelon on the southern Palestinian coast is named; it is a large, 50ha site surrounded by a semicircular wall and rampart; at the farther end of the country Hazor, also listed, is an even greater 80ha site, with formidable fortifications, a place which probably dominated all the land from the sources of the Jordan to the Sea of Galilee. In between twenty-four other places are named, to which can be added some other major sites not mentioned, such as Megiddo, Kabri, Gezer, Lachish, and others. It is clear that Palestine was more or less fully occupied by cities of various sizes, some of them the size of Ebla, others smaller. And so it is unsurprising that the Egyptian pharaohs should be both concerned about what was going on in Palestine, and exerted themselves to establish some control.

There are several other Egyptian references to the whole of the Syrian coastal area in the first part of the Middle Bronze Age. The Pharaoh Amenemhat II, the third king of the Twelfth Dynasty (c. 1876–c.1842 BC) is recorded to have conducted at least three naval expeditions along the Syrian coast. One went to Lebanon, another to 'Asia', a third probably to Cyprus and Kilikia. His grandson Senusret III made a raid by land as far as Shechem in Palestine, and was ambushed on his return march. The purpose of Amenemhat's raids, according to his own record, was purely loot – silver, gold, cattle, slaves, wood, oils – but Senusret's campaign may well have a more strategic-political purpose, just as Amenemhat's navy was also demonstrating the length of his reach.[7]

These are isolated instances, and it seems quite probable that there were other expeditions, both naval and military, into Palestine (called Retjenu by the Egyptians) during the time of the Twelfth Dynasty, to which both kings belonged. The reign of Senusret III's son Amenemhat III (a contemporary of Hammurabi, Zimri-Lim, Shamshi-Adad and Sumu-epuh) was long and generally peaceful; there are no records of trouble in Palestine in his reign, but this does not necessarily mean much since the campaigns of his two predecessors are known only from chance discoveries; we may confidently assume a continued Egyptian interest in controlling, or at least dominating, Palestine from a distance, and the use of naval and military strength to ensure it.

The background to all this is that Syria was evidently a rich land, rich enough in material goods – silver, gold, slaves, and so on – to tempt kings who could well claim to be already the richest men in the world. At the same time the Palestine area, and even north Syria, was obviously seen in Egypt as a threat, or at least as a potential threat. The defences of Egypt in Sinai – a line of forts along the route of Palestine, the 'Way of Horus', and an armed security zone – were clearly not merely for show. Along that Sinai trade route the old practices of infiltration were continuing, and the major centre of trade at Tell ed-Daba, in the eastern Nile Delta, was no doubt a means of exerting some control. By a century after Senusret's campaign to Shechem, when the Twelfth Dynasty's powers were fading, there was a substantial population of 'Asiatics' in the eastern Nile Delta. Part of this was composed of the descendants of immigrants from Palestine; others were descended from the 'thousands' of slaves captured by Amenemhat II in his naval raids to Phoenicia and beyond. The numbers had been increasing for centuries, but only the most recent arrivals were truly 'Asiatic' – those descended from earlier immigrants were Egyptians by now.

The normal method of powerful states when a threat such as that evidently felt from Palestine is to conduct a pre-emptive strike to scotch the threat. This seems to be what Senusret III was doing in his raid to Shechem, just as Amenemhat II was weakening the states of the Syrian coast by seizing their wealth and demonstrating his naval power. On the other hand, it does not seem that the Palestinian threat was more than blunted; and the immigration continued.

In north Syria, meanwhile, Yamhad emerged as the major power. An early contact with Mari, before Shamsi-Adad's conquest, turned into enmity when Yamhad's King Sumu-epuh was thought to have been responsible for stirring up trouble between Yadhun-Lim of Mari and the Amorite Yamini nomads. (Whether he did or not is now hardly clear, but it probably did not take much effort to cause the trouble.) However, the sanctuary given to the fugitive Zimri-Lim at Yamhad resulted in an alliance, or at least friendship, between the two cities after his return to Mari.

The third major state in its region was Qatna, also at intermittent odds with Yamhad, and so an obvious ally for Mari or Shamshi-Adad. This situation is one familiar to anyone who has considered the conduct of international relations. The three Syrian cities formed a balance of power, but with other states intervening. The revival of Mari under King Zimri-Lim, who expelled the Assyrian viceroy after Shamshi-Adad's death, brought a certain stability to the system, which also included Babylon, now under King Hammurabi. It was, of course, an unstable condition, but while it lasted it allowed all to prosper. The central figure seems to have been Zimri-Lim – at least it is his collection of correspondence which provides our information. In the end, he quarrelled with Hammurabi, whose assault on Mari was deadly. The city was captured, Zimri-Lim presumably died; after a rebellion, the city was then sacked and destroyed. (The archives were packed and ready to be sent to Babylon when the palace burned down.) Hammurabi emerged as the ruler of all Sumer and Akkad, from the Persian Gulf to Assyria, a land which now can be called Babylonia.[8]

It is always a hazard in any balance-of-power situation, that one of the participants would succumb in the constant intermittent warfare, and so unbalance the system. On this occasion, perhaps because Hammurabi was old by this time and had achieved his ambition, the complex of states survived. In fact, it was probably much more unstable than most such arrangements: as one of Zimri-Lim's correspondents summarized it, 'ten to fifteen kings follow Hammurabi of Babylon, Rim-Sin of Larsa, Ibal-pi-El of Eshnunna, or Ibal-pi-El of Qatna, but twenty kings follow Yarim-Lin of Yamhad'.[9] This was clearly before Zimri-Lim's elimination in 1762 BC, and he is not listed since his correspondent understood that Mari's followers did not need to be named. But the balance clearly depended on each overlord keeping control of his own region and his under-kings, and preventing others of the great powers from poaching. There were other kingdoms not included in this list, such as Ugarit or Byblos on the coast.

Each of the main kingdoms was a major city, but at the same time several of those cities owing allegiance to them were not negligible. For example, Alalah in the Amuq Basin was one of Yamhad's cities, but it was well fortified; similarly Carchemish and Ebla were eventually part of Yamhad's region, but were important cities in their own right. Ebla had revived and was now surrounded by a major fortification of the latest design. It is unlikely that the subject kings were always content to be subordinates, particularly if they had originally been fully independent. It would not take a great deal – an ambitious subject king, a greedy or lazy overlord, a military defeat – to unbalance the international system once more. The temptation was always present for ambitious kings to tempt his rivals' subordinates to change sides.

The archives recovered at Mari provide many details of this state system. The cities switched alliances as it seemed necessary and advantageous. Intrigue seems to have been constant. Troops were loaned by one ally to another. Temporary diplomatic victories were likely, as when Abba'el of Yamhad managed to install his brother Yarim-Lin as king of Alalah. Mari was the entrepôt for supplies of tin from Elam; the king appears to have used this position to distribute the metal to the other cities, being careful not to be too generous to any particular king. The whole diplomatic system extended through the Fertile Crescent, from Hazor in northern Palestine to Elam.

The system did survive for two centuries at least, perhaps three, from soon after the end of Ur III to about 1600 BC. Such systems tend to be self-correcting if given a proper chance, though any period of imbalance is dangerous. So when Mari was defeated and destroyed, its subject territories probably took shelter under the wings of Zimri-Lim's competitors, or perhaps shifted into independence. Babylon inherited some of these, including Assyria, perhaps Yamhad acquired others. But these local empires depended too much on the abilities of capable rulers. Hammurabi's descendents could not hold on to what he had won, and his empire broke up within a few years – just as had that of Shamsi-Adad. The main enemy of Babylon was in the south – the 'Sea-land' – so a preoccupied Babylon rarely bothered the Syrians after Hammurabi.[10]

It is unfortunate that the main collections of records for this period are from Mari and Babylon, since they provide only glancing information about Syria. For example, we know the names of only two kings of Qatna, one of the major cities, and that because they are named in the Mari archives; similarly we know only two from Carchemish. The products of the Egyptian raids along the coast show that it was a wealthy land, but they also show that it was a vulnerable land; and a land which is both rich and divided was liable to find itself in trouble. But Yamhad, with its 'twenty' subordinate kings, was surely a powerful state and fully capable of defending itself. Or so it might have seemed.

Palestine's relations with the Egyptian power were very similar to that of Yamhad's subjects to the king in Yamhad city. The pharaohs of the XII Dynasty had constructed a typical Bronze Age empire of a homeland dominating a series of subject rulers, usually domiciled in cities. At some point, we do not know exactly when, that domination had been imposed, and Senusret's expedition to Shechem has the appearance of an enforcement of his authority against a disobedient subject king. Such empires in part depend on overwhelming force projected from the dominant place, but also on enticements issuing from that same place. The subject kings were rewarded for loyalty by rich and prestigious gifts, or in particular cases by royal presents; they could also collect by way of trade valued Egyptian goods. In Palestine at least seven cities have produced Egyptian goods, or other evidence of contact – Gezer, Megiddo, Shechem, Beth Shean; scarabs and other seals have come from these places as well as Jericho, Gerar, Beth Pelet, Deir Alla, Lachish, and Tell el-Ajjul (which was probably Sharuhen); royal gifts have been found at Byblos and Beirut in Lebanon, at Ugarit further north, and at Qatna inland.

On the other hand there is evidence that contact was still continuing between Palestine and the cities of north Syria. Hazor is mentioned in the Mari archives as a player in the diplomatic game. Cylinder seals of Syrian type and make have been found at Tell Beit Mersim, Megiddo, Tell el-Ajjul, Beth Shean, and Pella. The influence of Syrian architecture has been noted in the major public buildings at several Palestinian cities.[11]

Another method of control, besides brute force or bribery, was direct supervision, not necessarily very intrusive, but one in which the supervisor would report on events to his master. In Palestine the Egyptian base at Sharuhen (Tell el-Ajjul) probably performed such a function, but one would expect at least one similar post in the northern part of the land. Sharuhen could supervise the kings in such places as Lachish and Gezer, but the main cities of Palestine were at places like Megiddo, Shechem, and Beth Shean, and a supervisor would be most useful there. For, the further from the Egyptian base he was, the more likely it was that a subordinate king would feel able to act individually or defiantly.

The land east of the Jordan had been largely empty, except for nomads, during the Early Bronze Age, but it now began to be developed. In the Hawran, where an area of higher land combined with a gap in the western hills to provide a better fall of rain, and this promoted agricultural settlement, as it did in the lands of the plateaux east of the Jordan Valley to the south. An elaborate water system designed to divert the occasional and seasonal flow from a nearby wadi has been found at Khirbet Umbashi. It originated in the Early Bronze Age, and lasted into the Middle. It appears to have been a society above all concerned with animal husbandry, and left a large quantity of animal bone for the archaeologists.[12]

After that site's final failure, about 1700 BC, possibly as a result of over-exploitation of the land, a number of smaller sites used by nomads have been located, quite possibly inhabited by descendants of those at Khirbet Umbashi. Newly founded sites, all of the Middle Bronze Age, have been found at several places in the Hawran proper: Ashtari (the former Ashtaroth) Bosra, and others; several of these are named in a curious story inserted into the book of Genesis, which appears to be of about this date. Clearly this area was now being settled by agriculturalists who had mastered the techniques of dry farming in a marginal land, possibly assisted by a small increase in rainfall.[13]

To south and north of the Hawran are two lands which, like the Hawran, had been scarcely occupied for a long time. To the north was the Damascus Ghuta, which had been inhabited for a time in the Neolithic, but then apparently deserted until at least one new and permanent settlement began in the Early Bronze Age, except for the visits of nomad bands. The first of the new settlements was at Tell es-Salihiyeh, a little north of the Barada River, but well to the east of the site of Damascus. Little is known of the size of the place, since the excavation only found a wall of the earliest settlement at the bottom of a deep sounding. It has been pointed out that the height of the walls on the tell would provide the inhabitants with a wide view and so an early warning of any raiding party's approach.[14] It seems to have lasted into the Middle Bronze Age, and was joined by another site at Tell Sakke, somewhat to the south, where a palace has been found, showing decoration in an Egyptian style; two or three other sites have been located, but little has been excavated as yet.[15]

The Ghuta was difficult to settle. Skills of irrigation were needed to make the land grow crops, otherwise it was merely undistinguished pasture. But at Khirbet Umbashi these skills clearly existed in a way, and Tell es-Sahihiyeh was both contemporary with that site, and had water available from the river. The river had to be canalized, irrigation ditches dug, and the techniques of using the water developed, a learning process which would clearly would take some time, but by the beginning of the Middle Bronze Age the area was recognized as distinct from any other, and had acquired a name, Apum, or Upu, in both Babylonian and Egyptian sources.[16]

South of the Hawran are the plateaux of high land west of the Jordan, divided into four roughly equal sections by deep-cut river valleys; from the north, the Irbid plateau, between the Yarmuk and the Zerqa, the Amman plateau (Ammon in the Bible), between the Zerqa and the Mujib, the plateau of Moab, between the Mujib and the Hasa, and the plateau of Edom, south of the Hasa, after which the land tails off into the desert to the south. The first two were occupied in the Middle Bronze Age for the first time for millennia, above all at Pella (one of the names on the Execration Texts) and the future site of Amman. The valley of the Jordan had been occupied for a long time, though whence came the settlers of the plateaux is not clear – they could be from the valley, from Palestine, or, more likely, they could be settling nomads. The culture of the settlements is close to that of Palestine, but there are fewer signs of direct contact in trade between the two regions; settlements east of the Jordan were largely self-sufficient.[17]

The history of Syria in the Middle Bronze Age splits the land very much into two parts. In the south much of Palestine and the Lebanon were under the influence, even domination, of Egypt. To what extent this amounted to political control is not altogether clear, but Egyptian pharaohs clearly had the ability to march into and through Palestine, and their navy could reach all the way to Cyprus. It is not surprising that the whole country shows signs of being politically, economically, and culturally strongly affected by Egypt.

North Syria on the other hand was out of Egypt's reach. With both Anatolia and Babylonia both fully occupied with their own affairs until the seventeenth century BC, the cities of Syria, from Byblos to the Euphrates, and from Qatna to the Taurus, conducted their own affairs in isolation. We know little about these affairs after the destruction of Mari, but it seems clear that they did not fear being threatened by any outsider.

The separation of north and south in Syria meant that the clear decline of Egypt from the mid-eighteenth century affected only Palestine and that slowly. The dynasty of the Senusrets and Amenemhats (the Twelfth Dynasty) expired in about 1750 with the death of the short-lived King Sobkhotep I. The following Thirteenth Dynasty was less of a dynasty than a series of kings from a succession of families who took it in turns to provide a candidate. Many of the men were presumably old when they achieved the kingship, which would explain why there were probably fifty kings in 130 years. In the circumstances it fell to the bureaucrats to keep things going, which they managed to do fairly well, but inevitably the kingdom decayed. This became particularly obvious from about 1700 BC, by which time the foreign contacts with Nubia and Palestine were being abandoned.[18]

The central administration then itself failed. By about 1650 BC a part of the delta had been proclaimed the seat of a new pharaoh; this drove the final rulers of Dynasty XIII away southwards, but the successor regime also faltered under the stress of a plague. Then, following the route pioneered by 'Asiatic' traders and slaves, an army crossed from Palestine. The new regime was that of the Asiatic invaders, called by the Greeks the Hyksos, a corruption of an Egyptian term meaning 'rulers of (or from) foreign lands'.

At least, invasion is the hypothesis claimed by ancient historians of Egypt, such as Manetho, but some doubt has been cast on this by modern researchers.[19] It is pointed out that there was a substantial 'Asiatic' presence in the delta region during the centuries preceding the Hyksos seizure of power, and that this may well have been sufficiently Egyptianized to know how to develop a kingdom. And yet it is also clear that it was the introduction of chariot warfare which was decisive in bringing the Hyksos to control of much of Egypt, and this was clearly something which arrived from Palestine. Condensing the two notions would suggest an invasion of chariot warriors who combined with the resident Asiatic population to form the Hyksos dynasty (Dynasty XV).[20]

Meanwhile just as southern Syrians were invading and seizing power in Egypt, so outsiders were invading northern Syria. The kingdom of Hatti was brought into being as a union of a series of small Anatolian states, about the middle of the seventeenth century BC, which we call the kingdom of the Hittites. The founder, King Labarna, was succeeded about 1650 by his grandson Hattusili, and between them they established control of the centre of Anatolia, and gained a precarious supremacy over the kingdoms of the west. Hattusili now aimed to add at least part of Syria to his kingdom.[21]

There were presumably preliminary moves, military and diplomatic, and plenty of warning, before the Hittite invasion of Syria came, for Hattusili was met by a coalition of eight northern Syrian states, under the leadership of Yarim-Lim III of Yamhad; or rather he was met by the armies of the kingdom of Yamhad whose king was supported by his subordinate kings – Carchemish, Urshu, Hassu, Ugarit, Emar, Ebla, Tunip, and Alalah – a range of princes which included all north Syria from the Mediterranean to the Euphrates. Some of these may in fact have been independent states and so outside Yamhad's system, but between them they constituted the full array of north Syria.

Hattusili mounted at least six campaigns against Yamhad and its alliance. The allies were his first target rather than Yamhad itself, which was very well fortified. Alalah was attacked in the first campaign, and captured and sacked (with the result that a cache of tablets was preserved, providing much of the information for this war). Yarim-Lim was apparently unable or unwilling to come to Alalah's assistance, even though its royal family was descended from his great-uncle – one might suggest a family dispute here. Later much of the fighting seems to have concerned the control of a series of small cities north of Carchemish which Hattusili had to control in order to reach Yamhad.[22]

Hattusili had the same sort of problem which had distracted Hammurabi of Babylonia and Assyria – trouble amongst those he thought he had already conquered, in this case in western Anatolia – and this made him vulnerable. There is no evidence for it, but one would suppose that an obvious move for Yarim-Lim would be to contact these lands and provoke them to fight, just as Hattusili was clearly operating against Yarim-Lim's allies. In the end Hattusili failed in his Syrian war, and was perhaps wounded in the final fighting.

As Hattusili lay dying, having been in effect defeated in his Syrian war, he changed his plans for the succession. He had already rejected his two sons as disloyal and unfit, and now he rejected their replacement, his nephew, for the same reason. He now nominated his grandson Mursili as his successor, a child; the officials crowded round the bed of the dying king were admonished to care for and educate the boy.[23]

The overall effect of this was that the Hittite menace was understood in Syria to have been seen off, at least while the new king was still a child. It was also clear that there were diplomatic means of preventing further invasions. And yet the situation had fundamentally changed. The emergence of a new and formidable military power in Anatolia had altered the political balance in Syria, just as had the emergence centuries before of a united kingdom in Babylonia. And the campaign had clearly weakened Yamhad, and had seriously damaged its alliance system.

Chapter 5

Battleground

The origins of the Hyksos kings are presumed to be in Palestine, and their success in conquering part of Egypt is to be attributed to the possession of horse-drawn war chariots. These weapons had been developed during the early part of the Middle Bronze Age, adopted in Anatolia from the peoples of the Eurasian steppe (hence the Hittites' war-making power) and was adopted throughout the Middle East by those who could afford them. The north Syrian area has also been identified as the country from which the use of chariots spread to the rest of the region.[1] For they were expensive, requiring skilled workers in metal and wood and leather to construct them, horses to be acquired and trained, and bred and fed, and soldiers to be trained in their use. The main method of warfare in using chariots was first as a mobile platform carrying an archer, or a spearman, and second as a shock weapon to break bodies of formed infantry.

Like all new weapons the use of the chariot by the Hyksos had an immediate effect in Egypt. They gained control of Avaris, the major commercial centre in the eastern Delta (Tell ed-Daba) with which the 'Asiatics' had long been familiar, approaching along the 'Way of Horus', the route along the northern Sinai coast, whose fortification system by Amenemhat II had probably been abandoned by the bureaucratic regime of dynasty XIII. From there they were able to gain control over much of northern Egypt. But not the whole country. Once again there is the same factor of extension and attenuation of power operating: unable to gain full control of all the land, the Hyksos were doomed to find that their kingdom eventually failed. Their new weapon was, as with all such 'revolutionary' weapons, something which could be adopted by their enemies, and as foreigners they could never expect more than toleration from their Egyptian subjects.[2]

In the circumstances they did well to last for about a century. Their initial success brought them as far south as Thebes, which may have been captured, but then they stalled. The regime at Thebes was for a time essentially a replication and continuation of the defeated Dynasty XIV, counted as Dynasties XVI and XVII (the Hyksos being XV), and so it was similarly as barely competent. With both the Theban and the Avaris regimes unable to make progress in (presumably) any attempts to either conquer the south or recover the north, a truce of sorts was accepted, permitting trade to exist: Avaris could trade into Nubia, Thebes into the Delta and Palestine.[3]

The extent of Hyksos interest in Palestine is never clear. Certainly there was trade, as a wide scatter of seals attests. How far this was accompanied by any political presence is the uncertain element. A 'kingdom of Sharuhen' has been suggested to have occupied the southernmost part of Palestine at the time. Sharuhen city is probably Tell el-Ajjul (but other places have been suggested as well, including Tell el-Fara'a (south)), and a dense set of fortified towns within the 30 or so kilometres of Gaza have been suggested as the components of the kingdom. Kingdoms based on Ashkelon to the north and Hebron to the east are assumed to be its neighbours. This is a marginal area for agriculture, but a likely region for interaction of cities and nomads, and the urban density was greatly increased just at the time on the Hyksos.[4]

The obvious explanation of a deliberate promotion of settlement by the Hyksos is not attested either by any texts of the time or by archaeology. The alternative explanation, that the presence of a sympathetic regime in the Delta encouraged trade and hence the urban expansion in nearby Palestine, seems more likely. After all the XVth Dynasty was much occupied by holding, expanding, and then defending its position within Egypt, so any foreign adventures seem unlikely. The latter part of Hyksos rule, when the tacit truce with Thebes allowed a resumption of trade, is perhaps the best explanation of the growth of towns and populations in Palestine.[5]

And, of course, this is only a fragment of the picture in Palestine as a whole, where the growth of communities which seem to be urban in nature covers much of the country. Tell el-Ajjul at 12ha is in fact in the lower range of major sites by size; at the other extreme, both geographically and in terms of size, is Hazor at 80ha. There are another 14 sites which lie between these two in size and position, covering much of the Middle Bronze Age, and with the last phase of that age seeing the largest sites. In other words, the country had developed throughout that period into a quasi-urban land, though it must always be recalled that much of the population still lived in villages. The assumption is further made that the major sites were the headquarters of independent city states.[6]

This perception is reinforced by the first appearance, and probably the first use, of writing in Palestine. Cuneiform written tablets of clay have been found at Gezer and Hazor and a few other places. It is odd that Egyptian writing practices, which must have been known for a thousand years and more in the region, and were visible on the numerous sculptures which were present, had not had any effect in stimulating the local adoption of writing, and that it was a cuneiform system which was in fact adopted. Presumably this was the result of the inapplicability of the Egyptian writing to the local Semitic language, which cuneiform could cope with; even so the adoption of writing took a long time, considering it was in use in north Syria by 3000 BC. But with the beginning of the use of writing came a development which often happens in similar conditions: the idea sparked research into the effective writing system for the local language. This had been the process in Egypt, of course. The result in Palestine was the development of an alphabetic script. It was used only sporadically at first, which suggests that writing was not seen as a particularly useful tool, but its use was also adopted in north Syria, where it was used at Ugarit to record religious texts.[7]

The connection with Palestine and the Hyksos kings provoked a strong reaction at Thebes when a new dynasty – a real one, this time, not the haphazard pass-the-parcel system used earlier – emerged. This was the XVIIth Dynasty. Initially it was as ineffective as its predecessor, but it did first of all establish a proper system of dynastic inheritance to replace the former method of transferring the crown in succession between different families. The three kings of the dynasty lasted less than ten years between them, with the second, Taa II, suffering death in battle, according to the grievous wounds on his corpse.[8] His son, Ahmose, however, proved to be a compelling commander. He inherited the crown young after a stopgap kingship by his uncle, Kamose. Ahmose, reckoned to be the first king of Dynasty XVIII, conducted a series of campaigns to 'expel' the Hyksos, using the new chariots-and-horses military technology, and a propaganda which branded the enemy as a set of foreigners. After a long series of annual campaigns Ahmose captured the Hyksos capital at Avaris, in part by first seizing control of the fortress of Tjaru, cutting the 'Way of Horus' route by which any reinforcements could reach Avaris. He then pushed into southern Palestine and laid siege to the city of Sharuhen. It took three years to take the city, a war which was clearly seen by the Egyptians as essential for their future security.[9]

The brief period in which Mursili of the Hittites grew to manhood and learned to become king left the Syrian victims of his predecessor weakened but surviving. It was perhaps a surprise when Mursili resumed the attack on Yamhad. His motives were probably to revenge his grandfather/adoptive father's death, and to complete his work against Yamhad. This he certainly did, achieving the conquest of Yamhad city, apparently in his first campaign. The sheer speed of the conquest suggests surprise by the Hittites and unpreparedness at Yamhad. Mursili then mounted a long-distance raid to Babylon, captured the city, and then left it; it was taken over by the Kassites from the eastern mountains not long after. Mursili returned home with riches and captives. Not long after that he was then assassinated by his brother-in-law, one of the fruits of his grandfather's tampering with the succession.[10]

The ultimate purposes of Mursili's wars are quite unclear. He made no attempt to hold Babylon, which was probably a hopeless possibility given the distance, and an outcome likely never contemplated. He may have hoped to hold Yamhad, which, after all, had been the object of all these wars, but his death effectively prevented that. His assassin King Hantili attempted to revive and retain control, and is known to have campaigned in the area north of Carchemish, but he soon found he had to fight Hurrian invaders of his own kingdom, and with his lack of success in this, other areas of his inheritance shifted into independence. The crucial area so far as Syria was concerned was Adaniya, which is probably Kilikia, and whose detachment from Hatti made access to Syria much more difficult.[11]

So in Syria the older kingdoms revived, but without the overlordship of Yamhad. The destroyed Alalah revived, under a new line of kings. Ebla, however, had also been destroyed and did not revive, though it is not known if its destruction was caused by the Hittites.[12] The condition of Yamhad city, which may now be called Halab, is unknown. The real beneficiaries of the Hittite wars and removal were the Kassites, who took over Babylon, and the unification of several small Hurrian states into the kingdom of Mittani, which now begins to emerge as a new power in north Syria.

The retirement of the Hittites into Anatolia after Mursili's murder came at the same time that the Hyksos in Egypt were fully occupied with their continuing problems with the Theban kingdom. For much of the sixteenth century BC therefore Syria in the largest sense, from the Taurus to Sinai, was free of outside interference. The Hittite invasions of the end of the seventeenth century had only been brief and although Yamhad, the greatest Syrian state, had been badly damaged, the rest had largely survived or recovered quickly. As after the Ur III collapse the several local states emerged from the shadow of Yamhad's suzerainty into full independence.

This condition lasted for only a couple of generations (say, 1590–1520), and it is yet another effective blank in our records. By the last quarter of the sixteenth century the defeat of the Hyksos in Egypt had brought the revived Egyptian state based on Thebes into southern Palestine to destroy Sharuhen, and in the Jazirah the Hurrians had been organized into the new Mittani state. The Hittites were still mired in dynastic disputes, with repeated assassinations of kings and kings' families during the sixteenth century, a situation which was followed by constant instability for another hundred years and more.[13] In these circumstances, although no doubt Syrians kept a wary eye on events in Anatolia, no Hittite king was able to mount a new southward invasion. The field was left to Egypt and Mittani.

The advances of the Egyptians and Mittani into Syria took place more or less simultaneously. Of the first we know a good deal; of the second virtually nothing, until the two powers met, and their conflict generated records. After Ahmose's conquest of Sharuhen, the same problem of the royal succession which was plaguing the kingdom of Hatti emerged in Egypt. Ahmose's son, Amenhotep I, was a child, and though he grew to be a competent king, he himself had no children.[14] At about this time (about 1500 BC) the Hittite King Telepinu issued a new regulation attempting to define the line of succession (though it hardly worked in the face of his too-ambitious successors), and Amenhotep chose a competent successor from outside the royal family, married him to a cousin and designated him as his heir. (The Egyptian problem may well have been due to the practice of pharaohs marrying their sisters – Amenhotep was the son and grandson of such marriages, and was himself married to his sister; his lack of offspring is not too surprising.)

In the north Mittani reached westward from its political base in the Khabour 'triangle' to establish an overlordship which certainly existed by c.1500 BC, and included the domination of Emar on the Euphrates, and Alalah to the west, but probably not Halab between them, and probably none of the states south of that city. Mittani itself appear to have been an aristocratic society, in which the lords lived in large 'manor houses', often perched on abandoned tells from earlier centuries. This had few or no other habitations, and the rest of the population lived in small villages or hamlets scattered widely.[15] On the one hand, this suggests a quasi-feudal situation, with the king having less than complete control; on the other, the wide and unfortified spread of the rural population implies a certain internal peace. No doubt it also means overbearing lords, who would monopolize military power in the form of the new chariots. This is a region where chariot warfare was developed, and like the Hyksos in Egypt (who may well be partly Hurrian in their origin) this gave Mittani a strong political and military advantage. Hence the distant domination of north Syria.

By the end of the sixteenth century the political situation in Palestine had radically changed. The major urban centres which had developed in the Middle Bronze Age were suffering decline. Many of them did not survive into the Late Bronze Age, and often suffered destruction. How this destruction was caused is not known. Both the Hyksos and their enemies have been blamed, as has a process of fission affecting the political units. For all of this there is no direct evidence. The destruction would seem to have happened at the point at which the archaeologists shift from the Middle to the Late Bronze Age, which is also when the Hyksos ruled in Egypt, but this is not a particular point in time and the city destructions were spread over a considerable period. The destruction of Tell el-Ajjul/Sharuhen marks the end of the Hyksos regime in Egypt by about 1520; this is also during the period of much destruction in Palestine. It would seem that the cause of the destruction of Palestinian cities was mainly due to internal warfare between the cities.[16]

Amenhotep I, without children, solved the succession problem by adopting, as an adult, a capable lieutenant of his. This was Thutmose I, who had plenty of government experience, but who had to make clear his right to the throne. One means to this end was to conduct a successful military campaign, and he began to do so in his second year. He campaigned furiously in Nubia, and then turned to Palestine. His justification was 'to destroy men of the foreign lands and to subdue the rebels of the desert' – the usual vague but unpleasant self-justification of conquerors.[17]

Thutmose I's expedition was a power play intended to impress on all in Syria and beyond (as well as Palestine and Egypt) the extent of his power. For the first time the geopolitical conditions in Egypt and north Syria were knitted into a single system which was not simply cultural and economic. The only reason for the expedition was that Thutmose regarded Mittani as a potential threat, which might seem exaggerated given the distances, but which he clearly took seriously. He understood that the growth of the power of Mittani in north Syria posed a political threat to his own rule and kingdom in the south. So his expedition ignored disturbed Palestine and aimed to make a spectacular campaign which would alert the whole Middle East to the arrival on the international scene of a new great power. A successful campaign might very well so impress his near neighbours that they might be more submissive. He attacked Mittani in its homeland.[18]

He carried his army by sea and landed at Byblos, then advanced inland along the gap between the Lebanon and the Bargylos Mountains, the Eleutheros Valley. From there he could turn north along the plateau east of the Orontes. On this route he passed through a series of at least three Syrian kingdoms, Niya, Nuhhasse, and probably Halab. There appears to have been no opposition to him from any of these; it would seem that Mittani was seen as an enemy of these kingdoms, just as it was of Thutmose. On his return he spent some time hunting elephants in Niya. This suggests he knew full well that Mittanian influence had been spreading south and that one of his aims was, at least in part, to bolster the international diplomatic defences of these small Syrian states. It may be assumed that his progress on the march had been negotiated in advance – he clearly knew where he was going and what his aim was. On the other hand he had no intention of staying in the north, so no specific political relations with these kingdoms were made.

At the Euphrates Thutmose indulged in some fighting, apparently across the river on the Mittani side, but it is likely that neither he nor the Mittani King Parattarna was keen on a long war. Thutmose would obviously be able to call up reinforcements if he became deeply involved, at least from the fleet at Byblos, and possibly from the local Syrian states, and Parattarna surely understood that his enemy would have to go home soon. No truce or treaty is mentioned, and since the sources are Egyptian, this probably means that Parattarna did not bother to negotiate nor did he submit. Thutmose set up a stele of celebration on the banks of the Euphrates and left. It was still there two generations later; Parattarna had not even bothered to destroy it. But surely Thutmose had made his point.

Mittani had expanded from its original base in the Khabour Triangle to control all the Jazirah as far as the Euphrates by the time Thutmose encountered it.[19] There is no evidence in Thutmose's expedition that Parattarna's power had spread across the Euphrates, but the curious story on King Idrimi of Alalah seems to indicate that it soon did, for King Parattarna installed Idrimi at Alalah as his ally and subordinate. Idrimi's father had been king in Halab and had been driven out by a local revolution several years before; Idrimi took refuge first in Emar and later at Ammiya in Canaan, that is, Phoenicia. After several years (he says 'seven') he gathered together a group of exiles from Mukish at the mouth of the Orontes, Halab, Niya, and Amae. He spent some time organizing his return, and clearly laid down several lines of intrigue. He built, or acquired, ships to transport his gathered forces. At last, when all was ready, the expeditionary force sailed from Ammiya and landed him and his men at the Orontes mouth. With local support he installed himself in Alalah. There followed another 'seven' years during which he was in conflict with Parattarna, but in the end they made peace on the basis that Idrimi would accept Parattarna as his overlord.[20]

This story indicates clearly enough that Mittani had by this time imposed a vague overlordship over all north Syria; Idrimi's expedition in fact may have been the trigger for that development. In another treaty with Parattarna, Idrimi indicates that his kingdom stretched to the Mediterranean at the mouth of the Orontes, and was bordered on the north by the kingdom of Kizzuwatna, which occupied Kilikia, and was one of the detached sections of the Hittite kingdom.[21] To the east he does not include Halab, not surprisingly; it thus seems to have been independent, and one of the reasons for Idrimi's war with Parattarna was to prevent the exiled claimant returning to Halab; confining him to Alalah would sensibly reduce the power of both cities, and perhaps promote enmity between them, which would make it all the easier to impose a Mittani overlordship on both. Halab had therefore resumed its role as a bastion of Syrian independence as against the invader, in this case Mittani, a situation now thoroughly undermined by Idrimi's seizure of Alalah. How far south Parattarna's influence extended is unclear, but the supporters of Idrimi stretched as far south as Niya and that area may be assumed to be within Parattarna's system – thus the region through which Thutmose I was able to march unhindered was now within the sphere of influence of Mittani. An emissary from the kingdom of Tunip is recorded in Egypt in Thutmose's reign, perhaps hoping for Egyptian support.[22] Tunip was inland in Syria, south of Niya. It would seem that the ease with which Thutmose marched as far as the Euphrates had persuaded Parattarna to stretch out his power as a means of defence.

It is worth pointing out that these events demonstrate some details not recorded by the rather staid and boastful official accounts. Three items may be adduced to emphasize the sea-aspect. In order to effectively intimidate any of the Syrian states which were likely to be hostile, and to have on hand a sufficient force to fight, if not actually to defeat, the Mittani army of Parattarna, Thutmose must have taken a substantial force north on his campaign. By using Byblos and the Plain of Akkar at the Eleutheros mouth as his base, he had presumably transported his army by sea, landing, it is assumed, at Byblos. The army consisted of horse–drawn chariots and infantry, and it would need a substantial quantity of stores; all of this is bulky, so Thutmose will have required a large force of ships.

When Idrimi launched his expedition to seize a kingdom for himself, he transported the force he had collected by sea. He is said to have been living at a place called Ammiya, somewhere on the coast of Phoenicia, in the second part of his exile. He clearly had access at fairly short notice to a substantial number of transport ships. He obviously did not need as many as Thutmose, but one may surely refer to it as a fleet.

The third example in this little catalogue is from some time earlier. When Kamose campaigned against the Hyksos in northern Egypt, he captured 300 merchant ships laden with gold, silver, weapons, and other goods, which are said to have come from Retjenu – that is, Palestine – and Avaris by this time was a substantial city and a major port of trade; the implication, however, of Kamose's captures is that these 300 ships were in the service of the Hyksos king, bringing war materials to him to enable him to continue the fighting.[23]

It is evident from these three cases that the eastern Mediterranean around 1500 BC was a major and busy trading region, in which large numbers of ships were active. Those captured near Avaris are said to be 'cedar-built', by which one may understand that they were ships constructed in the ports of Lebanon. Byblos was the major Levantine port of contact for Egypt, but Tyre and Sidon are known to have been in existence by the Middle Bronze Age,[24] while several others may be presumed to exist – later campaigns by Thutmose III mention several places, usually to report he destroyed them; farther north also was the city of Ugarit, where the excavations have produced evidence for contact with Egypt, Crete, Cyprus, and Greece.[25] Close by was Kilikia (the Kizzuwatna kingdom) and Cyprus, both of which had shipbuilding traditions throughout the ancient world.

The active trade of the Bronze Age is of course a well-understood phenomenon. Excavations at the ports along the Levant coast invariably produce examples of Minoan pottery; Ugarit and Alalah and Avaris have produced evidence of the importation of Minoan artists in the decoration of the walls of buildings. It is also clear, from circumstances of the naval expeditions of Thutmose I and Idrimi, that the possibilities of exploiting the ships of the region for military purposes had not escaped the rulers.

The foreign expedition of Thutmose I was not repeated by his successor, Queen Hatshepsut, though she is reported to have sent one or two expeditions into Palestine to suppress obstreperous princes.[26] The expedition to the Euphrates had perhaps dented the growing prestige and authority of the Mittani kingdom, but it had also stimulated that kingdom to expand into north Syria. By the time of Hatshepsut's death in 1458 Mittani's authority had extended south to the Upper Orontes.

Her successor was Thutmose III, who had been kept in subjection since his father's death, but who had also, like his stepmother, grown up to admire the achievements of Thutmose I. At once he was able to prove his mettle. For, like

Thutmose I, his claim to the throne was very slender if heredity was counted, and he had to demonstrate his prowess. He may also have felt it necessary to demonstrate his manhood after being dominated by his stepmother for fifteen years – and warfare was the obvious means. (Later he attempted to obliterate her memory.) He counted the years of his reign from his father's death, ignoring Hatshepsut's time, so his first campaign as sole king was in his '23rd year' (1453 BC). Within a few weeks of his accession as sole king he went on a decisive campaign into Palestine, one which determined the history of the region for the next two centuries and more.

The campaign's object was a large coalition of states which had gathered an army under the leadership and command of the king of Qadesh.[27] The Egyptian record of the campaign reports that the coalition comprised members from Palestine to Nahrin, the whole, therefore, of Syria from central Palestine to the Euphrates. Those which are mentioned individually, in part because some of the Egyptian prisoners came from there, are mostly from the northern part of Palestine and southern Syria.

So here is one of the results of the original expedition into the north by Thutmose I: until then Egypt had only been concerned with events in Palestine, together with occasional notices of the coast as far north as Byblos. But now, the city states of central Syria had become fearful of Egyptian power (Thutmose I's effect), or hopeful of Egyptian loot (the Hyksos effect). Whatever the reasons for the involvement of the Syrian cities in this alliance, they were now within the range of Egyptian concerns.

The reason for the campaign according to the Egyptian record is that the coalition threatened Egypt, and 'rebels' who should have been obedient to Egypt, had to be dealt with. One factor must surely have been the death of Hatshepsut. The accession of a new king was always the occasion for enemies to gather, and the fact that Thutmose had been kept out of power by his stepmother for fifteen years must have suggested that he was incapable – after all, she was a mere woman – and that his accession was a further sign that Egyptian power was waning.

The motives for both sides in that case would be clear: Thutmose was acting to pre-empt an attack by the Syrian alliance; the Syrians were aiming to exploit a moment of Egyptian weakness. The coalition had obviously been organized before Hatshepsut's death, since it could hardly have been conjured up in the few weeks between her death and the start of Thutmose's march. It was headed by a king whose territory, in the upper valley of the Orontes, had never been threatened by any Egyptian king, which tends to confirm the Egyptian claim that it was threatened by an attack; the geographical extent of the coalition is something which can hardly have been organized in only a few weeks; it must have been in contemplation for some time, perhaps years.

Thutmose marched north from Egypt, calling at Gaza, which had replaced the ruined Sharuhen as the main Egyptian base in southern Palestine.[28] He marched north along the coast road, clearly in the knowledge that his enemy was somewhere in the north or centre of Palestine. At a town called Yehem (Jemmeh) he discovered that it was gathered and waiting for him, camped along the route stretching south-east from the city of Megiddo. Between the two armies was the southeastern extension of the Carmel Ridge, a difficult obstacle through which there were only two routes, a relatively easy one, and a more difficult one along the Wadi Aruna. For good logistical reasons the enemy army was camped on the north side of the ridge in fertile and productive land where the flocks which were their logistical base could be pastured and food obtained. Thutmose chose the more difficult route for his approach march, whereas the Qadesh army probably expected him to use the easier route to the south. (Had he done so the enemy would have had warning and been given time to array itself in preparation.) His march was aimed directly at Megiddo, which was the centre of the coalition's position. Therefore his arrival – apparently by surprise – split the enemy army into two parts.

The Egyptian assault drove off the coalition forces, but the leaders, and presumably many of their followers, took refuge in Megiddo, a formidably fortified city. The Egyptian army had failed to capture it in the immediate aftermath of victory because the soldiers turned to looting the enemy camp; if that was so it is unlikely that the fleeing enemy had to be hauled up the city wall on ropes: they would have had plenty of time to reach the city. Without apparently even attempting an assault, Thutmose began a siege, surrounding the city with a rampart and ditch, and waited to allow starvation to force a surrender. Inside the city, the enemy commanders were probably waiting for the same effect to drive the Egyptian army away, together with the hope that relief would come from their forces still outside the city.

It was the Egyptian pressure which won out. Thutmose was encouraged by a steady flight of inhabitants out of the starving city, whom he ostentatiously pardoned, no doubt after extracting intelligence of the conditions inside. After five months the enemy leaders also surrendered. There was no pardon for them. They were all taken prisoner, and their goods became prize – over 2,000 horses, 1,000 chariots, over 1,700 slaves, 1,900 goats, 2,000 sheep, 2,000 cattle, 20,000 other animals, weaponry, prized ornaments, and so on. The kings were deposed, and new kings of their cities were appointed.

This marks the first Egyptian attempt to establish control over Palestine, as opposed to simply dominating it from a distance and sending raids to punish perceived 'rebels'. The participation of the king of Qadesh, and his presumed replacement by a newly appointed king, ensured that Thutmose' empire now stretched well into Syria. Whether the Mittani king was the instigator of the coalition or not, as has been supposed, his overlordship was now clearly in danger from the south.

It was, however, one thing to acquire an empire and another to keep it. Thutmose spent the next twenty years of his reign repeatedly campaigning in Palestine and later in Syria, to maintain the hold he had gained over the country at Megiddo. In the four years after the Megiddo campaign he had to besiege and capture the port of Joppa, and campaign, without apparently fighting, through inland Palestine. In other words the king of Joppa was unconvinced that the victory at Megiddo was decisive, and the rest of the country needed to be explicitly and repeatedly warned, by the presence of the Egyptian army, to keep quiet, and to produce the required tribute in full and on time. One would suppose that several of the newly appointed kings were themselves replaced during these years.[29] Thutmose was in the process of inventing methods of imperial control of a more rigorous standard than mere overlordships.

Some of the participants in the coalition of Megiddo were apparently from northern Syria. Kizzuwatna is mentioned, for example. 'Nahrin' is named, a term which is often the Egyptian word for Mittani, but is also a general term for north Syria, especially where it was under Mittanian rule. But just to the north of Qadesh were two cities, Qatna and Tunip, who seem to have been actively anti-Egyptian after the battle, though they had not been directly punished, presumably because their kings had not been captured. Thutmose seems to have identified them as causing trouble, perhaps by intriguing with his new subjects to promote rebellion. The two cities must have been apprehensive that, when he had become confident that he would have no more trouble in Palestine, Thutmose would move on northwards.

This he did in his fifth and sixth campaigns. Reverting to the methods of his grandfather, he transported his forces by ship to Byblos, and made the Plain of Akkar at the mouth of the Eleutheros his base. The fifth campaign was devoted to establishing control of this base area, by capturing the town of Ullaza north along the coast from Byblos. There the Egyptians found a garrison of soldiers from Tunip. Whether this was an allied force which had arrived to help out or a garrison established to maintain control over a town in a minor Tunipian empire, Thutmose was clearly now involved in a much wider war.

The capture of Ullaza, the possession of Byblos, and the capture of the nearby town of Ardata, established the Egyptian base. Thutmose may have been attempting to emulate his grandfather here, and aiming for a much wider campaign, but it was obvious from these initial events that he had a much more difficult task. Whereas Thutmose I had faced no opposition in his campaign until he reached the Euphrates, and indeed it is probable that Tunip was an ally at the time, Thutmose III half a century later was faced with opposition from every state in the area except possibly Byblos.

Whatever position Thutmose thought he had achieved in his fifth campaign (1451) had to be recovered in the next campaign (in his thirtieth year, 1450). Ardata and Ullaza had to be reconquered, but he did raid into the territory of Qadesh, following the route along the Eleutheros Valley. Next year again, Ullaza had to be retaken from yet another garrison sent from Tunip, and the area of Sumur north of the river in the Plain of Akkar was also ravaged. This time he left a garrison of his own in Ullaza, and from there he established Egyptian control over several other coastal towns, each of which was stocked with supplies in case of a new campaign. So at last, after three campaigns, he had achieved a permanent base from which he could campaign into inland Syria.[30] It is obvious that the Syrians were using the same strategy as had produced the battle of Megiddo, by holding on tenaciously to their most forward position (e.g., Ullaza) and so forcing Thutmose to fight there.

Sure enough, next year, the thirty-third of his reign, Thutmose made a major effort. He had finally come to the conclusion, like his grandfather, that the root of his troubles lay in Mittani, so, again like his grandfather, he mounted a new campaign as far as the Euphrates. Whether he was correct in this assumption is not known, for we do not have any records from Mittani itself; there is no direct evidence from the Egyptian side. On the other hand, with an Egyptian army planted permanently in northern Phoenicia, and Egyptian campaigns directed against Tunip and Qadesh, it is very likely that Mittani was at the very least seriously worried, and would be likely to have taken a direct share in the resistance.

Thutmose's new campaign first attacked Qatna, and then moved north to confront Mittani. Here the kingdoms of Niya and Nuhhasse presumably submitted readily to the pharaoh, as they had to Thutmose I, but when his army reached north Syria the Mittani forces were ready for it, and a battle was fought near Halab, at a place called Juniper Hill. Halab was thus presumably now one of Mittani's vassal states. Thutmose won the victory and set about the usual process of destruction of villages, of crops and fruit trees. He had brought dismantled boats with him, built at Byblos, and these were reassembled for the crossing of the Euphrates; the Mittani forces were withdrawn without fighting. Another stele was erected to boast of the king's achievement and placed next to that of Thutmose I. There was no reason for the Mittani king to continue fighting, for, as with Thutmose I, it was obvious that Thutmose III would need to return to the south soon. The fact that he had chosen to fight before Halab implies that he was defending Mittanian vassals.

The crossing had been in the neighbourhood of Carchemish, and when he turned back Thutmose marched south along the west bank of the river as far as Emar, devastating the land as he went. It is possible that he received the submission of several of the local kings, who had been Mittani vassals before, but any such submissions were clearly insincere and designed simply to get rid of the Egyptian forces; the Euphrates campaign implies that this area did not submit. Thutmose spent some time, like his grandfather, on an elephant hunt in Niya, but then had to fight against Qadesh, which was defeated in battle at 'Zinzar', which is probably Shaizar on the Orontes, and then captured and sacked Qadesh itself; he also faced enmity from Tahshi, the Bekaa Valley; thirty towns and villages were plundered in that land. The army, or at least most of it, then returned to Egypt by sea by way of Byblos.[31]

The Egyptians had been much impressed by the wealth they discerned in Syria. Booty on a large scale was collected, detailed lovingly by the king on his victory stelai, and many of his soldiers returned to Egypt with loot and wives and slaves. The number of Syrians who moved or were taken to Egypt in these campaigns was considerable, and many of the tombs constructed and decorated at this time, often for men who had taken part in the campaigns, show scenes of Syrian life, or contain trophies looted from Syria.[32]

This local wealth was substantially reduced as a result of the looting and plundering and destruction the Egyptians had committed. Their methods of warfare, which involved destroying crops in the fields, cutting down fruit trees, and destroying undefended villages, were clearly designed to impoverish their enemies. But it was not designed to establish Egyptian rule, which required that vassal states supply tribute on a regular basis – this was probably the reason for the repeated campaigns in which no fighting was recorded. The territory Thutmose had actually gained reasonably full control of was Palestine, probably as far as Mouth Hermon, but maybe not the Judaean hill country, Damascus (probably[33]), and the coastal region of Lebanon, called Djahy by the Egyptians. The Orontes Valley cities might be considered as Egyptian vassals, but Thutmose had to fight them more than once: Tunip and Qadesh were defeated. Towns in Djahy rebelled.

North of the Eleutheros Valley, Thutmose had to fight several times in the next years. Nuhhasse was his enemy twice, in his thirty-forth and thirty-eighth years, and in his thirty-eighth year's campaign he again fought troops from Mittani.[34] But in these affairs, Thutmose made no serious attempt to retain control; so the land between Qatna and Halab was becoming a frontier zone between the Mitannian and Egyptian parts of Syria; in the north, the Egyptian aggressiveness no doubt compelled Mittani to exercise a steadily greater control over its region. The Egyptian campaigns have the air of the old pre-emptive strikes, designed not to conquer, but to maintain control over what had already been seized, and unsettle those who might consider contesting his conquests. The Syrian enemy states were no doubt concerned to push Egyptian power further south, a desire surely reinforced by continued Egyptian interference and the tactics of devastation. A rebellion close to his Byblian base, maybe with Mittanian support, occurred in his seventeenth campaign, and in his forty-second year a town called Irqata was the focus, but Tunip was identified as the cause and was captured and its lands devastated. Among the prisoners captured were men from Nahrin.[35]

If Thutmose had been correct in identifying Mittani as the basis of Syrian enmity, he had gone to a great deal of trouble to achieve very little. Certainly he had extended his empire over a series of wealthy cities, though he had damaged them badly in doing so, but he had also committed himself to continued fighting to defend what he had gained at a great distance from his strategic base in Egypt. Mittani, on the other hand, did very little of the actual fighting in the face of Egyptian attacks, being evidently content to rely on its vassals to bear the brunt. Only twice during these campaigns does it appear that Mittani forces were engaged, at the battle near Halab and in fighting in Nuhhasse. Instead, most of the resistance to Egyptian conquest came from the Syrians themselves, with Mittanian encouragement and some participation.

How far these resisters were under Mittanian control or influence is not certain, but the fact that Mittani troops fought in Nuhhasse and in Tunip suggests that Mittani had at least considerable influence over them. Whether the rebellions in Djahy were Mittanian doing is less obvious, but they may very well have been. Probably Mittani did not have to work very hard to achieve its influence, since it was clearly Egypt which was the aggressor; and rebellions were apparently always likely.

The Egyptian empire was therefore an unsteady construction, dependent for its continuation on the brutal suppression of any rebellion and the devastation of any enemy territory the army could reach. Some princes and their heirs were taken to Egypt partly as hostages, partly in order to 're-educate' them into becoming loyal Egyptian supporters, but it was, as became obvious in the next two generations, not merely the princes whose opinions counted. Egypt, in building an empire, had constructed for itself a continuing burden.

Even after Thutmose's death (in 1425) the war continued. His successor, his nephew Amenhotep II, conducted a campaign in his third year in Tahshi, when he claimed to have collected as booty 54 tons of silver, 200 horses, 300 chariots, and almost 90,000 prisoners; if such figures are correct and not merely exaggerating boasts, the Bekaa Valley was left virtually depopulated.[36] The same fate befell a rebel in Palestine two years later. In his seventh year he campaigned against Qatna – this after a march through Palestine. In the Qatna fighting some of the Mittanian chariot men called *maryannu* were taken – though this might be a general term for such specialized fighters. He then marched against Niya, coming at it from the north, which suggests a campaign directed at Mittani; since no result is stated, probably the Mittanian forces again evaded direct contact. After capturing another town, the army was taken back to Egypt.[37]

Amenhotep could probably have made peace with Mittani at any time by accepting that Mittanian influence in the Orontes Valley was a legitimate matter; on the other hand it is clear that he enjoyed campaigning, just as he enjoyed displaying his physical prowess as an archer and a horseman. It was thus left to his son Thutmose IV to conclude a peace treaty, though it seems probable that there had been occasional discussions for peace since late in Thutmose III's reign.[38] In all likelihood it was the obvious recovery taking place in the Hatti kingdom under the latest man to seize the kingship which was the final persuader. Egypt and Mittani had in fact fought each other to a standstill years before, but their pride would not allow them to bring discussions for peace to a definite conclusion. The threat of another player in the game was decisive. The result was a Syria divided between the two outsider kingdoms, and much destruction.

Chapter 6

Divided and Ruled

The peace between Mittani and Egypt, which was probably concluded by kings Thutmose IV and Artatama, existed by 1390, the year of the former's death, but had been concluded some years before. It is possible that the revival of the Hittite kingdom under the new king, Tudhaliya II, who became king about 1400 BC, helped to bring the two states to a decision, but it is also likely that the kings had fully understood the impossibility of victory. As it happened, the Hittite revival was slow and irregular, but by about 1360, when a new king succeeded – Tudhaliya III – much of the essential recovery groundwork had been accomplished. Later the Hittites recalled that a Hittite invasion under Tudhaliya II had conquered Halab and had defeated the Mittani king, but the record was clearly thoroughly exaggerated in the Hittite memory, though some such raid seems quite likely.[1] It was a clear sign that Hittite ambitions for Syrian wealth continued.

Otherwise the Syrians, though controlled by Mittani and Egypt, had a respite after the Egyptian-Mittani peace treaty was agreed. The Egyptian region was partly under direct Egyptian rule and partly had its own kings, whose allegiance was claimed by Egypt, and who paid tribute. The direct rule was actually less than total, and depended largely on the presence of the Egyptian garrison and viceroys, whose task it was to maintain control over the various kings and princes, who were liable to 'rebel' if a chance offered. It was beyond the resources of any Bronze Age state to do more, and it is obvious that it was still a somewhat rickety system, depending very much on the continued interest of the pharaonic regime in Egypt, and on continued support, military and diplomatic.

The successor of Thutmose IV, his son Amenhotep III, was certainly diplomatically active. He sent missions to all the great powers of his time – Mycenae, Crete, the Hittites, Mittani, Babylon – and was active in the constant intrigues of his Syrian vassals.[2] The empire in Syria was dominated by his viceroys and garrisons. These were stationed at Gaza, guarding the essential landward entrance to Palestine, and at Sumur, in the Plain of Akkar, which was the seaward entrance used repeatedly by Egyptian expeditions. Other major posts were established as needed, notably one in the devastated Bekaa Valley at Kummidi (Kamed el-Loz), again guarding a major routeway, which was made all the more vulnerable by the destruction and deportations carried out by Amenhotep II. These were places where important governors were posted along with garrisons; garrisons were also placed at Joppa on the Palestinian coast, at Ullaza between Byblos and Sumur, and at Beth Shean in the Vale of Jezreel, where the valley was particularly open to infiltration from the east; a garrison there would also be convenient to watch events in the hill countries of Galilee and Judaea, just as Kummidi and Ullaza could watch the hill lands of the Lebanon and Anti-Lebanon. Altogether this was a carefully chosen series of position, well placed but few.[3]

Apart from the need to guard strategic places and watch difficult areas, it was necessary that the Egyptian posts be few and relatively inexpensive. If one thing had become clear to the Egyptian rulers in the previous fifty years of Syrian warfare it was surely that it was a very expensive matter, both to wage war at such a distance from Egypt, and to govern the conquered land, and that the major enemy, Mittani, had committed far fewer resources to the fighting than had Egypt, having apparently persuaded the Syrian states to bear the major burden. Each invasion by Egyptian forces had involved major expenses to provide for troops, supplies, and shipping, but the Mittani forces had usually avoided battle, and the Mittani homeland, in the Khabour Triangle, was too far off to be damaged – just as Egypt was essentially invulnerable to Mittani attack. Consequently the fighting on the Mittani side had largely involved Syrian forces, and the battles had taken place in Syrian territory – Megiddo, the Bekaa Valley, Ullaza, Qatna, Halab, the Euphrates Valley – and it was Syria and Syrians which suffered the devastations visited upon enemies, and paid the requisitions imposed by the pharaohs – and then had to pay the heavy tribute levied on the conquered lands.

The resilience of the Syrian countries under this burden is remarkable, but for a generation after the peace was concluded the Egyptians had few problems as the Syrians recovered from the warfare. Amenhotep III, though active in diplomacy, was more concerned with great building projects at home, and he was followed by his son, Amenhotep IV, who was seized by a religious passion and attempted to rework the Egyptian religion around his chosen god, Aten, after whom he renamed himself Akhnaten. He was followed by three short-lived and ineffectual kings, including Tutankhamun, and by much internal disputation. So from diplomatic action only under Amenhotep III Syria sank well below the horizon of the Egyptian concerns for another generation.

The results are demonstrated in a diplomatic archive known as the Amarna letters, discovered at the new city of Akhetaten (Tell el-Amarna) which was constructed by Amenhotep IV/Akhnaten as a new centre for his religious observances. (Incidentally, this shows the great wealth and organizing power of the country, in building a new city from scratch in little more than a decade; it also shows the carelessness of the whole system, in that it was then abandoned – a good part of the expense was provided by Syrian tribute.) The letters are from a variety of foreign rulers, and from a number of Egyptian subject princes within the empire, and they show the gradual decline of Egyptian power and the change in the political conditions.[4]

The foreign rulers include the Mittani king, Tushratta, whose increasingly frantic letters show that he was very concerned about the rise of Hittite power on his northern borders. He looked to Egypt for support, mostly in gifts of gold, which he no doubt needed to pay his chariot-riding warriors, perhaps to persuade the lords of the kingdom to turn out to fight. In exchange Amenhotep required sisters and daughters of his royal correspondents to be delivered to his harem. And yet none of these arrangements actually produced a working alliance and there seem to be no occasions when two of the great powers actually agreed to fight a joint enemy, but neither did their diplomatic disputes result in wars. An example is Amenhotep's approach to the king of Arzawa in western Asia Minor, who had recently won a war against Tudhaliya III of the Hittites. It looks as if Hatti was finished, Amenhotep commented in a letter, and asked for a royal daughter for his collection.[5] Indeed the Hatti state was certainly in distress at the time, with Kaska barbarians from the northern mountains having captured the capital Hattusa. But the Arzawan king refrained from inflicting the knockout blow, Tudhaliya recovered, drove out the Kaskas, and then turned to deal with Arzawa, but Amenhotep made no attempt to assist his political ally.[6]

The revival of Hatti from this crisis took place in the last years of Amenhotep III's reign and the early years of the reign of his son. It was this which was at the root of the growing panic of Tushratta of Mittani. The successor of Tudhaliya III in Hatti, Suppiluliuma I, made one attempt soon after his accession about 1350 to extend his territories by taking over a former province which had been taken by Mittani, but he was defeated.[7] This was clearly not the end of the matter, and Tushratta wanted Egyptian diplomatic, monetary, and possibly military support. He did not get it.

The nature of the Mittani overlordship of north Syria is much less clear than that of Egypt in the south. The directly-ruled kingdom appears to have reached as far as the Euphrates, but between that river and the Mediterranean the same set of kingdoms – Carchemish, perhaps Emar, Halab, Alalah, Ugarit, Nuhhasse, Niya, Tunip – continued to exist under their own kings. Presumably they paid tribute to the Mitanni king, but all the evidence from the Egyptian wars shows that they also maintained their own armed forces, which were not afraid to challenge Egyptian rule, and were often liable to fight on their own, with only a small degree of Mittanian military assistance. This suggests that Mittani's overlordship was much less onerous than that of Egypt (or, later, that of the Hittites); the contrast with the more rigorous alternatives, and the knowledge that were they independent the kingdoms would be very vulnerable, perhaps persuaded the kings to be loyal. Later when Ugarit attempted to switch from the Mittani to the Hittite side, the kingdom was quickly attacked by two of its neighbours; all three seem therefore to have enjoyed a considerable degree of independence, but in the context of a general loyalty to Mittani.[8] This suggests that Mittanian overlordship was a fairly light weight.

While the Hittite threat was thus growing after 1360 there were problems developing within Egypt's Syrian empire. In two areas in particular local rulers were using the neglect by the pharaohs from about 1360 onwards to develop their own kingdoms. Out of the northern Lebanon Mountains there emerged a lord called Abdi-Ashirta, who combined flattering letters to pharaoh with insidious expansion of his own area of rule. He was complained about by every one of his neighbours and eventually even seized control of the Egyptian base at Sumur, excusing his actions by claiming that he was rescuing it for pharaoh himself. He owed part of his strength to having enlisted groups of landless men, perhaps nomads, called Apiru, and he was able to appeal to the ordinary people of the cities over the heads of the kings, which suggests that he was believed to be aiming for full independence from Egypt or was promoting a social revolution, or at least of aiming to improve conditions. He was successful in passing on his power to his descendants, in particular his son Aziru, who secured recognition of a sort for the kingdom ('Amurru') from pharaoh and established a kingdom which lasted for seven generations.[9]

In Palestine a very similar situation developed somewhat later. Here the great culprit (from the Egyptian point of view) was Labayu, Lord of Shechem. He adopted the same tactics as Abdi-Ashirta in the north, loudly protesting loyalty to the pharaoh while expanding his own power over neighbouring towns and cities, expelling rulers who were loyal to Egypt, and employing groups of stateless people, Apiru, who could be hired either for pay, or more likely with a view to being allotted lands. As Labayu's influence spread, so did the area of disturbance around his territories. Eventually he made the mistake of attacking Megiddo, where there was an Egyptian garrison, and encroaching on the towns on the coastal highway, the Way of the Sea, which was the essential communication route by land between Egypt and the north. The Egyptian administration turned on him and he was soon murdered.[10]

The stories of these two insurgent princes reveal that a network of minor rulers covered the whole of Palestine. Each town had its chief, called variously the 'man of', or 'king', or 'prince', in a variety of languages. All were eager to intrigue against their neighbours and to extend their power if they could. Abdi-Ashirta and Aziru were the most accomplished at this, as was Labayu for a time, but the others were no different in essence. The pharaohs generally paid little attention, leaving the problem to their local officials, but understanding well enough that the constant bickering and intriguing between their vassals was the cheapest way of keeping overall control. No doubt it was necessary to see that the tribute was paid, and a general respect was awarded Egyptian authority – as the insurgents always did, at least in writing, if not in their actions – so that the overall system remained in balance. If some one king became too obviously hostile he could be, it was hoped, easily dealt with, either by his neighbours combining against him, or by a minor expedition. In extreme cases, the insurgent could even be recognized, as happened to Aziru in Amurru.

In many ways this governing system might seem not much of an advance on the original Egyptian system of sending an expedition into Palestine whenever a combination of rulers, or an individual prince, seemed to be becoming too powerful, and therefore a threat to Egypt. In fact the difference is profound. Direct Egyptian control over a substantial area of territory was now being exerted, and by means of governors and garrisons; the individual kings were no longer free to indulge in wars of conquest. That some, like Labayu and Abdi-Ashirta, succeeded in exploiting the diplomatic system to their advantage only demonstrated that the Egyptian imperial system remained flexible. The kings in Palestine and Phoenicia – 'Retenu' and 'Djahy' – were probably under closer control, or rather supervision, than the kings in the Mittani region, but it was the Egyptian system which marked a clear governmental advance, whereas that involving Mittani was loose and probably inefficient, and essentially, in comparison with the Egyptian system, old-fashioned.

On the other hand, it was probably less unpleasant to live in north Syria under Mittani overlordship than it was to live in Palestine and be subject to constant Egyptian supervision and interference. It is noticeable that in both Palestine and Lebanon there was clearly a division between the kings and their subjects. Abdi-Ashirta was able repeatedly to appeal over the heads of the kings to the populations of the cities he was menacing against those rulers; more than one city king was expelled by his people at the urging of the Amurru kings; no doubt this was a result of the rulers being too obviously identified with Egyptian rule and being the agents used by the Egyptian administration to collect and pay over the tribute; no wonder the kings were thereby rendered, at the least, unpopular.

The enmity between Hatti and Mittani blew up into a full scale war after c.1340 when Suppiluliuma launched a decisive attack on Tushratta. He aimed directly at the Mittanian political centre, Washshukkani, in the Khabour Triangle. Tushratta, taken certainly by surprise, and probably with very few troops available, escaped the rout. Suppiluliuma knew well enough how to exploit his sudden victory and moved at once to Syria. He had already made diplomatic preparations, of which Ugarit had been one target, though it had to be rescued from the enmity of its neighbouring kingdoms when they turned on King Niqmaddu for changing sides. Nevertheless it seems that the region had been well prepared diplomatically, and Suppiluliuma's 'Great Syrian War' was overwhelmingly successful: Halab, Alalah, Nuhhasse, Niya, Qatna, Tunip, and even Qadesh fell under his control, as well as

Ugarit. In fact King Niqmaddu of Ugarit was the only king to keep his throne, for all the rest were summarily dethroned and replaced by Hittite nominees.[11]

The two aspects of the campaign which were unsuccessful were that Tushratta survived to go on fighting, and the city of Carchemish held out against the Hittite campaign. Aziru of Amurru used the occasion to join Suppiluliuma and simultaneously to seize control of Byblos and Tyre, whose rulers preferred Egypt to Hatti; the man whom Suppiluliuma installed at Qadesh similarly seized Qatna by the same device. Within a year the power of the king of Hatti had expanded from the Taurus Mountains to the borders of Damascus.

These kings were clearly in the position of Hittite vassals, as they had been to pharaoh and to Mittani though one assumes that Aziru would need to be rather more circumspect in his actions with Suppiluliuma's eye on him. Suppiluliuma had in fact only just begun his war, and had to spend several more years fighting Tushratta. It may have been this continuing war, or perhaps a knowledge of the practices of the Egyptian imperial administration, which persuaded Suppiluliuma to install his son Telipinu as his viceroy in Halab, rather than leaving a local king in charge. The reputation of the city for independence and opposition to any outside powers must have also affected his decision.

The success of Suppiluliuma was partly due to the defeat and humiliation of Tushratta at the start of the war, but it was also due to the contemporary crisis in government in Egypt. Akhnaten died in 1336, while Suppiluliuma's Syrian war was still on. He was succeeded by two young kings, neither of whom had living children, and neither of whom lived long. Under the circumstances the Egyptian reaction to Suppiluliuma's victories was understandably slow to emerge, but he had definitely pushed his power into former Egyptian lands, seizing the allegiance of Aziru of Amurru (and so also gaining control of the Phoenician coast as far south as Tyre) and Qadesh, which brought the Hittite presence to the northern borders of the Damascus kingdom of Upu; a Hittite force had also penetrated into the Bekaa Valley, though, in the face of the Egyptian governor and garrison at Kummidi, it did not stay. The continued troubles of the Hittites in the north did provide a certain opportunity, however, and during the reign of Tutankhamun (who died in 1322) an Egyptian force attempted to recover Qadesh.

The Egyptian offensive had little effect other than to provoke a hurt letter from Suppiluliuma, who claimed that the Egyptian attack was unprovoked, even though both sides knew full well that Qadesh had been in the Egyptian sphere before the war. Suppiluliuma was involved in the final stages of the Mittani war at the time, besieging Carchemish. In the midst of all this the widow of Tutankhamen wrote to Suppiluliuma to send one of his sons to be her new husband. One was sent, but, not surprisingly, he was killed on the way. Suppiluliuma was furious but he could hardly invade Egypt while his Mittani war was unfinished.

Matters were partly resolved soon after. The Egyptian crisis eventually resulted in a new pharaoh, Horemheb, seizing power. He was a military man, who legitimized himself by marrying a daughter of Akhnaten. He had been involved in the Qadesh fighting and may well have been involved also in the murder of the Hittite prince. He was not of royal birth or ancestry, so he had to spend much energy and time in establishing himself in control within Egypt. Further, he had no children and eventually made a military colleague his heir – he became Ramesses I.[12] Ramesses ruled only a little over a year, but he did found a new dynasty (Dynasty XIX), being succeeded by an adult son, the first pharaoh to do so for forty years.

While this was preoccupying Egypt, Suppiluliuma finally captured Carchemish, and at about the same time Tushratta, who had continued to fight since his initial defeat, was murdered by some of his own people, including his son, Shattuwaza. Suppiluliuma sent a force to fight the Egyptians, capturing considerable numbers of soldiers, but they brought the plague into his homeland, of which Suppiluliuma himself died. He had installed Tushratta's parricidal son as his own vassal in the remaining fraction of Mittani, some of which was also taken over by Assyria.

Before he died Suppiluliuma established another of his sons as viceroy at Carchemish, to complement Halab. This was Piyassili, who tactfully took the Hurrian name of Sarri-Kusuh. These two men established their own subordinate dynasties, counting themselves as kings of their cities. What is particularly remarkable is that all the members of these families remained loyal to Suppiluliuma's successors and to each other. Suppiluliuma's second successor, his youngest son Mursili II, had to fight hard to secure his kingship. He and Horemheb, contemporary rulers, were therefore both fully occupied at home throughout their reigns, and had no time to pursue the old imperial quarrels.

Syria therefore remained divided between two outside powers. The boundary between the two empires had been shifted south, from the Eleutheros Valley to the southern end of the Lebanese Mountains, though it seems that the Bekaa Valley remained under Egyptian control, with the garrison still at Kummidi. Both imperial powers had had to tighten their grips on their sections, in large part because the war between Egypt and Hatti continued, even though there seems to have been little fighting because of their internal preoccupations.

Otherwise the pattern continued. In the north the two viceroys at Halab and Carchemish established Hittite dynasties of their own, but they were loyal to the Great King in Hattusa. The viceroys intervened in the subordinate kingdoms whenever they found it necessary, and in the Egyptian region the governors at Kummidi and Gaza acted in similar ways. But both empires suffered rebellions. Once they realized the Hittite regime was more rigorous than the Mittani, kings of Nuhhasse rebelled at least twice, once at the death of one of those kings, the other at the death of Sarri-Kusuh of Carchemish. At Qadesh the man installed by Summiluliuma, Aitagama, was murdered by his son, Niqmadu, possibly because the father had intended to rebel; Egyptian intrigues have been suspected in both of these rebellions.[13] Aziru of Ammuru carefully kept up good relations with both Egypt and Hatti, and this practice was continued under his successors; Ugarit had supported the Nuhhasse rebellion with money, but had not fully participated. It is clear that even with viceroys in place, the Hittite domain remained restless.

In the south Horemheb, who cannot have recalled his failed campaign against the Qadesh when he was still a general with any pleasure, was probably behind whatever intrigues were taking place. After he died his chosen successor, another general, Ramesses I, ruled for less than two years, but at least he had an adult son, Seti I, who was king by about 1290. In Hatti, Mursili II died about 1295 and was succeeded by his son Muwatalli II. Between them Mursili and Horemheb had succeeded in settling the problems of their homelands; but they had not made any real attempt to solve their mutual dispute in Syria; their sons resumed the fight.

Seti I was faced with the sort of rebellions in his part of Syria which Mursili had suppressed in the north. He had to clear the Way of Horus, along the north Sinai coast, of bands of 'Shasu', whose internecine conflicts had spilt over to bother the Egyptians. He went on to deal with a problem at Beth Shean, where a rebellious band had seized the city – a major Egyptian military base – and places on both sides of the Jordan had been drawn into the fighting.[14]

What was probably a later campaign brought Seti along the northern Palestinian coast and into Phoenicia, to Tyre, Ullaza, and Kummidi. This was Ammuru, and if he campaigned there he did so in the territory of the current successor of Abdi-Ashirta, his great-great-grandson Bentishima. It would seem therefore that the Ammuru dynasty maintained its normal practice of swaying with the political wind. Seti could thus claim to have recovered part of the lost Syrian lands.

The records of these campaigns are in pictorial inscriptions on the celebration monument to Seti I at Karnak in Egypt. Two places in northern Palestine, Hazor and Beth Aneth, are named, and there may have been another campaign into northern Palestine at one time; one of Seti's victory stelai was found at Tell es-Shihab in the Yarmuk Valley south of the Hawran, so he would seem to have campaigned east of the Jordan as well; these campaigns would fit either with that to Beth Shean or that to Hazor and Dan.[15] It is likely that after Kummidi Seti went on to recover control of Qadesh. The capture of Qadesh should, geographically, come after the visit to Ullaza, since Qadesh is at the inland end of the Eleutheros Valley route. The inscriptions are damaged, with the crucial section missing, so certainty is not possible.[16]

Nevertheless it seems probable that, in these two or three campaigns, Seti had resumed control of all the lost Egyptian lands in Syria. He seems to have fought at least one battle, presumably after gaining Qadesh, against soldiers from the Hittite sub-kingdoms to the north. He claimed victory, and certainly boasted of it on his inscriptions, though it is described in such formulaic terms that it is impossible to determine what happened exactly.[17]

Seti's restoration of Egypt's Syrian boundaries would hardly be allowed to stand by the Hittite king. One reason Seti had been successful was that Muwatalli had been busy fighting in Anatolia, and as soon as he could he returned to Syria. It seems that he recovered both Ammuru and Qadesh, perhaps by pressure rather than by conquest in both cases. At Qadesh the stele of celebration Seti had put up was not destroyed, but apparently just tidied away, perhaps in the knowledge that it could be brought out again when – not if – the Egyptians returned. So when Seti died about 1279 his Syrian work had been undone.[18]

His successor was his son Ramesses II, who came to the throne as a young man. The Syrian war was still on, of course, and it seems clear that Ramesses was intent on recovering the territories once gained by his father; but since lost again. In his fourth year he made the first move, sailing an expeditionary force to Byblos to persuade Amurru to change sides once more. He thus gained control of the old Egyptian base in the Plain of Akkar, and the Egyptian governorship was re-established at Sumur. Next year he moved to secure Qadesh, but, alerted by the previous year's campaign, Muwatalli also made preparations to defend that city. The main Egyptian army marched through northern Palestine and the upper valley of the Orontes, not the route usually used. Meanwhile a separate force was sent by sea to the Plain of Akkar. The intention may well have been to persuade Muwatalli to head for the sea along the Eleutheros Valley and so catch his army between the two Egyptian forces. Muwatalli, however, stayed in Qadesh, and instead it was pharoah's army which was surprised.

The battle which resulted is the best described of any from before the Greek historians.[19] Ramesses' advance force, under his own command, was deluded by false intelligence that Muwatalli's main army was still at Halab, and proceeded to make camp. The Hittite army, which was actually close by, drove round the city to attack the other divisions of the approaching Egyptian army, destroyed part of it, and then turned to attack Ramesses' own force. He was facing defeat when the seaborne detachment arrived, having marched from Sumur. The two armies fought to a standstill, then separated. Next day they faced each other again, but the Hittite infantry stood firm against the Egyptian chariotry. At the end of the day the two kings agreed on a ceasefire and Ramesses took his army home.

He might claim a victory on his boastful monuments, but it was a strategic defeat, and Muwatalli rubbed it in by recovering Amurru – replacing Benteshima, who had changed sides once too often, by a new king, Shapili – and then pushing up the Orontes to take over the old Egyptian government centre at Kummidi and then through the Barada Gorge to take control of Upu, the Damascus kingdom. So much for Ramesses' triumphant campaign. But Muwatalli had overstretched his kingdom's resources, though for a time it seemed that Damascus would be made into another Hittite viceroyalty under Muwatalli's brother Hattusili.[20] But Muwatalli died two years after the battle and Ramesses, having given his army a year to recover, marched through Palestine restoring order to the Egyptian empire where it had been thought his retreat marked a crucial decline in Egyptian power. In particular he sent a force south of the Dead Sea which campaigned north along the King's Highway, reducing Edom and Moab, while he took another force across the Jordan and joined it. Next year, while more succession problems paralyzed the Hittite regime, he moved north and regained control of Upu and the Bekaa Valley.[21] Then in his tenth year he returned once more to the northern battlefields.

Based at Sumur the Egyptian forces penetrated along the Eleutheros Valley and campaigned towards the north. Ramesses ignored Qadesh, but turned his attack on Tunip, north along the Orontes, and the town of Dapur. He also seems to have ignored Amurru, where the Hittite appointee Shapili was undisturbed. Given that situation, he cannot have expected Tunip to remain his for long, and sure enough as soon as he returned to Egypt, Tunip and Dapur swiftly returned to the Hittite allegiance, no doubt excusing their treason by *force majeure*.[22] What Ramesses had done was to demonstrate that he was fully able to march into the Hittite Syrian kingdoms without incurring any real danger, just as Muwatalli had been able to penetrate as far south as Damascus. It was actually a demonstration that for both sides the never-ending war was unwinnable.

Peace came as a direct result of yet another succession crisis in Hatti. The king who followed Muwatalli, his son Urhi-Teshub, whose throne name was Mursili III, was fearful of his uncle Hattusili (the former brief governor in Damascus), whom he worked to reduce to impotence. In reaction Hattusili defeated, captured and dethroned the king, and sent him into exile. Hattusili became the new king. But by exiling Mursili, presumably because he still had support in the kingdom, he had laid a burden on himself, for the deposed king inevitably intrigued to gain support for his return. Babylon and Assyria both recognized Hattusili. Yet the Egyptian war continued. Mursili escaped from his exile to Egypt, and appealed to Ramesses II to restore him.[23]

The prospect of a new war was real, and it seems that both Ramesses and Hattusili made preparations. While Hattusili was thus preoccupied, the Assyrian King Shalmaneser I struck at the remaining Mittani state, usually called Hanigalbat, ruled by a descendent of Tushratta. Hanigalbat had been technically a Hittite sub-kingdom since Tushratta's defeat, but now Shalmaneser succeeded in seizing it.[24] This altered the general strategic situation, for if he fought Assyria, Hattusili understood he would soon find Ramesses joining in against him. In addition the Babylonian king had taken the Hittite side, so he might join in also against Assyria; there was a real danger of a quasi-world war.

But none of this was of any interest to Ramesses, whose concern was not who ruled in the Jazirah, or even who was king in Hattusa. He required acknowledgement of his own rule in Syria, and a recognized and acceptable boundary between his and Hattusili's kingdoms. Hattusili finally appreciated this, and that peace with Egypt might well let him confront the Assyrian menace without the danger of incurring an Egyptian war as well. The way out of the situation was to make peace with Ramesses, which would neutralize the exiled Mursili III, who stayed in Egypt but was also prevented by Ramesses from causing trouble. With peace guaranteed in the Syrian provinces, Assyria was also neutralized, since Shalmaneser was not strong enough to take on the full might of the Hittites. And Hattisili could now attend to other problems, such as ensuring his domination of western Asia Minor and fending off the Kaska barbarians in the north. The peace was agreed in 1259.[25]

For Syria, of course, this was perhaps one of the worst outcomes. It was bad enough to be the object of military campaigns and invasions, and to have to face either conquest or destruction – or all too often both – and then foreign control, but when the invaders made peace, their joint control over their parts of Syria was thereby confirmed. The Egyptian–Hittite peace held so long as both powers existed; Syria was left under their divided rule for the next six decades, perhaps more.

Chapter 7

Independence through Disaster

T he imperial duopoly of Egypt and Hatti lasted about six decades after
        the peace of 1259 BC, but of course it had in fact already existed for over
        a century by that time, and the duopoly of Egypt and Mittani before
that. For Syrians the difference occasioned by the peace agreement was that it
was clearly more difficult to find occasions for attempts to break free of their
overlords' joint system when they were at peace. The succession of a new king in
the imperial capitals almost always presented a chance, but just as often it ended
in the suppression of the 'rebellion'. This happened in Palestine soon after the
death of Ramesses II in c.1213, when his son and successor Merenptah conducted
a campaign in which he had to take over Ashkelon, Gezer and Yenoam – implying a
march along the coast road and then east to the Sea of Galilee. He also encountered
a people called 'Israel', whom he claimed to have destroyed. The inscription is
in the usual bombastic style and is manifestly inaccurate, or rather exaggerated,
though the precision of the places named in Palestine is clear. There was clearly a
people called Israel in the area in the end of the thirteenth century. What relation
they had to the later kingdom of Israel is, however, quite unknown. Since they are
marked as a 'people' rather than a place, it is assumed that they were nomadic.[1]

    The lengthy period of the imperial duopoly had very largely preserved the
Syrian kingdoms which had existed much earlier – the imperialists did not like
change. Most of those which were part of the empires after the peace of 1259 had
been in existence since the collapse of the Ur III dynasty abound 2000 BC. Halab,
for instance, was the successor of the defunct kingdom of Yamhad; Ugarit can
be traced through the centuries under what seems to be a single dynasty; Alalah
we know was provided with a new dynasty by Idrimi, but it had been a city state
for centuries before the Idrimi's adventures; Carchemish features repeatedly in
events; Byblos is frequently noted in Egyptian records.[2] In other words, in north
Syria city states which had emerged from the wreckage of the Ur III collapse had
existed, either independently or as subordinates of Mittani or Hatti, for up to eight
centuries when the chaos of the Sea Peoples' adventures descended on them (i.e.,
from c.2000 to c.1200 BC).

    Elsewhere in Syria the position is less clear. In Palestine it seems that many
of the cities similarly lived through the same period, but their experiences were
much more difficult. The record of destructions in the end of the Middle Bronze
Age (say between 1600 and 1500 BC) is clear in the archaeological record, and not

all of the wrecks were reinhabited afterwards.[3] But some more prominent cities did survive, either by their continuing inhabitation, or by being revived soon after destruction. Shechem, for example, was more than once the object of Egyptian ire, but survived; Jebus in the Judaean hills (which became Jerusalem later) appears to have existed continuously, if in obscurity; Megiddo was continually inhabited, but subject to repeated attacks; the sea coast cities such as Acco and Joppa, Ashdod and Ashkelon, lived on. The difference between these cities and those in north Syria was essentially one of the size of their territories; those in Palestine clearly had only small territories to govern, partly because there seems to have been many more and smaller cities to divide up a smaller territory.

In the middle part of Syria, the cities had the most disturbing time of all. This became the frontier land between the empires, and the antagonists were liable to besiege, and at times to destroy the cities, not necessarily in order to hold them, but to prevent the enemy from doing so. And yet most of them survived. Qadesh, Qatna, Niya, Tunip were all fought over, and all still existed at the end of the Bronze Age (c.1200 BC). On the coast, Ugarit, Byblos, Tyre and Sidon either lived through the experience or developed during it. The Egyptian strongholds at Sumur in the Plain of Akkar, and Kummidi in the Bekaa Valley, were still in Egyptian control at the end of the period. In the Damascus Ghuta it is likely that the city of Damascus had now been occupied and had become the capital of the kingdom of Upu. This was also the area in which the only new state developed – the Amurru kingdom – during the duopoly, a clear mark of the disturbed and frontier condition of the area.

This implies that Syria from the Taurus Mountains to Sinai in the Bronze Age was a resilient and vigorous society capable of absorbing the conquerors who ruled it, and who fought over it with unpleasant frequency, but also essentially ignoring them, while also, of course, supporting their extra weight. As a society Syria had absorbed the Amorites, and accepted the infiltration of the Hurrians; no doubt considerable numbers of Egyptians and Hittites had taken up residence, married and contributed their DNA to the basic population without having much effect. As a cultural region Syria had accepted a number of Egyptian elements, but these were largely in the plastic arts; Minoan painting was more accepted than the stiff Egyptian imperial style; writing had been taken up, in the form of cuneiform from Babylonia, but the local version was radically different, the syllabic forms based on Sumerian or Egyptian writing being both rejected. Despite the continuing presence of Hurrians, Hittites, and Egyptians, all continuing to use their own languages and writing systems, the local Semitic language (or languages) continued to be spoken and were eventually written during the imperial period. It seems unlikely that either Hatti or Mittani contributed much culturally; rather it was the Syrian culture which they themselves absorbed – as did Egypt in many details.

Syrians moved out to inhabit the neighbouring lands. We know more about Syrians moving into Egypt than elsewhere, but the Hittite kings did drag numbers of their victims and captives into Anatolia to reinhabit devastated lands – one of the reasons for the kingdom's collapse was shortage of manpower. Syrians went to Egypt willingly in many cases, as traders, soldiers, migrants; and they were taken unwillingly as captives, prisoners, and slaves. In Egypt at least they integrated fairly well, though they and their descendents were always designated as, and denigrated as, Syrians, even or especially when they reached positions of power; not surprisingly the less privileged also tended to escape when they could, as in the story of the exodus of the ancestors of the Hebrews.

Syria therefore was a vibrant and creative society, productive of wealth and talent, but was much divided politically and so subject to conquest and exploitation by its more powerful and militant neighbours. And yet it did continue to exist, apparently largely stable in its society and culture and political organization, despite its troubles. In 1200 BC, when both Egypt and Hatti began to go through serious internal and external troubles, Syria was as stable as ever in political and social matters.

It was soon put to the test. The Egyptian king, Merenptah, had successfully maintained his empire against Palestinian rebellions and Libyan invasions, but there was a succession dispute when he died, followed by a series of short reigns, and the royal family descended from Ramesses I died out with another regnant queen, Tawosret, in about 1185 BC. Her main supporter was a Syrian called Bay. It was a perfect situation for a rebellion against the government. The general in command of the garrison forces, Setnakht, contrived a coup and then spent several months putting down opposition within Egypt. This in turn, together with the previous twenty years of crises, was exactly the situation to produce provincial rebellions.[4]

The crisis which enveloped Hatti (at the same time as the succession crisis in Egypt) was ultimately fatal to the main kingdom, but left the viceroyalties intact. The details of what happened in Anatolia are unknown, but the crisis involved a famine – Pharaoh Merenptah sent food from Egypt for the relief of Hatti, and peremptory demands for supplies were made of Ugarit – invasions from outside, and the continuing dispute between the descendents of Urhi-Teshub and Hattusili III.[5] One would assume that the Kaska barbarians from the northern mountains were involved, and probably others attacked from the west. There was also a clear increase in maritime raids about this time – 'pirates', of course, to the victims – which are blamed upon a variety of peoples whose origins can only be surmised, though the Aegean area is the obvious source. The effect on Hatti was to destroy the main kingdom, leading to the abandonment of the imperial capital at Hattusa but allowing the survival of a collection of minor kingdoms, collectively known as 'Neo-Hittite' states in Syria. That they survived and continued to use the Hittite language and script suggests that the main victims of the disruption were the imperial system itself, the Great King and his imperial administration (including the imperial language, called Nesite). No doubt to many this was no great loss. Since Suppiluliuma I over a century before the kings had struggled to maintain themselves, having to fight Assyria to the east, and the various hostile kingdoms in the west, hold on to Syria, fight Egypt, and even invade Cyprus, on top of which they clearly faced a continuing, or perhaps a growing, shortage of food and a manpower crisis. The empire was clearly greatly overextended, and in a condition where it was very liable to collapse.

The seaborne invaders, called by the Egyptians the Peoples of the Sea, were a different matter from the Hittite problem, though the two issues obviously overlapped.[6] In fact, it may be that the Sea Peoples included displaced people or refugees from the Hittite collapse, but the Sea Peoples' campaign was aimed at a different target; the collapse of the Hittite state probably helped their campaign to succeed, but without a direct connection. They were a collection of various groups, identified by the Egyptians by half a dozen different names, which coalesced into a nomadic force of considerable size. It moved by sea along the Syrian coast in parallel with a land force using horses and chariots and wagons. They were first reported to be approaching Ugarit by a letter from Eshuwara, grand supervisor of the king of Alashiya (Cyprus); Ammurapi, the Ugaritic king, wrote to the Alashiya king that they had reached his coast. He also appealed to the viceroy at Carchemish, who could only send advice, and since Ugarit suffered destruction and abandonment about the same time it seems reasonable to connect the two events.[7] An earthquake has been suggested also as the agent of the destruction, but of this the excavations have produced little or no evidence, and it is normal human behaviour to reoccupy and rebuild a wrecked town after an earthquake. This did not happen at Ugarit. It is only direct human agency that can wipe out a city and drive or kill the entire population.[8]

Further, several other places south of Ugarit but close to the coast show evidence of destruction at this time as well: Tell Sukas on the coast 20km to the south, Sumur and Irqata in the Plain of Akkar, and Kummidi in the Bekaa Valley. On the other hand, the coastal town and cities from Sukas to Tyre were unaffected, and many places show no signs of trouble archaeologically.[9] In the same region it is recorded in Ramesses III's inscription that Amurru was the site of the nomads' camp, the king of Amurru had 'become ash' – no doubt meaning killed – and that its people were dispersed and captured or subdued; the dynasty of Abdi–Ashirta disappeared, as did the dynasty at Ugarit.[10]

The destruction was clearly selective, not mindless. The invaders' concentration was on Egyptian posts and allies, including in these Ugarit, whose seapower had to be eliminated before further advances could be made. The fact that the Phoenician cities were ignored might suggest that they were not simply spared, but were complicit in the events. Byblos and Tyre for example had certainly been part of the Amurru kingdom, though whether this continued into the twelfth century is not clear. (The last king known by name, Shaushgamura, succeeded about 1230; he could hardly have lived beyond the end of the century; and an unnamed king in the Egyptian account is reported to have been killed.) Either the cities of the coast were under Amurru domination, in which case they may be thought to have resented it, or they were not, and were thereby under threat. Egypt at this time was much weakened by other threats and by the dynastic paralysis, and could provide no help, just as the viceroy at Carchemish could send no help to Ugarit. It would seem therefore that the Sea Peoples were probably allied with local elements in north Syria and deliberately set about removing Egyptian power from the region.

The invaders would not need to go further. If it was loot they were after their next move would be to return to their homes. If it was land to settle on they sought, they had acquired it. The lands from Ugarit to the Plain of Akkar and on into the Bekaa Valley were theirs for the taking, and the inscription of Ramesses III comments that they had 'pitched their tents' in Amurru. It seems probable that this is where they stayed, seizing the conquered land and the captured people, and the chiefs replacing with their own persons the former lords of Amurru. The Egyptian evidence suggests that they were a migration of people, men, women, and children. Yet they cannot have been numerous, and the best interpretation would be that they settled as a ruling group, and swiftly became absorbed by the more numerous original inhabitants.

It would be characteristic of such groups of invaders to split into two parts at this point. Some would be content with what they had already gained; others would for various reasons want to continue. The conquest of the Egyptian outposts was not the final word, for Egypt still ruled in Palestine and Egypt itself, and it could be argued that there would be an attempt to recover what had been lost. Some of the invaders were no doubt so imbued with the spirit of adventure and conquest that they wanted simply to go on fighting and travelling. Whatever division of lands had taken place in Amurru and the north some might be expected to be dissatisfied. There were certainly enough people – mostly men, probably – who felt the need or desire to go on to mount a new invasion force.

These were the people who sailed along the coast and landed in Palestine, but were soon after defeated by Egyptian sea and land forces under Ramesses III. Within Palestine this is a time of destruction just as it had been in the north, but yet again the destruction was not random – and of course there is no indication of the causes. Beth Shean, the Egyptian military base, was sacked; Gaza, the other main Egyptian government centre, became a city of the Philistines. In other words it looks as though, once again, the invaders were targeting the Egyptian empire. It would not be surprising to find that their attack on Egypt was assisted by Canaanites who had rebelled against the Egyptian imperial presence in their land.

The result of the attack on Egypt was a defeat for the invaders, followed by a diplomatic victory for the Egyptians, but at a cost. Some of the invaders were recruited into the army of Pharaoh Ramesses III as mercenaries, probably with the promise of land to settle on. The rest, who did not wish to be recruited, or whom Ramesses did not want, were driven out of Egypt into southern Palestine. There they settled in the coastal region from Gaza to Ashdod, with control of part of the inland areas. This may or may not have been done by arrangement with Ramesses, but it seems certain he could not remove them. Ramesses recovered control of other areas in Palestine, including Beth Shean where the Egyptian palace was rebuilt and reoccupied.

The evidence for the settlement of the invaders is a particular pottery of local manufacture but of a style most closely resembling that of the Aegean, and called 'Myc IIIc1b' – here 'Myc IIIc'. Pottery from the Aegean had long been a popular import into Syria, and the change from Myc IIIb to Myc IIIc is identifiable as the moment of the invaders. At Ugarit, for example, Myc IIIb was in use at the time of the destruction, but there is no Myc IIIc; on the other hand Myc IIIc appears at Dor in the layers of the rebuilding which followed the destruction. It also appears at several sites along the northern coast, such as Ras Ibn Hani and Sukas, and may be taken as evidence of the settlement there of the invaders.[11]

The Philistines in Palestine destroyed the cities they seized and rebuilt them on different lines and usually bigger. Each city was heavily fortified with powerful brick ramparts, a factor which suggests strongly that whatever arrangement was made with Ramesses in the immediate aftermath of the defeat of the invasion, the settlers soon asserted their independence. The fortifications were so strong that each of the cities so protected could have held up the whole Egyptian army for a long time.

This development must have taken some time. The rebuilding and fortification was the work of years, not months. The greater size of the new cities, as opposed to the earlier Canaanite Bronze Age cities they replaced, suggests that the urban population was now much greater. The mayhem associated with their arrival will have cost lives, and it is unlikely that the invaders themselves were very numerous. The answer seems to be that the whole population of the city, urban and rural, was concentrated inside the walls. Very few rural Iron Age settlements have been found in archaeological surveys, though it is obvious that the land continued to be cultivated. The advantages to the Philistines of such concentrations are obvious: they could impose their control over the Canaanite population, which may well have supported them against Egypt, but was unlikely to welcome them as lords.

But there was another good reason for the powerful development of the cities and the concentration of the population in them. Ramesses III, either from the start or perhaps after appreciating what the Philistines were doing in their cities, constructed a series of fortified cities of his own. These are marked by buildings such as the fortress at Tell el-Farah (S). To the north at Tell es-Shariah was a large governor's house, in which was found Egyptian pottery and other Egyptian items. It was placed very close to a major Philistine city at Haror. Similar Egyptian forts and administrative cities have been located at Lachish and Hesi, and at Tell Mor on the coast north of Ashdod. To the north and south of the Philistine area, at Aphek and Deir el-Balah, governors' residencies have also been found, probably in connection with controlling the major routes, the Way of Horus across Sinai and the Way of the Sea in Palestine. In total these Egyptian forts enclosed the whole of the Philistine territories.

This situation was not, however, stable. The Egyptian regime was unable to maintain the system created by Ramesses III. The succeeding type of local pottery, 'Bichrome Ware', a development of Myc IIIc with more decoration, is also Philistine in manufacture, and it is found over a considerably wider region than Myc IIIc, and this new area included some of the Egyptian posts established by Ramesses III – Tell Mor, Hesi, Lachish, and Tell es-Shariah. Clearly the Egyptian government had failed to keep up its guard in south Palestine and had yielded to Philistine pressure.

Farther north, a smaller version of these events is discernible. Megiddo and Beth Shean have produced evidence of occupation in Ramesses' time; on the coast Dor is known to have been the new home of a group of the Sea Peoples called Tjeker and they were still there and apparently still distinctive about 1070 BC when the Egyptian envoy Wenamon visited and was robbed. A second group may have seized Acco further north, where Myc IIIc pottery has been found.

The conclusion therefore is that, having accepted, willingly or not, the settlement of the Philistines, Ramesses III ringed them with forts to pen them in. How long the system endured is not clear. Presumably it lasted for the whole of Ramesses III's reign (he died in c.1156), but his successors all had short reigns and made little or no mark on events. This is the period of the production of the Bichrome pottery, so it is likely that during the half century after Ramesses' death the Egyptian posts were abandoned and the Philistines could expand their territory. When Wenamon went to Byblos in search of wood, about 1070, he could report no Egyptian presence anywhere along the coast and no courtesy from any of the local rulers. Egyptian power had clearly evaporated by that time.

It will be seen that the dating of the events in Syria, from Ugarit to Gaza, is not easy. Part of the chronology depends on pottery styles, whose dates can only be approximate, and elsewhere on Egyptian chronology, which is not fully determined yet. But it would seem that the reign of Ramesses III saw the main activity. Bay, the Syrian vizier in office under Queen Tawosret, wrote to the last king of Ugarit, Ammurapi, who was already under threat at the time, so that city fell about the end of that queen's reign; Ramesses' inscriptions show crucial events in his years five and eight, of which the second was the defeat of the invasion of Egypt, followed by the settlement of the Philistines in Palestine. So it seems probable that from the sack of Ugarit to the repulse of the invaders only about ten or a dozen years elapsed. By the end of Ramesses' reign (about 1156) the invaders had taken up their new lives in their conceded cities.

The destruction of the Hittite kingdom left the imperial viceroyalties in Syria on their own. They probably received large numbers of refugees from the collapse of the Anatolian kingdom, and these will have reinforced the existing Hittite population which had already moved into Syria. For several more centuries the Luwian language (used by the Hittites) remained in use in Carchemish, for example. This became the main Neo-Hittite city, where the descendents of the viceroys tended to take the title of Great King which had been borne by the emperors in Hattusa. Other Neo-Hittite states existed from southern Anatolia to middle Syria – fifteen have been counted.

The collapse of the main imperial power, however, had other effects. It seems, for example, that a new dynasty, originating from western Asia Minor, took over Halab and extended its control into the Amuq Basin (Alalah had been destroyed) and south along the Orontes. The first king, so it is thought, was Taita. He used Luwian in his inscriptions and others associated with him have been found at Tayinet in the Amuq Basin and at Shaizar on the Orontes. The area did not remain a single kingdom, and suggests that his family did not rule for long. But he called himself 'Palaistin-ean', which connects him with the Sea Peoples in some way, perhaps as a man who came from their homelands.[12]

The arrival of the Sea Peoples and the Hittite refugees disturbed and altered the political situation in northern Syria. One result was that the one major power left in the region was Assyria. Already in the last years of the Hittite kingdom the Assyrian king had defeated the Hittite king, Tudhaliya IV, but Assyria had also to attend to hostility from Babylon and was threatened by opposition from the hillmen to the north and east. The collapse of the Hittite regime, however, did provide Assyria with a clear opportunity to emulate its predecessor Mittani.

In the meantime another development was working to alter matters throughout Syria. The catastrophe which hit the Syrian cities was accompanied, according to Assyrian sources, by a widespread drought. This pushed the nomadic tribes who roamed the steppeland between the settled areas and the desert to move into the better-watered lands to save their flocks.[13] The combination of aggressive nomads and weakened cities and failing imperial governments had the same effect as a thousand years earlier when the Amorites had infiltrated the city land. This time the nomads were Aramaeans, and their movement was much more purposeful. By 1100 BC many of the old Bronze Age cities were regarded as Aramaean, probably because their rulers spoke the Aramaic language, a variety of the West Semitic language to which all previous tongues in Syria had belonged.

In all likelihood the Aramaeans had been moving into the cities and inhabiting the rural areas around them and intermarrying with the inhabitants for some time, probably centuries, before they become visible in the records. Their presence is not obvious in the archaeology, but it becomes clear in the written sources. By 1100 they and the Neo-Hittites divided all Syria between them from the Taurus Mountains to Damascus, with the exception of the Phoenician cities along the coast.

In the Palestinian area the people whom Pharaoh Merneptah had encountered in his campaign, and whom he called Israel, were probably part of the infiltration from the steppe into the land of cities. As with other such movements they joined the existing inhabitants and together gained control of the cities. And as with the Aramaeans elsewhere in Syria they founded new kingdoms, usually based on one of the cities they had come to control, though also they were often named from the tribe whose chief had come to rule. So Halab eventually became part of the kingdom of Bit-Agusi (the 'house' of Agusi, or Gusi or Gusu) which seems to have been the name of the first chief to become king; the Bit-Adini kingdom was established east of the Euphrates, and Bit-Bahiani in the Khabour Triangle. Samal was an Aramaean kingdom in what had been a Hittite region – it is evident that the peoples were much intermingled; Damascus, wide open as the Ghuta was to desert infiltration, became called simply 'Aram'. In the south a number of tribes who were later identified as Hebrews occupied the Judaean Highlands and Galilee. But in every case the basic population was descended from the Bronze Age inhabitants, who adopted the new languages, and who continued the old agriculture – to which iron implements were slowly added – and who continued to worship the old gods; the newcomers eventually adopted those same gods, and so the different peoples became one.

Syria thus became a patchwork of local kingdoms often with ethnic labels: Hittite, Aramaean, Phoenician, Hebrew, Philistine, while some retained the old name of Canaanites. The Sea Peoples/Aramaean invasions had shaken up the political system, but it had largely settled back into the same or a similar configuration as before, but with a new distribution of power, and with for the most part an absence of imperial overlords. The influence of the geography of Syria once again exerted its power.

The new distribution of power did make a difference. In the north the various Neo-Hittite states were generally small, but seem to have been able to keep the peace fairly well amongst themselves – but then we have little information about their relationships. The presence of Assyrian power stretching right across the Jazirah as far as the east bank of the Euphrates was very threatening, and sure enough the accession of a more than usually warlike Assyrian king, Tiglath-pileser I, in 1114 soon brought an Assyrian attack. The aim was, in formal terms, to collect cedar beams in Lebanon for a temple to be built in his capital city, Ashur; in wider, more political terms it was clearly aimed to establish Assyrian political supremacy in north Syria, and in his record of his reign he claims to have 'conquered .. to the Upper Sea in the West'. It was thus a campaign of a very traditional sort. Tiglath-pileser succeeded in collecting his wood and gathering tribute and loot, but did not apparently succeed in his wider political aims.[14]

Instead he became embroiled in a long conflict with Aramaeans, nomads who were infiltrating into his Jazirah territory between the Euphrates and the Khabour. In his later campaigns he was fighting them in this area and in the land to the south towards the oasis of Palmyra. Furthermore, he was losing, since it proved impossible to stop the infiltration, and the nomads soon were able to begin organizing themselves into their own kingdoms – this was the origin of the Bit-Adini and the Bit-Bahiani mentioned earlier. Similarly the Bit-Agusi moved into Halab's territory, and replaced the brief kingdom of Taita and (presumably) his descendants with their own. The Assyrian kings after Tiglath-pileser I became overwhelmed by the nomad problem and retreated to defend their homeland; but their ambitions had been stirred.[15]

In the south the Aram kingdom of Damascus emerged from the period of invasions and confusion as perhaps the strongest of the new states. This was because its neighbours tended to be later in becoming organized efficiently or because they were geographically restricted to a much smaller territory. The name awarded to Damascus – the kingdom of 'Aram' – suggests also that it maintained good relations with the nomad Aramaeans, giving it a larger availability of manpower than its size would normally suggest.[16]

The arrival of Aramaeans/Hebrews in the settled lands from Assyria to Gaza was clearly a time of great confusion. The infiltration of and takeover of many of the cities surviving from the Late Bronze Age converted them into Aramaic states, even if the basic population did not usually change. The process is invisible in most areas, and the one thing which can be done is to stand at the end of the period of change and consider the new situation which had come about in the meantime. It does not help that of the two written sources, the Assyrian annals concentrate on events in the eastern Jazirah and Babylonia, and the biblical account cannot be relied on since it was written so much later, and is quite evidently only a secondary source, if that. This affects the whole structure of politics and chronology, while the archaeological record in Palestine is subject to much controversy.

The process of settlement by the Aramaeans is invisible. In only one case do we appear to have evidence of a sort for it, and this is the biblical narrative concerning the Hebrews. However, this cannot be accepted as true evidence because it is so obviously both secondary and composed with a particular political and religious point of view in mind. It was not the intention of the authors of these stories to provide historically accurate information, but to lay out a scheme of narrative to 'prove' or demonstrate a point of view. Until and unless an independent source can be found which will validate the testimony of these biblical narratives, it cannot be used as a historical source for these early centuries. It is clearly more reliable for later events, and will be used in the next chapter.[17]

There are a few inscriptions from Syria which can be dated to the period between 900 BC and 745 BC. There are also the Assyrian royal annals, which boast of the conquests of a series of Assyrian kings. And there is one Egyptian inscription of the same sort. Each of these sources has been squeezed mercilessly to extract information, which is a natural process for historians, but in too many cases it has been done for the purpose of detecting a relationship with the biblical narrative. Further, that biblical narrative, being distorted and invented, has had a dire effect on the historical writing concerning all events in Iron Age Syria. For, if the biblical account is not acceptable as a verifiable historical source, then its chronological scheme has to be dismissed.

To take as an example, the case of the kingdoms in the Damascus area. There are several which are mentioned, some of which, such as Geshur and Maacah, are mentioned in earlier sources and which therefore clearly continued to exist through the time of confusion. But two are mentioned only in the story of King David – Bit-Rehob and Aram-Zobah. These are Aramaean states by their names, and therefore cannot have existed before the Aramaean infiltrations. Given the archaeology of the Judaean hill country it is not possible to accept that David was able to campaign in the Damascus area, or to construct his 'empire', which is said to have stretched as far as Palmyra. In that case his conquest of Damascus did not take place. And it follows that the whole construct of the history of the Damascus area in the Iron Age, based as it is only on the Bible, cannot be accepted.[18]

Archaeology, all too often dragooned into 'proving' the biblical accounts, has in fact done the opposite. It is clear that the settlement of the Hebrews is not something which necessarily ever took place. The inhabitation of the Judaean Highlands was woefully thin during the time the settlement was supposed to have taken place. There is also evidence of an expansion of population during the tenth century BC, though not before.[19] This is not to say that the infiltration of Hebrews into the highlands did not happen, only that if it did it was on a small scale and the arrivals were accepted into the existing villages.

The emergence in the region of a kingdom in the eleventh century BC similarly cannot be discerned. The population density is far too low to support a state structure or to provide the manpower for a major army. There is no indication at Jerusalem that there was a great phase of building – temple, palace, houses for the rich, military fortifications – in the period when David and Solomon were supposed to be active there. Despite the fact that this is negative 'evidence', the conclusion must be that, once again, the biblical narrative is invented.[20]

There are, however, clear signs of the emergence of kingdoms elsewhere in the immediate region. Across the Jordan a king of Moab, Mesha, set up a stele in which he gave an account of his kingdom's tribulations. In this he reports that his main enemy was Israel.[21] Israel is also mentioned in a very difficult inscription found at Tell Dan, in the north of Palestine. (This is a very awkward text, broken and incomplete, which certainly does not say what its earliest interpreters claimed, and whose date is uncertain; it may mention the 'House of David' as the rulers of a kingdom – or it may not – but this does not prove more than that such a kingdom existed, which we already knew.[22]) These kingdoms – Israel and Moab – are the only kingdoms which are independently attested by non-biblical sources in the Palestine area at the time.

And yet the biblical narratives of Saul on David and Solomon were not spun out of thin air. Whatever date is assigned to the Tell Dan inscription it does seem to mention a House of David of which a member was a king, and this can only be Judah. Israel is well-attested in Mesha's stele, by the Tell Dan inscription, and by the Assyrian annals. It is therefore reasonable to accept that at some point before 800 BC (the approximate date of Mesha's stele; the Tell Dan inscription may be a little earlier, or about the same date) a political leader called David existed. His story in the bible is so entwined with that of Saul that he also must been presumed to have existed. The stories of these men were clearly elaborated from a series of events, quite possibly in some cases originally unconnected with them, which may have occurred during the eleventh and tenth centuries. What may not be accepted is that these elaborations are anywhere near historical accuracy.

So, to return once more to 900 BC, when independent evidence concerning Syria first exists, the political situation in Syria had reverted to a series of variously-sized city states. Some were particularly small, such as the Phoenician cities, two of which were actually located on small islands, or Geshur and Maacah to the north-east of Palestine; some were already dominated by outsiders, such as the Philistines' cities in south Palestine. The largest were, as ever, in the more open spaces of the north. Bit-Agusi, whose founding king was in office in about 1100 BC, was perhaps the largest, but as a relatively newly established king, an Aramaean ruler in what had probably been a Hittite state, he may not have been too secure on his throne as yet. The Carchemish kingdom, under a line of kings probably descended from Suppiluliuma I, and so who might still claim the old Hittite status as the Great King, was one of the more powerful, holding territory on both sides of the Euphrates River, as did Bit-Adini, though that kingdom's political base was east of the river, and its people may have been responsible for the destruction of Bronze Age cities about the Euphrates Bend, such as Emar.

To the north of these three were kingdoms based at Malatya (Melid) and Samsat in the Euphrates Valley (Kummuh); to the west were Gurgum, Unqi (also called Patin – the effective successor of Alalah), and others south along the Orontes. That river's middle section was controlled from Hamath, another state of the same status and weight as Carchemish; then Damascus, called Aram, which had probably (the evidence is biblical, and so suspect) absorbed several smaller states around it. In the south was Israel, perhaps the largest state in Palestine, then small and weak Judah, the Philistine cities who had expanded their territories at the expense of the Egyptian areas in Palestine, and several states based in cities along the coastal area between the Philistines and the Phoenicians – these were to be fairly easy prey for Israel. East of the Jordan was a string of small territorial states, such as Mesha's Moab; Ammon and Edom were probably in existence by now; there were other small states between them and Damascus.

These city states, insofar as they were literate, had all adopted the alphabetic writing system which had emerged in the Late Bronze Age. Most of them used Aramaic, though the Neo–Hittites tended to use Luwian, probably to emphasize their supposed imperial heritage. The Aramaic script was capable of being used for any Semitic language, and became the vehicle for Moabite, Phoenician, and Hebrew as well as Aramaic, though the ease of its use on papyrus or hide or parchment means that little survives.

The Phoenician cities were developing, or reviving, their trading links with the Mediterranean lands. Tyre was the leader in this enterprise, under a series of kings. The regal regime was no more stable than any other, and kings were liable to be overthrown, and the overseas enterprises were liable to turn hostile – events which were not unconnected. The Tyrian colony of Kition in Cyprus, for example, had to be subdued by an expedition under King Hiram as early as the 950s,[23] which puts the date of the foundation at least a generation before him, and the elements of the royal family fled to North Africa in the time of King Pygmalion a century and a half later;[24] a Tyrian colony was also founded at Botrys, probably with the aim of ensuring access to the Eleutheros route to the Syrian interior.[25]

Tyre and Byblos have produced evidence of contact with Egypt in the tenth century. The new dynasty (XXII), which came to power in 945 with Shoshenq I, was aggressive, probably because since Shoshenq was by origin a Libyan, as a means of legitimizing his rule in Egyptian eyes. Shoshenq was in contact with Byblos, perhaps choosing that city for traditional reasons; his successor Osorkon I did the same.[26] Shoshenq also conducted a campaign in Palestine, eventually returning to Beth Shean, and raiding the lands on either side of Jordan in that area. He also sent raiding parties through the Negev and into southern Judah. His route north, avoiding the Philistine area, more or less replicated the line of forts established by Ramesses III a century before, if a little to the east; this is hardly a coincidence, and presumably was an attempt by Shoshenq to revive the old Palestinian province. Yet his work was of no permanent value, since he died soon after the campaign, before his victory monument was finished.[27]

This raid does give some idea of Shoshenq's priorities: his raiding force followed the trade route which linked Gaza with the copper sources in the Wadi Arabah, and destroyed a recently developed settlement at Tell Masos, which may well have been imposing extra taxes on the trade. Gaza itself was ignored, as were the other Philistine places, making it probable that they were allied with, or even still subject to, the pharaoh – or perhaps too strong to be even menaced. No mention is made of either Judah or Israel, even though the expedition's forces penetrated into what should have been their territories, making it likely that those kingdoms were not yet organized; both Hebron and the traditional homeland of King Saul were attacked. Jerusalem was ignored.[28]

So it seems that Shoshenq's aim was to recover control of the trade routes, to possibly reaffirm the alliance of the Philistine cities, and suppress some hill tribes which may have been perceived as a threat; it was in this period that archaeologists have detected a serious growth in settlement, and hence in population, in the highlands; the pressure on resources of any population growth in the area might prompt migrations and raids.

The date c.900 for this brief survey marks the beginning of the renewed and determined invasions by Assyrian kings, which continued on and off for the next two centuries. Internally Syria was as fragmented as ever, yet clearly the society was vigorous and expanding economically. When the Assyrians attacked (and when Shoshenq raided) they were able to acquire wealth, either as loot or as tribute. So despite the effective blank in the records of the two centuries after the arrival of the Sea Peoples it is certain that the productivity of Syria had not ceased. It was, as the Egyptians and Hittites had known, and as Shoshenq and the Assyrians perceived, a rich land.

Chapter 8

Conquest and Tribute

The invasion of the Sea Peoples was unusual in that it had come from the sea; all previous invasions of Syria of such size had arrived from the south, from Egypt, from the north, from Anatolia, or from the north-east, from the Jazirah, though Egypt had sent forces to Byblos on several occasions. Invasion from the sea was always inherently unlikely since it would take a large number of ships to carry a sufficiently large force of soldiers to have an effect. But the divided nature of political Syria was always a temptation, and the collapse of the Hittite power and the simultaneous weakening of Egyptian authority provided the opportunity. The result was paradoxical: the confusion resulted in a simultaneous revival of the independence of the city states into which Syria had long been divided, and the momentary emergence of a new military and imperial threat in the form of Assyria.

The other 'invasions' which had affected Syria as deeply were the continuing seepage of people from the steppeland into the settled lands. This had probably been going on without any interruption for thousands of years; it can be detected quite often by archaeology, though the idea of migrations is now all too often discounted in archaeological interpretation, it having been overworked in the past. The movements into Syria have acquired ethnic labels – Amorites, Aramaeans, Hebrews – and later Arabs – only when it became obvious that the infiltrations had begun to affect the cities and their rulers, but to consider these as sudden changes is to misunderstand the situation. The movement was continuous, and the changes it imposed on the cities were only gradual, as it was in the matter of language.

Generally these gradual movements had been accepted with little argument. Ebla had been noting Amorites for decades, even centuries; Aramaeans had been arriving with little fuss into the settled lands for years before notice was taken – the earliest notice is in Babylonia about 1450 BC.[1] It was only the turbulence occasioned by invasions and imperial collapses which brought some Aramaeans to power in individual cities, and even then this was a slow process. At Halab, for example, the Hittite rulers were in firm control until about 900 BC; it was not until shortly before that date that the Aramaean Gusi became king of the area. This is an infiltration process taking at least a century before the migrants were able to take power.[2] The same may be assumed to have happened elsewhere; in Palestine the Hebrew infiltration took even longer to emerge as a political entity.

This was all essentially normal. In the past there had undoubtedly been conflict between the immigrants and the residents, but with the Aramaeans one kingdom in particular, Assyria, took umbrage; Assyrian kings campaigned extensively with the aim of preventing the Aramaeans from taking over what the Assyrians presumed to be their lands in the Jazirah. The pattern was set by King Tiglath-pileser I (reigned 1114–1076), who campaigned through north Syria, but then turned his attention to the Aramaeans, whose settlements were proliferating in the land between the Assyrian homeland and the target of his original campaign. He reports that he crossed the Euphrates twenty-eight times in pursuit of Aramaean bands and tribes. In this case it was that part of the river between the bend and Babylonia to which he refers, and his campaign was thus in the steppeland to the south of his kingdom; he says he campaigned as far as Tadmor (Palmyra).[3]

All this may well have caused Aramaean casualties, but it did not stop their infiltration. Tiglath-pileser's son Ashur-bel-kala (1073–1056 BC) reports fighting and 'uprooting' Aramaeans on the Tigris, and other groups whose locations seem to be north of the Euphrates. His boastful inscriptions include a long description of his hunting prowess and an account of his zoo, which may be in part copied from his father's account; it is therefore doubtful that he really made an expedition as far as the Mediterranean as he claims, though a conflict with Carchemish is a little less unlikely.[4] From this reign on, however, Assyria was beset on all sides. An alliance with Babylon was no help, except in ensuring peace on one boundary, and the Aramaeans founded their states in the Jazirah from Assyria to Carchemish with scarcely any interference for at least a century.

These Assyrian kings, no matter how short-lived or powerless they were, repeatedly referred to themselves as 'king of the four quarters', an old Sumerian term used by Sargon the Great, and 'king of the universe', though it has to be said that the full range of titles used by Tiglath-pileser I was rarely employed by his successors until the reign of Ashur-dan II (934–911 BC), who began the process of Assyrian military recovery.

This digression concerning Assyria is intended to help explain the conduct of the Assyrian kings in their campaigns of conquest, which restarted so far as Syria is concerned, with the reign of Ashur-nasir-apli (883–859 BC). For two centuries, therefore, Assyria had been reduced to a minor power, beset by enemies who were usually identified as Aramaeans. But Assyria was also, in effect, the only state in the region surviving from the preceding Late Bronze Age. Every power of any size from the Persian Gulf to Sinai had been overturned or destroyed; even Babylon fell to an Aramaean dynasty in about 1067 BC.[5] Perhaps the only state of any size which could claim the same continuity as Assyria was Carchemish, but that was only a fraction of the old Hittite kingdom.

The Assyrian kings traced their own ancestry back for several hundreds of years. Shamshi-Adad I, the old conqueror of Mari in the eighteenth century BC, was mentioned as a royal predecessor by more than one later king, in terms which implied that he was seen as a major inspiration. Several kings make the point in their annals that they spent resources on the restoration of temples originally built by one or other of their ancestors. In other words, the Assyrian kings were powerfully motivated by the history of their dynasty, which fed their royal pride; the claimed titles of 'king of kings', and 'king of the universe' and so on were more inspirations.

The aims of the kings were thus in part the restoration of their old territories, which had been taken by the infiltrating Aramaeans, and in part a claim to a superior position over other kings, based on their longer ancestry, but also the removal of enemies from their doorstep. This latter seems to have been engraved into the royal minds, part of their heredity, and, of course, there is no answer to the problem of such enemies, for unless some king really becomes 'king of the universe' there will always be enemies. The conduct of the kings and their armies during their campaigns of conquest ensured that enemies were always present.

The first target for Assyrian conquest had to be those Aramaean states which had seized lands formerly Assyrian, notably in the western half of the Jazirah, the Khabour and Balikh valleys. Campaigns along the Khabour River Valley and the middle Euphrates secured that route and territory. The kingdoms of Laqe (at the confluence of the Khabour and the Euphrates) and Bit-Adini (between the Balikh and the Euphrates) were reduced to vassalage by King Ashur-nasir-apli II in his first years (the 870s). He also took his army over the Euphrates to attack Carchemish, whose King Sangara gave him tribute but had also to hand over much of his army to assist in the rest of the Assyrian campaign. This opened the way into Syria, for both Carchemish and Bit-Adini held lands on both sides of the river. Ashur-nasir-apli set out on the traditional march to the western mountains, accepting submissions from kings, and receiving their tribute offerings on the way.[6]

After he returned to Assyria (with quantities of wood from the mountains for his temples and palaces) several of his victims continued to maintain tributary relations with him. Unqi, at the mouth of the Orontes, 'Hatti' – that is, Carchemish – Tyre and Sidon, Gurgum, and Melid (Malatya) were the Syrian states who sent congratulatory envoys to participate in a great banquet marking the completion of new buildings in the city of Kalha; naturally Ashur-nasir-apli considered this a mark of their vassalage.[7] In fact it is more likely to have been a policy decision by the cities involved to avert more demands for blackmail (tribute) and so keep him from repeating his campaign. At the same time they could demonstrate that he was their ally – it was thus in all probability more a move in the political relationships within Syria than respect for the Assyrian king which persuaded them to attend. This was thus the total real effect of Ashur-nasir-apli's adventure, apart from setting a marker for his successors' later aspirations.

Several of the Syrian states had escaped serious danger in Ashur-nasir-apli's campaign by tendering submission, but three in particular had been treated with especial savagery. Bit-Adini, always the first target because it lay astride any route taken by the Assyrians towards the west, had had to pay several lots of tribute. The king, Ahuni, had also promoted early resistance to Assyrian expansion by sending a new leader to Suru, further down the Euphrates (in the region of defunct Mari), though he had not succeeded in maintaining that kingdom's existence. When the Assyrian forces reached Unqi, King Luburna (a Hittite royal name) attempted to defy the invader from inside the walls of Kunulua (Tell et-Tayinet), his main city. The sight of the enemy army menacing the city unmanned him and his people; he paid a huge ransom, plus tribute, and conceded the use of his army in the rest of Ashur-nasir-apli's campaign. Luash, a kingdom to the south of Unqi, was then raided for food for the inflated army. The soldiers, sent to reap the local harvest, hardly surprisingly met resistance. They reacted by burning several towns, massacring their populations, and impaling the survivors next to the ruins.

This was unusually savage behaviour for a conquering army. It had long been normal for kings to destroy cities and towns which resisted, but it does not seem to have been normal to do so in such a thoroughly unpleasant way. Massacring the inhabitants of the conquered country was, of course, counterproductive, if the conqueror wished to go on receiving tribute from it. It is possible that Ahsur-nasir-apli was using the time-worn tactics of staging a preliminary example of one place – rather, two – in order that later campaigns would provoke only submission, though Luash was one of the last places he attacked. Since he did not return to Syria for the rest of his reign, the Syrians' wounds had time to heal, though it is possible that Luash was so badly damaged it fell under its neighbours' control.

So Syria had twenty years to reflect on the Assyrian raid. The result was that when a new attack was launched, in the first years of the reign of Shalmaneser III (858–824 BC), the Syrians knew what to expect and were in a frame of mind to make their arrangements for meeting him. An alliance of Syrian cities was formed, though probably not until he had begun his campaign.

The first target for the Assyrians, as ever, was Bit-Adini, whose King Ahuni was defeated and driven to take refuge in his capital, Til Barsip.[8] Leaving him there, apparently helpless, Shalmaneser's army crossed the Euphrates northwards into that part of Bit-Adini across the river. The king of Kummuh, Bit-Adini's northern neighbour, submitted, as did the king of Gurgum, both paying tribute. It was when the army approached Unqi, which had resisted Ashur-nasir-apli before, that the next episode of serious opposition appeared. A coalition had by this time been formed to resist the Assyrian campaign. It included King Hayanu of Sam'al, King Supalulma of Unqi (i.e., Suppiluliuma, another Hittite royal name), and King Sangara of Carchemish, together with the organizer of the whole coalition, Ahuni of Bit-Adini, who had left the security of Til Barsip to do this.[9]

It is clear that a diplomatic campaign complementary to the Assyrian army's campaign had been going on, and that Ahuni had been the organizer. He had been so successful that the coalition had mustered an army to confront their oppressor in Sam'al. They did not win the battle, and Shalmaneser went on to collect wood in the Amanus Mountains and set up a commemorative image of himself as victor. Despite this, the coalition, its leaders and much of its forces, survived. Shalmaneser made another attack on Unqi, and was confronted by the coalition army again. Supalulma was this time assisted by the four original members of the coalition, together with King Kate of Que (a kingdom across the Amanus from Unqi), King Pirihim of Hilakky (also in Kilikia) and the kings of Yasbuq and Yahan. He won another battle, but the victory was by no means total. Shalmaneser received tribute from only one more of the north Syrian states, for King Arame of Bit-Agusi, who joined the alliance late, perhaps because the Assyrian army was marching home through Arame's land.

The issue remained therefore undecided. Shalmaneser campaigned in Syria again the next year, 857, captured several small towns in the upper Quweiq Valley, which were probably part of the Bit-Agusi kingdom. He was bought off by most of the former allies, though it is obvious that he had hardly achieved more than collecting tribute, and thus this was no longer a sign of vassalage, but merely a blackmail payment.[10] Shalmaneser, it was clear, could go on campaigning in this way, collecting tribute, marching through north Syria, but each time he would need to redo the same work. In his third campaign, in 856, he changed his methods. He attacked and captured Ahuni's main city east of the Euphrates, at Til Barsip. Ahuni himself escaped, which was awkward, but Shalmaneser's main intention had been achieved. Taking up a policy which Tiglath-pileser I had pursued briefly two centuries before, Shalmaneser drove out the population of Til Barsip and repopulated the city with Assyrians, and then renamed the city after himself, Kar-Shalmaneser. Five other towns were treated in the same way.

The Assyrians therefore now had a major presence right on the Euphrates, commanding one of the main fording places, and so giving their army the facility to invade north Syria at will. It was especially threatening to Carchemish, only a short distance north of the ford. The land of the kingdom of Bit-Adini on the east side of the Euphrates had therefore been annexed to Assyria. At his new city, and perhaps even as it was being organized, Shalmaneser accepted the submission and tribute from the various kings of north Syria, men who knew they were beaten even before they fought.[11]

The next year Shalmaneser campaigned against Ahuni once more, but this time Ahuni could only operate north of the Euphrates in the fragment of his kingdom which was left to him after the previous year's campaign. The Bit-Adini army was defeated and its king was captured. He was sent to live as a captive in Assyria; his captured soldiers – 17,500 men according to Shalmaneser's own annals – were also sent into Assyria, there to be settled in Assur, in place of the Assyrians who had been moved into Bit-Adini's former lands.[12] Shalmaneser's new policy was partly annexation and settlement, and partly domination and taxation.

The rest of Syria had taken due note of all this. The lesson was that division amongst the Syrians rendered them vulnerable; alliances gave them a chance. The coalition wrought by Ahuni had come close to success, but it had not survived into the next campaign. When Shalmaneser, after a year in which he campaigned elsewhere, turned once again to Syria, he found that a much firmer alliance was prepared to fight him.

The instigator was Urhilina, king of Hamath (called Irhuleni by the Assyrians), which would be the next kingdom to be attacked in Shalmaneser's new campaign. He controlled the middle course of the Orontes, south of Luash, the kingdom which had been so badly damaged earlier (and which he may well have annexed). His southern neighbours clearly understood that if Hamath fell they would then be attacked. Urhilini brought into his alliance King Hadad-ezer of Aram-Damascus and King Ahab of Israel, together with two of the Phoenician cities, Arwad and Byblos, who had paid Assyrian tribute in the past, but who were presumably weary of working only to find their profits siphoned off into Assyria. It may be that some Egyptian forces were also sent to help, and other forces came from Irqata, near Byblos, Shianu and Usanatu, in the former Ugaritic territory, and from Beth-Rehob in the Bekaa Valley, and from Ammon in Transjordan. A desert chief, Gindibu, contributed a thousand camels to help with the transport. In all the alliance army, according to their Assyrian enemy, it is said to have included over 40,000 infantry, 4,000 chariots, and 2,000 cavalry, which may be approximately correct, though some of the individual contributions listed are impossible. It is a sign of the wealth and populousness of Syria (as was the continual production of tribute). This was an army bigger than that of the Hittites at Qadesh in 1274, which had been recruited from all north Syria and much of Anatolia.

Shalmaneser had an army of about the same size, recruited from the same north Syrian region as the old Hittites, several of whose kingdoms had already submitted, plus his own homeland. He conducted a preliminary campaign in northern Hamath, capturing three cities and destroying them. He then met the allies at Qarqar, on the border of Luash and Hamath. The alliance, in other words, had been formed well before Shalmaneser's campaign had begun. Urhilina had clearly gathered reliable intelligence about Assyrian movements and plans. The resentful north Syrians were no doubt well aware of both Assyrian intentions and quite willing to pass on information to the intended victims, even if they were compelled to fight on the Assyrian side.

The allies were defeated in the battle, but as in the defeat of the northern coalition in 856, not decisively. They did, however, suffer badly enough to be compelled to pay tribute. Shalmaneser did not apparently invade the central parts of the kingdom. The Assyrian king could learn lessons also: the alliance had not broken up, as the northern coalition had, and its continuation would mean he would need to fight another battle if he moved south. This would mean still more casualties; he must also have had doubts about the loyalty and steadfastness of his north Syrian forces when he failed to win decisively. He withdrew, taking his tribute profits with him.[13]

The formation of an alliance stretching from north Syria (Shianu and Usanatu) to Egypt is an indication of the wide understanding which existed throughout Syria and beyond about Assyrian methods and aims. This understanding spread through the Assyrian region as well. The less than successful Qarqar campaign in 853 stimulated rebellions and defiances from several of Shalmaneser's tributary states. He had already had to compel submissions from some of those in the Khabour and Balikh valleys, and now a small state in the Euphrates bend, Til-Abni, rebelled, probably by refusing to provide tribute. Its main city and other towns were destroyed, and probably most of its people were killed. A region to the north, about the sources of the Tigris, had to be similarly suppressed; its neighbour Nairi was compelled to pay tribute.[14]

The methods of the Assyrian kings were now clear. Tribute was required from every state within reach. If it was refused the army would destroy much of the civilized infrastructure of the refusing state, despite the fact that this would clearly prevent that land from producing the requisite tribute in the future; deportation of large numbers of inhabitants might also happen if a state proved obdurate. It had become a predatory kingdom, determined to secure the wealth produced by the others' work. As all this had become clear in Syria, so resistance had hardened.

Assyria's essential problem, however, was the same as the Hittites'. It faced the hostility of every Syrian state, but it also faced the same hostility from states on its northern borders and from those of the eastern hills. In 850 a new front opened up, when the Babylonian king appealed for assistance against his rebel brother; Shalmaneser suppressed the brother and then took his army south to collect tribute from some small states near the Persian Gulf. This was not a campaign he needed to repeat, and the friendship he had with the Babylonian king continued, but the range of the Assyrian army – to the Gulf, into the northern mountains, as far as Hamath – was formidable and clearly threatening.

Shalmaneser had to spend two years over the Babylonian campaigns, and his absence from Syria stimulated risings, just as his presence in Syria had let others rebel in the north earlier. This was to be the greatest weakness of the Assyrian kingdom; the usual overstretch which had contributed to the collapse of Hittites and the Egyptians. Assyria, as it happens, proved able to endure for longer, but in the end it also failed.

The targets in Syria in 849 were Carchemish and Bit-Agusi. The same methods were employed as against Til-Abni: cities and towns were assaulted and destroyed, including the main city of Arame of Bit-Agusi.[15] Neither kingdom was, however, suppressed. (Bit-Agusi was now to be referred to as 'Arpad', from the name of Arame's new capital.) Shalmaneser's savagery only succeeded in provoking a new rebellion next year, which was again suppressed. It is hardly possible to accept the Assyrian annals' account of what happened as they stand, as they repeatedly claim the same places to have been destroyed year after year – '100 towns of Bit-Agusi', for example, were destroyed at least three times. Yet repeated destructive raids and the continual extraction of tribute can only have worn down the Syrian kingdoms in the end. The eventual target in each state, of course, was the king himself; if a Syrian king could be persuaded to submit, his city would follow automatically, and the Assyrians would have access to tribute. The king would then be supported by Assyrian forces, certainly from a distance, and possibly even with a garrison or a royal guard. This would leave him divorced from his people, but still enjoying the wealth and status of royalty.

Shalmaneser went on southwards in 849 after devastating the north, and had once more defeated the southern alliance, but with as little overall effect as before. He had to repeat the whole campaign in 848, and defeated the allied armies in a battle well within Hamathite territory, but again there was no further political result. The alliance this time included Damascus and Hamath and '12 kings of the coast' but not, it seems, Israel.[16] Three years later in 845 the greatest Assyrian army yet assembled mounted a new campaign – Shalmaneser claims to have commanded 120,000 men, though this is certainly an exaggeration. Again the allies met the attack in battle and again were defeated – at least according to the Assyrians – and again there was no political result, and the report of events is unusually downbeat, and repetitive in many details from other campaigns.[17] Probably the result was far less decisive than he claimed, just as it clearly had been for the past several campaigns.

The original coalition formed by Ahuni had lasted only one campaign. Why it was not renewed later we do not know, but probably Shalmaneser's concentration on attacking Bit-Adini in the next campaign allowed the rest to feel safe for a time. The southern alliance had a better record, probably because it was more consistently threatened. It either continued, or was renewed several times, to meet the Assyrian campaigns, though it seems to have changed membership each year. The essential members, however, were always Hamath and Damascus. The repeated claim that it included '12 cities of the sea shore' is too vague to inspire confidence in its accuracy.

These southern states were not merely opponents of Assyria's occasional raids. Once Pharaoh Shoshenq's brief campaign was over, there had been no outside interference in the south for two centuries, and by this time, when the Assyrians mounted their threat to the southern states, it is possible to rely – cautiously – on the bible for information. It still gets details wrong, and has to be checked where possible against non-biblical sources, but the spread of writing clearly assisted memories and accuracy, and permitted the writers of the relevant biblical books to refer to source material.

The three main members of the original alliance controlled between them all the land from the Ghab marshes to middle Palestine. Boundaries between and around these states are little known and were probably fluid, but these states also dominated their smaller neighbours. Israel, for example, had control of Moab across the Jordan, and Damascus had come to control, or perhaps absorb the smaller states which had been its neighbours – Geshur and Maacah, for example. This gave Damascus a considerable territory in the Bekaa Valley and south along the east side of the upper Jordan Valley. Meanwhile Israel expanded into the north Palestinian coastlands, and acquired Dor and Joppa, which were originally Philistine cities.

Israel had probably emerged as an organized kingdom about the beginning of the ninth century under the leadership of King Omri (whose name was used by the Assyrians to identify the kingdom – Bit-Humri, as in Bit-Agusi). It was based at Samaria, in the same area as earlier states had developed, close to Shechem. It controlled much of a best land of Palestine, in the vales of Jezreel and Esdraelon.

The only other kingdom of some significance in the south was Judah, but it had been organized as a kingdom later than Israel and found itself at enmity with the Philistine cities along the south Palestine coast; it was also liable to fight Israel, with which it had a continuing feud. East of the Jordan were the kingdoms of Edom, Moab (currently under Israelite domination), and Ammon, none of them of any size or power, and liable to have to fight Israel or Judah for their independence. In Palestine therefore Israel was the most important state.

None of these kingdoms was particularly stable internally, and the kings were liable to be overthrown by *coups d'etat*. This happened, so our sources claim, in Damascus in about 845, and it also happened in Israel about 841, when King Jerhoram was murdered by the usurper Jehu. The king who had been a member of the alliance with Israel and Hamath, Hadad-ezer, either died or was murdered, and Hazael took his place. He was described by the Assyrians as a 'son of a nobody', which in fact was a standard Assyrian insult directed at awkward enemies.[18] Hazael, however, was also disliked by his allies, perhaps because of the way he seized power, and the triple alliance was not reformed when Shalmaneser returned to the attack in 841. The failure to revive the alliance meant that Hamath was exposed to the Assyrian attack even more than before. Urhilina was thus persuaded to submit to Shalmaneser rather than have his city and his kingdom destroyed.

Hazael therefore was Shalmaneser's next victim, but proved to be a hard nut to crack. Assyrian invasions came in 841, by which time Hazael had been king for three or four years and so was firmly seated, and in 838. Despite defeat in the field, Hazael held on to Damascus' city, which was clearly well-fortified. The sheer distance from his Assyrian home base made it difficult for Shalmaneser to maintain the pressure on the city for long, so Hazael's regime survived. After this Shalmaneser concentrated on fighting the kingdom of Que and other kingdoms in and about Kilikia. Given his earlier attacks on Hamath and Damascus it seems that he had no fears for his supremacy there. He also had to send a general to recover supremacy in Unqi, where the king was murdered and a usurper seized power; the usurper was in his turn killed and an Assyrian appointee made king in his place.[19]

The breaking of the southern alliance had left the Assyrians free to attack Damascus, but their failure to take the city left Hazael in power and with a certain enhanced prestige. He was also isolated by the apparent hostility of his neighbours Hamath and Israel. Israel had taken the opportunity of the Assyrian war to seize some of Hazael's territory, and when he was free to do so he turned to recover it. This is the context of the Tel Dan inscription, which is in fact a record by Hazael of what happened. He recovered his lost lands and appears to have defeated both Israel and (probably sometime later) Judah. That is, he constructed his own empire of tributary states as far south as the Philistine cities. It may also be that Hazael was behind the installation of the usurper in Unqi. In effect, Syria was divided between the Assyrian-dominated states of the north and those in the south dominated by Hazael's Damascus.[20]

That Shalmaneser sent a general to do the work in Unqi suggests that he was feeling his age (he had by then been king for almost thirty years). In the last years of his reign Assyria was engulfed in a civil war, and then his successor Shamshi-Adad V apparently conducted no campaign into Syria, perhaps because the tribute payments were reasonably regular. The kingdoms of north Syria remained under their own kings, usually of the local dynasties, but also under distant Assyrian domination. Shamshi-Adad campaigned once as far as the Euphrates where he reinforced Kar-Shamaneser (Til Barsip) which therefore continued to be a standing menace to the rest of Syria, but the internal disturbances in Syria continued, preoccupying the king.[21] By 814 he had turned to campaigning in Babylonia where two successive Babylonian kings were defeated and captured, resulting in that country being reduced to disorder for the next half century. It thus remained no threat to Assyria, but the Babylonians had been assisted by several other kingdoms in their fight, which was clearly a problem. As one enemy was beaten, so others were always apprehended.

Shamshi-Adad's successor was Adad-nirari III, who took control in 805 (after his mother's five-year regency – she became the model for the legendary Semiramis). The neglect of the west, as the Assyrians might have put it, had allowed the north Syrian states to revive. They were therefore now once more wealthy enough to make it worthwhile to cull their riches. But they had also revived militarily in the interval, and in their aspirations for independence, and when Adad-nirari led his army across the Euphrates northwards towards Kummuh, whose King

Suppiluliuma was in dispute with the king of Gurgum, he found that he faced another north Syrian coalition.

It is worth noting that this is yet another dispute between Syrian states, to go along with those between Judah and the Philistines, between Judah and Israel, and between Israel and Damascus. The Assyrian domination was thus not intended to enforce peace; indeed it is quite likely that the Assyrians fully appreciated that such Syrian arguments and petty wars left the door wide open for their own interventions – as this dispute between Kummuh and Gurgum is a classic example. The alliances and coalitions which were formed when an Assyrian attack was anticipated were also the opportunities for Assyrian loyalist kings to take their own chances of advantage. The Assyrian victory – overwhelmingly likely in all cases – might not bring the Syrian state an immediate profit, but it would surely reduce the resources of its neighbours – as the ravaging of Luash seems to have been ultimately to the advantage of Hamath.

This new coalition in 805 was led by the king of Arpad, Attar-shumki, the son of Arame, and included the kings of seven other states, collectively referred to as 'the eight kings of Hatti'; these are not named individually by the Assyrians, but, apart from Arpad, they will have included Gurgum (the object of the Assyrian expedition) and probably Que, a recent victim. Unqi under its Assyrian appointee, like Kummuh, might be assumed to be on the Assyrian side. Samal and Melid are other possible members of the coalition. Adad-nirari claimed a victory and set up a commemorative stele on the boundary of Kummuh and Gurgum, probably as a sign of his victory, but also as a clear marker of the disputed boundary.[22]

The sequence of Adad-nirari's several Syrian campaigns is not clear. He provided summaries of his achievements rather than an annual statement, and claims in one that he received tribute from all the states from the Euphrates to Philistia, though we do not necessarily have to believe him.[23] But it does seem that he succeeded in conquering Damascus, or at least in compelling the king there to accept vassal status. The date of this success was somewhere between 805 and 796, probably nearer the latter date.

However, also involved in this is a war between King Zakkur of Hamath, who was probably the successor of the last of Urhilina's family and was an Assyrian loyalist, against a coalition of northern kingdoms led by Attar-shumki of Arpad and Bar-Hadad II of Damascus. The cause of the war is not known, but Zakkur ended up under siege in the city of Hatarikka in the old kingdom of Luash (not far from the ruins of Ebla). He appears to have ruled Luash along with Hamath, possibly a gift from Assyria for taking its side. He survived, giving thanks to his god for his deliverance, though it is more likely that he was rescued by the approach of the Assyrian army.[24]

This affair rather floats free from the general context of the time and place, but it must be included with one or another of Adad-nirari's appearances in Syria.

Since the enemies of Zakkur were the northern coalition plus Damascus, it seems probable they were attempting to prevent him from attacking them from the south while they confronted Adad-nirari. Since Zakkur emerged victorious, and the coalition was thereby defeated, the way to Damascus was opened for Adad-nirari, while the king of Damascus had clearly provoked the Assyrian attack by his alliance with the coalition.

The northern coalition against Zakkur included, besides Attar-shumki of Arpad, the kings of Que, Unqi, Samal, Gurgum, Melid, Tabal and 'Ktk', and 'seven kings of Ammuru'. The king of Damascus, whether it was Hazael (who died about 803) or his son Bar-Hadad II, was also the overlord of most of the Palestinian and Transjordanian kings. No doubt their forces were called up to serve and were defeated both at Hatarikka and Damascus. This explains Adad-nirari's claim of receiving tribute from as far south as Philistia, and the huge tribute the Damascus king is said to have paid (though different totals are given in the Assyrian inscriptions, almost as though it was too big to be counted.)[25]

The actual Assyrian Empire had not grown as a result of all this. All the Syrian states still had their own kings, and the Assyrian boundary stopped at the Euphrates. The achievement of clear Assyrian supremacy by the conquest of Damascus was apparently sufficient for the moment. There were further problems for Assyrian kings. In the north a new and powerful kingdom, Urartu, had developed in the last half-century, while Babylonia was always difficult. It is perhaps this spread of problems which led to the internal developments in the time of Adad-nirari. The kings now tended to confide command of the army to generals, and powerful provincial governors emerged, guarding sections of the boundaries, but they were, of course, hardly able to initiate campaigns of conquest. Sometimes these were the same men. For Syria the usual governor to take note of was Shamshi-ilu, who was also at times the commander of the whole Assyrian army. He was often based at Kar-Shalmaneser, and was a potent force there for half a century. He was able to suppress risings and command the army, and act in the king's name when necessary.[26] The assumption is that this indicates a time of weak kings, but that is based on the supposition that it was the job of the Assyrian king to go on regular campaigns and to initiate conquest.[27] In fact, the system looks to be an interesting experiment in government, with the king presiding at the centre. It is, of course, more or less what both Egypt and Hatti had done in their last decades before the Sea Peoples smashed their joint system.

The Assyrian state therefore consisted of its home territory and its directly ruled provinces, all ruled by the king and his governors. Beyond this were the tributary regions, still under their own kings. But it had been clear from the reign of Shalmaneser that only by constant and repeated insistence on the delivery of the tribute required by the Assyrian king was it possible to believe that Syria was still under some sort of Assyrian control. The local kings had no wish to be vassals and evaded payment where possible. The king of Damascus, probably Bar-Hadad II, demonstrated his defiance by leading a raid as far as Kummuh, stealing the stele put up at the Kummuh-Gurgum border by Adad-nirari, and taking it home to Damascus.[28] It was a clear demonstration of his independence and of his defiance of Assyria; no doubt no tribute was forthcoming from Damascus after that.

The conflict between Zakkur and the coalition was a sign that the Syrian kingdoms were hardly friendly towards each other, and the conflict between the southern kingdoms was another. The relaxation of Assyrian pressure after the death of Adad-nirari in 783 allowed them all to go their own ways. Some, such as Bar-Hadad II of Damascus struck out for complete independence, though in his case this perhaps also meant imposing tribute on his southern neighbours. Some clung to Assyria as their protector, which may have been the attitude of Carchemish, which was very close to the local centre of Assyrian power and influence at Kar-Shalmaneser. In the north the kingdom of Melid fell under the influence of Urartu and then under its control.[29] Into all this, which was probably very confusing for all those involved, the Assyrian army lunged every now and again. In 775 Shalmaneser IV sent an expedition to the Amanus Mountains to cut cedar, the traditional method of asserting Assyrian supremacy over the intervening territories. This was followed by Shamshi-ilu's campaign to attack Damascus in 773. He was successful, and rescued the stele which Bar-Hadad appropriated thirty years before. There was a new king in Damascus, Hadyan II; he had to surrender a daughter and a large dowry.[30] Next year, however, the new Assyrian king, Ashur-Dan III, brought a royal army to attack the city of Hatarikka. This was still part of Hamath's lands (which had taken over Luash), but was close to its northern boundary; it would seem that Hamath was now hostile to Assyria once more. It is probable that Zakkur was dead by now, so perhaps there was a new king in the palace and a new policy in place. Whatever the result of this campaign it was unsuccessful in the long term, for Ashur-Dan had to repeat it in 765, and again in 755.[31]

Next year a new Assyrian king, Ashur-nirari V, campaigned against Arpad, perhaps as an inaugural celebration of his accession, but again this had no obvious results. The impression one receives is that these campaigns were in the nature of showing the flag, demonstrating the ability of the Assyrian army to march through Syria. But each one involved a shorter march than the last, and no kingdom south of the city of Hatarikka needed to be too alarmed; in effect Assyrian suzerainty was limited to the lands north of Hamath. Arpad had been, so far as can be seen, loyal to Assyria until the attack in 754; its territory had been marched through by the Assyrians to reach Hatarikka, presumably by agreement with, or at least acceptance by, Arpad's kings. But it was evident that Assyria was not feared to anything like the extent it had been in the previous century.

By this time Urartu was in control of Melid, and was able to intervene in Syrian affairs. Ashur-nirari's campaign to Arpad seems to have involved in a clash with Urartu in which the Urartian King Sarduri II is said to have inflicted a military defeat on Ashur-Dan's forces. Such a defeat is not something acknowledged by the Assyrians. The fighting ended in a treaty by which the Arpad King Mati'ilu acknowledged in formal terms that Ashur-nirari was his overlord, which does not sound as if Arpad was on the winning side. The prospect of an alliance between Urartu and the strongest of the Syrian kingdoms was presumably why the Assyrian king attempted to bind Mati'ilu so closely to him. By this time Sarduri was overlord of Melid, and by now of Kummuh as well (which last may have been a result of the fighting). This was clearly encroaching on Assyrian preserves and an Assyrian defeat would probably be needed to achieve this.

So for half a century after Adad-nirari, Assyrian domination of Syria was exerted and enforced only occasionally, and the Syrian states were able to indulge in their internal disputes without much Assyrian interference. But Assyrian lethargy had also permitted the growth of Urartu, which suddenly seemed to be becoming a major threat to that domination. Once again Syria had become a battleground between great powers, each eager to seize and control its riches.

Chapter 9

Destruction

The Assyrian period of near paralysis ended abruptly in 745, when Tiglath-pileser III carried through a *coup d'etat*. He had probably been the governor of the capital city, Calah,[1] and so was familiar with the royal court and with the kings and their policies; he had probably seen at least three kings in operation during his life so far (Shalmaneser IV, Ashur-dan III, and Ashur-nirari V – collectively reigning from 782–746). He was probably a member of the royal family, but he clearly had no right to the throne under normal conditions. There seems to have been trouble of some sort in the city, of which Tiglath-pileser took full advantage in seizing power; he was supported in this by at least one other city governor in the Assyrian heartland.

The result was what generally happens when a usurper seizes power, only to find holding onto it was more difficult: he deliberately turned Assyrian energies outwards, appealing to the old aggressiveness which had been largely in abeyance for the past half-century. That is, he identified the internal problems of the kingdom as being related to the less aggressive foreign policy of the previous kings, whereas the problems may well have been one of the results of that previous vigorous policy, particularly the practice of living on the loot and booty and tribute of the enemy and vassal states, a practice which is guaranteed to sap the will of the beneficiaries.

The practice of devolving authority to provincial governors was another policy he disliked, because the governors could not use their powers to do other than govern. For an expansionist empire such as Assyria, this had meant a slow decline – as was seen in the retreat of the Assyrian authority in Syria. Tiglath-pileser removed the old provincial system, and replaced it with small units whose governors were required to send in regular reports to the capital. To assist them in this, a speedy and efficient postal system was set up; in addition, inspectors visited the provinces to see that all was as it should be, and no doubt that the reality corresponded with the governors' reports; they would then make further reports. This established the king in much firmer control of his whole territory.[2] Tiglath-pileser was in fact inventing the type of bureaucratic imperialism which has been standard practice ever since; it was, of course a much more costly system to operate, yet another fuel for the new aggression.

The external situation included several perceived difficulties, of which relations with Babylonia and Urartu were the most pressing. And Urartu involved Syria.

The treaty between Ashur-nirari and Mati'ilu of Arpad ended when the former died. Instead Mati'ilu made an alliance with Sarduri II of Urartu. Babylonia was easily dealt with by establishing a clear boundary, and another region facing Urartu was rapidly conquered, so providing a clear defence line. But by the time Tiglath-pileser had dealt with these issues, the situation in the west had, from his point of view, deteriorated.

The Arpad-Urartu alliance had been formed, and it included Kummuh and Melid, which were already subject to Sarduri, and Gurgum, an old Assyrian adversary – most of north Syria, in fact. Tiglath-pileser took his army directly into the alliance territory in Kummuh, clearly having identified Sarduri as the main enemy. He defeated the allies in battle and drove Sarduri back into his homeland, which suggests that he had inflicted serious casualties. Gurgum suffered a nasty ravaging, and the kings of Kummuh, Gurgum, and Melid submitted and were confirmed in their posts, at least for the time being.[3] Tiglath-pileser commented that King Kushtashpi of Kummuh was a loyal vassal, not a rebel, which seems to imply a swift change of sides on Kummuh's part, and perhaps messages of loyalty were sent even when he was under Sarduri's thumb. For now, Sarduri having been driven away, the main enemy was Arpad, and it was necessary to make certain that there should be no interference from any of the others of the alliance, hence the momentary generous treatment of the three kings.

Arpad city was clearly a strong place, and it took three years to conquer it. An active siege of assault and bombardment is perhaps not to be understood, despite Assyrian expertise in siege warfare, but rather a blockade and the destruction of the resources of the nearby territory.[4] The length of time required is a mark of the importance Tiglath-pileser attached to the possession of the city. It was certainly a difficult enough fight to persuade Tiglath-pileser to take one more step on his route to a modern empire: the kingdom was abolished and made into a new Assyrian province.[5]

In the kingdom of Sam'al, south of Gurgum, between that kingdom and Unqi, King Bar-Sur was murdered by a usurper, whose name is not known. This happened in about 745, which was the same time as the alliance of Arpad and Urartu was formed. There was a surviving legitimate claimant Panamuwa II, the son of Bar-Sur, who appealed to Tiglath-pileser for help in being restored. The Assyrian king seems to have ignored him until he had finished with Arpad, then Panamuwa was enthroned, and the usurper was killed. The kingdom suffered serious damage during the usuper's time, which suggests that Panamuwa did not simply wait for Assyrian assistance, but that the kingdom was badly damaged in the fight between their supporters.[6] Panamuwa II was also rewarded – or bribed to stay loyal – by being given some of the territory of Gurgum, whose King Tarhulara had been retained after joining the anti-Assyrian alliance, but was now punished for his earlier transgression. Much of his land had been ravaged by the Assyrians during the war, so it is quite likely that what Panamuwa got was in a bad state; nevertheless he was grateful, and proved it later.[7]

The crucial nature of the siege of Arpad becomes clear when these surrounding events are taken into consideration as well. Tiglath-pileser was clearly in a very dangerous position, with his army committed to the siege, and potential enemies all around him. Had the anti-Assyrian alliance survived the initial defeat, he could have been in deep trouble. It is a tribute to his diplomatic skills that he succeeded in warding off any interference, but it is also an indictment of the allies that they allowed their alliance to be so easily outfoxed. It may be that it was the potential for trouble from these neighbours, as well as the threats from other regions, which made it impossible to lock the army into a close siege. As it was, the neighbours now found themselves being closely watched by the Assyrian governor, and his garrison and agents, at Arpad, and with much less room for independent manoeuvre than before.

In 739 there were reactions to this among the new province's neighbours. To the west the King Tutammu of Patin (called by the Assyrians Unqi), ceased to observe his loyalty oaths, perhaps by omitting to pay the annual tribute; at the same time, and quite probably in concert with the usurper in Patin, just to the south a large-scale rebellion broke out in Hamath. The causes of these events were different, though they were probably connected in more than timing. Tutammu evidently wished to become free of Assyria, and took advantage of Tiglath-pileser being on campaign against Ullaba in Urartu. The rebels in Hamath, led by a man called Azriyau, appear to have been more interested in becoming free of the Hamathite king, Eni'ilu, who was, it seems, an Assyrian loyalist, or at least he said so when it became clear that Tiglath-pileser was coming west to deal with these rebellions. In Patin, Tutammu was quickly captured, many of his people were deported, and the kingdom became another Assyrian province, Kullania (named, like Arpad, from the main city).[8]

Azriyau was similarly defeated, but Eni'ilu's professed loyalty (if he did profess it) did him no good. The long hostility of Hamath to Assyrian ambitions, and the size of the kingdom and its evident strength, meant that Tiglath-pileser immediately took advantage of the civil war to diminish its power. The rebel territories were taken over and formed into two new Assyrian provinces: Hatarikka and Simirra. Eni'ilu was left with the remnant, only a third of the original kingdom.[9] That Hatarikka was involved in the rebellion might suggest that Azriyau's cause was the reconstitution of the old and defunct kingdom of Luash, which had become annexed to Hamath earlier; in a sense he achieved this, since the new province was the old kingdom in a new guise. The province of Simirra brought Assyrian territory to the Mediterranean. The province was essentially the Eleutheros Valley plus the coast facing Arwad city on its island. It gave Assyria an assured access not just to the coast, but to the coastal route connecting the Phoenician cities to the south, places which had often figured in Assyrian tribute lists, but which Assyrian campaigns had so far remained clear of. It is of interest that this is exactly the place chosen by the Bronze Age pharaohs for their governorship of Amurru – for Simirra is the former Sumur, whose capture by Abdi-Ashirta signalled his Amurru kingdom's emergence as an important and permanent power within the Egyptian sphere. Now the place was occupied by an Assyrian governor, who, it turned out, had wide responsibilities.

By 735 Tiglath-pileser was able to attack Urartu in its homeland, where, though he won a battle outside Sarduri's capital city Tushpa, he was unable to capture the city itself. Nevertheless this was enough to stop Sarduri's progress for a time. Next year Tiglath-pileser took advantage of a crisis in Syria, this time in the south, to launch a new campaign there. The king of Damascus, Rasyan, had assembled a new alliance to defy Assyria, consisting as before of King Pekah of Israel, the Philistine cities, and King Hiram II of Tyre. Judah under King Ahaz could not be persuaded to join. This disagreement led to a war, so that Ahaz appealed to Tiglath-pileser for help, supposedly sending a large treasure taken from the temple in Jerusalem as a helpful bribe, though this is more likely to have been the regular tribute. Tiglath-pileser arrived to break up the alliance, and would have probably done so even without the Judaean bribe (if it ever existed).

Judah complained that it was beset not just by Israel and Raysan, but also by the Philistines and Edom. This time, faced by another Syrian alliance, Tiglath-pileser chose a very different strategy than against Arpad-Utartu. Instead of attacking the most powerful of the allies – Damascus – he chipped away first at the rest. He must have assumed that this alliance was more solid than that in the north. It was, in fact, an alliance which had existed in some form or another for several decades, whereas that between Arpad and Urartu was new, and linked two powers with very different priorities.

The campaign against the south began in the new Assyrian province of Simirra. Tiglath-pileser had evidently decided that he would take the opportunity to regularize the position along the Phoenician coast. He first dealt with the island city of Arwad. This could have been difficult, since the city was on an island a kilometre offshore. The advantage of success was commensurately greater. There was certainly fighting, and apparently at sea, according to the fragmentary Assyrian record; Tiglath-pileser prevailed, and extracted both submission and an interesting array of tributary items, giving a sign of Arwad's trading links.[10]

From there he marched south along the coast road. He was faced by the hostility of Tyre, another Phoenician city perched on an offshore island, but one with a mainland settlement (Usnu) which was clearly vulnerable to his army. He assaulted and captured a hill fort called Mahalab (Mahlib), some 6km north of Usnu, and this seems to have persuaded King Hiram to give in before his city was attacked. He paid a large tribute, of course.[11]

Tiglath-pileser went on to deal with Israel, whose instability may have been one of the main causes of his expedition. Pekah was the latest of a series of several kings to have seized the throne by murdering his predecessor. In Pekah's case he had killed King Pekahiah, the son of King Menahem, both of whom had paid tribute to Assyria. Pekah refused to do so.[12] Since Ahaz of Judah did pay tribute, this inevitably put Judah in the pro-Assyrian camp when the new southern alliance was formed. The reason for their attack on Judah was thus not simply that he refused to join the alliance, but that his refusal meant that Judah would be actively on Assyria's side in the coming war. Tiglath–pileser employed the usual methods in his attack on Israel, devastating the countryside, sacking the towns and deporting parts of the population, and eventually annexing three quarters of the kingdom. Three new Assyrian provinces were formed from the annexed lands: Dor on the coast, Megiddo, and Gal'aza (i.e., Gilead, the Transjordanian area). Pekah was left with an area around Samaria for his kingdom.[13]

The Assyrian expedition went on to attack the Philistine cities, of which there were four of any importance – Ashdod, Ashkelon, Ekron and Gaza. The king of Gaza, Hanuna, fled to Egypt. This is the first time since the battle of Qarqar over a century before that Egypt had become involved in Syrian affairs, but the approach of Assyrian power to its very doorstep was an awakening call. The Assyrian king penetrated as far as el-Arish, halfway along the Way of Horus towards the Nile Delta. The other cities – and indeed, presumably Gaza, to which Hanuna returned – were made tributary.[14] From now on, one of Assyria's main concerns in Syria was to be reactions from Egypt. It is presumably while he was on this expedition that Tiglath-pileser received the submission from King Qaushmalaka of Edom and is said to have more or less ignored Ahaz of Judah. (But this is a biblical account which is concerned to blame Ahaz for the country's problems, so its testimony is more than suspect.[15]) Moab and Ammon were also now, or next year, tributary states.

Next year and the year after (733 and 732), Tiglath-pileser turned to attack Damascus, now weakened by the loss of its allies. Having defeated Rasyan's army, as usual, the Assyrians attacked the city, but failed to take it. Next year Tiglath-pileser returned and this time succeeded. In the course of the fighting King Panamuwa of Sam'al was killed, thereby all too drastically proving his loyalty to Assyria. Only by his death is there any indication that the Assyrian army had been supplemented by Syrian forces; no doubt other kingdoms had furnished contingents as well. Tiglath-pileser deported large numbers of the people, destroyed their orchards and villages, and then converted the kingdom into another Assyrian province.[16] Then Pekah of Israel was murdered by Hoshea, who seems likely to have been, if not an Assyrian agent, then certainly an Assyrian ally.[17] In the meantime, in 733 Ashkelon had 'rebelled' and was defeated, a war which included the Assyrian capture and destruction of Gezer, a powerful fortified site dominating the route south along the Palestinian coast. The rebellious Ashkelonite King Mitinti was replaced by his son Rukubti as an Assyrian appointee.[18]

Tiglath-pileser had achieved his main aim, which was the elimination of the main centre of hostility to Assyria at independent Damascus. With that city under his direct control, the enmity of the surrounding kingdoms – remnant Israel, Judah, Hamath, the Phoenician and the Philistine cities – would be of no account. Damascus as an Assyrian province was even more powerful locally than it had been as the basis for Hazael's south Syrian empire.

Tiglath-pileser was the real founder of the Assyrian Empire, second only to Adad-nirari II who had organized the initial period of expansion across the Jazirah. He was also clearly a particularly able military commander. And yet it was still no more than the outline of a correctly governed state. Many of the necessary elements were present – a strong and bureaucratic central government, governors of relatively small provinces (and so not powerful enough to rebel) controlled by reports, postal instructions and inspectors – but there were also grave flaws in the system as Tiglath-pileser had constructed it.

The first was the sheer brutality of the process of conquest. The Assyrian army was clearly a well-trained force accustomed to victory in battle, and was repeatedly successful. It had some difficulty in capturing cities, but the long sieges of such places as Arpad were usually due to factors other than military prowess. The kings resorted to frightfulness to persuade their enemies to surrender – massacring, deporting, destroying. It is no wonder that after Tiglath-pileser's reign his successors had to repeat his conquests and when the end came, that the kingdom, the empire, and its cities were wiped out by vengeful subjects and victims.

There was no pretence that the empire was being constructed for the benefit of anyone but the Assyrians, particularly the kings and their courtiers – though it was all done supposedly to honour their gods. The constant insistence on the production by vassal states of tribute, and by subjects of taxation was directed at the enrichment of the core of the kingdom, which was not subject to such demands. It was also a successful method of funding the campaigns; each one usually began by extracting tribute from some hapless city; this could then be used to finance the next stage. Further, once the brutal and extortionate system had been set up, it was impossible to end it, except by dismantling the whole thing – Assyria had placed itself on a treadmill of constant effort to go round in circles, in which campaigns were launched to subdue a recalcitrant kingdom, whose tribute was and thus used to finance more attacks, thus creating resentment so that it was necessary to repeat the campaigns to get more tribute to finance more campaigns. Naturally the system did not last very long, for it led inevitably to impoverishment.

Tiglath-pileser may have set his kingdom on a new round of annexations, but when he died in 727 the work was only partly done. From Melid to Gaza Syria was politically a complex mixture of provinces and tributary states. Tiglath-pileser had a list of tributaries drawn up: it included ten Syrian states – and this was before the conquest of Damascus, and did not include any kingdom south of Israel.[19] What is more, the tributaries resented their position (and no doubt the tribute they had to pay), and the people of the annexed provinces resented their new status. Every state or province had suffered devastation and deportation as well as looting and massacre. It is hardly surprising that not only was Syria halfway between independence and total subjugation but every part of it was liable to 'rebel' when the chance arose.

The tributary states were the most liable to rise, having their own local leaders and their own armies, and once that happened, provinces may well join in. A string of these states, from Carchemish round to Sam'al, half encircled the provinces of Arpad and Kullania; south of these were the two provinces taken from Hamath, then Hamath itself, still a kingdom but much smaller than before. In the Bekaa Valley were two new provinces, Mannusuate and Subite, probably formed during the Damascene war; south of Damascus were two more new provinces, Hauran and Qarnim, lands which were split off from the Damascus kingdom when it was also made a province. South again was the remainder of Israel, centred on Samaria, and the fragments taken from it, which had been formed into three new provinces. The Philistine cities, Judah and the Transjordanian states were all tribute-paying kingdoms. Along the coast were the Phoenician trading cities retained as tributary states; they could always be compelled to disgorge large quantities of tribute.

The mixture of states and provinces in Syria was still new when Tiglath-pileser died. He was succeeded by his son Shalmaneser V. The death of the old conqueror encouraged the king of Israel, the Assyrian agent Hoshea, to try his luck, probably encouraged by his people, to go for complete independence. No doubt he hoped for support from the people of the new Assyrian provinces which had been part of Israel, and perhaps from those of the former Damascus kingdom. He contacted one of the Egyptian kings, Osorkon IV, who ruled in the north-east delta from the city of Tanis, but whatever assurances were given did no good, and no Egyptian assistance arrived. Shalmaneser arrived and laid siege to the city of Samaria. The siege lasted some time, no doubt because of the possibility of Egyptian interference, but the land was ravaged and many of the people were deported. When finally taken by Shalmaneser's successor, the city of Samaria was destroyed. Sargon continued the annexation policy by making Samaria into a new province.[20]

Shalmaneser had proposed to subject the Assyrian home territory to the same government regime as the provinces, in particular by requiring forced labour from the population.[21] In a sense this was logical, for by now a large part of the population of the metropolitan territory was no longer Assyrian. 'Assur' had been the destination of many of the deported peoples, especially under the Tiglath-pileser III, under whom the forced movement of the population became a normal part of conquest and punishment. He sent at least eleven groups of exiles from several different regions to Assur during his reign; and of course considerable numbers of true Assyrians were also moved out to nearby conquered lands.[22] No doubt to Shalmaneser V these newcomers were not really Assyrians at all but imported provincials, and possibly serfs. Yet the Assyrian population – the lords, no doubt – objected to his plan, no doubt assuming that they would also be subject to the forced labour provision in the end. No doubt many of the exiles had been assigned to lordly Assyrians to work their estates, and feared a minor reduction in their living standards. As with his father, Shalmaneser discovered that unrest in Assyria was far more dangerous to the king than any war or battle. The disturbances were seized on by Sargon, who deposed the king and presumably killed him, and made himself king in his place. He claimed to be another son of Tiglath-pileser, but few now believe him, and perhaps few even in his lifetime did so; he was, however, as ferocious as Tiglath-pileser, and it would be too dangerous to voice doubts.

Trouble followed, as it did after every disputed succession. Sargon (now referred to as 'Sargon II') had to fight an alliance of Babylon and Elam, and was soon worried by Urartu's advances as well. In Syria the king of Hamath, Yaubidi, became the leader of a widespread rising. Samaria, only recently conquered, joined in, and so did Damascus and Gaza. There was a rebellion in Simirra, formerly part of the Hamath kingdom, and another took place, most ominously, in Arpad. It is probable that Yaubidi had deposed the previous Hamathite king (possibly still Eni'ilu, a known Assyrian loyalist) acting in the name of an anti-Assyrian policy. If so this proved popular in many parts of Syria, much of which had only recently felt the heavy hand and tread of Assyrian forces. The new alliance gathered sufficient forces quickly enough to meet Sargon's forces in battle at Qarqar (suggesting that Arpad had not put up much resistance). The allies were beaten, Hamath was burnt and its people were deported; the same happened to Samaria – no doubt the other allies suffered similarly. Hamath became a province.[23]

Sargon went on south to deal with Gaza, and there fought and defeated a rather tardy Egyptian army at Raphia. Raphia, of course, was sacked, though it was hardly involved in the fighting. Not long after he returned and planted an Assyrian garrison and trading post near Gaza. Ashdod rebelled in 713, and its king was replaced. The replacement was then deposed by the citizens. They chose a new king, who then led them into rebellion again. An Assyrian army recaptured the city, in the meantime also destroying several of its constituent towns.[24]

The tributary kingdoms in north Syria, having been loyal since the conquest of Arpad in 740, now rose one by one and broke into rebellion, and were crushed serially. The basic problem, as so often, was Assyrian aggressiveness, which alarmed its more distant neighbours, in this case Urartu in the north and north-east, and Phrygia to the north-west. These powerful states could offer the Assyrian vassals possible protection, though in the event, like Egypt in Palestine, they usually failed to do so, the Assyrians always moving much faster.

In 717 King Pirisi of Carchemish, after a century of the city's loyalty to Assyria, was detected corresponding with Mita, king of Phrygia (that is, Midas); Sargon fell on the city and destroyed it.[25] Melid's king about this time was deposed by Sargon, probably for the same crime, but in 712 his appointed successor Tarhunazi also contacted Mita, was detected in this, and his city was 'smashed like a pot' as Sargon put it, followed by the usual deportations and killings. Next year the king of Gurgum, Tarhulara, who had been pardoned by Tiglath-pileser after his first Syrian war, was assassinated by his son Muwatalli. Sargon removed the assassin, though this time apparently without the same violence. All these kingdoms were broken up and made into new Assyrian provinces, though part of Melid was handed to the king of Kummuh, another Muwatalli, who had been designated as 'no rebel', by Tiglath-pileser back in 743. He may well have been loyal to that king, but Sargon was, as his neighbours had appreciated, a different matter. Muwatalli was reported to Sargon to have been in contact with the Urartian king, he was rapidly attacked and his kingdom conquered and annexed, its people deported and replaced by transportees from Babylonia.[26]

Sargon's work in Syria reduced the tributary kingdoms to one in the north – Sam'al, eventually provincialized at some unknown date – the Phoenician cities along the coast, and the small kingdoms in Palestine. One of the reasons for these survivals was, of course, their distance from the Assyrian base, which might have been enough to allow them to continue in existence if they had stayed quiet, but the presence of Egypt next door was a constant inspiration to reflect on the merits of independence.

Egypt for some time had been split among several kingdoms, of which the kingdom centred on Tanis of Osorkon IV was one. In 716–715, however, a new dynasty, the XXVth, out of Nubia, reunited the whole kingdom, though local strong men continued to exert influence. The reunifier, Pharaoh Shabako, carefully watched the conquests of Sargon, at one point returning a Philistine king who had fled to him for refuge. Yet the new strength of Egypt was encouraging to the dissidents in Syria and Palestine. This is probably one of the origins of the new series of rebellions which occurred in 701 BC, the year after Shabako's death.

Another reason will have been the death, probably in battle in Anatolia, of Sargon II in 705 BC. He was succeeded by his son Sennacherib, who seems to have acceded without dispute, but who was faced at once with trouble in Babylonia; this he put down in a campaign lasting perhaps two years. No doubt this was yet another reason for trouble in the west, for the Assyrian army was clearly fully occupied in Babylonia. There were now concerted moves to repudiate Assyrian authority by the Phoenician cities, by some of the Philistines, and by King Hezekiah of Judah; all of these were backed by Egypt, and possibly also by the leader of the

Babylonian independence movement, who was in communication with Hezekiah – but who was also losing his own war.

Sennacherib arrived in the west in 701. He identified the first enemy to be dealt with as Tyre. The king at this time was Elulaios, called by the Assyrians Luli, who governed a state stretching along the coast from about the Nahr el-Kelb near Beirut to Mount Carmel in Palestine, including Sidon and Acco. The cities of Arwad and Byblos submitted quickly to the Assyrian, and when he was faced with the Assyrian forces Luli fled to the Tyrian colony of Kition in Cyprus. It seems also that in Sidon the Luli's rule was repudiated, clearly a pro-Assyrian action, which was rewarded when Sennacherib appointed a King for Sidon, so decisively separating the city from Tyre's rule.

Egypt meanwhile had a new king, Shebiktu, who succeeded his uncle Shabako in 702. The approach of Sennacherib and the fighting in Phoenicia was clearly ominous, while Shebiktu was also more imperially minded than his predecessor, and accepted the proffers of alliance made by King Hezekiah and his fellow rebels. As Sennacherib came south after expelling Luli from Tyre, an Egyptian army under the command of the pharaoh's brother Taharqa moved into Philistia.

The cities of the Philistines were divided in their response. Gaza and Ashdod refused to join the rebellion; Ashkelon expelled its King Rubukti (an Assyrian appointee) and rebelled under his brother Sidka; Ekron rebelled, but its King Padi did not, and he was taken off to Jerusalem as a prisoner by Hezekiah. This was hardly a condition of affairs in which victory was likely – and Sidka of Ashkelon was captured by Sennacherib even before the Egyptian army arrived.

The two armies met in battle at Eltekeh, north of Ashdod. The Assyrians were, as usual, victorious; Taharqa withdrew. Sennacherib captured a series of Philistine and Judahite towns and then laid siege to Lachish, while a detachment of his army, commanded by the Rab-shakeh, a high military official, went against Jerusalem. Lachish was captured by siege, but Jerusalem was not; on the other hand, Hezekiah did make terms with Sennacherib's general, agreed to pay tribute, and released King Padi. Taharqa, realizing that the Assyrian forces were divided, advanced once more, only to discover that they had reunited. He returned to Egypt.

Sennacherib rewarded the three loyal Philistine cities with slices of Judah's territory and probably took over a separate section of Ashkelon's lands north of Ashdod to add to the province of Dor. At some point also the mainland territories of Tyre were taken over. Those near the city itself now became Sidonian land – Tyre on its island remained untaken, and so independent – while the southern territory, between Ras en-Nakurah (the Ladder of Tyre) and Mount Carmel, may have become a new province.[27]

There was further trouble in the next half-century or so, but this campaign by Sennacherib had clearly demonstrated that it was highly unlikely that any rebellion, even when assisted by a major external power, would succeed. This is the same situation as in Anatolia, where Phrygia was fended off without difficulty, and where Urartu was destroyed by Assyrian victories and by the invasion of the Cimmerian nomads, and in Babylonia as well, where Elam was similarly defeated and conquered. Of course, this left Assyria at full stretch, dealing with problems on ever extended frontiers, but for the present it was coping.

The means of exerting internal control were, of course, by visiting destruction on rebel communities, by destroying their settlements, and by deporting and dispersing their people. Archaeology can locate the destructions though there have been too few excavations in north Syria or the Lebanon to generalize. The much more extensive archaeological work in Palestine, however, can provide an indication to the extent of the Assyrians' actions. Almost twenty sites have been identified as having been destroyed by Assyrian action. Not all may be precisely dated, but for once it seems possible to fasten the blame for destruction on a particular attacker. At Hazor, for example, the burnt level was 3ft thick, and was followed by a thin Assyrian level; Samaria and Shechem show comprehensive destruction; Megiddo similarly.[28]

The destruction by the Assyrian was evidently aimed above all at removing the urban basis of Iron Age Palestinian society, and it was comprehensive. Some cities did survive, but most suffered either destruction or at least serious damage. And those which were destroyed were not repopulated, at least not to anything like the same extent as before. At several places – Hazor, Tell Chinnereth, Megiddo – Assyrian 'palaces' were built on the ruins. At Megiddo, which became the name-city of an Assyrian province, a small town developed, presumably to service the Assyrian governor and his staff in his palace. Elsewhere it is normal to find no remains, or a short-lived settlement (as at Taanach, which was reoccupied for about half a century) or an occupation by poverty-stricken farmers. This was the result of the fairly short campaigns between 734 and 701; it is probable that even more extensive damage was done in north Syria, where there were campaigns spread over a much longer period. Even a single campaign could result in total destruction, as, it seems, at Hamath.

The repopulation of these places did not happen because the people who had looked to the cities as their economic and political centres had gone. The price of rebellion in Syria was to be either killed or deported. The practice is known from the earliest period of Assyrian campaigns in Syria, with Adad-nirari II, but it became particularly extensive in the reign of Tiglath-pileser III. There were two processes involved, first the initial deportation of the resisting populations, their wealth having been confiscated before they left, and then the importation of replacement groups from elsewhere. There are essentially two records, the Assyrian and the biblical, of which the former is incomplete, and the latter deals only with Palestine. Even so the Assyrian record shows that Tiglath-pileser III deported over a third of a million people in a reign of seventeen years, Sargon II well over 200,000 in the same length of time, and Sennacherib over 400,000 in a quarter of a century.

There seem to be two purposes in these population movements: to break up resisting populations by removing them from their homeland, eliminating their leaders, and sending them to foreign lands, where many of them were put to forced labour, for example in construction palaces for the kings. Those who remained were largely rural village dwellers, farmers and peasants, who no longer had a local city in which to market their surplus produce, or where they could buy manufactured goods. The process of conquest also often involved the destruction of orchards, the theft of burning of the crops, and damage, if not worse, to rural habitations. The empty lands were partly repopulated by similar deportees, who were no doubt similarly disoriented, and had to settle on devastated lands. Sargon, for example, deported 27,280 people from Samaria in 720, sending them to 'Halah, and in Habor by the River of Gozan and the cities of the Medes', that is, to the Assyrian city of Calah, to the Khabour Triangle, and to Iran.[29] Tyrian deportees were put to work on the construction of ships on the Tigris.[30]

The net result varied over the empire, as one would expect. Judah, for example, suffered relatively little from Assyrian attentions, despite the invasion by Sennacherib, and few of its towns were damaged (though Lachish was destroyed in the siege) – presumably the distraction caused by the Egyptian invasion stopped the worst destruction. It seems clear, on the other hand, that large parts of the former Israel were seriously depleted of population. In some cases the Assyrian kings seem to have been especially vindictive. When Sargon conquered Kummuh, for example, he seems to have deported almost the entire population. There are nineteen separate instances in the (incomplete) Assyrian records concerning Kummuhian deportations; the people were sent to nineteen different places, many of them in Babylonia, but others went to Elam, to the Zagros Mountains, the Khabour Valley, and Assyria proper. This was in contrast to its neighbours: only one deportation from Melid is listed, only one from Sam'al, and only two from Gurgum. Maybe the reputation of Kummuh for loyalty made Sargon particularly incensed when it proved false. Also in contrast is the fact that only two groups are recorded as having been sent from Bit-Jakin in southern Babylonia to repopulate Kummuh. The land became an Assyrian military region; it seems to have been left largely desolate.

When the deportees arrived in their new locations, no doubt large numbers simply died. It is doubtful if the Assyrians cared. The land they arrived in had, of course, been cultivated by its previous inhabitants, but the conquest had probably involved considerable destruction, and whether they had seed or animals is not known. It would of course be in the Assyrians' interests to ensure that these were supplied, but it is by no means clear that this happened. In some instances they were allotted plots of land, and some of the refugees arrived with money of their own, and were able to buy land; most, however, had nothing, and many were townsmen with no agricultural skills – indeed it seems that the Assyrians were intent in some regions of eliminating towns altogether and imposing a purely agricultural regime. The movement of people from one region to another was also not one from like to like: the Kummuhians sent to Babylonia had to learn a new agricultural method; the Babylonians sent to Kummuh had to learn a new agriculture as well as coping with an Anatolian winter. This disorienting experience was repeated in every single case.

Syria was evidently fully and finally subjugated by the campaign of Sennacherib in 701. His deportations were virtually the last by any Assyrian king from the whole region, though both of his successors, Esarhaddon and Ashurbanipal imposed one deportation each – from Acco and from 'Arza'. They did not cease the practice: Esarhaddon carried out twenty-one deportations in his reign of only eleven years, and Ashurbanipal no less than eighty-eight in his reign of forty-two years; Arabs were the object of both kings' ire, but Ashurbanipal carried out half of his deportations from Elam. The contrast shows quite clearly that Syria had been cowed and definitively conquered, ceasing to resist.[31]

This is not to say that Assyrian rule had become accepted in Syria, only that the land, after almost continuous warfare for over two centuries, had finally been reduced to prostration. But its agony was not yet over.

Chapter 10

A Time of Desolation

The result of a century and a half of Assyrian warfare was to leave Syria a shattered wreck. Of the dozens of cities and kingdoms which had existed in, say, 900 BC, there were barely a single dozen left by 700 BC, and these were almost all geographically marginal – the Phoenician cities, Judah, Sam'al for a time – all of them well away from the major military routes by which the Assyrian army would march to fight Egypt.

The land of the Nile, rich and populous, had become one of the most feared enemies on Assyria's frontiers. There were others, in Iran and Anatolia, but Egypt was the most awkward so far as Assyria was concerned, because it was the most distant from the imperial base in the upper valley of the Tigris. The early collisions, in the time of Pharaohs Osorkon IV and Shabiktu, had been cushioned to some extent by the intervening Palestinian states such as Israel and Judah, and the Philistine cities, but as these were crushed, or pushed aside, the Assyrians came face-to-face with the Egyptians. From the time of Sennacherib's successor, Esarhaddon (680–669) war broke out regularly, almost always involving the Assyrian invasion of the Nile Valley. Assyrian armies penetrated steadily more deeply into Egypt with each campaign until Ashurbanipal reached and sacked Thebes in 664, but they were never able to complete the conquest, and the Egyptians eventually eased the Assyrians out when a new pharaoh (Psamtek I of the XXVI dynasty) developed from a local ruler favoured by the Assyrians to a ruler of the whole country.[1]

So from 700 BC onwards Syria was the scene of tramping armies marching to and from Egypt, a place in which Assyrian garrisons were alert for an Egyptian invasion, or for an Egyptian-inspired rebellion. And meanwhile other Assyrian armies were fighting on other frontiers farther and farther from their base, and Assyrian kings were shifting populations about in hopes of, presumably, defusing internal hostility. This may well have successfully prevented rebellions for a time, but it failed utterly to secure support. Instead, the wars, the deportations, the looting, and the 'tribute payments', continued to generate a constant hatred and a continuing and deepening impoverishment outside the beneficiary region of the Assyrian homeland.

In the end, of course, the whole structure collapsed. Babylonia detached itself under a native king, Nabopolassar, in 626, and, in alliance with the Medes, inflicted defeats on the remnant Assyrian kingdom until it finally vanished.[2] As they did so, the Egyptian enemy fished in troubled waters for choice morsels; the main intention of the Egyptians was to gain control of Syria. The new Egyptian dynasty was in fact an Assyrian ally, and this was its means of gaining control in Palestine.

For perhaps a generation before the end in the Assyrian heartland, the Egyptians were able to operate more or less freely in southern Palestine. When Assyria was tottering to its final collapse after the capture and sack of Nineveh in 612, the final Assyrian kings were assisted by Egyptian forces. Egyptians and Assyrians were fighting together against the Babylonians in the western Jazirah and along the Euphrates as early as 616, which suggests that the Assyrians had ceded control of some Syrian territory to Egypt before then. In 609 a combined Assyrian-Egyptian defence of the final Assyrian fragment in Harran in the Balikh Valley was eventually destroyed.[3] In 605 the Babylonian army under Nabopolassar's son Nebuchadnezzar defeated the Egyptian army under Pharaoh Necho II at Carchemish, then again in the region of Hamath. The Egyptians were driven back into their homeland.

In the last century of Assyrian control, after Sennacherib's campaign in 701, the Syrians who still had some autonomy were inevitably regarded with suspicion. Tyre was besieged by Esarhaddon (680–668) when his main army invaded Egypt in 671; several years earlier he had captured and sacked Sidon, then founded a rival port nearby, presumably to compete with the older city. Esarhaddon set up a stele to celebrate his Egyptian wars in Sam'al, which may suggest that the kingdom still existed; the king was making it clear how powerful he was to his vassal.[4]

When Ashurbanipal (668–c.627) campaigned again against Egypt he ensured that the kings of Tyre, Byblos, and Arwad were among those contributing to his forces. Tyre and Arwad later joined the Egyptian side, but were gradually reduced to political dependency on Assyria. Later Acco and Usnu, both in the mainland territory of Tyre, rebelled and were crushed, their people deported.[5]

It is notable that in all this there is no mention of trouble from the people living inland from the coast. It seems probable that the Assyrian devastations had been efficient in deterring any further demonstrations of independence, and that the massacres, deportations, and destructions had so thinned the population that the region was not well enough populated to be able to muster a rebel army. The kingdom of Judah survived, as did at least some of the Philistine cities, but only by avoiding any declarations of hostility to their overlords.

Nevertheless, no recovery from the Assyrian devastations was possible. Syria remained a battleground between Assyrians and Egyptians, with occasional Syrian rebellions, from 700 onwards. And when Egypt penetrated into southern Syria on a more or less permanent basis in the last Assyrian decades (perhaps from c.640) it was not with the aim of liberating Syrians from Assyrian control, but in order to rule the land itself as part of a revived Egyptian empire; this would include establishing Egyptian suzerainty over any surviving local states. In 609 Egyptian forces were fighting Babylonians at Carchemish, and Necho was established at Riblah in the territory of Hamath, clearly ruling Syria; King Josiah of Judah, who had been king since about 640 and was therefore under Egyptian suzerainty, was executed at Megiddo at Necho's orders in 609, presumably for rebellion against Egypt.[6]

The surviving minor kingdoms in the south lived on until the Babylonian Empire. The Ammonite kings were repeatedly called on by the Assyrians to provide tribute, and dutifully did so; in return the Assyrians provided help in defending Ammon against its enemy, in particular the Arab nomads. The land appears, from the archaeological remains, to have enjoyed a period of prosperity as a result. The same can be said of a kingdom to the south, Moab, one of whose kings defeated and captured the king of Kedar, an Arab kingdom. To the south of Moab was Edom, which took advantage of Judah's troubles to seize control of the southern part of Judah, the Wadi Arabah and the route to Egypt. Again, as with the other kingdoms, the Assyrian period is seen as a time of local prosperity.[7]

The contest of Egypt and Babylon for control of Syria turned into a Babylonian war to establish control of the disputed land, with Egypt only occasionally intervening. Repeated campaigns between about 610 and 580 BC by the Babylonian king Nebuchadnezzar II were needed to conquer Syria. After defeating Necho's army at Carchemish in 605, he campaigned for the next four years in Syria, supposedly collecting 'rich booty', each time. He claimed in 603 that 'all the kings of Hatti' had submitted to him. Who exactly these kings were is not clear; they were probably the kings of the Palestinian area, unless local kings had re-emerged in the wake of the Assyrian defeats. It is possible, like the repeated claims to have collected 'rich booty' from Syria, that whoever composed the *Babylonian Chronicle* from which this information comes, was merely using the phraseology expected of victory, taken over, like their war methods and their treatment of conquered populations, from their Assyrian predecessors.[8]

In the campaign of 603, however, Nebuchadnezzar marched as far as Ashkelon, so at least one or two kings were encountered – Ashkelon at least was still ruled by its own king; he opposed the invasion and his city was captured and destroyed. In 603 it was Gaza's turn to fight and be destroyed. The Babylonians had to fight an Egyptian army at some point in 601, without apparently either side being victorious, and two years later they had to fight Arab tribes in north Syria. No doubt the devastated land had attracted the attentions of the nomads, and the Transjordanian kingdoms already had. Nebuchadnezzar was back in Syria in 598, and laid siege to Jerusalem where King Jehoiakim had rebelled, on the assurance of Egyptian help, which did not arrive. Instead the Babylonian army, joined by forces from Ammon, Moab, and Edom, forced the city of Jerusalem to surrender. Jehoiakim had died in the siege; his successor Jehoiachin was packed off to Babylon city with a selection of the Judahite elite, supposedly to the number of about 3,000 people. The new king, Zedekaiah, was imposed by the Babylonians.[9]

Judah had been one of the kingdoms caught between Egyptian and Babylonian claims to suzerainty during the last years, and once the city was taken, a new king, called Zedekaiah, was installed. Nebuchadnezzar campaigned again in Syria three more times in the next four years, as was recorded in the *Babylonian Chronicle*. He marched only as far as Carchemish in 596, but the next year, after a brief rebellion in Babylon itself, he reappeared to collect tribute in Syria, no doubt also reinforcing his authority there, and reminding any who felt they might take advantage of the troubles in Babylon that he was still in control. Another campaign of sorts, though no fighting is recorded, took place in the next year. It is possible that some of these campaigns were merely tribute-collecting occasions, but the fact that Nebuchadnezzar used his army to ensure that the tribute was produced suggests strong reluctance by the Syrians.

Judah's semi-independence was extinguished by the siege of 598–597, and by that time the remnants of independence in the Philistine cities, had also disappeared – indeed the cities themselves had gone, all destroyed. The Babylonian methods of conquest were copied from those of the Assyrians – destruction, depopulation, and massacre. One result was to allow the infiltration of Arabs, the next tranche of nomads to come in from the steppe, who had already threatened the kingdoms east of Jordan in the Assyrian times. Arabs gained control of the site of Gaza.

Judah's last flicker of defiance came in 587, when the city of Jerusalem was captured yet again, after the rebellion which had been encouraged by Egypt, and their former enemies, the Transjordanian kingdoms. This time the city was destroyed. King Zedekaiah and his family were killed and the defiant part of the population deported – some had already left for Egypt in advance of the attack. A selected set of towns were destroyed, though an area north of Jerusalem, inhabited by the Benjaminites, was spared, the leaders of the communities – among them the 'prophet' Jeremiah – having argued that resistance to the Babylonians was pointless. It was in this area that the governor appointed by Nebuchadnezzar, Gadaliah, established his government centre, at Mizpah.[10]

The Transjordanian kingdoms were ignored in 587, but Nebuchadnezzar turned on them five years later. Ammon and Moab were his targets. No king from either of these is recorded again. Edom was ignored, yet Edom was now no longer protected against Arab attacks and seems to have succumbed to them not long after. The region was not wholly destroyed, and the main centres of Ammon and Edom (Rabbath-Ammon and Buseirah) survived, though the region's earlier prosperity now failed.[11] Of course, the prosperity of this region depended largely on similar prosperity on the west side of Jordan; with that area destroyed, the east also faded.

By 580 there were probably no autonomous states left in Syria apart from perhaps three of the Phoenician cities. The urban superstructure of the country had been destroyed, the skilled workers, the artisans, the wealthy, had mostly been removed by deportation and most of those people had become domiciled in their new homelands. So far as we know only the last of the deportees, the Jews of Jerusalem, were able to maintain their ethnic cohesion in exile, and this was probably so because their deportations being late in the process, their exile was relatively short. They were in exile in and after 597, with further groups being sent off over the next fifteen years, and the first groups able to 'return' did so in the 530s; some of those driven out will have still been alive at the end of the exile, and will certainly have been able to maintain their culture.

This period of Syrian desolation lasted for four centuries. Without any real sources of wealth or wealth-creation the surviving population had become rural village dwellers. The number of urban sites which existed at the end of the period of desolation numbered not much more than half a dozen – the Phoenician cities of Tyre, Sidon, and Arwad, and possibly Tripolis and Byblos, Gaza, possibly Damascus, and the town of Bambyke in the north. Thapsakos, the crossing point of the Euphrates, may have had a larger population than a village, but not much more. Gaza revived to defy Alexander's army for two months; it had been handed over to, or acquired by, the Arab Kedarites and became a major trading centre, exporting spices brought up from south Arabia to the lands around the Mediterranean.

The country of Syria was still fertile, the people were generally as inventive and vigorous as ever, given the chance; the reason for the continuing poverty was undoubtedly the policies of the several imperial governments. The taxation system was as greedy as that used by the Assyrians and the Babylonians, and culled any surplus wealth quite effectively. The irregular military campaigns which were conducted through Syria were no doubt just as efficient at removing even non-surplus products as ever, as Nebuchadnezzar claimed. The constant enmity of Egypt ensured that such campaigns came repeatedly, and the frequent alliance of Egypt with one or other of the Phoenician cities – once other dangers had been destroyed – ensured that the fighting was not confined to the Egyptian border. A 'thirteen-year' siege of Tyre by the Babylonians (c.585–c.572) will have scraped up any food and other resources in the neighbourhood – a term which no doubt can imply the whole of Syria. The siege, which was probably intermittent rather than continuous – no ancient army could keep the field for thirteen years – ended with the destruction of Tyre, leaving Sidon as the pre-eminent Phoenician city.[12] Phoenician shipbuilders and sailors were employed by the Egyptian pharaohs in the early sixth century to develop a serious Egyptian maritime capability; some of the ships and sailors went on a voyage round Africa.[13] It may well have been the relations between the Phoenicians and Egypt which contributed to the hostility between the Babylonian king and Tyre; there are signs that Nebuchadnezzar had to campaign in the Lebanese mountains to remove Egyptian forces who were harassing his men.[14] Once again the sheer power of the Babylonian Empire finally ensured that its internal enemy was crushed.

On the other hand, a king of Tyre continued to rule. Baal II, who became king at the end of the siege, and so was presumably appointed by Nebuchadnezzar as a Babylonian loyalist, died in 564, and only then did Nebuchadnezzar change the government of the city, appointing a succession of 'judges' rather than installing a new king. This did not last long, and about 556 or so a king was once more appointed.[15] Hostility towards Egypt continued, and when that country was plagued by internal troubles, Nebuchadnezzar attempted a new invasion, unsuccessfully; he had received as a refugee the deposed Egyptian Pharaoh, Wahibra/Apries (589–570 BC), but when he attempted to restore him – as a Babylonian puppet, of course – his invasion was defeated by the man who had driven Wahibra out; Ahmose II/Amasis. Whether it was that Nebuchadnezzar was now convinced he could not win in Egypt, or that he was now too old to go campaigning, or that he felt threatened by rival states to the east, he and Ahmose appear to have now made peace.[16]

Nebuchadnezzar died in 561, and his death was followed by a period of dispute over the Babylonian succession, with four kings in as many years. One item which emerges from this is that at least two of the deposed Syrian kings still lived at Babylon, kept there no doubt so as to be available if their restoration might be useful. Jehoiachin of Judah was briefly promised such a return by Nebuchadnezzar's son Abel-Marduk, but his royal sponsor died before the policy could be put into effect. The deposed King Aga of Ashkelon was also still living in Babylon with him, as were former kings from Tyre, Sidon, Arwad, Gaza, and Ashdod (and others whose names are missing).[17] It was, no doubt, the knowledge that a king of the House of David still lived, even after the comprehensive elimination of Zedekaiah and his family, which sustained the hopes of return of the Jerusalem deportees, who appear to have been concentrated in and near Babylon.[18]

The reign of the last Babylonian king, Nabonidas (556–539), who was put on the throne by his fellow officials in place of a son of a usurper, is a blank so far as Syria is concerned. He lived for much of his reign at the Arabian oasis of Teima, and he installed his daughter as priestess of the god Sin at Harran in the Balikh Valley, but even this relative proximity brought no Syrian reaction. The only signs of Babylonian military activity in Syria are an expedition to Kilikia in 557, and the use of the army to collect cedar from Lebanon in 553, and an attack on Edom.[19] It would seem that the peace negotiated with Pharaoh Ahmose II was maintained, and without Egyptian meddling and encouragement, the prospects of a Syrian rebellion were never good.

The Assyrian practice of deporting populations from their homes was complemented by importing other populations to replace them. Therefore, many of the places in Syria which show evidence of destruction in Assyrian times also show evidence of resettlement soon afterwards, if invariably on a smaller scale than the original inhabitation. The Babylonian practice, however, seems to have been simply deportation and destruction, perhaps because there were relatively few rebellions so that the removal of populations became less common. The Jews of Jerusalem, of course, were deported, and in fact no new inhabitants were brought in to take their places in Judah. The site of Jerusalem was left desolate, as were many of the places in the kingdom, such as Lachish and sites in the Negev. The findings of archaeology are generally negative: 'no material finds' of the Neo-Babylonian period, or finds are 'meagre'; these levels can, in fact, only rarely be detected in a site, except in the ruins they created. These conclusions are confirmed by the implications of the written record, or the absence of it.[20]

This apparent quietness – or 'vacuum'[21] – in Syria during the later Neo-Babylonian period may be due as much to the absence of source material as to the lack of activity, but the lack of sources is also a symptom of that very quietness, and the absence of archaeological remains tends to confirm it. And this quietness continued after the collapse of the Babylonian Empire. For during the following centuries when the land was part of the Akhaimenid Empire, the sources are similarly absent. The fact that no Akhaimenid Great King went to Syria until 526/525, when Kambyses II campaigned to conquer Egypt, gathering his forces at Acco, suggests that Syria was still quiet, or perhaps prostrate. Dareios I probably made the land a separate satrapy ('Ebir-nari'),[22] but very little activity is recorded in the area until the end of the fifth century, other than the passage of armies.

The lack of activity in the region is reflected in the lack of interest in it shown by its rulers. The Assyrians had valued it more as a problem to be solved than for itself, though loot was always welcome; the Babylonians cannot have been able to acquire much of the latter once they had finished their work of destruction, and anyway they seem to have spent it mainly on building and decorating Babylon itself. For the Persians of the Akhaimenid Empire the Syrian interior seems to have been seen as a region in which the members of the royal family and the nobility could establish substantial rural estates, and 'paradises' where they could indulge in massive hunts – some of the lands were presumably cleared of inhabitants for the purpose.[23] Archaeologically their presence is revealed mainly by burials, and by palaces built on such places as Ebla and Lachish, ruined tells which gave a splendid view over the surrounding country – the Persians were great admirers of natural beauty. Another palace is known outside Sidon, which was probably for a governor, or possibly for the Sidonian kings. There was one north of Aleppo, where the governor of Ebir-nari, Belesys, had his palace burned down by the soldiers of Cyrus the Younger in 404 when he refused to join the potential usurper.[24]

The only region where economic activity more than rural and peasant life existed was along the coast. The Phoenician cities still survived, and were able to trade throughout the Mediterranean; their ships were valued by the Achaimenids as useful adjuncts to their military power during the Greek wars, and in their wars with Egypt. At the same time, those very Greeks were active in trading with Syria, and some settled at places on the coast. Greek pottery is relatively common on Persian period sites, no doubt because of its quality – there can have been few skilled potters left in Syria, and certainly none with the resources to produce for a bigger market than a village.[25]

One of the more curious events in Phoenicia is the foundation of a new Phoenician city, Tripolis. It was literally a 'three-city', in that Tyre, Sidon, and Arwad each contributed to it. It may have been a place in which the Phoenician kings met to discuss mutual problems, which may have been called a 'synedrion', though it does not seem to have had any institutional basis. Perhaps the oddest thing about the place is noting that it had a Greek name, whereas a Phoenician name would be the more likely.[26]

The city was founded in some point in the fourth century BC, no doubt before the destruction of Sidon in 360 BC. It is perhaps just about possible that it was founded as a meeting place, but communal and political considerations are much more convincing. It was sited on the southern side of the mouth of the route along the Eleutheros Valley from the Syrian interior, more or less where there had been other cities in the Bronze Age (Ullaza) or earlier in the Iron Age. This in turn suggests that Syria was beginning to recover a little from the centuries of neglect and exploitation and destructions, though this was also the main land route from Phoenicia to Babylonia, which was the main Phoenician market; perhaps where effect on Syria was minimal. The revival of the city of Gaza, evident by its stout resistance to Alexander in 332, is another sign of recovery. In both cases the initiative was local – the other Phoenician cities at Tripolis, the Arab traders at Gaza; the imperial authorities were never interested.

The lack of interest in the region shown by its imperial masters is suggested by the failure of either the Babylonians or the Persians to do more than continue to use the same governing system that had been installed by the Assyrians. There is little enough evidence for this, of course, but enough exists to show that there was an essential continuity. In the Khabour Valley some cuneiform tablets from Dur Katlimmu (Tell Sheikh Hamad) show that the same administrative practices continued through from Assyrian to Akhaimenid times. In Palestine, the old Assyrian province system evidently was taken over by their successors without alteration. When Judah was finally conquered and reduced to a Babylonian province, it just became another sub-province, apparently with no boundary alterations.[27]

Even more startling and indicative of a failure of the Persian imagination, the Persian conquest of Babylon was succeeded by the appointment of just one man, to rule of the whole of the former Babylonian Empire, from the Persian Gulf to Sinai, which clearly precluded any change in the administrative system or probably any change in the personnel running the system – the first governor, after all, was Ugbaru/Gobyras, a renegade Babylonian.[28] The Syrian section was in fact evidently separated off by Dareios I into a new province, a satrapy called Ebir-nari, meaning 'Beyond-the-River', the Euphrates, that is. Even so, this was a huge area for one governor to control; no detailed changes are to be expected.

When the Persians captured Babylon and thereby extinguished the Neo-Babylonian Empire, Cyrus II the conqueror was faced with ruling a new territory which was largely devastated, and with much of the imperial wealth concentrated in and about Babylon. One of his responses was to give permission for the Jews who had been exiled to Babylonia, or rather their descendants, to 'return' to Jerusalem.[29] The Jewish interpretation has always been that they were favoured in this, and this favour was a mark of Yahweh's influence; from Cyrus' point of view, however, it may have been largely another deportation to remove a disenchanted group from the geographically important region of Babylonia. It was also, of course, a political manoeuvre designed to plant a group which was loyal to Persia in a useful place in southern Palestine as a check on Egyptian ambitions in the area.[30]

The 'returnees' arrived with the same ambition as other Syrian populations: to re-establish their local temple, which then became the centre of the community. Their god Yahweh thus returned to Jerusalem as the local god of the Jewish community around Jerusalem, just as Hadad had remained as the city-god of Damascus, the god Dagon of Ashdod, or Atargatis at Bambyke, and the Hittite storm god in what had been Arpad and Patin and Carchemish and other states, and so on. These local gods filled the place in local loyalties of the extinguished dynasties – the House of David was probably the last to be snuffed out, by the Babylonians, though the leader of the first Jewish returnees, Zerubbabel, is said to be a grandson of King Jehoiachin, and later the governor Nehemaiah could claim the same descent; that the Persian government should permit these men to have authority in Judah implies that their loyalty to the Akhaimenid kings was absolute.

Nevertheless, it must be emphasized that the Jews' 'return' – there can have been very few who actually 'returned' to Judah – was only a minor matter in the Akhaimenid scheme of things. It was, however, a typical gesture in that the kings were never insistent on imposing their own beliefs and ideology on their subjects, which may or may not be regarded as toleration, though it is more likely to be a realistic assessment that the crushed populations were unlikely to rebel if they were not pressed too hard. At the same time, and probably incidentally, the revival of local loyalties in the persons of the local gods proved to be even more effective in fashioning local communities and their stance of hostility to their rulers than the more fallible dynasties.

It is necessary to resort to the Jewish experience because any other evidence from Syria between 700 and 300 BC is so very thin. The Jewish refugees, or perhaps those left behind in Judah, preserved a good deal of their written history, which the exiles added to, revised, and altered, both in exile and afterwards. It is in these remains that there occur the mistakes and deviations, the alterations and additions and reinterpretations, which so concern we later historians. Such preservation is apparently not something other destroyed communities managed to do. The Phoenicians, at least according to Josephus much later, whose communities survived, though battered, held on to their chronicles and king lists and myths, just as did the Judahites, and these two instances give some notion of what has been lost.

It would be of interest to know if Cyrus permitted other groups to return to their ancestral homes. A group of tablets found at Neirab in north Syria seems to suggest that a group there also 'returned' to their ancestral homes.[31] It seems unlikely that many others succeeded in doing so. The great majority of the deportations from Syria had taken place under the Assyrians in the eighth century BC, at least a century and a half before Cyrus took Babylon; integration, death, and forgetting had by then probably extinguished more than any legendary memories.

It is, in these circumstances, impossible to delineate a connected history of Syria in the four centuries covered by this chapter. All we have is a series of disconnected incidents, some already detailed earlier in this chapter, which may be significant in the overall imperial histories, but which say little or nothing about Syria itself.

The Jewish returnees have a history of a sort. They had been deported to Babylonia in at least three sections, and returned in at least as many, spread over almost a century. Yet only those, it seems, who had been sent to Babylonia were permitted to 'return'. Any who had been deported to other parts of the empire appear to have been absorbed there – the former Israelites who were sent to 'Halah', the Khabour area, and Media certainly were.[32] The early returnees were commanded by Zerubbabel, apparently a grandson of the former king, Jehoiachin (who was either dead by this time or was not permitted to go). Their activities were inspected by a governor of Ebir-nari, Tattenai, who was concerned at their building activities and asked for an archive search at Babylon to determine exactly what they were allowed to do. The relevant decree was found, actually at Ekbatana in Media, and the building of a new temple was permitted.[33]

In the middle of the fifth century, over half a century later, more exiles turned up, guided by Ezra who had letters of permission addressed to various officials, in effect imperial permits. The rebuilding, which appears to have earlier been very limited, was now restarted, but the neighbours objected to Jerusalem becoming a walled city, and so did the king when it was reported to him. A new governor, Nehemiah, said to be a descendant of the former kings, was successful in both protecting the Jewish community from its neighbours and in ensuring that it was well founded. The city wall was too dangerous a concept to be allowed, according to the neigbouring communities, but it appears to have been built anyway. The two biblical books in which these events were recorded include references to a number of places in the region which were evidently occupied, though it is not obvious how large or important they were – the area north of Jerusalem, the Benjaminite area, had never been as badly damaged as the rest of Judah, and remained reasonably well populated.[34] The proximity of Egypt and its propensity to fight against, or rebel against, any outside control, rendered southern Palestine a sensitive area, and Egypt's full independence in the fourth century only enhanced that.

The extent of rebuilding in Jerusalem is not very obvious. The texts are unclear, the archaeology difficult. The wall completed by Nehemiah enclosed only the old site, and the temple is somewhere under the Herodian platform. This was a small settlement, and probably fairly poor. Other areas resettled in the Persian period show only small communities. Along the coast Phoenician influence helped to maintain several towns, including Tel Dor, where excavations have produced evidence of Persian period buildings, though the town was relatively small – about the size of the resettled Jerusalem, in fact.[35]

The Phoenician cities were also involved in the problem of Egypt, as the Persians would perhaps have put it. They had participated with some enthusiasm in the wars in Greece under Dareios and Xerxes, where the Sidonians in particular distinguished themselves. They also acquired control over a series of coastal stations, such as Acco and Dor, presumably to ensure that their trade could continue.[36] Quite possibly the imperial destructions had left much of the coastland towns ruined. The control of a regular series of ports along the coast would allow Sidonian ships to voyage safely. It seems likely that the Persian period saw a degree of recovery among the residual communities in the inland coastal area, but this was distinctly limited.[37]

And yet, despite this hollowing out and immiseration of Syrian life and society, the influence of Syrians was wider spread than ever. One of the results of the dispersal of Syrians which was accomplished by the Assyrians and the Babylonians was to spread them throughout the whole Middle East. They took with them above all their Aramaic language, which they appear to have retained, and which was accepted by others as a useful *lingua franca*. It is even the case that those who replaced the deportees in Syria itself appear to have taken up the language, perhaps because they were a heterogeneous mixture of exiles and since the surviving local population spoke Aramaic, it became the one necessary and common tongue. It was so influential that it was eventually adopted by the Akhaimenid regime as one of its official languages, reaching the borders of India – and there the Aramaic script was adopted as a model for the first Indian script, modified, in the usual way, to accommodate the peculiarities of the Indian languages. Persian Aramaic was still one of the local languages in Kandahar in Afghanistan in the third century BC.

At the same time the local languages survived, and were used by the imperial administration. In a way this was a complementary policy to go along with the tolerant religious approach, by not interfering with local communities so long as they remained loyal and paid their taxes. But it was also, of course, a useful divisive measure. It did mean that interpreters and translations were constantly needed – and that a language such as Aramaic became steadily more important.[38]

This extension of the Aramaic language was essentially a movement to the eastward, as the Assyrian deportees were driven from their homes. A westward movement of the language also went on, by way of the Phoenician cities, whence other refugees followed the old trading routes to the west. The result was the spread of the Phoenician variant of Aramaic to North Africa and Sicily and Spain, and the growth of a major political power centred at Carthage. The Phoenician cities were regarded with suspicion by every imperial regime which ruled Syria, no doubt because of their chronic assumption of independence as their default political condition, their contacts with an independent region speaking their language, and because of their propensity to commerce, which was another activity regarded with suspicion by the rural-dwelling Persian aristocracy. And yet it was presumably their ability to accumulate wealth which brought their survival (in most cases). Their trading interests and activities around the Mediterranean, and in particular their ability to acquire metals from Spain, made them essential to the several regimes which alternately battered and favoured them, but constantly took tribute from them. The voyages of exploration around Africa, and the explorations set on by the early Akhaimenid kings, were other Phoenician achievements at a time when their Syrian hinterland was in ruins.

In such circumstances of original destruction and continual neglect, the several Syrian communities were quite unable to revive, and wholly unable to develop an urban dimension. In 404, for example, the Greek mercenary army of Cyrus the Younger marched through north Syria from Kilikia to the Euphrates. Xenophon's account does not mention a single town in the region in which independent city states had been numerous four centuries earlier.[39] The surviving Syrian population in their villages were reduced to a peasant economy, rendered vulnerable by the open nature of their settlements, though they still possessed the usual resources of an oppressed peasantry: evasion and concealment to preserve their possessions and food from the taxman, and their gods.

The old Syrian gods had survived the destruction of temples and shrines and cities, and received continued devotion from their people, no doubt in part this was an assertion of their continued identity and as a defiance of their rulers. New shrines developed, assisted by the usual superstitious fears of outsiders, who had no wish to bring down misfortunes on themselves by interfering with the local gods. These gods were probably the one surviving element of the past which linked together the village communities of a locality, and with their ancestors. These were the basic religious beliefs of the population, inherited from long in the past. In north Syria, for example, the Hittite storm god, who was essentially the same as the old Syrian thunder god, was venerated throughout the region from the

Euphrates to the Amanus and from the Taurus to the Orontes. It was in fact the local shrines which maintained what remained of Syrian culture through the long period of the desolation.

The Phoenicians put considerable resources into distinctive temples. Open air temples are known at Sidon (to the god Eshmun) and Amrit; these are in the territories of Sidon and Arwad respectively, no doubt there was also one at Tyre, where the local god was Melqart; another, to Astarte, has been excavated at Sarepta. The temple for Atargatis at Bambyke was wealthy enough to have its chief priest make a claim to kingship in the 330s. The returning Jews eventually built their new temple for Yahweh at Jerusalem, and there are a number of shrines and 'chapels' at sites throughout southern Syria. The Samaritans, despised by the Jews as Yahweh-deviants, built their temple on Mount Gerizim. Such buildings tend to have been constructed rather more durably than ordinary domestic buildings, and to have stayed in use longer, which is why they have survived to be excavated.[40]

The political history of Syria in the Persian period consists in part of the re-establishment of the Jewish community in Judah, but otherwise the country was, as in the later years of the Assyrian and Babylonian Empires, a passageway for armies heading elsewhere. Egypt repeatedly rebelled against Persian rule, and each time this meant that a great Persian army came marching through, and camping in Syria, usually in coastal Palestine, before launching a new invasion of Egypt. Such armies were like swarms of locusts, gobbling up all resources in their path, no respecters of property or persons, and each campaign resulted in damage, looting, killing, and requisitions of food.

The deaths of Akhaimenid kings were usually the signals for an Egyptian rebellion, though the first happened a year before the death of Dareios I, which meant that this was one of the first problems his successor Xerxes had to deal with. Xerxes' own death produced another rebellion, and this took the Persians ten years to suppress – the satrap of Ebir-nari was one of the commanders involved, no doubt drawing his supplies from Syria.[41] This man, Megabyxos, himself soon rebelled, assisted by his sons. Based in Syria, he succeeded in defeating two expeditions sent by King Artaxerxes I, and was then forgiven. The whole affair no doubt cost Syrians rather more than either of the principals involved.[42]

A complex succession dispute lasting most of a year followed the death of Artaxerxes I in 424. This was followed by another civil war, in which the satrap of Ebir-nari, Artyphios, the son of Megabyxos, fought against the winner of the succession fighting, Dareios II. The satrap of Egypt moved with his forces to fight Artyphios, only to find that Egypt rebelled in his rear.[43] A much more serious rebellion began in 410, without this time the stimulus of the royal death. It lasted long enough, however, to result in the proclamation of a new pharaoh when news arrived of the death of Dareios II in 404.[44] Another dispute over the Akhaimenid succession now helped, and involved Syria when the army of Cyrus the Younger marched through the north of the country in order to attack the incumbent king, his brother Artaxerxes II.[45]

This time the Egyptians succeeded in maintaining their independence, but for Syrians this was even worse news, for their country now became the battleground between the two powers. Southern Palestine was invaded and occupied by Pharaoh Nayfaurud/Nepherites (399–393), according to a seal impression and a broken inscription found at Gezer. His successor Hagar/Achoris (393–392 and 391–380) moved northwards into northern Palestine and took control of Tyre and Sidon for a time, in alliance with King Evagoras of Salamis in Cyprus. Again there is epigraphic evidence for Hagar at Acco and at Sidon.[46]

This invasion, of course, eventually produced a Persian response, and between 385 and 380 the Egyptians were driven out of Palestine, after which the Pharoah Hagar's son, after a reign of only four months, was overthrown by a more prudent commander and rival, Nakhtnebef/Nektanebo (380–362). A new Persian army was concentrated at Acco from 385 under the satrap of Ebir-nari, Abrokomas, and by 380 the Egyptians were driven from Palestine. Then another army was organized to invade Egypt itself, together with a fleet of 300 ships, many of which will have come from the Phoenician cities. When the army, after at least four years spent in organizing and gathering supplies, finally attacked Egypt, it was stopped at the frontier fortress of Pelusion, and then, short of supplies, had to withdraw.[47] It was also hampered by the unwillingness of King Artaxerxes II to allow any of his generals to gain real credit and renown by success.

In this, of course, Artaxerxes was fully justified, both by past performance and rebellions by Persian aristocrats, and by what happened soon after, with a long crisis called the 'satraps revolt', mainly in Anatolia. Pharaoh Djedher/Tachos (365–360) took advantage of Persian distraction to return in arms to Palestine, but then found himself overthrown by his brother who put his own son on the throne at Pharaoh Nakhthorheb/Nektanebo II (360–343).[48] Although the Egyptians withdrew to their homeland, the next Akhaimenid king, Artaxerxes III (359–338), made a serious attempt to recover Egypt. His first attempt failed, and this was followed by a rebellion by the Phoenician cities, no doubt encouraged by Nakhthorheb, but mainly, it seems, because of the constant pressure to provide supplies to Persian armies; the rebellion began when the Sidonians raided a local royal estate, or paradise, where supplies had been stored.[49]

This rising was led by Tennes, the king of Sidon, whose city was now the most powerful of the Phoenicians. It spread its violence over all Syria, and for a time was successful in detaching much of Syria from Persian rule. Artaxerxes painstakingly gathered an army at Babylon, and returned to attack Sidon in 345. The city was betrayed by its rulers, many of the citizens committed mass suicide and the city itself was razed to the ground. It may be that Judah participated in this revolt, which certainly affected all Syria.[50] This cleared the way for a new invasion of Egypt, which at last succeeded in recovering control of that land for the Persians.

This catalogue of warfare has not been complied just to illustrate the difficult and violent political history of the Persian period in Syria, though that is one of the points to be made. It also shows that, except for the occasional king of a Phoenician city, no Syrians had any control over any of these events, a factor which had been constant in the land's life for a long time. In such circumstances, with an army marching through and/or camping in Syria every few years any serious recovery from the destruction of the previous regimes was hardly possible. And worse was to come.

An Egyptian rebellion started once more in 338, with the death of Artaxerxes III. This was followed by another royal succession crisis, which eventually was resolved by the seizure of power by a distant member of the royal house, who became Dareios III. In Egypt the rebellion was then swiftly suppressed. But yet another crisis came on top of all this, with the Macedonian invasion led by King Alexander III. This reached Syria in 333, with the defeat of Dareios at the Battle of Issos. Dareios then withdrew to reassemble his army in Babylonia, while Alexander moved south through Syria. In one way this was a clear sign that Alexander was determined on the conquest of all the empire, and he was thus allowing Dareios time to set himself up to be beaten finally. Meanwhile Alexander had plenty of time to devote to Syria.

It turned out that Syria as a whole was unwilling to become part of the Macedonian kingdom. The city of Arwad had to be blackmailed into surrender, and Byblos and Sidon joined him (the latter's sack by the Persians was a fairly recent memory).[51] The city of Tyre, however, had to be conquered in a long and ferocious siege which ended in the city's destruction and the massacre of most of its inhabitants – thus Alexander behaved in exactly the same way as the Persians only a decade before at Sidon.[52] His senior general Parmenion captured Damascus, but the hillmen of the Lebanese mountains harassed the Macedonians during the siege.[53] The city of Gaza resisted almost as valiantly as Tyre, and suffered the same punishment.[54] On his return from Egypt (where he was welcomed, not surprisingly), Alexander had to suppress a rebellion in Samaria, the governing centre of that part of Palestine.[55] In the north the chief priest of the temple of Atargatis at Bambyke claimed the title of king, but only briefly – no doubt he was suppressed when Alexander heard of it.[56]

Alexander marched off to the east, never to return to Syria – an outcome no doubt the Syrians generally welcomed. But he had in effect completed the latest work of the Persians by his similar destructiveness. It is clear from the reaction of the Syrians to his campaign through their country that as a whole they were loyal to the Persian regime. The reasons would include enmity towards the Egyptians, whose interferences in Syria had repeatedly brought armies down on them, dislike of Macedonian destructiveness, familiarity with the Persian government, and sheer inertia, for the Akhaimenids had been their kings for two centuries, and the Jews at least always recalled Cyrus and Dareios I with gratitude. If such memories also activated others who had 'returned' from their Assyrian and Babylonian exiles, then other memories of invasions and campaigns will have warned them that disasters were likely to follow – the last time the country had been conquered, it had been followed by destructions and deportations and massacres, from which the Persians could be claimed to have rescued them. No matter that this rescue had been inadvertent, it had happened, and the Syrians were clearly willing to stand up and be counted as loyal subjects of the Great King. It did not, of course, benefit them.

Chapter 11

Assisted Recovery

This chapter covers a smaller period of time than almost any other in this book, perhaps a century and a half. The reason is that this period (c.330–170 BC) was crucial for the future history of the people of Syria. And indeed, as will become clear, within that period just two decades was the vital part – literally, since it was then, between 301 and 281 BC that life came back to Syria. It was the accomplishment of one man.

For the thirty years following Alexander's brutal conquest of Syria in 333–331, the Syrians suffered the same sort of violence and oppression as had been their lot under the preceding Persian Empire and before. Armies marched through the country every year or so, and this meant, as before, repeated requisitions, violence, destruction, and looting.

The violence began almost as soon as Alexander was dead. Part of the Macedonian army under the command of Krateros had already passed through the north of Syria and then camped menacingly in Kilikia in 322. Ptolemy, the satrap of Egypt, sent a raid to Damascus in 321 to seize Alexander's catafalque, which he diverted to Memphis and then installed in Alexandria, in defiance of an earlier decision by the regent Perdikkas.[1] This provoked an expedition by the main Macedonian army through Syria under Perdikkas, designed to bring Ptolemy to heel; instead Perdikkas himself was assassinated after a considerable number of his men were killed in the fighting.[2] A conference followed at a place called Triparadeisos, a former Persian estate somewhere in the Phoenicia area; the whole Macedonian army camped there, and, of course, had to be supplied; requisitions of local produce followed.

This meeting attempted to set up a government for the Macedonian Empire, but it succeeded only in dividing the empire among the commanders, so it also essentially failed, since it only encouraged conflict.[3] In 320 Ptolemy kidnapped Laomedon, the governor of Syria, and seems to have made himself its unofficial governor.[4] Two armies, led by Antigonos and Eumenes, followed each other into Syria and spent the winter of 318/317 in the north, which meant more requisitions and looting.[5] When these forces left Syria Ptolemy, who had pulled out to avoid clashing with either, returned to occupy most of the country.[6]

By this time the major players in the west, Ptolemy in Egypt, Kassander in Macedon, and Lysimachos in Thrace, had been alerted by Seleukos, who had been driven from his satrapy of Babylonia. He reported that Antigonos was rich, powerful, and ambitious, so when Antigonos, having eliminated Eumenes, came back to Syria in 315 and Ptolemy's forces were driven out, he again held on to the city of Tyre, which had only just begun to recover from Alexander's destruction. Antigonos began building a fleet in the Phoenician ports, but was hampered by the need to lay siege to Tyre, a siege which lasted a year. Ptolemy's forces were driven out of Palestine, his garrisons in Joppa and Gaza having little effect in slowing Antigonos' conquest.[7] Tyre fell in 314.

In 312, Ptolemy's army faced one of Antigonos' armies under the nominal command of his son Demetrios, in battle at Gaza, and beat it, and the whole invasive and destructive process was repeated. Tyre was besieged yet again, but only briefly this time. Ptolemy's victorious army reached as far north as Phoenicia, then was forced out again, and on his retreat he systematically destroyed the fortifications of every place with walls.[8] (Seleukos, who was one of Ptolemy's commanders in the battle, rode off with a small force and succeeded in recovering Babylonia.)

Six years later, in 306, Antigonos mustered a huge new army, said to be 80,000 strong, and a fleet of 150 warships, for an invasion of Egypt, which failed.[9] Antigonos and his warrior son Demetrios located a new source of wealth in the Arab trading community of Petra, and raided it, with only moderate success.[10]

A few Syrian towns survived the battering delivered by all this campaigning, principally as usual those in Phoenicia, which were especially valuable to these warriors for their peoples' shipbuilding and maritime skills. Antigonos had returned from his eastern expedition in 315 with a huge treasure, much of it originally accumulated by the Persians. When he spent part of this hoard on building a new fleet in the Phoenician ports some of the treasure will have trickled down to the workmen, sailors, woodcutters, and the merchants.

Syria may well, however, have continued to manifest its hostility to its occupiers, whoever commanded them, which would not be surprising, given the behaviour of those conquerors. Antigonos ruled Syria, apart from the several Ptolemaic interventions, for fifteen years (315–301), and it seems that he distributed garrisons throughout the country, partly to control it, and partly to defend it. The men of these garrisons were generally Macedonian, though some were Greeks. They gave names taken from their homelands to the places where they were stationed. Most of these places, after the long desolation of the previous four centuries, were no more than villages. Sometimes they adapted local names to their Greek speech, or they saw a resemblance to a place at home and applied that place's name. So Fihl, in the old kingdom of Ammon, became Pella, the name of the royal centre in Macedon; a spring of water, in Arabic and Aramaic 'ain', became Ainos, the name of a small city in Thrace. A mountainous area leading down to the sea became Pieria, a name brought in from Macedon. A local shrine to the storm god in the hills north of Aleppo was named Doliche for a similar site in Macedon, and the god became Zeus, at least to the Macedonians. There are a couple of dozen of these places scattered through all Syria, and each one will have been held by a group of Macedonian or Greek soldiers.[11]

It has to be admitted that this is only theory, but I voiced it over twenty years ago, and so far as I know it has not been challenged, and at least four of these Macedonian/Greek names were demonstrably in use before 301 – Pella (which was later Apameia), Larissa, Kyrrhos, and Chalkis. The cities founded later by the kings almost invariably were given names from members of the royal families – Ptolemais, Antioch, and so on – a practice begun by Alexander and his father, and continued by Antigonos. Accordingly the names imported from Greece and Macedonia were not bestowed by the kings, but by men of the lower ranks who lived there. Seleukos kept many of these names when he organized north Syria (see later in this chapter), and some were awarded royal names later, just as the surviving Syrian cities were often given dynastic names, presumably as an honour.

So there are three layers of place names in Hellenistic Syria: first, those with the old Semitic names such as Gaza, Damascus, Tyre, and so on, many of which survived, and some of which, like Ainos, were adapted into the Greek. Second, the garrisons with Greek and Macedonian names which were planted between the time of Alexander and the definitive division of Syria between Ptolemy and Seleukos in 301; and third, those with dynastic names awarded from 301 by the two kings (and one earlier by Antigonos). Thus the city names may be used to make some points about the development of Syria after the fighting died down.

The persistence of these names, even though some were replaced later, implies that the men who awarded them stayed in place for a considerable length of time. No doubt some had retired from the army through age, or may have been disabled, and most of them will have acquired wives and children during their campaigns, or when they settled down. Any man who began his military career as a member of Alexander's army in the great campaign will have been at least 40-years-old by the time Antigonos gained control of Syria in 315, and will have added another fifteen years by the time Seleukos did so. His homeland had by that time been long under the control of Kassander, an enemy of Antigonos, and he would scarcely have been allowed to return to it; settling in Syria, no doubt with land to farm or rent out, would have been a satisfactory option.

This, as it happens, was the beginning of Syria's recovery from its time of desolation. The Persians had used Syria as a source of large noble estates; there is little sign that they placed any garrisons there, though they must have existed. There were the occasional military burial grounds, as at Deve Huyuk, north of Aleppo, but it is unlikely that the soldiers settled in the country.[12] Garrisons which were more or less both permanent and numerous, however, were new, and their people constituted large villages or small towns. They were the first stage in the recovery of Syrian fortunes, for these men were vigorous and active, and had money. A second stage came in about 307, when Antigonos began the construction of a new city in the Amuq Basin in north Syria. This was to be called Antigoneia, and it was to commemorate his assumption of the title of king, which came the next year. In fact, this was a false start, for he was defeated and killed in the Battle of Ipsos in 301, and the city was later dismantled.[13]

This was the war which had promoted a new invasion of Syria. Ptolemy had marched his army north from Egypt, as far as Sidon, to which he laid siege, something he had done frequently in the past twenty years. He then withdrew to take up winter quarters in Egypt; it was later said in a rumour that Antigonos' army, victorious over his allies, was marching south to fight him.[14] Some of Antigonos' forces were clearly based in Syria, and resisted Ptolemy's attack.

Antigonos' kingdom was divided up between the victors of the final battle at Ipsos, Kassander, Lysimachos, and Seleukos. Ptolemy had not been present at the decisive battle, but he had once again occupied that part of Syria (Antigonos' territory) which he wanted. He had been attacked in Egypt from Syria three times by enemies in the previous twenty years and on four occasions he had marched into Syria to take control of the southern part of that country as a defence for Egypt; he could probably recall from his childhood and adolescence that the Persians had been prevented for years from attacking Egypt because they had to take Sidon first, and once the city was taken, Egypt had been successfully invaded. He clearly had no intention of allowing that to happen again. He was able to occupy all Palestine and Damascus before Seleukos arrived to take over Syria, but had difficulty in Phoenicia. He had been unable to take Tyre and Sidon, though the towns to the north of Sidon – Berytos, Tripolis, Byblos – had become his. His advance stopped at the Eleutheros River.

In order to reach this northern Phoenician section, Ptolemy must have taken control of the Bekaa Valley, for the road along the coast between the sea and the Lebanon Mountains was blocked by Demetrios' cities of Tyre and Sidon. The Bekaa Valley will have become his main communication route between Damascus and Tripolis, and this will have required him to control Damascus as well, since the way from Palestine to the Bekaa lay through that city and the Barada river gorge. It is striking how the geography of Syria asserts itself repeatedly when invasions come. The Eleutheros River route between the sea and the Syrian interior – the 'Homs Gap' – had been repeatedly used as an imperial base for the last 2,000 years and more before Ptolemy, and at times as an imperial boundary.

The Phoenician cities had been constantly independent of, or hostile to, whoever controlled the Syrian interior, and if they had fallen into the control of that imperial power they had usually attempted to get free of it. They were now divided between the three of the Macedonian kings: Ptolemy held the northern cities, all of them fairly small; Demetrios held Tyre and Sidon; Seleukos found he had one city, Arados (Arwad) in his section.

Antigonos' conquerors had assigned Syria to the portion of Seleukos. This was a man who had already defeated Antigonos in battle more than once. After he had gained control of Babylonia in 311, he seized Media and Baktria, and had attempted an invasion of India. His military contribution to the victory over Antigonos at Ipsos had been a large cavalry force, a force of 400 trained military elephants acquired from the Indian Emperor Chandragupta Maurya as part of their peace settlement, and the cunning of an accomplished commander who tended to win his battles by subterfuge rather than brute force, which no doubt made him popular with his soldiers. Syria was the obvious part of Antigonos' kingdom to be assigned to him, since he already held the lands to the east.

It cannot have been unexpected by any of the victors, least of all Seleukos, that Ptolemy had already occupied much of the territory assigned to him. The other two victors, Kassander, who was king in Macedon, and Lysimachos, who took over Asia Minor, were probably quite content to contemplate the possibility of hostilities between Ptolemy and Seleukos. The defeat of Antigonos had not expunged Macedonian power politics but only shifted the context. But Seleukos had certainly come out of the war with the smallest reward: a thinly populated and impoverished land, hemmed in on three sides by potentially or actually hostile territory – Ptolemy to the south, Lysimachos in Asia Minor to the north-west, while Kassander's brother received Kilikia, though Demetrios soon seized it from him.

However, Seleukos was the most politically astute of the various successors of Alexander who had attempted to acquire their own independent kingdoms. When he arrived in Syria to find that his share of the booty from Antigonos' kingdom was only north Syria between the Taurus and the Eleutheros River, he of course complained to Ptolemy. But he must have known that Ptolemy would prove obdurate, for they had worked together previously, and it was no secret that Ptolemy wanted to control southern Syria. So, after Ptolemy refused to yield, instead of flying into a rage, Seleukos took three carefully calculated decisions.

First, he announced that he would not fight Ptolemy, who was his friend.[15] In effect this meant that Ptolemy could continue in occupation of southern Syria without Seleukos formally renouncing his rights to it, and leaving open the possibility of later taking it over; at the same time it drew attention to the fact that Seleukos had done the hard work while Ptolemy's campaign had been comparatively easy. It put Ptolemy subtly in the wrong. Second, Seleukos made an alliance with Antigonos' son Demetrios, who retained control of various ports, islands and cities from Athens to Syria, including Tyre, Sidon and Cyprus, all of which Seleukos knew Ptolemy wished to gain, as well as Kilikia, seized when Demetrios came east to meet Seleukos, and to present him with his daughter Stratonike as his second wife. The meeting was deliberately spectacular, on board Demetrios' largest ship, as another public demonstration of Seleukos' policy.[16]

Demetrios controlled the most important and powerful fleet in the Mediterranean, and this was clearly a standing threat to the whole of Ptolemy's coastline, from the Eleutheros River mouth to Cyrenaica, and he launched a raid from Tyre into Palestine as a demonstration.[17] These diplomatic manoeuvres provided Seleukos with protection. He had first of all put Ptolemy in the wrong by his refusal to fight, making the Egyptian king seem greedy and ungrateful; his alliance with Demetrios extended his protection to the north, and since Demetrios was more or less still at war with Lysimachos and Kassander, Seleukos was protected from them as well, especially when Kilikia was taken from Kassander's brother by Demetrios.

The alliance with Demetrios had another aspect. Many of Antigonos' soldiers who fought for him in Asia Minor had long been settled in Syria. When Antigonos' army was disbanded, these men returned home to the many places in Syria to which they had given Macedonian and Greek names. These men had been loyal to Antigonos to the end, and many of them may well have felt a continuing loyalty to his son Demetrios, who was a very inspiring commander. The marriage of Demetrios' daughter Stratonike with Seleukos, who had been recently widowed, and the alliance with Demetrios was clearly a sensible political manoeuvre which would help to defuse any obvious hostility by these men. And this leads to the third of Seleukos' measures, the most creative of them all.

Seleukos' forces in the war against Antigonos had been mainly cavalry recruited in Media and elephants from India, both of whose personnel had probably been mainly non-Macedonian. The infantry he commanded was the smallest contingent of foot soldiers in the field. Therefore when he arrived in Syria it is likely that the former enemy troops outnumbered his own, for the Median cavalry probably went home, while the Indian mahouts and elephant-carers were never involved in the internal politics in any Hellenistic kingdom. It was clearly uncomfortable, if not dangerous, that his soldiers should be less than obviously in charge. Seleukos' solution to this was to bring in immigrants from Greece.

These people would wish to live in cities, of a similar type to those they already knew. Seleukos set about founding cities throughout his section of Syria with the simultaneous objects of creating communities of Greeks who were loyal to him only and who would soon outnumber any who might have preferred Demetrios to him, and at the same time he created a powerful set of fortified cities from which he could defend both his part of Syria and the new population.

There were three types of city which he founded.[18] The first was a group of four major cities of considerable size, equivalent to Republican Rome or Ephesos in population and area, and larger than Athens. They were placed very carefully in a great quadrilateral to control half of the land Seleukos had acquired, facing both the sea and Ptolemy's territory, but at some distance from the latter. This was clearly a very defensive configuration. They were all named for members of Seleukos' family, his father, his mother, his first wife, and himself, and so he laid his own personal stamp on the region, which in fact soon became called the 'Seleukis'. Seleukeia was founded just to the north of the mouth of the Orontes River, at the northern edge of a small fertile plain. A harbour was dug out for it, and its fortified walls climbed the hills above. The city included a temple, high on the acropolis, which became the shrine of the dynasty, and where Seleukos himself was eventually buried. It was clearly designed, with its temple and its name, to be the major government centre for Seleukos' new territory.[19]

Inland, in the Amuq Basin, where the former kingdoms of Alalakh and Patin had been, the city of Antioch was founded. This is also the area where Antigonos had been building his own new city of Antigoneia, whose building materials were now taken for the construction of Seleukeia, a gesture both practical and symbolic: the old city was transformed into the new, and the former king was replaced by the new – and the stones were not wasted. Antioch was placed in an advantageous position, for the Amuq Basin had a large lake, fed by three rivers including the Orontes, and the basin was a major source of food.[20]

The other two cities were to the south. The city of Apameia, named for Seleukos' first wife, was situated at the southern end of the Jebel Zawiye, the plateau east of the Orontes which slopes away eastwards into the desert. The marshlands of the Ghab and the Orontes itself were on its west and south. It was situated in a defensive position and at the same time it overlooked the inland end of the Homs Gap and the Eleutheros route, and controlled the major inland roadway which followed the line of the escarpment to the north, and Antioch.[21] The fourth city, Laodikeia-ad-Mare – 'on-the-Sea' – was on the coast, in a fairly awkward position with the Bargylos Mountains behind it, rather like the situation of Seleukeia. It was also provided with a substantial harbour, and it controlled the coastal route, though this was a difficult route and less commonly used than the central route between Apameia and Antioch. Laodikeia was not far from the Phoenician city of Arados (Arwad), the only one of these cities to fall within Seleukos' sphere; like Seleukeia it was clearly established above all for defence, but it was also so placed as to watch over Arados, one of the more independent minded of the Phoenician cities.[22]

These four cities enclosed that part of north Syria which fronted directly on Ptolemy's lands, and on the sea which he and his successor, Ptolemy II Philadelphos, soon dominated. They were designed to form a major obstacle to any attempt at conquest, either from the south or from the sea. Each one of them was provided with a substantial city wall of the very latest military design, was large enough to hold a large population of several tens of thousands of people, and each was placed in an agriculturally fertile area and so had access to good supplies of food; all had well-fortified acropolis planted in one corner of the site, both as a defence and to proclaim royal control of the city itself.

Beyond these four major cities, Seleukos also organized the development of half a dozen more cities to the east of the 'big four'. Most of these had clearly originated in Antigonos' time, for they all retained their Macedonian names: Beroia (which eventually became Aleppo), Doliche, Kyrrhos, and Chalkis. All of these were smaller than the four greater cities to the south and west, but they were all clearly placed on rivers, and across lines of communication (as was to be expected of garrison towns). Walls, acropoleis, and a new population were all installed by Seleukos. Two urban places already existed in these regions when Seleukos arrived, and were extended and converted to Macedonian-type cites; one was Bambyke, the city of the temple of Atargatis, which became Hierapolis (Holy City);[23] the other was at the crossing point of the Euphrates at Thapsakos, which was renamed Seleukeia, to be distinguished from all the others by the nickname 'Zeugma' (the Bridge); it was the first time the river had been bridged; a fortified suburb was established on the east bank, and called Apameia, the names recalling the marriage of Seleukos and Apama, Seleukos from Macedon to the west, Apama from Sogdiana far to the east; it seems that Seleukos laid considerable emphasis on the value of such symbols.[24]

The cities were populated during the two decades following Seleukos' acquisition of the territory. The population came from Greece and Macedon as immigrants or as discharged soldiers of Seleukos' army. Others were Syrians who moved into the new cities from their villages, or whose home was a village which had been taken into one of the new cities. The plan of Beroia, for example, shows that the new city was laid out with a grid of straight streets, but in one corner the old winding streets of the village remained;[25] Apameia had been a garrison of Antigonos' soldiers who called the place Pella, and before that it had the Persian name of Pharnake, and earlier still the local name of Niya.[26] It would, of course, be impossible to build a new city anywhere in Syria without encroaching on somebody's village, and Syrians were sensible enough to understand that life in a city would be easier and better than life in a village.

It will have taken some time for these cities to be founded and developed and built but also populated. Seleukos himself seems to have remained in north Syria for most of the next two decades – his son Antiochos went off to govern the eastern provinces from about 292. Seleukos indulged in no wars between 301 and 285, though he was able to take control of Kilikia from Demetrios in 294 BC, without more difficulty than marching his army into the province. Presumably he spent much of his time overseeing the development of his new cities. He had to provide building materials, food supplies, and land for the immigrants, who probably arrived with only the minimum of resources. Probably the new arrivals were responsible for building their own homes, but Seleukos was responsible for the city walls, the public buildings, the temples, and so on.

Each city seems to have had a citizen body of about 6,000 men. This is uncertain, but a century later Seleukeia-in-Pieria had a citizen body of 6,000 and Kyrrhos also one of probably 6,000.[27] (Antigoneia seems to have had a citizenry of 5,300, which has been also applied to Antioch, though this is not an acceptable argument.[28]) These men will have been Greeks and Macedonians in the main, immigrants persuaded to move, soldiers of Seleukos' and Antigonos' forces. The numbers imply an initial citizen population for each city of 20,000-plus by including wives and children. Given that he had developed at least a dozen cities this means a minimum male Greek and Macedonian population in north Syria of about 70,000 men, and so an initial immigrated population of perhaps 250,000. To these must be added their slaves and their servants and any dependants, and other inhabitants, Greek and Syrian, who were not citizens. There must have been a population getting on for 500,000 inhabiting the cities by the time they had been fully founded.

Two other cities which fit into this intermediate group seem also to have been founded by Seleukos. One was in the valley of the Kara Su, north of Antioch and east of the Amanus Mountains. It was called Nikopolis – 'victory-city' – (the modern town of Islahiye) and was probably founded to commemorate Seleukos' victory over, and capture of, Demetrios in these mountains in 285; this is, however, merely an inference from the name of the city and its proximity to the battle site; no ancient evidence exists for its origin, other than a general list in Appian.[29] Another city, Nikephorion, was founded at the junction of the Balikh River with the Euphrates (modern Raqqah). Again the name implies that it commemorated a victory of some sort. No obvious battle is known in the area, but it may have been a reminiscence of an exploit of Seleukos' in 312 when he succeeded in crossing the Euphrates on his way to seizing power in Babylon. This is again quite uncertain, as is the attribution to Seleukos, though the city certainly existing during the Hellenistic period.[30]

There was a third set of settlements, of which the garrison towns inherited from Antigonos were the main part. These did not generally develop into bigger settlements. Between the Euphrates and the Balikh Valley were several places of varying size, all of which received Macedonian names. Anthemousias is explicitly said to have been founded by a group of Macedonians, which must date it to Antigonos' time; it lies on the road leading east from Seleukeia-Zeugma through the Jazirah.[31] Edessa was presumably, from the name, also a Macedonian foundation, on another urban site; there was a strong tradition that Seleukos built this city walls and towers; it also lay on the main eastward road.[32] Further east was Harran, a survival from the previous centuries; it was renamed Karrhai, actually on the Balikh River; to the south along the river was Ichnai, a garrison founded by Antigonos, which is noted as a 'Macedonian' foundation, and both were named for places in Macedon.[33] Nikephorion was placed still further south where the Balikh joins the Euphrates.

This set of clearly Macedonian foundations – all their names come from Macedon, forms an obvious pattern. They are placed along the road leading east from the crossing at Zeugma (probably the former Thapsakos) towards the upper valley of the Tigris, which from 308 certainly and probably from 311 was under Seleukos' control. The other posts had established a defensive line along the valley of the Balikh from the Euphrates northwards. Combining the layout of those and their origin as Macedonian foundations, the best interpretation is that Antigonos organized them as the forward defence for Syria against Seleukos, when Seleukos controlled the east. As it happened, when they went to war again, Seleukos attacked by way of the northern road, through Armenia – thus it could be said that Antigonos' defence line had served its purpose, even though he lost the war.

The other smaller settlements were spread through the rest of Seleukos' lands. Along the Euphrates the site of Carchemish had been occupied by a garrison and had acquired the name of Europos.[34] Further south along the river was a town at Jebel Khalid, whose Hellenistic name is not known; it had a solid wall, an acropolis – unusually placed within the city, not as part of the outside defence – a 'governors' palace', and a temple, but there was relatively little space for domestic housing and shops; perhaps the inhabitants lived on their estates. Also somewhere along the Euphrates was a town called Amphipolis; it is possible that this was Jebel Khalid, or it is more likely to be a separate place.[35]

Along the Orontes south of Apameia there were three or four small towns each occupying a strategic point, Arethusa (modern ar-Restan, on a plateau three quarters surrounded by the gorge of the river),[36] Larissa (modern Shaizar, where the survivors of a regiment of Alexander's Thessalian cavalry had settled),[37] and two places probably but by no means certainly founded by Seleukos, at Laodikeia-ad-Libanum, built on Tell Nebi Mend, the ancient Kadesh,[38] and the unlocated Seleukobelos.[39] This line of fortified posts established Seleukid control over the middle course of the Orontes in the same way that Antigonos' posts controlled the Balikh Valley.

There were other places founded during Antigonos' time or that of Seleukos, whose locations are not known, or whose origins are uncertain. Several were strung along the coast, and probably originated even before Alexander as minor trading posts. Several had Macedonian or Greek names. They are included in a long list by one historian, Appian, as Seleukos' work, but some places in his list clearly were not his, and others may well not have existed. Later many places claimed to have been founded by Alexander, but he did not really spend long enough in Syria to do any such work.

This work of Seleukos was a tremendous achievement. It is impossible to find anything comparable in the ancient world, or even in the modern world, with all our resources. Seleukos had, at a stroke, in no more than two decades reversed the destruction and neglect of four centuries. His work in north Syria between

301 and 281 BC set Syria on a new course for prosperity, power, and importance, which lasted for the next 1,500 years. The cities he founded, and the establishment thereby of north Syria as a centre of power, made it one of the foundations for a series on empires – Seleukid, Roman, Byzantine, Arab – during which the local population acquired wealth, political weight and influence, and was inventive. That is, Seleukos' work revived the Syria which had been in existence until the destructive Assyrians arrived.

In social terms, what Seleukos had done was in effect to import a new middle and upper class population, and so he reinstated the usual social system of rich, middle and poor in place of the solely peasant population which had existed under Persian rule. The upper class would be the royal family and the government; the ruling group were, as always, few in number and wealthy and were concentrated in the main cities; the middle class were mainly Macedonian and Greek immigrants and lived in the cities on rents from their estates or on commerce; the poor were the peasantry in the countryside and the mainly Syrian working class in the cities. To these latter groups, of course, the change was essentially one of opportunity; the existence of cities had opened up the chances of a poor man acquiring wealth.

The immigrants and the former soldiers will have been given land by the king, land which had been Persian royal estates, and which thus fell to Seleukos as king, and those of the Persian nobles, none of whom seem to have remained in Syria – they seem in most cases to have been absentee lords anyway – and which will have been royal land under Seleukos by confiscation and/or abandonment. The land was, of course, already inhabited by the Syrian peasantry who would have to pay rent to the new landowners, and at the same time continue to pay taxes to the government. It is unlikely that these impositions were particularly onerous. The tax system appears to have been relatively fair, based on taking a regular percentage of income, rather than a fixed quantity, and no doubt the rents were either fair or controlled.[40] We hear of none of the rural revolts which took place in Egypt, at least until the Seleukid kingdom was failing, or perhaps until the Judaean rebellion; this negative evidence may well be an indication of a fairly contented peasantry. Since many Syrians went to live in the new cities, it seems unlikely that they were pinned down to their village homes in some sort of serfdom.

The Phoenician cities had been divided for a time between Seleukos, who had Arados and its *peraia*, which included several small towns; Demetrios held Tyre and Sidon; Ptolemy controlled the northern Phoenician coastal cities from Berytos to the Eleutheros River. Ptolemy seized Demetrios' cities in 288 and, along with Cyprus, this gave him substantial resources in wood and in shipbuilding expertise through which to develop a dominating navy, in which he was helped by seizing control of many of Demetrios' old ships. By this time Tyre had recovered somewhat from its various troubles, as clearly had Sidon, but the Phoenician cities must have been always conscious that they were in fact the front line defence for Ptolemy's lands in case of a war with Seleukos. Their governing systems changed: Sidon's last known king, Philokles, became Ptolemy II's naval commander-cum-viceroy in the Aegean for a time;[41] the kingship was probably abolished when Ptolemy seized the city. The last known king of Arados either died or was deposed in 259;[42] Tyre appears to have had no king even before Alexander's siege, and his destruction of the city prevented any reinstatement; the rest probably ceased to be monarchies in this period as well. How far this was at the insistence of the cities' suzerains, and how far it was an internal decision of the citizens – or perhaps both – is not clear, but the result was to convert the Phoenician cities into city states more or less on the Greek, or rather Macedonian, pattern.

Seleukos and Ptolemy maintained their mutual peace while they lived, Ptolemy until 282, Seleukos until 281. There had been some trouble, perhaps in Syria, when Seleukos died, though we know no details and it did not last long.[43] War did break out between their successors, Ptolemy II and Antiochos I. The details of the war are not known, but any fighting must have taken place in the Eleutheros Valley and northern Phoenicia rather than in the Seleukis. This was the first of a series of 'Syrian Wars', which lasted until the end of the second century BC.[44] Later we know that invasions from the north captured the Phoenician town of Orthosia, and another raid reached as far as Damascus; in the other direction Ptolemy III succeeded in invading and gaining control of all north Syria for a couple of years in the Third War (246–241 BC).[45] But these wars were by no means on the same scale or ferocity as those conducted by the previous imperial regimes, and, although looting certainly took place – Ptolemy III boasted of having gathered property worth 40,000 talents from his expedition into the Seleukis – none of the cities were deliberately destroyed in the way the Assyrians, Babylonians, and Persians (and Alexander) did. In fact in four wars waged by the two dynasties between 277 and 217 only one city changed hands on a near-permanent basis – but this was Seleukeia-in-Pieria, captured by Ptolemy III in 246 and retained until retaken by Antiochos III in 219; its retention by Ptolemy for over twenty years only made it more certain that a vigorous Seleukid attempt at recovery would eventually be made.

Ptolemy's areas of Syria, Phoenicia and Palestine, with Damascus, collectively known as Koile Syria, did not receive the same degree of care and attention that Seleukos lavished on north Syria. To some extent this was due to Ptolemy's necessary attention towards his main kingdom, Egypt, but also to its not having suffered quite so badly from previous conquerors. It had, however, certainly been badly damaged, as Tyre and Sidon and Gaza could testify.

Ptolemy's section of Syria had only a few of the Antigonid posts with Macedonian names, and they were substantially fewer than in the north: there was another Chalkis in the Bekaa Valley, Dion and Pella east of the Jordan, possibly an Arethusa in Palestine.[46] Anthedon was in Philistia, probably originally a Philistine town wrecked in the past.[47] A place called Hellas is recorded; its location is not known, but the name might suggest a settlement by a mixed group of Greeks who either chose the name, or found that it was awarded by people nearby.[48]

There were also other places which were certainly founded in the early years. Alexander punished Samaria for rebellion on his way back from Egypt, and left a group of Macedonians there as a garrison.[49] The place was damaged or destroyed twice more in the next forty years, by Ptolemy in 312, and by Demetrios in 296. How much remained after this is not clear, but it probably continued to exist for some time. Across the Jordan, the city of Gerasa claimed to have been founded by either Alexander or Perdikkas. The first is most unlikely – he was never in the area – and the second is so curious it may well be true; it would seem therefore to have been one of the early garrisons.[50]

Many of these places retained or later revived their original Semitic names, which rather suggests that they were continuously inhabited, with Greeks and/or Macedonians added; there is a strong suspicion at times that the Greek name is an adaptation of an earlier Syrian name. This, of course, is something which could be said of most of these places, and in all parts of Syria, but it seems more prevalent in the south than in the north.

The threat, albeit for some time unlikely, of a Seleukid invasion of the south compelled Ptolemy to fortify his territory. The Phoenician cities were all walled and garrisoned, as were several places in the Bekaa Valley, which is the upper waters of the Orontes. Thus those places faced those strung along the middle Orontes in Seleukos' lands. There was not a great deal of scope for new settlements in Phoenicia, but two places in the Bekaa, Gerrha and Brochoi were later developed as a fortified line of defence; the site of the local god, the Baal of the Bekaa – Baalbek – received the Greek name of Heliopolis.

In Palestine Ptolemy I, or more likely Ptolemy II, refounded Acco as Ptolemais-Ake, and this became the administrative centre of the region.[51] It had, of course, been originally a Sidonian town, but had also frequently been the site of the Persian military headquarters when invasions of Egypt were in prospect: this was a neat reversal of the city's role. Gaza, wrecked by Alexander, and again by Ptolemy I, inevitably was rebuilt, fortified and garrisoned as the penultimate defence point for Egypt; it was paralleled on the Egyptian end of the Sinai route (the old Way of Horus) by Pelusion. Antigonos had used it as his base for the failed invasion of 306.[52] Within Palestine itself Ptolemy does not seem to have founded many places, but the most notable was perhaps Philoteria at the southern end of the Sea of Galilee, named for his daughter.[53] This may actually be an indication that it was founded in the reign of Ptolemy II, who also refounded Rabbath-Ammon as Philadelphia, and so it became a Greek-type city, but based on a pre-existing Syrian population.[54]

As in north Syria, it was the long period of peace after 300 BC which did as much as any government initiative to foster the recovery and development of the country. There were, as mentioned, several Syrian Wars in the third century BC, but they tended to be less destructive than in earlier wars, partly because they did not involve the rebellion of a Syrian community, which always seems to call out the worst in a conqueror; being contests between dynastic armies, the civilian population tended to submit quickly on the approach of an enemy army, suggesting a less than total feeling of allegiance to the kings. Nor, of course, was it in the interests of any king to gain control of a land which was ruined. In 219–217, and again in 202–198, however, Antiochos III conquered Phoenicia and Palestine; on the first occasion he was eventually defeated in the Raphia battle on the Sinai coast, but he completed the conquest successfully at the second attempt.

It is of considerable interest to consider why it was that rebellions against the rule of Assyria, Babylonia, the Persians, and Alexander, had regularly punctuated the history of Syria, whereas rebellions against the Seleukid and Ptolemaic kings were non-existent between 301 and 167 (when the first Jewish rebellion began). The rebellious communities under preceding regimes had generally been the Phoenician cities – the rest had been largely destroyed – and one good reason for their quiescence under Hellenistic kings was that they were not being instigated to rebel by the Egyptian ruler – and yet neither were they being instigated to rebel by the Seleukid kings. Two other reasons suggest themselves: that the rule by the Macedonian dynasties was much milder and less oppresive than that by the Babylonians and Persians; and that the general rise in prosperity, combined with the less destructive warfare of the Syrian Wars, conduced to a general satisfaction, and an assumption that even better times were coming. On the other hand, the history of Arados shows repeated attempts by the city at least to enlarge its area of autonomy, and in the end all the Phoenician cities seized the opportunity of the final decline of the Seleukid kingdom to seize their independence.

The refoundation of Rabbath-Ammon as Philadelphia, and the presence of Macedonian settlers at several places, is an indication that the land east of the Jordan was responding to the general rise in prosperity. This region always depended on receiving the stimulus from the rest of Palestine. A line of cities, in general fairly small in size, developed along the great ancient route, the King's Highway, which followed the top of the plateaux, while to the south the place raided unsuccessfully by Antigonos in 312, Petra, grew into a major mercantile centre specializing in incenses imported from south Arabia. This was the area of the former Edomite kingdom, but the rulers were now an Arab people called Nabataeans. They exported their goods through Gaza, and may be considered to be the inheritors of the similar system which had operated during the Persian regime, and indeed may well be descendants of the same people. In their desert land they also developed considerable expertise in water management, in order to cultivate their dry home.

The Nabataeans were the first sign of another political development which was brought about by the increase in prosperity resulting from the peace and the Hellenistic kings' deliberate policy of development, particularly by the Seleukids. For the prosperity was not restricted to the Greco-Macedonian population, but spread among the native Syrians. The increased wealth of the Phoenician cities is another indication of this, while the Jews in the upland Judaea also grew in numbers and prosperity.

In 195 the Seleukid king, Antiochos III, concluded a peace treaty with Ptolemy V which ended the Fifth Syrian War (202–195), in which the Ptolemaic section of Syria was transferred at last to Seleukid rule. Despite several attempts over the next century the Ptolemies never succeeded in recovering their lost lands, and, sure enough, they found that their kingdom of Egypt became vulnerable to invasion as a result.

The reduction of Ptolemaic Egypt to the second class in the international power stakes was decisive, though the Seleukids soon bumped into Rome and were accordingly also reduced in power and status. By this time (188 onwards) the will and wealth required to continue the development work in Syria was fading, though occasional new foundations were still made. Instead the main royal activity with regard to the cities was to honour the existing cities with royal names, and to allow some of them to mint their own coins. So Gerasa became Antioch, and the small town of Abila became a Seleukeia, and so on, until almost every city had a royal name. One result was a necessary reversion to their original names as a means of distinguishing them from one another.

This was all very well, but of little importance. In fact by this time all that was required of the kings in internal matters was to keep the peace, tax lightly, and not to interfere in the impetus given to the growth of the cities and the expansion of the economy which had been provided; the land was able to develop in wealth without further help. And, of course, that was exactly the moment when things began to go wrong.

Chapter 12

Disintegration and a New Conquest

Antiochos III's defeat of Ptolemy V in the Fifth Syrian War allowed him to annex Koile Syria at the peace they concluded in 195. One of the elements which brought him victory, was that the Ptolemaic Governor General of Koile Syria, Ptolemaios son of Thraseas, had defected to Antiochos; he was then confirmed in office as Antiochos' own Governor General for the same territory.[1] As a result the administrative system in the area remained virtually the same under both kings.

Syria was thereby reunited once again to a single polity, though still under alien rule, and this remained so for only a single generation. Macedonian rule was by no means as brutal and oppressive as its imperial predecessors. By leaving the cities with a large area of autonomy, each supervised by an official called an *epistates*, who acted as liaison between city and king, the weight of government was lessened. The taxation system appears to have been relatively fair and not too onerous. The release into circulation by the first Macedonians of a large quantity of the hoarded treasure of the Akhaimenid kings had stimulated the whole Mediterranean economy, and the implantation of new cities, particularly in north Syria, further assisted the growth of local wealth, for Seleukos had necessarily poured out money to finance their foundation.

However, the society which Syria had become consisted of a Greco-Macedonian class of citizens and rulers who were the controlling groups in the cities, the army, and the royal administration. The lower levels of society were the Syrians, descendents of those who had endured imperial oppression in the previous four or five centuries, and who distinguished themselves from the Greeks by adhering to their Syrian languages, and similarly adhering to their local gods. To what extent these societal layers integrated is very difficult to discern, largely because the issue does not seem to have been considered worth investigating at the time.

There was also a distinct geographical division between these language groups. It becomes clear in considering the century and a half after Antiochos III's conquest that the Greco-Macedonians were concentrated in the cities, and those cities had been planted in the lower lands. The highland areas, of which Syria has many, had been left alone both by the Ptolemaic and the Seleukid governments. This applied also in the marginal areas where the steppeland to the east faded away into the desert. These regions were also the most difficult parts in which a Macedonian-type army could operate, and were more suitable for light cavalry.

A series of problems for the Seleukid state began in 175. In that year King Seleukos IV was murdered by his chief minister, a man called Heliodoros. Heliodoros had clearly hoped to rule the kingdom in the name of Seleukos' son, still a child, but he was overthrown by Seleukos' brother, who made himself king as Antiochos IV. Antiochos was not the true heir, and if primogeniture operated, as it had so far in the dynasty, Seleukos' successor should have been his elder son Demetrios, who was being held in Rome as a hostage. Demetrios did not abandon his claim to the kingship, and, as usual, a succession dispute within the royal family proved to be a disaster for the kingdom as a whole.

Five years later, Antiochos had the child-king murdered. He was also soon afterwards attacked by the government of Ptolemaic Egypt, whose members, a regency for another child-king, appear to have believed that he was vulnerable. In this they were wrong. Twice in the next few years Antiochos invaded and occupied large areas of Egypt, eventually withdrawing in 167, partly at the behest of the Romans, but largely because he had achieved his main aim, which was to bring the Egyptian government to a condition of subservience.[2] Next year he celebrated his triumph with a great military parade in Antioch, which emphasized the military power and wealth of the kingdom.[3]

However, during the course of his Egyptian war, Antiochos had mistaken a local dispute in Jerusalem for a rebellion in favour of his enemy. He had reacted with some violence, and this stimulated further opposition, which this time really was directed against the Seleukid government. The basis of the problem in Jerusalem lay in the conflict between the worshippers of Yahweh, the local god, and the attractions of life in a Greek city, which required abandoning Yahweh for Zeus and other Greek gods. The Jewish community in Jerusalem had become divided in a way which was very similar to that of the kingdom as a whole, but in this case the disputants were both Jews, an upper class which had adopted many Greek ways, including exercising in the nude, games – technically religious actions, hence the religious problem – and the use of the Greek language, as opposed to the traditional religious basis of the society centred on the temple in Jerusalem, the worship of Yahweh, and the use of the local language, Aramaic.[4]

Antiochos' solution was to convert Jerusalem into a normal Greek city, with the upper class placed in control of both civic and religious affairs, in the same way as the descendents of the Macedonian immigrants ruled the other cities of his kingdom. Antiochos in fact had a record of encouraging the cities, by allowing them to establish mints, among other matters. Several were upgraded in status during his reign. Hamath, for example, was renamed Epiphaneia, after the king's assumed title; it must be presumed that the place had developed in size and population sufficiently to justify such a promotion.[5] It was originally a native Syrian settlement, so acting in the same way at Jerusalem would have seemed reasonable, and he no doubt assumed that by doing so the troubles in Judaea would subside.

The conversion of Jerusalem, however, included rededicating the temple in Jerusalem to the worship of Zeus Olympios, and the sending of commissars through the countryside to persuade the inhabitants to sacrifice to Zeus in the normal Greek way – or to insist. For most of the population this seems to have constituted no difficulty, but there were objections, of course, though the only one we know of in any detail was by a man called Mattathias, from Modiin in the north-west of the Judaean Highlands. He murdered the official sent to conduct the sacrifice for Zeus on an open air altar, but then found that nobody in the town, except his six sons, would support him. From occasional references in the Jewish account of these events, it is clear that there were other objections in other parts of Judaea, but it is also clear that the population of Jerusalem generally and much of the rural population took the government's side. So the conflict was between Hellenizing Jews and traditional Jews, and to a degree also between the city and the countryside.[6]

The king's government inevitably took the side of the Hellenizers and the city. Unable to prevent this, Mattathias and his sons staged a rebellion. Other groups turned to violence in other parts of Judaea as well. It would probably have been best if the king had left the situation alone, but he wanted to set off on a great expedition to the east, for he allowed the local governors to use their forces in an attempt to suppress the troubles. The governor of the Samaria region, then the governor of Koile Syria both sent forces into the hills, and both were defeated. In the process the sons of Mattathias, led by Judas, called Maccabee, gained control of other rebel groups, and then seized control of Jerusalem and 'cleansed' the temple. Eventually a competent Seleukid commander, with a competent army, arrived and defeated the insurgents, and took back the city.[7]

King Antiochos IV died in 164 during his expedition to the east. His regent left in command in Syria, Lysias, succeeded in gaining full control of Judaea and the insurrection declined to a minor problem.[8] It was not, however, eliminated. Lysias himself was overthrown when Demetrios returned from Rome and executed both Lysias and the child-king for whom Lysias was working.[9] Of the Maccabee brothers two survived, Jonathan and Simon, apparently living quietly in a village in Judaea. In fact Jonathan was carefully organizing the Judaean countryside by purging his enemies by terrorist tactics – thereby using the same methods on behalf of Yahweh, but with much more violence, than Antiochos had used on behalf of Zeus. In 152 the problem of the royal succession revived, when a pretender, Alexander Balas, was promoted by Ptolemy VI, and established himself at Ptolemais-Ake.

This was Jonathan's opportunity. He succeeded in gaining concessions from the royal contenders to extend his authority so that he became an autonomous ruler within Judaea.[10] The succession problem also had ramifications elsewhere in Syria. For the first time in nearly half a century there was extensive warfare in Syria, and a serious attempt was made by Ptolemy VI to re-establish his control over Koile Syria, as his price for assisting Alexander. In the end this attempt failed, but it is clear that the loyalty of many of the cities to the royal house had been severely shaken.[11] There is some indication that the four great cities of the Seleukis made a league amongst themselves, which can only have been in defiance of royal authority.[12]

One of the casualties of the warfare was Jonathan Maccabee, whose youngest brother Simon succeeded both to his position inside Judaea and in defending that position against attack. The contending kings were also killed, either in battle or by murder, and the eventual successor was the teenage Demetrios II. He recruited a mercenary force from the Jews, whose major exploit was to burn Antioch when they were not paid.[13] For a time the whole of Syria was divided between two contending kings, and when Demetrios finally went off to the east to attend to another crisis there, his brother, Antiochos VII, arrived and swiftly and efficiently cleared up the situation in Syria. But then he himself also went off to the east and after a brief period of success, was killed. Demetrios II, who had been imprisoned by the Parthians, then returned but was undermined by yet another pretender promoted out of Egypt when he prepared to invade Egypt.

This was a period of almost continuous warfare in Syria, lasting two decades. During that time, much of the eastern territories of the kingdom were lost, and within Syria Simon Maccabee established Judaea's complete independence of all outside authority in 129 BC. His title was high priest, which emphasized the religious basis of his authority, but he was also the political heir to his brothers and his father, and when he was murdered, his successor was his son John Hyrkanos.[14] A new dynasty of rulers had become established.

In other parts of Syria it was the Phoenician cities which took the lead in moving into independence once it was clear that the kings rarely had the power to enforce their full authority. It was Arados which took the lead. The city had attempted several times over the previous century and a half to expand its autonomy towards full independence. In 139 it gained more powers from the king, and in 129 it demonstrated its full independence by establishing its full control over the adjacent mainland, its *peraia*, where it destroyed its mainland rival Marathos and parcelled out its lands among the Aradians.[15]

This aggressiveness was unusual, for no other Phoenician city indulged in it. On the other hand, the new Judaean state proved to be extremely aggressive, once its homeland was secure. Simon Maccabee was firmly in control by 142, when Jonathan was killed, and by 129 his son was able to take advantage of the great defeat in the east and the death of Antiochos VII to secure full independence. John Hyrkanos was, however, cautious, and attacked in all directions, except towards the Seleukid lands, and then waited for two more decades before deliberately extending his boundaries into those lands. During the fighting between the rival kings in the 140s, however, the Jews had sacked more than one city, notably Ashdod, and had shown a determination to secure a port, preferably Joppa, as a means of gaining access to the seaborne trade of the Mediterranean.[16]

This aggressiveness had also been turned eastwards. Judas in the 160s had contacted or clashed with various Arab groups, and the menace was such that by the 140s the Nabataeans had consolidated themselves into a kingdom.[17] The ideology of the Judaean state demanded that all worship by Jews be concentrated in the temple in Jerusalem. Accordingly the private temple which had been built by a wealthy Jewish family, the Tobiads, at Iraq el-Amir in Ammon became a target to be destroyed by Judas.[18] The development of monotheism among the Jews rendered the old Samaritan community not merely dissidents but heretics and rivals. John Hyrkanos organized an expedition to destroy their temple on Mount Gerizim, and in 109 launched an attack on the city of Samaria.[19]

This was a new development. Samaria was a Greek city, the site of an old Macedonian colony established by Alexander; it is unlikely that many of the original colonists and their families had survived the unpleasant early years of the colony, but it was a well established Greek city. The Judaean attack took the form of a siege, which lasted a year. When the city was taken, it was deliberately destroyed, and any survivors were driven out. The city was destroyed, that is, partly because it had given shelter to Samaritan refugees, and partly because it was a Greek city.[20]

Three times the Ptolemaic kingdom sent expeditions into the Seleukid kingdom between 152 and 100 BC, twice with the aim of recovering control over its old province of Koile Syria. For a time in the 140s Ptolemy VI did succeed but he was one of the casualties of the final battle, and his troops then swiftly evacuated the land. At the end of the century Kleopatra III campaigned in the Palestine area and gained control of considerable areas, in the process comprehensively defeating the Judaean kingdom, but she soon died and once again the Ptolemaic conquests evaporated.[21] Two of these interventions were directed to disrupting the Seleukid kingdom when it looked to be becoming too powerful for Ptolemaic comfort.

The poison inserted into the Seleukid succession system by Antiochos IV in 175 worked its way through until there were succession crises from 164 onwards. It was these crises which gave the Ptolemies their opportunities to intervene with the aim of weakening the Seleukid state, and perhaps recovering Koile Syria. Of course, the Seleukids themselves contributed greatly to this state of affairs. Three times between 164 and 129 great armies were lost in attempts to recover the lost eastern provinces. On the third occasion Antiochos VII took an army reputed to be 80,000 strong to the east and very little of it returned. This was an army recruited almost entirely from Syria, and gives some notion of the importance of Syria by this time.[22]

It was these losses above all which prevented any Seleukid recovery. John Hyrkanos immediately took his small Judaean state into independence, Arados did the same, Tyre was independent within three years, and in north Syria at least two sections of the country became autonomous, and possibly even independent.[23] This was a slow process, for Syria remained locally powerful, and the kings were obviously unwilling to allow real independence for any local area. But an Arab kingdom centred on Edessa, east of the Euphrates, eventually dated the dynasty's independence from 132 BC,[24] and to the north the territory of Kommagene (which had been the kingdom of Kummuh in the Iron Age) became ruled by a single family from 163 onwards, and was not probably effectively independent by 130.[25]

Succession disputes among the Seleukid royal family continued from 129–121 BC (four murders), and resumed from 113 BC (civil war for two decades). After that year there was never one single Seleukid king; always there were two or more kings disputing the loyalties of their subjects, and in effect each king came to rule a separate section, so that some regions became effectively independent under Seleukid kings. In fact, of course, it was this division which allowed John Hyrkanos to attack Samaria in 109–198; twice Seleukid armies arrived to attempt to break the siege, but neither was strong enough to do so. It was in fact the nadir of Seleukid power.

Gradually Syria broke up into a series of independent kingdoms and independent cities, some under Seleukid kings, some under Greek rulers, some under Syrians. There were still kings in north Syria until 83 BC, and they seem to have been able to hold on to the loyalty of many of the cities. By contrast the regions inhabited by 'native' Syrians – those speaking Aramaic, that is – were the areas which became independent. Judaea had been the first, of course, and the Phoenician cities were now tending to re-emphasize their Phoenician identity, at least on their coins, and presumably in their language. The hills and the desert regions formed themselves into kingdoms, as the Nabataeans had done.

Many of these new states were formed around a local shrine, in this, of course, mirroring the Jewish experience in Judaea. In the Bekaa Valley, it was the local Baal, whose shrine was at Baalbek/Heliopolis whose high priest became the local prince of the people of the area, the Ituraeans; it seems likely that they could count themselves independent by about 100 BC, though the dynasty dated its power from 115 BC. A second Ituraean group was centred on Tell Arqa in the northern Lebanese Mountains.[26] Inland of Arados an Arab dynasty emerged in the 90s centred at Emesa on the Orontes.[27] Again close to Arados a people called the Nazerini in the Bargylos Mountains formed an independent principality. Even the Ghab marshes north of Apameia seem to have been the home of an independent group.[28]

Impatience with the incompetence of the later Seleukid kings prompted several of the cities eventually to break away into independence. Seleukeia-in-Pieria several times had been separated from the interior under kings who held the place for a time, and in 109 received a royal charter of special autonomy.[29] Beroia and Bambyke/Hierapolis became part of an independent principality originally under control of a general called Herakleon, who was disgusted at the lackadaisical attitude of the king, staged a coup which failed, and then seized Beroia to make himself the first of a local dynasty.[30] Damascus became an independent kingdom under one of the last Seleukids, who gave it his own name as Demetrias – this did not last long.[31] East of the Jordan Philadelphia and other cities were effectively abandoned by the Seleukids; a principality including Philadelphia and Gerasa emerged under a Greek dynasty.

Some of the new states were aggressive, in particular the Judaean state, whose rulers called themselves kings from 103, and who attacked, not always successfully, in all directions. For some time any Greek city which was captured suffered destruction and its people were massacred or enslaved. Since this proved to be counterproductive by stimulating even greater resistance, the policy changed. Under King Alexander Jannaeus (103–74) massacre and destruction were eventually replaced by suzerainty. As a result the Judaean kingdom spread throughout Palestine, but it had become an almost normal Hellenistic kingdom. It was also notably unstable, suffering coups and civil wars – just like other kingdoms.[32]

The Nabataean kingdom proved to be similarly aggressive, but directed much of its enmity at Judaea. On the Orontes the Emesan kings gained control of at least one Greek city, Arethusa. In the north of the Lebanese Mountains a Greek called Dionysios created a minor state by taking over several of the smaller Phoenician cities, including Byblos and Tripolis and eventually Berytos – a curious repetition of the activities of Abdi-Ashirta in the same region in the Bronze Age. In the north, the kings of Kommagene spread south and gained control over the Euphrates crossing at Zeugma. Some Greek cities thus fell under Syrian rule, and others succumbed to tyrants as a means of preservation. On the Palestinian coast Dor and Strato's Tower were briefly ruled by a 'tyrant' called Zoilos.

That is, in more general terms it is clear that there was a general sorting out of power going on. For the time being the most vigorous states were those ruling kingdoms based in the hills, but it did not follow that this would always be so, for it was in the cities where the majority of the population lived, and where most of the wealth was concentrated and generated. But the cities had to be organized, and the failure of the Seleukid kings to provide that leadership by continuing their dynastic disputes, left the cities in unasked-for independence, and often subject to 'tyrants'.

Meanwhile an array of greater powers lay just beyond Syria's borders. Ptolemaic Egypt had fallen into the same sort of dynastic squabbling which afflicted Syria, but the country was rich enough that if it came under the rule of a capable king, it would again provide a major threat to southern Syria. For the moment, however, the greatest threat came from the north, where three expanding powers were approaching. From the north-west the Roman Republic had been slowly advancing further into Asia Minor since 133, and by 95 BC one of its magistrates had met a representative of the other major approaching power, the Parthian kingdom, on the banks of the Euphrates north of the Taurus Mountains. The Parthians were in fact able to penetrate some way into Syria not long after this meeting, but its internal instability ensured that an early lunge across the Euphrates was no more than a temporary appearance.[33] As it happens instability also afflicted in the Roman state, and thereby delayed its appearance in Syria as well. So it was the third of the northern powers, Armenia, which was the first to make a serious attempt to exploit the confusion in Syria for its own benefit.

King Tigranes V of Armenia began moving south into Syria in 84/83 BC following the death of the Seleukid king, Philip I, who had ruled in the north for a time. There were two contradictory traditions about his campaign, one which emphasized the violence, the other which reported that he established his rule more or less peacefully and by negotiation. This progress began when the Antioch city council met and chose to submit to Tigranes. Other cities followed, but one or two certainly resisted; he never did get control of Seleukeia-in-Pieria, nor of Herakleon's principality at Beroia. The various kings succumbed rapidly, apparently on the assurance that they would retain their thrones; Tigranes was clearly aiming at suzerainty rather than direct possession. In Palestine he came up against two ruling queens. Queen Salome of Judaea moved with almost indecent haste to surrender, offering riches; in Ptolemais-Ake, Queen Kleopatra Selene, a Ptolemaic princess who had been married to several Seleukid kings, defended the city with greater determination.[34]

It had proved to be all too easy. Tigranes had advanced through Syria meeting virtually no opposition, all the way to Palestine. Many of the cities and kingdoms had become part of his empire. On the other hand, he did very little towards integrating his conquests into a single state. All the kings seem to have stayed in place, all the cities retained their autonomy. And as he was besieging Ptolemais, the Romans arrived.

The Roman Republic had only occasionally paid any attention to Syria. The Senate had sent occasional commissions of inquiry, which had toured the various kingdoms and reported back, usually taking two or three years over the journey and enjoying themselves as they went. An officious envoy in 163, C. Octavius, had claimed to enforce the defunct treaty of Apameia, and had compelled the regent Lysias to begin killing the elephants he was said to have been maintaining illegally. The animals' agony was such that there was general Syrian approval when Octavius was assassinated.[35] The Judaean rebels contacted Rome and were given some encouragement, though no practical help.[36] Rome was simply not interested in Syria once it was clear that the Seleukid kingdom was no longer capable of mounting a serious power challenge to it.

Tigranes had stumbled into a war in Asia Minor with Rome while his forces were advancing through Syria. Defeated in his homeland he had no choice but to withdraw his forces, leaving Syria to its own devices. To the Romans this put Syria for the first time within their reach and the man who arrived to sort out the whole Middle East on Rome's behalf, Cn. Pompeius Magnus, was quite unconstrained by the wishes of the Syrian people.

And yet, Pompey was no more thorough in his takeover of Syria than Tigranes had been. He arrived, so it is said, assuming that it was a land threatened by 'Arabs and Jews'.[37] In other words he felt he was rescuing the Greek cities from the threat of conquest or destruction by the native Syrians. This, however, did not include supporting the Seleukid royal family. He found that there were two contending kings, and he dismissed both of them from consideration. Cities were freed of tyrants, more than one being executed.[38] Kingdoms were cut down in size by being forced to surrender any Greco–Macedonian city they had taken over, though Samsigeramos of Emesa kept Arethusa;[39] but the Jewish kingdom was reduced to its Judaean heartland; the Ituraean kingdom in the Bekaa Valley survived only by making a massive tribute payment.[40] The cities were declared free, which meant that they were now part of the Roman Empire.

Pompey's rearrangement of Syrian affairs had rolled back the advances of many of the Syrian kings which had taken place in the previous century. But he did not always convince all of them that they really were part of the Roman state. In the cities the acceptance of their new situation was much easier, for it was, after all, very similar to that which they had enjoyed, or endured, under the Seleukid or Ptolemaic regimes. They paid their taxes to a distant city rather than to a close-by king, but otherwise they continued managing their own internal affairs in the old way. In the kingdoms, this resigned attitude was less likely, for the kings, by definition, had aimed for independence and power. At the same time, the kings had a much more acute appreciation of the realities of power than some of the city councils, and rebellion against Rome was never a sensible proposition for Samsigeramos of Emesa or Ptolemy of the Ituraeans.

The result of Pompey's expedition, therefore, was a radical reorganization of power in Syria. The cities could be confident that they were now under the protection of the greatest power in the Mediterranean world, and no longer feared to be attacked and destroyed by a neighbouring Syrian king. Many of the cities which had in fact already been conquered by their Syrian neighbours were now freed, and no doubt the experience will have persuaded them to favour Rome. The kings on the other hand were in a much more precarious situation. The cities might maintain a militia, but the kings had professional armies several thousand strong. They were inevitably seen by the Romans as a potential threat, and it would not take much to convince them that any particular kingdom merited extinction.

Nevertheless the kingdoms largely survived, though all Syria had to go through the civil wars which racked the Roman Republic from soon after Syria became part of it. The Judaean kingdom, having been the largest and most important of the kingdoms, and the one most cut down by Pompey, was the most troublesome. Pompey had to use force to insist on his dispensation, which included a three-month siege of Jerusalem, and damage to the temple there.[41] In north Syria the Roman civil wars involved a siege and serious damage to Apameia, a siege of Laodikeia,[42] and a long and unsuccessful siege of Samosata,[43] the main city of the Kommagene kingdom, and all Syria was impoverished by the requisitions of the various armies and the tax-collecting *publicani*. Large numbers of men were also conscripted, particularly for the armies of Brutus and Cassius which were defeated at Philippi. And Syria was invaded by Parthian armies several times between 51 and 42, on the latter occasion in alliance with the Judaean kingdom.

Judaea had the additional experience of a civil war between the survivors of the Maccabean royal house and the upstart Herod. Both sides ravaged their opponents' territories, helped by intrusive Parthian and Roman forces, and Jerusalem was besieged and again captured by Roman forces after the civil war in Judaea had reached a stalemate.[44] The opposition to Herod had been strong enough to compel him to clamp on a bitter control over Judaea, and he spent the rest of his long life looking suspiciously at and for conspiracies.[45]

The presence of Marc Antony as Roman controller of eastern affairs meant that Egypt's Kleopatra VII was able to revive aspects of her ancestors' empire in Koile Syria. She and Herod were enemies, to the point of military conflict at one stage, but he survived both of them by ostentatious obsequiousness to Octavian, the final victor. In the end the elimination of Antony and Kleopatra brought Herod to heel and Egypt into direct Roman rule. But for thirty years Syria had been racked by warfare of a nastiness not seen since Alexander.

The net result was the subtraction and destruction of much Syrian wealth, and of many men, and the installation of the most notable of the Roman client kings of the east, Herod, as king of a much enlarged Judaea. Other kings had been compelled to choose sides and had, almost inevitably, given the complications of the situation, suffered for it. The kingdom of Emesa was abolished for a decade, and two of its kings were executed, one by Antony, the other by Octavian/Augustus, an odd way of balancing the risks.[46] Herod was more adept at political somersaults, and put forward a convincing case that he was the only man who could control Judaea.

By the time the Roman civil wars were over, in 30 BC, and any threat from Egypt was ended by its annexation, Syria was still a complex mixture of cities in the Roman province, and kingdoms. The encyclopaedist Pliny the Elder located a list of places in Syria which seems to have been compiled during the reign of the first emperor, Augustus. It listed the cities, which are relatively well known, but also, probably separately, it listed the kingdoms of various sizes. The obvious ones are these: Kommagene, Edessa, Emesa, Ituraea, Judaea, but there were also a series of names which hardly impinge on the general history of the time. Some of these can be located. The Gabeni in the Ghab marshland, as already mentioned;

the Nazerini were in the Bargylos Mountains. The Gindareni were presumably centred on the town of Gindaros, between Antioch and Kyrrhos. Also in the north were the Gazetae, the Tardytenses (around Tarutia), and the Rhambaki, in the desert area south-east of Chalkis.

Others are now no more than names, and cannot be located even by the halfway guesswork employed for these last. Further Pliny gives up his listing with the despairing comment that the list continues with seventeen more names which he cannot transcribe because they were so barbarous – that is, they were Aramaic names.[47] It also follows that these were small principalities, ruled by men with such titles as tetrarch and ethnarch by the Romans, whatever titles they gave themselves. If they had been large they would have been important enough for Pliny to know of them apart from his bureaucratic list. Further it is probable that by the time he was compiling his *Natural History* many of these small states had already vanished.

This was usually the doing of the Roman governor of the province of Syria. This was one of the most important posts in the Roman government.[48] The governor had the responsibility of governing the directly ruled province, which was composed entirely, at least at first, of the cities, and so he was in the position of the defunct Seleukid kings. He also had to supervise the numerous kingdoms, which were technically part of his province – that is, his area of responsibility – but these had to be handled with some diplomatic care. He had in his province one of the larger factions of the Roman army, four legions, together with an equivalent force of auxiliary regiments. This large army was required in part because of the many kingdoms he watched, and watched over, which had their own armies, but also because he faced the Parthian kingdom, which had extended its authority as far as the Euphrates, having brought the kingdom of Edessa under its distant control.

The establishment of Roman control over Syria had abruptly stopped the process of disintegration and conquest which had been going on in Syria since the beginning of the Jewish rebellion in 166 BC, and had reversed many of the most recent changes. The unity the country had achieved under the Seleukid kings had vanished, of course. It was a patchwork of minor states. An independent principality had even come into existence at Gindaros, on the main route between Antioch and the river crossing at Zeugma, a stark comment on the failure of the last kings to maintain any sort of control outside the main cities.

However, it has to be said that there had never, so far as can be seen, been any feeling of 'unity' among Syrians, quite apart from the social division within Greeks and Syrians. There was certainly a community of culture among 'native' Syrians, and a knowledge that they worshipped the same gods, but no indication exists that it was felt that they should stand and work together as a community. The geography is perhaps to blame, since it obviously promoted division in a way that the Egyptian Nile Valley and the valley of the Tigris-Euphrates tended to promote unity. The beginnings of the disintegration of the Aramaic language had also promoted division: Phoenician, Nabataean, Hebrew, and other dialects were approaching the status of different languages.

Nevertheless, there was a good deal of fellow feeling amongst the kingdoms, based on their shared languages, and their shared subjection to Roman, and before that to Greek, rule. The royal families of the various kingdoms intermarried, though the Jewish Herodians had problems in marrying to non-Jews; they did manage to develop their own rules, of course. The result was that by the mid-first century there was an interlinked network of royalty covering every existing kingdom between Thrace and Judaea.[49] The one kingdom which seems largely to have refrained from becoming involved was the Nabataean. This was a political development which may well have increasingly concerned the Roman authorities, and eventually in AD 44 the Roman governor C. Vibius Marsus had to interrupt a meeting between several of the kings, and send them off home.[50]

For the Greeks of the cities, who remained in control of the local governments, the Roman control had been clamped on Syria just in time. The advance of Syrians towards full control was stopped and reversed, and from the time of Pliny's list the number of Syrian-ruled states gradually diminished. This was not a steady process but, so far as we can see, took place irregularly. Each time a king or tetrarch died, the question arose as to whether his state should be inherited by the dead king's heirs or annexed by Rome. The best known case is, of course, Judaea. This was broken up when Herod died, and separate sections were handed out to several of his children, a process which included rebellions in Palestine, a Roman governor's armed intervention, and a decision by Augustus to accept most of the provisions of Herod's will.[51] Some of these proved to be satisfactory rulers, from Rome's viewpoint, and some were not. The main kingdom, Judaea itself, lasted as a kingdom for only ten years under Herod's son Archelaus, and then was taken over to be ruled as part of the province directly under the governor.[52] Other parts remained as kingdoms for much longer under two other sons, Philip and Antipas, largely it seems because they were in desert or hill country, and as such did not have the urban development which Romans felt was necessary, and a local king that could suppress banditry more easily than the Roman forces from far off.

Other kingdoms were similarly treated as items to be changed, dismantled, or disposed of as perceived Roman necessities dictated. The Emesan kingdom and the royal family were reinstated after ten years' suspension, in 20 BC. This took place when Augustus came to the east to sort out various problems. The major issue was the hostility of Parthia, and there he succeeded in arranging a peace, which was portrayed at Rome as a triumph.

It may well have been at this point that the king of Kommagene was deprived of two Greek cities he had gained control over in the confusion of the previous decades. One was Doliche, whose shrine to Zeus began to develop in importance from this point on. The other city was Seleukeia–Zeugma, the main Euphrates crossing, which was clearly too sensitive a position to be left under the control of even the most obedient client king – and the kings of Kommagene were hardly the most enthusiastic clients of Rome. The king had taken the side of the Parthians when they invaded Syria, and had successfully resisted the siege of their capital Samosata by Marc Antony in 38 BC. It was clearly more comfortable for the Romans themselves to control the bridge.

There were four legions stationed in Syria, all of them in the north. Once Zeugma became Roman, one of the legions was shifted there, from its original post at Kyrrhos. Antioch was another legionary station, no doubt partly as a guard for the governor and partly to ensure control of the great city; Apameia, the former military base of the Seleukids, was a third station. The fourth legion was, however, on a new site, at a place called Raphanaia. This was a telling position, squarely in the Homs Gap, controlling access from the interior and from the sea. That route had been largely dominated to that point by Syrian kingdoms, while the sea was also, of course, dominated by Phoenician cities.[53]

Central Syria had, in fact, fallen almost entirely under the control of 'native' Syrian polities before the Romans arrived. The Phoenician cities controlled the coast, from Arados to Tyre, the Bargylos Mountains were the domain of the Nazerini, and the Lebanese Mountains of the Ituraean states based at Chalkis and at Arqa; inland was the kingdom of Emesa, and further east, in the desert, was the oasis of Palmyra.

Palmyra had first emerged into political prominence in 41, when Marc Antony had attempted a raid on the place, in a rumour of wealth to be stolen.[54] He was largely unsuccessful, just as Antigonos had been many years before in his raid on Petra. The oasis had an abundant spring which allowed the establishment of a local irrigation agriculture, and the community had been developed into a major trading centre, connecting southern Babylonia with Syria. The trade across the desert avoided the potentially difficult northern route across the Jazira, where there were many cities and two empires faced each other, and all collected taxes and customs duties, and where armies marched. The route from Palmyra to the west went through Emesa, and on to the Phoenician cities where the goods were exported to the lands of the Mediterranean; it was a conduit of wealth.

The relationship of Palmyra, a city state ruled by the mercantile elite, with Rome was as edgy as was that of the Syrian monarchies, and it was as liable to change as theirs. By the reign of the second emperor, Tiberius, the city was reckoned to be part of the Roman province, at least by the Romans, though it is probable that the Palmyrans were less convinced. Their mercantile links with the Parthian Empire and its subordinate kingdoms will no doubt have promoted a certain independence of view.[55]

The concentration of the Roman legions in the north of Syria was clearly a precaution against Parthian attack, but it was also a means of maintaining control over the richest and most populous region of the province. As wealth increased also in the areas not directly ruled by the governor, it became steadily more likely that they would be brought into direct rule as well. The establishment of peace had had the usual effect of encouraging production, trade and innovation in the Syrian cities. This had happened, of course, in the early part of the Iron Age, until such activity was snuffed out by the Assyrian conquest – except in the Phoenician cities – and it had revived in the peace brought by the dual rule of Seleukids and Ptolemies from 300 BC onwards.

Now the Roman peace – a reversal in fact of the Seleukid-Ptolemaic peace – was acting to have the same effect. The export market for the products of Syria had expanded with the growth of the Roman Empire, and the result was a major development of the production of olives and wine in Syria, particularly in regions which seem to have been hardly using them earlier. It is in this period that the foundations were laid for the great production of olive oil in the regions north of Apameia, which the French archaeologists called the '*villes mortes*', the limestone region which is now littered with the ruins of a whole series of towns – a region populated almost exclusively, it seems, from the names and graffiti, by Syrians, rather than Greeks, though it is likely that Greco-Macedonians were the ultimate landlords. Wine was a major producer of many coastal regions, inland of Laodikeia, for example, and about Ashkelon.

The Phoenician cities were long famous for their production of dyed cloth, notably that rich red which became known as imperial purple. It was a colour which was both appropriated by the emperors and used to distinguish senators and other Roman magistrates. Sidon was the innovator in the technique of glass-blowing, in the late first century BC, and this technique spread quickly through the whole Roman Empire, in part by Sidonians themselves, who set up manufactories wherever they could locate supplies of the right quality of sand.

Perhaps above all Syria became the interchange for international grain, which brought in spices from south Arabia and from India, silk from China by way of central Asia, metals and slaves from the east and north, and which sent goods produced around the Mediterranean in return – coins, statuary, works of art, cloth, and so on. And to accomplish this, the Syrian population continued to increase and began to expand its control of its environment.

The contrast within Syria was between the prosperity of Phoenicia and the north and the constant disturbances of the south. The troubles of Palestine are in general put down to the developing conflict between the Roman rulers and the Jews who were being ruled. This is true as far as it goes, but the rest of Syria did not have such difficulty in accepting Roman authority. Of course, there was an implicit alliance between the Greek city rulers and the Roman power, and between the Syrian kings and the Roman governors, all on guard against the Syrian native population, of whom the Jews were a part. Yet it was only the Jews who took matters to the extreme of a great rebellion.

The centre of the matter was, of course, religion. Since their exile in Babylonia the Jewish priests and thinkers had been developing exclusivity in the way of worshipping their particular god, Yahweh. For a variety of reasons, partly for internal political reasons, partly to distinguish themselves when weak and small in numbers, Yahweh had become portrayed as exclusively a Jewish god, and other gods were excluded, even hostile, and certainly to be shunned. This had proved to be a difficult exercise to accomplish. It was against the general tradition in Syria to have an exclusive god of a particular people or place, though it was quite usual for one god or goddess to be the talisman of a city or a nation. And where Hadad may have been the main deity of Damascus, he was not the only one worshipped there. Yet the Jews elevated Yahweh to exclude all others. It was partly the result of Antiochos IV's attempt to convert Jerusalem into a 'normal' Greek city, and the defence of Yahweh in the temple which had been staged by the Maccabee rebels; it was also in part a defence of the independent Judaean kingdom against Seleukid and Ptolemaic and Roman assaults; and it was partly an imperialistic impulse which had been thwarted first by the royal family's failure to impose forced conversions, then by Pompey's deconstruction of the kingdom and then by the Roman patronage of the Herodian dynasty, whose Hellenistic orientation permitted more toleration, if only in the lands surrounding Judaea, than the fanatics could accept.

It has to be said that the Romans, within their own limits, and by their own lights, did make several attempts to conciliate Jewish opinion. They were not prepared to allow Judaea complete independence, but up to that limit they tried installing kings, they tried governing directly, they tried appointing governors for Palestine separate from the man in Antioch, and they even appointed a governor (Felix) with connections to the Herodian family. Several governors of Syria acted to thwart inconvenient or dangerous initiatives emanating from Rome. In the end, of course, much of this was seen by the Jews as Roman weakness, and the intransigents seized on a particular dispute to make their bid for independence.[56]

It turned into an expensive disaster, and not only for the Jews. What was interesting when the fighting finally broke out in AD 66 and began with a comprehensive Roman defeat, was that in the rest of Syria support for the Jews was minimal; indeed, had the phrase anti-Semitism been appropriate one would have characterized Syrian reaction as just that; Jews were harassed, murdered and imprisoned in several places, from Palestine to Antioch (and on to Alexandria and Cyrenaica). This was in part a reply to Jewish attacks on the Greek cities around Judaea, so there were mutual massacres. The ferocity of some of the attacks, on both sides, attests to an accumulation of dislike which had hardly existed a century before.[57] In addition many of the Syrian kings sent contingents of their soldiers to assist the Romans in the fighting – 4,000 men from Emesa, for example – as did numbers of the cities.[58] It is plain that the Jewish rebellion was seen by the rest of Syria, kings and cities, Greeks and Syrians, as profoundly disturbing, unpopular and unwelcome.

One of the reasons the Romans were apprehensive of the Jews was that the temple had become very wealthy. The obligation laid on Jews of the Diaspora to contribute regularly to temple funds had piled up a substantial treasure; it was, of course, confiscated for Roman use at the end, such as was left, but no ancient government could ever be comfortable when a disaffected group had access to such resources – for gold was the fuel of war, as every Roman in authority was aware. The Jews of Judaea had really done everything possible to rouse Roman suspicions and enmity; their destruction, given known Roman military capability and methods, was a foregone conclusion. And they had been warned. King Agrippa II had explained to them in a public speech exactly what they were up against – or so the historian Josephos claims – but they hardly needed such a warning.[59] Every Roman provincial knew the power and expertise of the Roman army, and that a single Roman defeat did not mean the end of a war. The fanatics, however, as usual were convinced of their rightness, and impervious to sense. Jerusalem was destroyed in the fighting, in part by the Jews themselves, and became the site of a legionary camp afterwards.

Another result of the war had been to draw Roman attention to the continuing existence of the Syrian kingdoms, and to their potential military power. Suppose the kings had come out in support of the Jews, all Syria would probably have been lost. The Jewish Revolt had coincided with an imperial crisis which had developed from a revolt against the Emperor Nero, and the ultimate winner of the contest which followed was Vespasian, who had been commanding against the Jews. For the first time for a century a ruling emperor had direct experience of affairs in Syria, and reforms followed swiftly.

The Emesan kingdom was suppressed, probably in 73, perhaps even before the fighting in Judaea was over.[60] By this time it is likely that the smaller, anonymous tetrarchies and other principalities had also been largely absorbed into the directly ruled province as their rulers died or their dynasties faded away. The Kommagenian kingdom had been suppressed once already, by Tiberius, and had been restored by Emperor Gaius, probably on a whim, for he quickly changed his mind, only for the king to be reinstated by Claudius in 41.[61] The kingdom was now suppressed permanently, a matter which involved a short military campaign (in which an Emesan contingent took part).[62] A legion was moved forward from Syria to take station at Samosata. The heirs to the kingdom had fled to refuge in Parthia, so a guard was obviously necessary to maintain control of the former kingdom; the two men returned quickly enough – life in the Roman Empire seems to have been more agreeable – and one of their sons became a Roman consul later.

By this time there were only two Syrian kingdoms left: the Ituraean, by then under the rule of one Agrippa II, the grandson of Herod, whose kingdom was steadily enlarged by his friend the Emperor Claudius, and lasted until the 90s, and the Nabataean, which lasted a little longer. The area between the Nabataeans and Damascus, called for short the Hawran, a difficult region of basalt rock and desert, littered with caves and pockets of fertile land, had been passed around between various members of the Herodian family since Herod, and then handed to Agrippa.[63] A king of the Nabataeans died in AD 70, most opportunely, since that was no time for the Romans to indulge in a new campaign, and the kingdom was thus allowed to last another long generation; the king had also supplied 6,000 auxiliaries to Vespasian's forces.[64] The new king, Rabbel II, therefore ruled his semi-independent and wealthy kingdom until he died. Then, finally, in 106, the last Syrian kingdom was taken into the Roman Empire, after a short resistance.[65]

The latest era of independent kingdoms in Syria had lasted for about 270 years, from the Judaean revolt of 166 BC to the annexation of Nabataea in AD 106. For many of the kingdoms, of course, their histories were much shorter than that, and all had succumbed without much resistance to Roman annexation when pushed. The Jewish resistance was in some ways noble and inspiring, but in others it was exceptionally stupid, while the methods used by the Yahweh-fanatics to enforce obedience to their interpretation of their religion was a chilling pre-echo of similar methods used by later monotheistic religions.

The period demonstrated, once again, that Syria was a country which could only be united from outside. The geography encouraged division, a condition happily accepted by the inhabitants, even when faced by total conquest by an outsider. But at least this conquest, like that of the Macedonian kings (except Alexander), had been relatively benign – Judaea excepted – and had opened up a new period of prosperity.

Chapter 13

Province of Rome

The last chapter was devoted to the way in which a united Syria broke up as the Seleukid dynasty failed and then its slow reintegration as a province of the Roman Empire. In addition this had also been a time of vigour and innovation in Syria in many fields; religious, architectural, commercial, manufacturing. It is in fact always during periods of division and conflict that Syrians have been most active in these fields. Some items – blown glass vessels, widespread trade, Syria as a commercial entrepôt – have been noted already. There were other developments, notably religious, but from the Syrian viewpoint probably the most important was the climate-assisted expansion of settlement and agriculture.

Syrian agriculture was, and is, very climate-sensitive. Archaeologists frequently adduce a period of increased heat or of decreased rainfall as the cause of changes they observe in the settlement pattern, though this may really be no more than an easy way out; just as often the cause is human action. During the late Hellenistic and the early Roman periods, however, it is clear that there was a major movement outwards from the well-settled regions of western Syria and into the less favoured area of the steppe, and that this was partly the result of an improvement in the climate, but also in part a result of the imposition of peace; in other words, the improved climate provided the occasion for an expansion of settlement, but it was human agency which took the opportunity.

The movement had begun from a low base. The devastations of the Assyrian and Babylonian rulers had been fairly indiscriminate, but a major effect was to open up the better-watered and more fertile lands, and to discourage attempts to farm the steppe. Arable farming in the steppe was always likely to be a precarious activity, and when the population of the western part of Syria – the Orontes Valley, the Phoenician coastlands, Palestine west of the Jordan – was so substantially reduced by massacres and deportations that people of the steppe drifted west into the lands which were more profitably cultivated. To archaeologists, and to the inhabitants at the time, this may well be seen as the infiltration of nomads, which had happened repeatedly in the past – and indeed probably continuously since farming was invented – but it was also due to a reduction of the resident population brought on by the ending of settled times.

At the same time the perceived insecurity of some areas concentrated the settlements on high ground, the better to provide defences. In north Syria this was unlikely to be required, partly due to a generally less hilly topography, partly because of the well-populated and defended new cities, and partly therefore because the general insecurity was lessened. But in Palestine it was not until the Roman period and in some cases the second century AD that the hilltop settlements ceased to be required and new villages were planted on lower land.[1]

The establishment of peace took place from 300 BC onwards, though this took effect at different times in different places. This applies, for example, early in north Syria, for even if Syria as a whole was divided between hostile Seleukids and Ptolemies it was subject only to relatively minor wars from 300–150 BC. This peaceful period, together with the infusion of Greek immigrants and new money being spent on the new cities, provided the conditions for an increase in agricultural production. Needless to say, at first this was concentrated in the lands surrounding the new cities, but by the mid-second century BC tentative moves were also developing to expand into the steppe. Since this was also the time of renewed public disturbances, with the spread of wars and civil wars amid the disintegration of the Seleukid state, the expansion of agriculture into vulnerable areas did not at first get very far. Some parts, however, did gain encouragement from the new conditions, in particular many of the newly independent states were situated on or close to the very territory which had become the target for development – the Nabataeans and Emesa are obvious examples.

The emergence of cities along the abandoned borderlands during the Hellenistic period is part of the story, notably the cities of Hamath and Emesa. At Hamath archaeologists have found pottery of the mid to late third century, which means that the site was reoccupied during the early Seleukid period, when the nearby garrisons at Arethusa and Larisa could provide some protection. Emesa is not reported in any source before the beginning of the first century BC, but by then it was important enough to be the seat of a Syrian monarchy; meanwhile Hamath was important enough to be made into the city of Epiphaneia by Antiochos IV in the mid-second century. The growth of both of these places requires that the nearby land had also been developed for agriculture in that time. This was also the time when the old frontier between the hostile kingdoms had been cancelled by the victory of Antiochos III, and so the area between Apameia and the fortified lines in the south of the Bekaa were open for settlement.[2] In the area south of Apameia, where Raphanaia became the Roman legionary base, there were a large number of villages in the early Roman period, many of which were founded in the late Hellenistic. Several places east of the Orontes have provided evidence of occupation in the second half of the Hellenistic period.[3]

The same may be said about the land east of the Jordan, though here the process seems to have begun earlier, during the Ptolemaic period. Gerasa claimed to have been founded in the late fourth century, and to the south Rabbath Ammon was refounded as Philadelphia in the early first; these would presuppose expansions of the local agriculture to supply the cities' populations. In the Bekaa Valley, as the land was retaken by the farmers, one result was the rise in importance of the temple at Baalbek, whose high priest emerged as the Ituraean king during the Seleukids' slow collapse; this man was rich enough by the 60s BC to pay 1,000 talents to Pompey to avoid being evicted.

In the northern area, between the Orontes and the Euphrates, several sites were reoccupied, and this collectively pushed the frontier of settlement south into the country of the salt lakes. This was land which was part of the territories of three of the cities, Chalkis, Beroia, and Hierapolis/Bambyke; the unnamed Hellenistic town at Jebel Khalid, newly founded in the early third century, was in this area as well. In the steppe to the east of the middle Orontes several places besides Hama and Emesa have produced evidence of occupation in the Hellenistic period. Most of these were on old abandoned tells, which may have been chosen because they were the more easily defendable, but the occupation may also have been noted because these are the places which are automatically examined by archaeologists first of all.[4]

The recolonization of these lands was obviously begun during the Hellenistic period, but the wars and other disturbances from 150 BC onwards will have retarded the process. In the Roman period, with internal peace re-established from 30 BC onwards, it was possible to reclaim much more of the steppe. The reclamation seems to have been largely an individual enterprise, but was probably encouraged by the cities; during the first three centuries of Roman rule, the whole of the steppe was retaken, out to the edge of the desert. This had substantial social effects, in that with virtually all the steppe under cultivation, the nomads who had roamed that land were now confined to the desert; the cultivated land did include plenty of animal husbandry, but this was in fact now a sedentary occupation.

The need for peaceful conditions is illustrated by the fact that in Palestine internal colonization was a much slower process than elsewhere. The first moves were obviously to expand the settlement within the already-settled regions west of the Jordan, reoccupying abandoned lands and reclaimable waste, but in Palestine that was still going on into the second century AD, whereas in the north, so far as can be seen, the reclamation process had by then moved out to the desert margins.

The reduction in the availability of the steppe for nomad herding meant that those who chose to continue as nomads had to change to be dwellers in the deserts and their oases; those who settled down continued herding animals, but had to give up their wandering. The latter probably predominated. The contrast between the account of the Nabataeans given in connection with the attack on Petra by Antigonos I in 312 BC, and that of Strabo three centuries later is instructive: the Nabataeans had given up their tents for houses, and had adopted agriculture, but still herded sheep and cattle.[5]

The increased production which resulted from the colonization movement encouraged permanent occupation. All through the steppe from the Euphrates to the Red Sea there are the remains of villages built at this period. They are largely stone-built, as would be expected in a land with few trees, and some are still substantial enough to be reoccupied now. The food produced also encouraged the expansion of cities, and the foundation of new ones, sometimes in the most unlikely places, and for unlikely reasons.

It was one of the marks of royalty for kings and emperors to build: some of them built megalomaniac palaces or tombs, others built cities. Herod was extravagant in paying for adornments in many cities around the eastern Mediterranean, and in Palestine he built a great new city at Strato's Tower, renaming it Caesarea for Augustus.[6] At Samaria, ruined by John Hyrkanos, he built Sebaste, again by its name honouring Augustus.[7] His son Archelaus built a new city called Archelais, north of Jericho in the Jordan Valley;[8] another son, Philip, developed the Greek shrine at Panias (close to the battlefield where Antiochos III finally won Syria) into the city of Caesarea Philippi,[9] and Antipas founded Tiberias; both of these were named for emperors. Antipas also rebuilt Sepphoris, which had been burnt down in the disturbances following the death of Herod the Great, renaming the place Autokratoris.[10] The other extreme is the foundation of Philippopolis in the Hauran; it had been the Emperor Philip the Arab's birthplace, no more than a village called Shahba, though a prosperous one and situated in an area which was well-populated – precisely the sort of place which was occupied, or reoccupied, as a joint result of the improved climate and the Roman peace; he promoted it and built it as a whole city; the city was built in less than five years, a strong reminder of the resources which could be deployed by the Roman Empire even in its bad days.[11]

The Roman preference for organizing the population in cities ruled by local oligarchies encouraged attempts in Palestine to restore the Greek cities which had been destroyed or damaged in the various wars and rebellions. This began at Dion with Pompey in 64 BC, and went on through to the first and second centuries AD. The stationing of a substantial garrison after the revolt of 66–73 eventually turned several of its stations into cities, such as Emmaus and Eleutheropolis. Hadrian refounded Jerusalem as Aelia Capitolina (which helped spark a new revolt). Generally the Roman system was to allow a community to develop and then give it a formal status – and so the ports of Ashkelon and Ashdod and Gaza eventually emerged as separate cities. All these places were, of course, surrounded by well-cultivated and -populated farmland, a process which was part of the expansion of settlement.

Not only were there new cities, but the older ones grew in size and population. Antioch had already expanded in the Hellenistic period, with the development of a palace quarter on an island in the Orontes. The wider growth was in part the result of the occupation of Seleukeia-in-Pieria by Ptolemy III's forces from 246–219 BC which concentrated growth in the one city, and where refugees from Ptolemaic rule settled; in the Roman period it grew to three times its original size or more, the growth stimulated by the presence of a substantial garrison and the governor's court. Herod's gift of a colonnaded street was built parallel to, but outside, the boundary established by Seleukos I, and later under the Emperor Tiberius (AD 14–37) a new wall was built to enclose a much larger area.[12]

Emesa was no more than a provincial royal centre when Pompey passed by, but had become a major city two centuries later when the future emperor, Septimius Severus, married a noble lady from the city; here the growth was due in part to the encouragement of the dynasty, but also to the presence of a major temple, which attracted pilgrims. In Phoenicia Berytos was taken over and made into a Roman *colonia* with veterans of two legions established there; its territory was soon expanded to take in Baalbek, whose gods then took on Roman names. The presence of the Latin-speaking veterans converted the city into the only Latin-language city west of Italy, and it developed into a major centre of legal studies;[13] it was capable of fielding a militia force of 1,500 men in the Judaean troubles which followed Herod's death.[14] The city developed into a major and wealthy place during the Roman period, and this was maintained well into the later Byzantine period.[15]

These are the most notable growths, but most cities benefited in much the same way. The spectacular temples built at Baalbek were only one example of a heavy investment in religious buildings throughout Syria. The temple of Atargatis at Hierapolis/Bambyke became famous as the scene of a pilgrimage, where the rites were elaborated into a public display for the tourists.[16] The temple in Jerusalem was another product of the first century AD, only to be destroyed in the war in AD 70, though the great limestone platform remained to be used by later religious buildings, the Roman temple of Jupiter Captolinus and present Muslim mosques.[17] The temple, having been under construction for almost a century, was finished only a few years before its destruction. In a more secular sense the new fashion of colonnading the main streets of the greatest cities was given a major boost by Herod's patronage, and spread to many cities.[18] In Damascus the old temple of Hadad, which had become a temple for Zeus under Macedonian rule, was developed further as a temple of Jupiter, at least to the Romans, no doubt it was still Hadad to the locals; the city acquired a colonnaded street ('the Street called Straight') as well.[19]

The early Roman period was thus a time of expansion and prosperity, generally peaceful, though there were occasional bursts of violence. Apart from the minor campaigns to incorporate the local kingdoms into the provincial system – Kommagene in 73, minor states probably continuously, Agrippa II's kingdom in the 90s, Nabataea in 106 and after – it was in Palestine that the major uprisings occurred, in Judaea first in 66 – 73, and again in the 130s. North Syria and Phoenicia

and Damascus were spared any internal violence for over two centuries, perhaps
the longest period of peace they had ever enjoyed. On the other hand, north Syria
in particular was occupied by a major Roman force which was necessarily alert for
any threat from across the Euphrates frontier.

Both of the Jewish wars resulted in major destruction in Judaea and Palestine
generally; the first war also brought serious damage to cities around Judaea, which
were (correctly) seen as hostile to the Jewish rebellion. The Judaean countryside
only slowly recovered after the end of the war, only to suffer massive destruction
in the second (Bar-Kochva) rebellion of AD 132–135. Much of the hill land was
deserted afterwards, either because of the destruction or because much of the
population fled to the lowland.[20] The centre of Jewish life and culture also moved
down to the lowlands, for Jews were forbidden to live at the site of Jerusalem,
occupied from AD 71 by a Roman legion, while substantial Roman forces were
present elsewhere. The occupation forces in north Syria, however, were largely for
defence; in Palestine they were mainly for control.[21]

There were also intermittent external wars, concerning the apparent threat from
the east, and internal crises concerning the problem of the imperial succession, but
they had relatively little effect on the Syrian population. In both of these issues the
control of the army was a major issue, rather than control of the territory.

Syria was the station of one of the largest sections of the Roman army. There
were probably 40,000 men in the region, and most of them were concentrated at
first in the north, but they gradually spread to other areas.[22] Such a force could
be decisive in a dispute over the imperial succession, but it was also in the present
instance a force mainly designed to defend Syria against attack. A secondary
purpose was to control Syria itself, which was clearly originally seen from Rome as
a potentially dissident province.

These interlinked problems were demonstrated in the succession crisis of 68–
69. The Syrian army, reinforced by two extra legions and a substantial number
of auxiliaries, both Roman and Syrian, was already locked into a difficult war to
conquer the Jewish rebels on Judaea when the succession crisis broke. The army
commander Vespasian at first continued the fight in the name of the new Emperor
Galba, but when Galba was murdered he was soon persuaded to make his own
attempt at the throne. To do this he had to suspend the fight in Judaea, ensure by
diplomacy that the Parthian Empire would not take advantage of the crisis – which
was surprisingly agreed to – and then had to use a large part of the army to attack
the current ruler in Rome.[23]

As it happened Vespasian got away with it, but it was clearly a major gamble
on his part, one which no later contender was able to repeat. He was fortunate
in that he had a large enough force to hold the line in Judaea, to keep a major
force facing Parthia, and at the same time to send an army to Italy – which was in
fact reinforced by forces from the Danube garrisons, another result of Vespasian's

successful diplomacy. This was never possible again. In the next imperial crisis, in 96 – 98, the Syrian governor, M. Cornelius Nigrinus Curiatius Maternus, made some moves indicating that he was aiming to claim the throne, but in the event he could not do so.[24]

The actual winner on that occasion, M. Ulpius Traianus – Trajan – decided that he would attack Parthia. This may be connected with the threat Curiatius Maternus had posed on his own accession, a means of ensuring the loyalty of a potentially hostile local army. In actual fact, it is more likely to be the personal decision of an emperor who felt it was his duty to campaign constantly to expand the empire, and who felt a certain guilt at the murder of his predecessor Domitian, who had been killed just as he was about to launch a great new campaign to conquer Germany. And of all the enemies of Rome, Parthia was the most powerful and the most difficult.

Crises had erupted more or less regularly in Roman–Parthian relations, the most recent being concerned with the overlordship of Armenia in the reign of Nero (in which Syria had been the logistics base for the Roman army campaigning in Armenia). From the Roman point of view this war had ended unsatisfactorily, in a negotiated peace which left Armenia largely under Parthian influence. This was a situation Trajan intended to change.

He made extensive preparations for the attack. The conquest of Nabataea and its conversion into the province of Arabia was part of those preparations, presumably on the assumption that the Nabataean kingdom might well take the opportunity to join in the war on the Parthian side, in a sort of repeat of Vespasian's problem with Judaea in 69. In fact it was the Jews of Egypt, Cyprus, and Cyrenaica who seized that chance, by developing an extensive rebellion while Trajan was in Parthia. The Parthian War was a Roman victory in a tactical sense, but strategically Trajan was too ambitious.[25] (The Jewish rebellion did not help, but was not the cause of his failure.) Trajan died in the course of the war, and was succeeded by Hadrian, his cousin, whom he had placed as governor of Syria to guard his base. Hadrian therefore also inherited the command of the major part of the Roman army and succeeded his cousin as emperor without serious opposition. He was also clearer-eyed in imperial affairs than Trajan. He gave up the Parthian War and evacuated Trajan's conquests.

For the second time an emperor had emerged from Syria at the head of an army. This was a factor which tended to confirm the fears of every emperor. Augustus had paid very careful attention to Syria, visiting the place for two long periods, and sending his trusted co-emperor, M. Vipsanius Agrippa, or members of the imperial family there several times. Nero had ordered the successful general, M. Domitius Corbulo, who had commanded in the war in Armenia in the 60s, to kill himself because he feared that he might have imperial ambitions. Curiatius

Maternus seems to have had similar ambitions. Syria was quite correctly regarded at Rome as a danger.

The Parthian War meant that there was for a time a largely increased force of soldiers in the region, which enhanced the market for Syrian goods, particularly such items as were needed by the forces – food, wine, olive oil, leather, clothing, and so on. One of the major reasons for Syrian prosperity was the continuing presence of a large army in the province, whereby the taxes extracted from the population were mainly expended within the region rather than being sent to, and spent, in Rome or other frontier provinces; a large army, a demand for provisions, and the expenditure of public moneys on public works, all combined to pump ever more cash into the province's economy.[26]

The Bar-Kokhva War in Palestine in the 130s and another Parthian war in the 160s will have had much the same effect. Then in the 190s another Syrian governor, Pescennius Niger, set himself up as emperor during the succession crisis following the murder of the Emperor Commodus, before being suppressed by Septimius Severus. Severus then went on to conduct a successful war against Parthia, which resulted in the conquest of much of the Jazirah. Again these campaigns can only have brought still more monetary resources into the province. It was in this period that the greater expansion of the *villes mortes*, the colonization of the hill country south-east of Antioch, took place. This was a region which became a major producer of olive oil and wine, no doubt in part as a result of the great demand generated by the presence of the army and the imperial court; it later also became a major exporter of these products to other parts of the empire.[27]

The army was not merely present in Syria in large numbers; it was also greedy for recruits. In the early years of the province, and in the years following each annexation of a kingdom, large numbers of young men were taken into the Roman forces. Many of these will have been members of the armies of the annexed kingdoms, enrolled, probably forcibly and automatically, as auxiliary regiments, or possibly in some cases as legionaries. Ituraeans, Emesans, and Nabataean Arabs all suddenly appear in the lists of *auxilia* soon after the annexation of their kingdoms, or even before.[28] Thus the Romans simultaneously acquired reinforcements, and reduced the numbers of fit young men in the former kingdoms who might have staged rebellions against the annexation of their homelands. These regiments were then despatched to distant parts of the empire – Ituraeans went to Egypt,[29] Emesans to Hungary[30] – as garrison troops, while other regiments from other regions arrived in Syria. Syria became, partly because it was to a degree already militarized, a major source of Roman military manpower.

The various wars had not merely added lands to the Roman Empire; they had expanded the Syrian province to an unwieldy size. In 106 Trajan had seized Nabataea but had then left it as a new province – Arabia. Even earlier, the Jewish war in 66–73 had ended in Palestine becoming effectively a new province, though it was still within the Syrian government in formal terms; it was shifted into a full province by Hadrian. Yet this still left a major and disturbingly well-garrisoned Syrian province. The winner of the next civil war, Septimius Severus, finally split it into two separate provinces, Syria Coele and Syria Phoenice, and made his new conquests east of the Euphrates into the province of Mesopotamia. (This had also been a province of Trajan's brief conquest earlier.) So where there had been a single province during the first century of Roman rule, in 195 there were five, and the army was divided between them. This was clearly a major concern for Severus, reasonably enough considering the penchant for Syrian governors to lunge for the throne he presently occupied.

Severus' successful conquest of the Jazirah moved the Roman frontier away from the Euphrates for the first time. He had to cope with a series of communities, none of which were especially keen to become Roman subjects. East of the Euphrates was the kingdom of Edessa, or Osrhoene, which had performed a successful balancing act between Rome and Parthia for two centuries. Severus reduced the kingdom, taking some territory to form the province of Osrhoene, but left the king on his throne; further east he created the new province of Mesopotamia, which was essentially the valley of the Khabor River, the old 'Khabor triangle'. Strategically, from Syria's point of view, this formed a helpful frontier defence; at the same time it allowed the emperor to move large parts of the Syrian garrison forward into this new territory.[31]

Even before his conquest the legions had been moved to the Euphrates, and now they were stationed further east. Trajan's conquest of Arabia had also resulted in the move into the new province of another legion, III *Cyrenaica* from Egypt to Bostra, the latter-day capital of the Nabataean kingdom. Trajan had also established a formal imperial road, with milestones, along the line of the old King's Highway, which dated originally from the Bronze Age, or earlier. This forward movement brought responsibility for policing the steppe to the Roman army. At first it seems that auxiliary regiments and detachments from the legions were posted at temporary camps, but it was not long before the army began to develop a series of permanent forts, especially to guard the roads.[32]

The victory of Septimius Severus, both over his rival for the empire and in his Parthian War, was thus decisive, though Syria had become even more central to the imperial policy as a result of other factors. Severus' wife, Julia Domna, came from Emesa, possibly a descendant of the old royal dynasty of that city, and she brought to Rome with her own Syrian attitudes. Her sons, Caracalla and Geta, hated each other, and when Severus died, it was no more than a year before Caracalla had his brother murdered.[33]

The presence of a Syrian family at the centre of imperial power was the culmination of the slow penetration of Syrians into the Roman administration, though it has to be said that they were still relatively few by the time Severus became emperor. Berytos was the origin of the earliest man to reach the Senate,[34] in large part because it was a Latin-speaking city (as a Roman veteran colony) and from Antioch where the oligarchs of the city were in contact with the governors and their patronage – one Antiochene married into the family of Marcus Aurelius.[35] It must be said, however, that it was easier for Latin-speaking Gauls and Spaniards, or Greek-speaking men from Asia Minor, to become senators than it was for Syrians. The connections of Severus and his wife in Syria, however, provided the patronage to bring more Syrians to the centre.

The Parthian War of the 160s had brought the joint Emperor Lucius Verus to Syria; his army's victory in capturing Seleukeia-on-the-Tigris also brought a plague into the Roman Empire. Cities such as Antioch suffered particularly.[36] Verus also collected a following of Syrian doctors, actors, and entertainers who returned with him to Rome, and brought to the imperial city a taste of the luxury and decadence for which Syria had become notorious.[37] (The cantankerous poet Juvenal had already a century before claimed that Syria was decadent, and had complained about the presence of Syrians in Rome, as the Orontes poured its waters – contaminated, of course – into the Tiber.[38]) Another result, perhaps indirect, of Verus' presence in Syria was the attempted usurpation, ten years later, of the Syrian governor, Avidius Cassius. He had been a successful commander on behalf of Verus, and had been made viceroy of much of the east by Marcus Aurelius, Verus' imperial colleague. He was the first 'native Syrian' – by which is meant a Greek Syrian – to aim so high. He was, as it happened, only a little premature.[39]

The Emesan arrival at Rome was thus something of a jolt, both for the Syrians and for the Romans. The family maintained its grip on power for forty years, even during the curious rule of the mothers, Julia Mammaea and Julia Soaemias, of two child emperors, M. Aurelius Antoninus, originally Varius Avitus Bassianus, and nicknamed Elagabalus (216–222), and Alexander Severus, originally Gessius Alexianus Bassianus (222–235). The sexual and religious antics of Elagabalus, who brought to Rome his own god, El, from Emesa, are especially striking.[40] Even after the elimination of these later Severans, Syria produced other emperors – Philip the Arab, for example, and several pretenders, above all from Emesa, a city whose imperial pretensions remained active for another generation. Clearly the Severans' career had brought Syrians to the centre of affairs at Rome for the first time, and their presence and patronage had maintained that Syrian presence for another generation after the family's fall.

The penetration of Syrians into the Roman power structure was in fact only one part of their movement into all aspects of the society of the Roman Empire, and in fact it was one of the latest. The transfer of soldiers recruited in Syria to all parts of the imperial frontiers has been touched on, but it should be emphasized that Syrian regiments were stationed all through the empire, in north Africa, in

Dacia, on the Rhine, and even on Hadrian's Wall in Britannia.[41] Not only that, but the legions which were stationed in Syria adopted Syrian ways. The legions left in Syria by Augustus stayed there for a long time. When *legio* III *Gallica* arrived in Italy to help put Vespasian on the imperial throne, it was noted that the men performed a dawn ceremony of greeting the new sun, apparently a ritual they had acquired in Syria[42] – Elagabalus' transfer of El to Rome was by no means the first religious importation from Syria.

The soldiers stationed in north Syria adopted other religious traits from the local environment. The shrine of the old Hittite storm god at Doliche became that of Zeus in the Greek time, and then of Jupiter Dolichenus, who became a popular god with soldiers; his shrines and temples spread along the frontiers.[43] The Baal of the Bekaa became Zeus, then Jupiter Heliopolitanus; he was not as popular as his contemporary at Doliche, but almost as widely spread. This was a generally peaceful penetration of the rest of the empire. The presence of Jews in many parts of the empire similarly was part of the same religious expansive movement.

So was the expansion of Christianity. From being no more than a minor Jewish sect in the first generation after its foundation, it had established a presence in north Syria – 'Christians' were first so-called in Antioch, within a decade of Christ's death[44] – in Greece and Asia Minor, thanks to the missionary work of Paul of Tarsus and others, and in Rome, all by the end of the first century; they had been numerous enough and disliked enough for Nero to enlist them as scapegoats for the fire of Rome in 64,[45] and Trajan similarly blamed them for an earthquake at Antioch in 115.[46] The expansion of Christianity was among civilians, whereas Jupiter Dolichenus and Heliopolitanus were largely military deities, as was Mithras, who seems to have emerged from eastern Asia Minor; the worship of Yahweh remained largely confined to Jews, in part because of difficulty of conversion, and the exclusivity of the Jews. Only Christianity had the political nous to appeal to civilians and to make it notably easy to join. Hence its success.

The spread of these religions out of Syria to colonize many parts of the empire followed the movements of soldiers and commerce. The presence next door to Syria of the intermittently hostile Parthian Empire made it certain that Syria would always also be a major political centre. But that empire was battered very badly by Severus in the 190s, and came under other attacks in the following years, from Caracalla and his brief successor Macrinus. Neither of these wars was as successful as that of Severus, but the constant battering eventually so weakened the Parthian state that it fell fairly easily to an internal revolution in the 220s.

The result was the new, tougher, more resilient and militarily capable Sassanian Empire, which faced Rome across the Jazirah. And it was then the turn of the Roman Empire to fall on the evil days. The imperial succession system, such as it had been, failed entirely after the murder of the Emperor Alexander Severus in 235. Soon there were not merely a rapid succession of brief emperors in Rome, but several other emperors who ruled just parts of the empire, and numerous 'usurpations', though many of those men recognized as 'legitimate' emperors began as usurpers. In Syria there were several attempts at seizing power in the generation after the murder of Alexander Severus, but the real problem was the growing menace of the Sassanians. The second Sassanian king, Shapur, was a capable commander and was able to conduct the defence against a series of invasions in the Jazirah area directed by successive emperors – Alexander Severus, Gordian III, Philip the Arab – and eventually Valerian, and to reply with even more devastating return invasions of Syria. Fighting was not actually continuous, but gradually the Sassanian forces came closer to Syria.

This therefore was a different matter than the several Roman invasions towards the east which had eventually so damaged the Parthians. The wars against the Sassanids were harder to fight and much more expensive that any Parthian war. The resources of the emperors were now significantly reduced by the loss of territories in the west, and the exploitation of Syrian resources was inevitably much greater and more oppressive. War had ceased to be a Syrian economic stimulus and had begun to drain wealth away. The defeat and death of Gordian III, followed by the defeat of his successor Philip the Arab deep in Persian territory in 244, stopped Roman aggression for a time,[47] but discontent in Syria was presumably behind an attempt by a local, Jotapian, to make himself emperor in 248. His name suggests a Syrian, specifically a royal Syrian, descent.[48]

This all became worse after about AD 250. In that year the Emperor Decius instigated the first empire-wide persecution of Christians, which undoubtedly caused considerable disturbance. Next year he was killed in battle against the Goths; his successor Trebonianus Gallus lasted less than two years, but in that time he so angered King Shapur, who accused him of 'lying', presumably in not carrying out earlier peace terms, that a new Persian war began in 252. The Persian attack was unexpectedly successful, considering that earlier wars had generally been confined to fighting in the Jazirah.

A Roman army was defeated at the junction of the Euphrates and the Khabour, and the Persian forces moved along the Euphrates capturing or bypassing Roman posts in what was evidently a new Persian strategy. This route allowed the Persian forces to avoiding the need to capture the crossing at Zeugma, entering Syria south of that city. They passed by or through Hierapolis and Beroia and Chalkis, and then south to Apameia and Raphanaia. A subsidiary raid was sent south along the Orontes, capturing Larisa, Arethusa, and Hamath, but a locally recruited force of 'peasants' – so it is said – stopped the raid from reaching Emesa. It seems that this raid was not in full force, or the 'peasant' army was more skilled than the term implies. Antioch and Seleukeia-in-Pieria were taken and looted, but not held on to. Most of the cities of north Syria feature in the campaign as Persian victims, though it is not clear how many of the places named were really taken.[49]

This was essentially a great raid, presumably by mobile forces rather than infantry, and once having broken into Syria the Persians were basically unopposed – though grave stelai found at Apameia suggest that Roman forces there put up a fight.[50] The raiders will have then withdrawn, no doubt laden down with their loot, almost at once; it is clear that Shapur had no intention of annexing any Roman territory. He only retained Dura-Europos, the most advanced Roman position on the Euphrates, though it seems to have been soon abandoned. The commander of the 'peasant' army in the battle outside Emesa – if such it was – was a priest called Samsigeramus; he was proclaimed, or proclaimed himself, emperor as Uranius Antoninus. These names suggest, as with Jotapian, connections back to the old royal family, and to the Severans.[51]

The crisis of this raid brought the Emperor Valerian to Syria in 254, and he remained in the east for much or all of the time until 260. The gravity of the situation which had emerged from the Sassanid seizure of power is illustrated by the frequency of imperial visits in this period. It was apparent, however, that the lack of fighting after 253 was only a respite. On the Roman side preparations were made, either for an attack in reprisal, or for defence. Supplies were being gathered for the Roman forces in Syria from far afield – Egypt, for example – and towns in Syria were being fortified. Adraa in Arabia built walls and towers at this time, and work went on rebuilding at Antioch, which had been badly damaged by the Persian occupiers.[52]

One city which evidently felt particularly threatened by the Persian advances and methods was Palmyra. If a Persian raid could reach close to Emesa, which was Palmyra's western desert port, then Palmyra itself was clearly vulnerable. The conquest of Dura-Europos, which took place probably in 256, was a further threat, for it was the closest Roman town to Palmyra on the route along the Euphrates. Palmyra organized itself militarily, and the richest merchant in the city, a senator whose son was also already a senator, Septimius Odenathos, emerged as the 'governor' of the city, with or without imperial sanction.[53]

The next Persian attack came in 260. It was met in the Jazirah by the imperial army commanded by the Emperor Valerian. The fight took place west of Edessa, and so not far from the Zeugma crossing. Shapur had laid siege to both Karrhai and Edessa, but was able to meet the Roman relief attempt well to the west of the latter place. The battle was a comprehensive Roman defeat, in which the emperor himself was captured.

The invasion then turned into another great raid. It seems that the Persian army crossed the Euphrates at Samosata and campaigned in Kappadokia and Kilikia before withdrawing through Syria. Much of the area of Syria which had been attacked in the earlier raid was not threatened, though the raid's route for its withdrawal is not known, and Antioch is said to have been captured again. The object thus would seem again to have been loot rather than conquest, and the sieges at Edessa and Karrhai were presumably designed to bring out Valerian and the army, defeat them, and so open the way for the raid. Valerian's defeat did not apparently leave Syria vulnerable, and he had presumably left considerable garrison forces in the cities.[54]

His capture, however, was an event which was unprecedented, and Syria descended into difficult times once more. The early reaction in Syria was for two men, Macrianus, one of Valerian's officials, and his son Quietus, to be proclaimed emperors by another official, Ballista. But they were not acceptable to all Syrians, and Odenathus came out of Palmyra to attack them. Macrianus died campaigning in Asia Minor, attempting to reach Italy; Quietus and Ballista stood siege in Emesa until the former was killed in the fighting, and the latter was murdered by the citizens. The result was that Odenathus secured control over Syria and the Jazirah, where he recaptured Nisibis; again it seems that Shapur was not interested in annexing Roman territory. Odenathus probably operated in the name of the Emperor Gallienus, Valerian's son, who controlled Italy and some of the nearby regions until 268. Odenathus is also said to have captured Ctesiphon, the Persian capital, which seems very unlikely, though it is possible he led a reprisal raid to the area.[55]

The lands ruled by Rome before the Persian raids were thus quickly recovered. Odenathus appears to have accepted some sort of official position from the Emperor Gallienus, over and above his position as governor, and the few inscriptions of Syria dating to the 260s instance Gallienus as the sole Emperor. Odenathus was assassinated in 267, however, and his son Vaballathus, only a child, was soon proclaimed as his successor. This was the doing of Odenathos' widow Zenobia, who retrospectively endowed her dead husband with a set of extra titles, which descended to her son, and Vaballathus soon became variously senator, king, consul, general, king of kings and emperor, depending on the inscription being consulted.[56] This was a challenge to Gallienus and his successors, one which Odenathus had not issued.

Odenathus had in fact operated more or less as part of the Roman governing system, if in exceptional conditions. That system was altering and adapting as a result of the long crisis the empire was going through, and Odenathus' actions were consistent with those of a loyal governor who was coping with a major crisis. But seizing the title of emperor would never be an acceptable action while another emperor with much more legitimacy existed, and certainly not another Syrian mother ruling in the name of her son; no matter how proud Syrians were of Julia Domna and her Emesene successors, the rest of the empire detested their memory. The emperors who were emerging in Italy and the Balkans – Gallienus, Claudius II, Aurelian – were stern military men, and were not willing to accept such people as their co-rulers.

Zenobia managed to seize control of Egypt, and pushed her army into Asia Minor, but this brief success soon evaporated.[57] Emperor Aurelian (270–275) was at last able to march east in 272, recovered Asia Minor without a serious fight, defeated the Palmyran army outside Antioch, and again near Emesa, and then launched a raid to take Palmyra. The whole 'Palmyran Empire' thus collapsed with scarcely any resistance, especially when Aurelian made it clear in a proclamation at Antioch that he would not be punishing anyone who had supported the Palmyran regime.[58]

Zenobia was captured and carried off to Rome to be exhibited in Aurelian's triumph. A rising in Palmyra when Aurelian was on his journey west was swiftly put down, the city was sacked, and a Roman fortress was established to maintain control.[59] Through all this it seems clear, from the little evidence there is, that the trade between Babylonia and Syria by way of Palmyra simply continued. It was, of course, the lifeblood of Palmyra. The more surprising thing, however, is that the Sassanid King Shapur, after twenty years of raids and battles, ignored the obvious opportunity presented by the Palmyran regime. But then Odenathus and Vaballathus were not serious threats to Persia, and Shapur had shown that he was fully capable of a distinctive and devastating response if he was attacked. It would seem that for a time the Roman government was content to be peaceable.[60]

The episode of the 'Palmyran Empire' is essentially unimportant, despite the romantic Zenobia. Below the level of Odenathus and Zenobia the government of the provinces of Syria functioned as normal, so far is can be seen. The edict of Aurelian promising no reprisals implies as much, and even Palmyra was not severely punished until the city rebelled. But the whole episode did have some influence in the hands of the subsequent events which brought a major revolution in the imperial government.

Chapter 14

Prosperity and a Crash

The Roman imperial complications of the middle years of the third century were gradually brought to an end under the ministrations, often violent, of the military emperors. Their periods of rule tended to be short, since they were very subject to assassination or to deposition by another general. In the end Diocletian devised a system of self-protection, and capitalized on the weariness of populations and armies with the constant conflict.

Inevitably he came to power in a process by which his predecessors were murdered, but he was then successful in holding on to power and developing a new system of government, which permitted the Roman Empire to continue in existence for the next century or so in the west, and in the eastern half of the empire for twice that length. As the west fragmented and broke away, Syria, therefore, as the richest part of the empire, became all the more important.[1]

Diocletian reformed the provincial geography, by increasing the number of provinces but reducing their size. In Syria the provinces went from half a dozen to eleven. North Syria was now divided into three, with a province along the Euphrates, and Syria Coele divided into two; Syria Phoenice and Palestine were similarly split into two; Arabia lost is southern part which was made into a third Palestine province. The object was to enable governors to exercise a much more detailed governmental control, but at the same time to reduce their access to armed strength, and so help to prevent provincial usurpations.[2]

Religion was identified as one of the glues which would hold the empire together. This was hardly a new idea, and several emperors during the previous century had attempted to use religion as a means of improving imperial cohesion – Elagabalus with his god from Emesa, Aurelian with his worship of the sun. Now Diocletian devised a new theology, the worship of Jupiter and Hercules, which mirrored the arrangement of emperors, where he took a colleague, and each emperor took a junior partner, who was intended to be his successor.

One of the sources of division and therefore of imperial weakness was Christianity, whose unusual beliefs insisted that rulers be not venerated. This had been one of the unifying themes of the Roman government ever since the divinization of Augustus, and Christianity's negative response to this time-honoured practice had drawn upon it popular enmity and official and unofficial persecutions in the past.

Christianity was, of course, one of the innovations out of Syria. The concept of monotheism, the exclusive worship of one god, which was combined with the demonization of all others, had been developed originally by the Jews, partly under the influence of the destruction of the Judaean kingdom and royal family – and the temple at Jerusalem – by the Babylonians, and their exile in Babylonia during much of the sixth century BC. This was followed by the pressure of Greek culture, which was so far superior to their own that in defence the Jews developed the worship of Yahweh. This concept was, of course, inherited by the Christians, whose early expansion was very largely as a Jewish sect from within the Jewish diaspora.

Exclusivity in religion was incomprehensible to Roman or Greek minds and it was not difficult to identify monotheism as hostile to the imperial system. The problem was that the Christian message was of some comfort to those who had no real stake in that imperial system, and that persecution, bravely borne, might evoke sympathy rather than support for the persecutors. And during the third century the Roman system appeared to be failing, so that the Christian alternative was increasingly attractive. Diocletian's promotion of the worship of two of the traditional gods, Jupiter and Hercules, was once again a ruler's religion, and not one to appeal much beyond the Roman elite. He also resorted to the traditional means of suppressing the rival religion, persecution, and having gained control over the whole government system his instructions could be carried out.

The effect on Syria was perhaps more profound than for any other region. This was a land in which Christianity had struck deep roots fairly early, probably in part because of the presence of a large number of Jews throughout the country, but also because it is likely that the monotheism of the Jews and of Christianity appealed to the Syrian population. A sort of monotheism had long underlain much of Syrian religion, for the predominance of Hadad and Atargatis under various names was widespread – indeed Atargatis is referred to by the Syrian writer Lucian as the 'Syrian goddess'. The concentration in each city on one particular deity as the city's god was another tendency towards monotheism, one which had been at the basis of the worship of Yahweh. The Christians' monotheistic exclusivity was at first disliked, but once that was accepted, it was not difficult to shift to Christianity, with the promise of freedom from the current life, and its tendency to egalitarianism. This was especially so when it became one of the more popular religions, and when it was seen to be disliked by the Roman government, an example shared by a large part of the population.

For one of the constants of Syrian history since the time of the Assyrian conquest had been the latent and at times open enmity between Syrians and their foreign rulers. None of the imperial conquerors – Assyrians, Babylonians, Persians, Egyptians, Macedonians, Romans – had made any effort to identify with their Syrian subjects, and Syrians had responded by holding firmly on to their identity as Syrians. Whenever it was possible, groups of Syrians had acted to free themselves from foreign rule, led, in many ways, by the Jews, whose monotheism could thus be seen as advantageous. Hence the repeated rebellions against every set of rulers, though in many cases such rebellions might be more gestures of despair than hopeful attempts at independence. It is in the nature of the situation that such rebellions should be local, but, to take the collapse of the Seleukid state as an example, it is not too difficult to see that one of the results, had the Romans not intervened, could well have been the emergence of a Syrian-wide polity, or perhaps no more than two or three. The success of the Maccabean kingdom in coming to control all Palestine was one indication; the intermarriages of the royal families of Syria were another.

The existence of a Greek ruling class from 330 BC onwards had, still six centuries later, not succeeded in imposing its language and religion on the people it ruled. This is a clear demonstration that the Syrians were determined to hold on to their regional and individual identity – one is tempted to use the term 'national'. The fact that there is no indication that this was a fully articulated 'ideology' is all the more impressive, since it would seem to have been the instinctive reaction of the Syrian population. Certainly the Jews reacted by shunning Hellenic religion, if not the Greek language, though they kept their holy books in part in Hebrew and partly in Aramaic as well as Greek. The local kingdoms had also emerged amongst surviving shrines and temples where the old language had also survived – El at Emesa, Baal for the Ituraeans, the temple of Baitokaike in the Bargylos Hills, Atargatis at Bambyke, Hadad at Damascus, and so on. The persistence of Aramaic is impressive, although it tended to split into local languages, and under the Roman Empire evolved into Syriac. Yet it was clearly still written, and no doubt it was often because it was the local religious language that it was kept alive.

Diocletian's persecution was a failure. In fact, it was only very late in his reign that the emperor instituted his persecution of Christians, and other new religions had incurred his annoyance earlier, the Manicheans by 297, for instance, branded as a 'Persian' religion, and so traitorous. Not only that, but the application of his decrees depended on his imperial colleagues and on the provincial governors who were not always keen. As it happens Syria was ruled from the time of the institution of the persecution decree by a series of emperors who were relatively keen persecutors – Diocletian himself, Maximinus, and Licinius – but the imperial action was only intermittent, and once Constantine had elected to take the Christians into partnership as his own solution to the problem of governing the empire there was little point in continuing.[3]

The experiences of the victims of the persecutions were recorded with rather unpleasant relish by the Christian writers, but there is no guarantee that they were accurate, or were not inventing cases, many of the accounts were written out much later. Constantine's toleration was as imperial an action as the original persecution, and with equally dire results for the Christian Church, which had thereby almost at once become a part of the Roman imperial system. The emperor claimed the right of appointing bishops just as he had the right to appoint provincial governors. Therefore it followed that those parts of the population which were already antagonistic to the Roman Empire continued to be so, but manifested their opposition by means of other religions. As soon as the persecutions ceased divisions among the Christians arose – Donatists in 314, Arians in 318. The development of these and other particular interpretations of Christian beliefs happened in various regions and were promoted by various theologians. These men turned out to be as avidly intolerant as any persecutor, both of their pagan adversaries and their Christian colleagues. The experience of persecution had in fact in some cases brought this Christian division about: in Egypt one part of the argument was over the treatment – harsh or forgiving – for those who had deserted under the pressure. Within only a few years, at least three schisms in the church had become obvious, and more were to emerge. The dogmatism of theological controversy ensured that they were never solved.

It seems unlikely that many Syrians were seriously affected by any of this theological controversy or by the persecutions; in the former case the argument tended to become arcane and to be one between prominent churchmen, often almost in private; in the latter case it was prominent Christians, bishops and writers, who were the obvious targets. But the gradual change in the status of Christianity, from not being persecuted to being tolerated, to being the preferred religion of the government, had its effect. In the cities it was now possible to build new churches without the risk of having them pulled down – and at least three new churches were built in Antioch in the last decade of Constantine's reign;[4] also in the countryside, though the adoption of Christianity seems to have been much slower, one of the effects was to develop veneration for 'holy men', and for the accompanying and consequent development of monasticism.

The experience of the Syrians in this period is difficult to sort out amid the polemics from either side. It will have varied with the opinions of the governor, and even of the city councils more than with the pronouncements of the emperors. Antioch, as a major imperial centre of government, probably had to react more immediately to imperial whims and decision than the more distant cities. Some cities had major investments in pagan sanctuaries, such as Jupiter at Baalbek, part of the *colonia* of Berytos, or Pan at Caesarea Philippi, and both of these continued in operation as pagan shrines for centuries after the Emperor Theodosios decreed their closing.[5]

Diocletian became involved in a Sassanid war in 297–298, but very carefully worked to ensure that it did not become too serious. A defeat for his general and deputy Galerius in a battle in the Balikh valley in 297 was followed by a Roman victory at Satala on the border of Armenia next year. A peace was then made which lasted several years.[6] Two further measures tended to confine future conflicts to Mesopotamia and Armenia. One clause of the treaty of 298 nominated Nisibis in

Mesopotamia as the preferred contact and transit point for inter-imperial trade. This effectively and finally sabotaged the position of Palmyra, which had been declining anyway since the defeat of Zenobia. But now that both empires chose to cooperate in regulating the trade at one point, it was hazardous to use any other route, and the Palmyrene monopoly was broken.

The other measure was Diocletian's decision to fortify the Roman desert frontier, in effect changing it from a frontier – a zone – to a boundary – a line. A road was constructed, or improved, from Damascus to Palmyra and then on to Sura on the Euphrates. The road was then lined with twenty or so forts at more or less regular intervals; two legions and several cavalry vexillations were stationed behind the line.[7] This system will have taken several years to construct, though many of the forts are not large, but the knowledge that they were being built would have a chilling effect on those who felt threatened or deprived by it.

A second system of the same sort, or perhaps it was all part of the same overall organization, was constructed south of Damascus, providing protection for the Hawran and for the line of settlements along the old King's Highway, now the Via Nova Traiana. Both of these systems were protecting the expanded settlements and reclaimed steppe which had developed since the Roman acquisition of the lands to the west.

Another reason for this measure must also have been the emergence in the previous generation of at least one and perhaps two Arab polities in the desert of north Arabia between Babylonia and Syria. The Sassanids were the first to pay attention, when they recognized an Arab kingdom centred on al-Hira in the Iraqi desert, under the Lakhmid dynasty. This had been established since the later third century, and was normally friendly with the Sassanids,[8] though in Aurelian's campaign against Palmyra his forces were accompanied by an ally, Amr al-Adi, the first really effective Lakhmid king, who was a rival to the Arab clan headed by Zenobia.[9] (Her marriage to Odenathus had been the alliance of her clan with the city of Palmyra, which was one of the strengths of the city in the crisis of the 260s.)

Amr's son Imr'ul-qays claimed on his tombstone set up at Namara in the Hawran in 328 to have been 'king of the Arabs', with influence if not authority among the desert clans of both north and south Arabia.[10] The new power manifested in such a title suggests an obvious reason for Diocletian's new borderline, but since Imr'ul-qays was buried on the Roman side of the desert, and actually in Roman territory, it would seem that he was still a Roman ally, like his father. And that alliance may well have been a source of his power. In the Sassanid War of 296–298 Galerius marched his army into Babylonia, and passed close to al-Hira on his return march; evidently they were not at enmity at that time.

There was a long period of peace along the Persian front after the war of 297–298. Occasional threats, even occasional fighting, developed, but it was not until 338 that serious fighting took place. The Emperor Constantine I had been preparing to attack Persia in a dispute over the treatment of Christians in the Sassanid Empire, but died before an attack could begin. The Sassanid king, Shapur II, therefore took advantage of a period of imperial succession confusion after the death of Constantine to conquer Armenia. The war then grumbled on for another twenty-five years, with much of the fighting centred on fortresses such as Nisibis and Amida in Mesopotamia. It ended with another Roman invasion of Babylonia, ironically by the last pagan Roman emperor, Julian, and another smashing Roman defeat.[11]

By this time the solid fortifications of Mesopotamia had made it very difficult for the Sassanids to penetrate as far as Syria, since they tended to be held up besieging one or more of the fortress-cities. The main object of the wars by now was control of Armenia; so this combination left Syria very largely insulated from the fighting. After the peace of 364 long wars were avoided for over a century, and only occasional disputes erupted until the beginning of the sixth century.

These wars affected Syria in the same way as the Parthian wars which punctuated the history of the Roman Empire between Augustus and Caracalla. The fighting was kept well away from Syria, but Syria was the source of much of the logistic support for the fighting forces. When the Roman system worked this meant that money collected in taxation was returned to the country in government spending. This is certainly one of the sources of the considerable prosperity which is visible in fifth century Syria, but probably not the whole story.

This prosperity, of course, was a continuation of that which had been building from the Hellenistic period, and which had been interrupted by the Seleukid collapse and, less seriously, by the Persian wars in the mid-third century. This wealth creation spread even more decisively into the countryside, where the dead villages of the plateaux of north Syria and of the Hawran show very clearly that they were doing very well. They are well-built houses, so much so that many of them still stand, often with inscriptions on them, which implies a fairly widespread literacy. They became Christian during the fourth century and built churches in large numbers – one village had thirteen.[12]

The source of the prosperity of these villages was partly their self-sufficiency in basic food products but also their ability to sell their surplus produce to the cities. The combination is clearly necessary, since self-sufficiency alone is a recipe for poverty. It has been thought that they were exporters to the wider empire, but this is now discounted in some of the latest interpretations, though the question is open.

The sheer number of olive oil and wine presses in the villages argues that production of these eminently marketable crops was more than was locally required. It has been argued that the road system consisted mainly of tracks between the villages, but production was not necessarily individually large, though in total it certainly would be; and there were roads leading to the cities which passed close to the region, and indeed one road, between Apameia and Chalkis passed through it. It seems therefore that the villages were producing oil and wine for a wider market. The obvious nearby destinations would be the local cities – Antioch, Apameia, Chalkis, Beroia – but it is worth noting that the newly expanded city of Constantinople required provisioning: grain came from Egypt, and wine from Palestine; oil from Syria seems probable.[13]

The villages appear not to have been owned or at least controlled by large landowners as was the case in the lower land around Antioch, for example, so their produce would be sold in small quantities to middlemen, who could well have exported it. These middlemen could have acted as patrons, to whom appeal could be made to judge disputes. One of such men whose details are known was Abraham, who took up residence in a village in the Lebanon Mountains. His object was to convert the people to Christianity, but his method involved being useful. He became the agent for the crop of walnuts; that is he either bought the crop himself and sold it on, or put the farmers in contact with their market; he was able, because he had contacts with wealthy people in Apameia, to arrange the village's tax affairs. Of course, his evangelization succeeded, but the point here is that Abraham was also an entrepreneur, apart from being a hermit. One of his achievements was thus to increase the flow of money into the village, and when the tax collector arrived he could smooth over any disputes and arrange a loan for the village, so preventing sudden impoverishment.[14]

The cities show plenty of evidence of similar prosperity. Berytos for example maintained its reputation for legal education into the sixth century, and developed a manufacturing capability in expensive cloth – silk and linen especially – which was widely in demand in the rest of the empire.[15] Gaza was the centre of a substantial wine-exporting industry, based in vines planted over a large area of southern Palestine.[16] Many parts of Syria – Laodikeia-ad-Mare, Apameia, Berytus – were major wine exporters.[17] Caesarea was a government centre and had a garrison; it grew to expand beyond its walls in the fifth century.

Most of the cities from Gaza to Samosata in fact grew, as did the population of the countryside. The inflation of demand which followed was another obvious source of the land's prosperity. At the same time, the capacity of the land to eventually feed all the people in it was clearly limited, especially since the demand from the rest of the empire was also growing. By the fourth century there cannot have been much land left to bring under cultivation, so the only way of increasing food production would be by more intensive agriculture. For instance, some of the central government's policies were detrimental. Inland of Berytos, for example, some land, especially on the Lebanon Mountains, was converted from arable to grazing land, probably because taxation of arable was much heavier than for grazing land, and herding animals was less labour-intensive.[18]

The villages of the limestone plateaux contain some of the earliest inscriptions relating to Christianity anywhere.[19] This is unusual since it seems that it was in the cities that large-scale conversion to Christianity first occurred. It has led to a theory that the Christians in the villages were in fact refugees from Antioch, or perhaps colonists, though it seems unlikely that Antiochene townees would move out of the city where Christians were generally welcomed to live in a countryside village. The alternative, of course, is that the village populations were converted by missionaries, and this seems the more likely explanation. This conclusion, however, also emphasizes that the conversion of the Syrian population, urban or rural, was a process which took a long time.

The conversion took place during the third and fourth centuries very largely, partly by the personal example of people like Abraham in his pagan Lebanese village, partly by the example of the central government when Constantine had gained control of the whole empire (the east from 324), and partly in the end by force.

A good example of the individual effort is that of Thalaleios at Gabala, a small city between Arados and Laodikeia on the Mediterranean coast. The city, small but neat, had become Christian, but a pagan shrine only a few miles away continued to exist, and the people living in the area continued to sacrifice there. Thalalcios was a monk, originally from Kilikia. He arrived and took up residence in the temenos of the shrine, living in a hut he built himself. There he contended with the local gods, whom he called daimons, of course, which must mean he performed acts which did not bring down on him any censure from the old gods. He was not, curiously, attacked by any of the local pagans, who presumably stood aside and watched the contest, no doubt with attitudes varying from jokey amusement of awe and fear; they must by this time (c. AD 400) have been fairly familiar with Christianity, and the activities of such men as Thalaleios. In the end, of course, Thalaleios won out (for it is only Christian successes which were celebrated), the locals were converted, and the temple overthrown, either physically or by mere abandonment. His success included the destruction of sacred olive grove. The description of this event is too vague to be interpreted rationally, but a storm is implied – that is, Thalaleios interpreted a natural phenomenon as an act of his own god in opposition to the gods of the sanctuary.[20]

This sort of event clearly took place in many areas. Before c.320 it will have been accompanied with much more danger than afterwards, when the government had shifted onto the side of the converters. In the cities even before Constantine's time the Christians probably had numbers on their side; in the country the evangelists were probably able to work in obscurity; and once a village had been converted in total, the fact could well be concealed from the government in times of danger.

Such local alterations culminated in the majority of the Syrian population becoming Christian, but it was a slow process. At the same time the rural political landscape was being changed by these activities. Thalaleios' doomed temple may have been destroyed, or it may merely have been allowed to decay; alternatively it could have been converted, like its local followers, into a Christian church. But, whatever happened, the religious landscape changed.

Several notable cases of temple destruction occurred. It needed a legal justification, fanaticism in both the ecclesiastical and the governmental establishment, and often force, even military force, to accomplish the destruction of an old and staunch building. Bishop Marcellus of Apameia was at first unsuccessful in using troops borrowed from the *Magister Militum per Orientis* to bring down the temple of Zeus in his city; he finally achieved it by employing an artisan from the east, who used his building and chemical skills to destroy the place. On the other hand, when he went out to the destroy temples in the countryside, for which he did not have any legal authority, his unofficial army of retired soldiers and gladiators, and monks was defeated, and he himself was killed in the fighting. His sons attempted to gain legal redress, met with no sympathy.[21]

Temples were powerful centres of pagan resistance to the adoption of Christianity. Zeus at Apameia was brought down because the bishop had law and force on his side, but other temples were simply abandoned. At Baalbek the strength of the pagans could only be thwarted by quasi-military intervention by the governor, a notorious anti-pagan fanatic called Theophilos, as late as 579/580.[22] The temple of Artemis at Gerasa, for example, was still standing at the beginning of the twentieth century AD, though it had been surrounded by several churches before the Arab conquest.[23] The temple of Marnas in Gaza was brought down by Bishop Porphyrios in 402, using very similar methods to those of Marcellus at Apameia, to the annoyance of the Emperor Arcadius, who pointed out that it was a prosperous city which paid its taxes.[24] In many cases the agents of destruction might be monks or hermits – the distinction is not always clear. If a single man was the agent, as Thalaleios in Gabala, the result was probably more acceptable all round than if the bishop used force. In more rural and less obvious cases, the pagan worship seems to have continued until it was absorbed into Christianity or Islam, for example at Caesarea Philippi, whose present name is Banias, a corruption of Pan.[25]

The prevalence of individual actions in the conversions in the Syrian countryside was in part a result of the individuality of the monks themselves. Ascetic rigour was the preferred demonstration of sanctity in Syria, probably based on the local popularity of the *Gospel of Thomas*, an apocryphal work in which much emphasis is laid on such practices. It was at the basis of the development of monasteries in both Egypt and Syria in the second century, but practices in the two regions diverged, so that the Egyptian version consisted largely of organized monasteries, and the Syrian of hermits. In Syria the admiration these men generated encouraged emulation, and innovation in ways of being ascetic – living on pillars, in caves, in ruined forts, wearing iron collars and chains, living on curious diets. These men gathered followers who might plant themselves as a monastery on a permanent basis even while their hermit lived. And, given that asceticism was the preferred local route to sanctity, the preferred location was frequently at the borders of the desert with the sown. Many of the monasteries were built on the very edge of farmed land; in Palestine they were often in inaccessible caves or on cliffs.[26]

The individuality of both monks and monasteries fed into the varieties of Christian beliefs and practices which existed, especially in Syria. This became especially important in the later fifth century when controversies developed between the varieties of Christianity. The monks and hermits were clearly regarded, and regarded themselves, as the shock troops of their sects. In Palestine, for example the founder of the Great Lavra monastery and several others, Sabas, is credited with preserving the land for the Chalcedonian sect by opposing and then converting a member of the imperial family.

All this – monasteries, hermits, conversions and destructions of temples – was the Christianization of the country. The presence of ascetics and then of communities of monks was the start of the process, but it was the action of Constantine I which compelled the process onwards. Having become a Christian himself, he set about ordering the construction of great churches which could compete in architectural terms with the greatest of the temples. His church in Antioch was octagonal, and was called the 'Great Church', and was clearly a distinctive building.[27] At Jerusalem, now to become a Christian city in place of its earlier identity as Aelia Capitolina, the site of the burial of Christ was located at a small cave-shrine of Aphrodite; this was destroyed and the Church of the Holy Sepulchre built in its place.[28] The emperor's mother, Helena, went into Palestine to identify sites of biblical and Christian significance, and in the next century these became the sites of commemorative churches. The example of the royal archaeologist stimulated pilgrimages to visit such places, from Sinai to Edessa, pilgrims arriving from all over the Mediterranean.[29]

This was hardly a coordinated development, any more than was the monastic movement. In fact one might suggest that this was as typical a development in Syria as the tendency to break up into independent states whenever the pressure of an outside government was relaxed and disappeared. The fragmentation of Christian effort was thus a normal Syrian development just as was the appearance of independent states after the Seleukid collapse. It would happen again.

There were, of course, also several varieties of Christianity in vogue in Syria, but unlike in Egypt or North Africa there was not a countrywide reaction against outside pressure, or an insistence on uniformity or orthodoxy. But in the end there were the two main varieties of Christianity which contended in Syria. The Monophysite version captured the north Syrian countryside in part by using the local language, a development of Aramaic called Syriac, which had first been written down in Edessa in the early third century. The holy men who emerged in the Syrian countryside when Christianity spread became intermediaries in village disputes and between villagers and villages in disputes with the governing authorities. The monks could be used to enforce episcopal authority, or to terrorize the surviving pagans into converting, or to defy the ecclesiastical authorities, depending on individual belief and the general context. Conversion was a patchy process, and the most resistance came from the great temples. Baalbek was a strong hold out, for example. In the end, once the government of Emperor Theodosios I pronounced an end to toleration it became possible to physically destroy the temples, and men such as Marcellus of Apameia and Porphyrios of Gaza took advantage.

Syria in the fourth to the sixth century was therefore a disturbed and complex society, with enough antagonisms to occupy the attentions of many holy men. The major one was between the Christian sects, the government and the cities adhering to the Chalcedonian interpretation which was announced after long sessions of discussion between several hundred bishops in 451, as against the Monophysite interpretation which had been defeated at Chalcedon, but only there. This gained adherents in both Egypt and Syria, but especially in the countryside; it was thus to a large extent, but not exclusively, a division between Syrians and Greeks. It was clearly only in part a religious disagreement; it was as much an expression of detestation for the imperial government itself.

The tensions in Syrian society therefore had originally been between pagans and Christians and later were between Christian sects, but all the time they were also between Syrians and Greeks, and between the cities and the countryside. All this was typical Syrian internal division. But so long as the government was able to collect its taxes, put down any peasant risings, and make efforts, generally inadequate and unsuccessful, to suppress the endemic banditry, the tensions were unlikely to become serious enough to amount to a full rebellion or a civil war, but they existed all the same. The government, for example, made no serious attempt to suppress the Monophysites, since they were far too numerous. The holy men who intervened to solve disputes were valued by all sides, since they acted to relieve the internal societal tensions. The government knew very well that these men, many of whom were originally from the landowning class, were useful in oiling the wheels of control. Some had direct access to the royal family in Constantinople.

There were still other tensions. The overall expansion in the population was not confined to Christians. The numbers of Jews, Samaritans, and Arabs also grew, and this was probably one of the sources of tensions in Palestine between Jews and Samaritans, and between Samaritans and Greeks. The population of the city of Caesarea was divided between the three groups. It was also the government centre for Palestine. Three times between 484 and 555 the Samaritans of Caesarea staged risings. One possible cause is likely to have been the construction of a great new church on top of the Samaritans' temple on Mount Gerizim, but there were many tensions within the city, including a slow economic decline typified by the gradual silting up of the harbour.[30]

The Arab tribes and clans of the Syrian Desert were converted to Christianity during the fourth century, with some having adopted the faith even earlier. The connections and communications between the settled lands and the desert were evidently easy, and the Arabs appear to have followed the Syrians of the countryside into the Monophysite camp; they also spread slowly and almost tentatively into the settled lands.[31]

There was therefore any number of possible causes of internal conflict in Syria by the beginning of the sixth century. To this was added a new round of Persian wars beginning in 502. The Sassanid king, Khavad, king from 499, was affronted when the Emperor Anastasius refused him a subsidy to be used to fend off another enemy. The war which followed centred in Mesopotamia, where Khavad captured the fortress city of Amida. Difficulties elsewhere compelled Khavad to make peace in 506, returning all his conquests in return for a subsidy.[32] The emperor had learned his lesson though, and more up to date fortifications were built along the frontier in the subsequent period of peace. The development of a major fortified city at Dara-Theodosiopolis, fairly close to the mutual boundary contributed particularly to Sassanid annoyance, but the peace held for twenty years.[33]

Another war, essentially fought along the frontier, happened between 526 and 532, ending once again in a compromise of peace once both rulers had died, both sides returning from their conquests. The peace was called the 'eternal peace',[34] and so – naturally – it lasted only a few years. The two new rulers, Khusro I in Persia from 531 and Emperor Justinian I in Constantinople from 527, were both ambitious, both capable, and these qualities almost guaranteed more conflict. Justinian's successes in recovering control of North Africa and Italy understandably were of concern to Khusro – and provided him with a new opportunity.

The Sassanid ally, the Arabian kingdom of the Lakhmids, had grown in power and was capable of raiding the whole of the Syrian Arabian frontier, apparently at will, and did so even during periods of official peace. The Lakhmid king in the first half of the sixth century, al-Mundhir, was unusually loyal to the Sassanids and the Syrian frontier more than usually harried.[35] During the new war which had begun in 526, Justinian had organized his own Arab kingdom, under al-Harith V, usually called the Ghassanid or Jafnid state.

Al-Harith was promoted to the status of patrician, and assigned to defend the desert frontier. His position gave him an equal status and authority with the governor, but the succession of kings maintained their headquarters at Jabiya, north-west of Bostra, which rendered them largely independent of any other Roman official. The kingdom included all the Arab clans and tribes along the Syrian frontier as far south as the Red Sea, all of whom had presumably been subject to the Lakhmid raids. These were now able to indulge themselves in revenge raids.[36]

Justinian also spent lavishly on the fortification and embellishment of many of the cities in Syria. Antioch's rebuilding after the earthquakes of the 520s was funded by imperial money, and at Apameia more buildings were constructed. At Bostra a considerable area of the city was rebuilt at this time, not all funded by the empire, but several major buildings were paid for, and the city walls were certainly paid for by the emperor; a smaller contribution came from the archbishop.

The apparent increase in Roman power from the reconquest of large parts of the west was accompanied by a realization on the Persian side that the Roman concentration on this work had left the eastern Roman defences less than fully manned. In 540 Shapur II took advantage of this situation and launched a surprise attack. He carefully avoided the earlier strategy of attacking in either Armenia or Mesopotamia, and by leaving untaken the fortresses in Mesopotamia and Osrhoene and marching along the southern bank of the Euphrates he took the Romans unawares. This was, of course, a repetition of the strategy followed in 252 by his predecessor and namesake Shapur I, probably a conscious and deliberate reprise. The result was much the same: he bypassed the Roman frontier fortress of Circesium at the junction of the Khabour and the Euphrates, then took, ransomed but then sacked Sura (the Euphrates terminus of Diocletian's fort-line), ransomed the cities of Hierapolis and Beroia, less well-defended than the trans-Euphratean fortresses, and then the Persian army reached and laid siege to Antioch.

There was confusion in the city, with competing plans and competing authorities pursuing contradictory policies as the Persians inexorably came closer. The emperor promised reinforcements, which did not arrive until the last minute. The Persian approach was relatively slow, allowing large numbers of people to leave the city before they arrived, but it was still well-populated when the siege began and to begin with it was defended by a combination of regular forces and the city militia. But the atmosphere was uncertain, and the previous disagreements between the authorities had sapped morale. It took just one accident during the defence to cause panic. The regular forces pulled out through a gate deliberately left available by the Persians.[37]

The city thus fell very quickly and the Persian army then sacked and burned most of it. Those inhabitants they could catch were taken captive – it seems that large numbers had already left the city before the capture. Khusro tried to sell back the captives when he got to Edessa, but the city, despite having raised a large sum of money for the ransom, was forbidden to pay it over; so Khusro took the captives off to settle them in places in Babylonia and Iran, which he ostentatiously named for himself.[38]

Other cities were captured or ransomed, including Apameia – another echo of Shapur's campaign in 252 – and Edessa. The whole disaster was clearly due to

Roman imperial overstretch, for even though Justinian's generals had conquered Africa and Italy with relatively small forces he had taken them from the eastern frontier, and then had failed to ensure that the Persians were neutralized.

Antioch had had a bad time in the recent past, and this sack and burning was almost the final blow. The city had been damaged by several severe earthquakes: a bad one in 478 had been followed by two more in 526 (after a bad fire in the previous year) and 528, and another minor one in 531.[39] The sack of the city in 540 was followed, as with the others, by a major rebuilding effort financed by the imperial government. This is described in some detail by the contemporary historian Procopius of Caesarea. His account makes it clear that the city was now reduced in size, by at least a quarter and perhaps more, by the abandonment of the island in the Orontes which had been the palace area and by the failure of many of those who had fled to return – not to mention the captives who had been removed.[40]

What probably had as much influence on the reduction in the size of the city as the damage it had suffered, was that two years after the sack and the kidnapping of the majority of the population, the city, and indeed the whole empire, was struck by a severe plague. It was probably bubonic plague, according to the symptoms described by the historians Procopius and Evagrius, the latter of whom had survived an attack as a boy. It arrived from Ethiopia by way of the Nile Valley and the Red Sea – it is thought to have been first noted at Pelusion in Egypt – and spread from Egypt to the rest of the empire and beyond. It reached Britain within a few years. In Antioch it is said that two out of every four or five inhabitants died. These were people who had returned to the city after having fled the siege, and men who had been drafted in to help in the process of rebuilding.[41]

This will have set back any work on rebuilding, and still further disasters were in store. Earthquakes struck in 551, and again in 557; another outbreak of plague came in 560. The city walls, which had survived the Persian attack, were badly damaged in the 557 earthquake, and were still unrepaired in the 570s.[42] All this rather suggests that Procopius' account of the rebuilding of the city was more in the nature of an aspiration than an accomplishment.

The general situation cannot have been helped by the final disruption of the church at this period. It had proved impossible to bridge the divide between the Chalcedonian and Monophysite sects. Antioch, as the birthplace of the Monophysite intellectual Severus, and as a decisive ecclesiastical centre, was at the heart of the dispute. During the reign of Justinian the Monophysites gradually inserted their own bishops and metropolitans into many dioceses, and eventually into the patriarchate of Antioch. Thus the church developed two hierarchies, and the Monophysites placed their men where they had congregations. By the end of the century there were in effect two churches.[43]

The change which had taken over Syria in the period between Diocletian and Justinian was therefore more socially profound that any other period in the country's history since the destructions of the Assyrian and Babylonian times. It had become a Christian country, if of a particular sort – but in being different it was in fact typical – but it had also recoiled even more than before from the authority of the imperium. It would be very difficult in the late sixth century to believe that this was a loyal province of the Roman Empire. On the other hand there was no evidence that the country was hoping for a rescuer to come along and expel the Roman power and take over. During the siege of Antioch in 540, King Khusro put forward as his negotiator a man called Paulus, an Antiochene who had defected to Persia. Whether this was intended as a conciliatory gesture or an insult, the Antiochenes took it as an insult, and eventually shot him. Antioch may not be typical of all Syria, but it seems probable that their reaction to the defector would have been approved by most other Syrians.

Chapter 15

Twice Conquered

The heady rise of Syria between 300 BC and 280 BC, from a conquered and devastated land to a country of cities and a new population was unique in its day, and scarcely ever repeated since. The reverse process, from prosperity to destruction, was always much easier to accomplish. However, Syria was to go through the upward process again, between AD 600 and AD 661 – a longer period than the first, and starting from a higher base, but the country did go through two destructive conquests in those years, only to end as the centre of the world, the ruler of an even greater empire than Rome. The conquests have to be considered first.

The successive disasters which laid Antioch low in the sixth century were not as destructive to the rest of Syria. Many of the earthquakes, that of 551 in particular, were very extensive, but it seems that Antioch was the worst hit. The plague was just as selective in its killing spree – Epiphaneia-Hama, for example, appears to have largely escaped both onslaughts. On the other hand, the plague recurred at irregular intervals, and those communities which escaped one attack were likely to suffer in another.

And there was the Persian War. The withdrawal of the Sassanid armies from Syria in 540 was followed by a long series of wars which happened intermittently for the next century. Generally the fighting was confined to the empires' mutual borders in Mesopotamia and Armenia, but the periods of open war were succeeded by periods of pseudo-peace, or even in one case by an armistice in one region and continued fighting in another. The intervals between wars were occupied by both sides with intrigues in search of allies or clients. The range of intrigues spread from the Turks of central Asia to the kingdom of Ethiopia to the wars in Italy.[1]

After the disaster of 540, Syria was clearly constantly menaced. Another Persian raid broke through in 573 and caused much damage. The invaders stopped short of taking Antioch again but took and sacked Apameia, burning the city and carrying off the whole population.[2] The two greatest cities in north Syria were thus both wrecked and depopulated, and did not recover. Dara, the most detested Roman frontier fortress by the Persians, was taken and then the Persian raid had used the old surprise route along the Euphrates to avoid the Syrian Euphrates crossing. The next period of peace was followed by a serious tightening up of discipline in the Roman army, so that the next war was much more evenly fought. Roman successes were also due to the general in command, Maurice, who succeeded as emperor in 582.

Maurice had been betrayed in one campaign by his ally al-Harith of the Ghassanids, and when he became emperor he exiled his betrayer. This, needless to say, caused further trouble amongst the Ghassanids, who rose in rebellion, and laid siege to Bostra where the accumulated Ghassanid treasure had been deposited in supposedly safe keeping. Once the city handed the treasure over and the emperor had installed al-Harith's son as king, the siege was abandoned, but much of the local countryside had suffered from the Arabs' negative attentions. Al-Harith's son al-Numar was no more loyal to the emperor than his father and he was also exiled; the kingdom then broke up into its constituent clans, some of whom, however, did continue as Roman allies.[3]

The Persian War which began in 572 continued until 590, in part because when Khusro I died in 579 his son Hormizd IV decided that he would abandon the peace talks which had begun, and continued the war all through his reign, though less successfully and less competently. For once some details of the effects on Syria can be detected in the story of the fighting. The Emperor Maurice had considerable trouble finding competent commanders, and his financial resources were apparently dwindling, in fact as a result of the current warfare. He resorted to reducing the pay of the soldiers; as surely everyone expected, this produced a mutiny in the army in Mesopotamia. The soldiers elected their own general, choosing a man called Germanus, who was already a military commander in Phoenicia. The soldiers' action is particularly interesting in that at almost any other time they would have made Germanus a usurping emperor. Instead Maurice accepted Germanus as commander, and he used the mutinous army to defeat a Persian army which had taken advantage of the confusion to score a success; the booty collected was used to pay the soldiers.[4]

The crisis brought everyone of authority into play. Germanus was clearly quite prepared to take command at the soldiers' behest, but was also at the same time loyal to Maurice and Maurice evidently understood that. The soldiers' action was actually more a strike than a rebellion. The patriarch of Antioch, Gregory, was an effective intermediary, and was clearly in a position of both secular and religious authority in his city, and was in charge of the logistic system of supplying the army, which gave him the necessary power in his role as intermediary.[5] (Similarly, at Apameia in the crises of 540 and 573, it was also the bishop who appears to have been in charge, and who negotiated with the Persian king or commander; no suggestion exists of any secular government.)

A not dissimilar crisis struck the Sassanid Empire not long after, in 590. A successful general, Barham Corbin, suffered a defeat and King Hormizd dismissed him. His army followed the general into rebellion and other disenchanted groups joined in. Hormizd was deposed and blinded, and Barham became king. However,

Hormizd's son Khusro escaped to Roman territory. He offered Maurice a restoration of conquests along their mutual boundary if the Roman would support Khurso's restoration to the kingship. Maurice surprisingly agreed, and Barham was defeated. Khusro kept his bargain, and for a decade the frontier of the two empires saw peace.[6]

The archaeological evidence from the country districts of Syria, and indeed from the great cities, indicates that the expansion of population and settlement had more or less come to an end by about 550. The exact population of any part of Syria is, of course, unknown for this period, but in the villages of the limestone plateaux of the north, and in the Hawran the expansion can be seen in the steady increase in the number of rooms in each house, where extra rooms were added as the extended family grew. This suggests that the population in these areas had expanded by a multiple of four between c.350 and c.550.[7]

The cessation of the expansion from c.550 can be accounted for in part by the damage done to the cities by the Persian invasions, but perhaps even more and by the plague which swept through the country in 541–542.[8] It is not known how badly the villages were affected by either of these events, but there seems to be little destruction which can be attributed to the Persians – unlike in the cities, which have been more widely excavated. But the cities, both in Syria and beyond, had been the markets for the surplus produce of the villages, and the drastic reduction in the urban populations obviously reduced the demand for those goods.

This was especially the case where the Persians had enslaved and removed the cities' populations, as they had at Antioch and Seleukeia, and perhaps other cities. Just who was taken is not clear, but those who were still in the cities when they were captured were removed, while others had removed themselves beforehand, and of these some will not have returned. Khusro I then visited Seleukeia-in-Pieria which may have been deserted by then.[9] In Apameia and in Antioch the great palatial villas in both cities which have been excavated show abandonment at the time of the Persian conquests and destructions. Furthermore these great buildings were not reoccupied to anything like the same extent, and probably not by the original owners after the Persians left.[10] The middle and upper classes of the cities will have been a major part of the market for the village produce, and when they vanished or fled or were transported, the villages were left without a place to sell their goods, or at least with a much diminished market.

The reaction in the villages was a cessation of new building in many areas. Gradually, without a market, they became impoverished. In the cities the abandoned houses of the rich were occupied by peasants, probably immigrants from the countryside. They were divided among several, even many, families, who stabled their animals in the courts, and lived in a few rooms which were walled off. The great churches kept going, but repairs were badly done, and the part of the buildings used for worship was reduced. Cemeteries encroached on the collapsed sections.[11]

The whole of Syrian society was clearly much weakened by the experiences of these disastrous decades. But it seems probable that the most serious effects were felt by just one section of the population. The most profound division in the society was between the Monophysites, who were mainly concentrated in the countryside, and the followers of the Chalcedonian rite, also called Melkites, the official imperial Church, whose adherents tended to be concentrated in the cities. This city–country division of the sects was not complete, but the power of the imperial government could be most effectively exercised in the cities, and this had kept those places loyal to the official Church. In much of Palestine the countryside was Melkite, but Monophysitism was hardly unknown. The development of a parallel hierarchy among the Monophysites after the failure of Justinian's regime to reconcile the two groups hardened the division.

The persecution of the Monophysites in the 520s had removed many of the priests of that rite, and their scarcity pushed the members to insist that bishops loyal to them be created. Their leader was Severus of Antioch, who had already used the idea of roving bishops to service isolated congregations; now another, John of Tella, arranged new ordinations, and found the response overwhelming. The twists and turns of imperial policy drove the two groups apart. In the end two Monophysite bishops were created: Theodore for Bostra, where he ministered to the Ghassanids, and James Bar'adai, who had a wider commission over much of Asia Minor and Syria, and travelled about in secret ordaining and consecrating. He it was who in effect created a separate Monophysite Church with its own hierarchy. (After him, it is sometimes called 'Jacobite'.[12]) This division was exploited by the Persians as early as the invasion of 540, and was a constant factor in the Persian Wars ever after, and in the Arab invasions which followed.

The Emperor Maurice was brought down by his soldierly arrogance. The mutiny in Mesopotamia had been overcome; in the Balkans another mutiny, occasioned by unreasonable imperial orders to campaign, without supplies, in the dead of winter, resulted in the proclamation of a new emperor, a centurion called Phokas. But Phokas was both violent and incompetent as a ruler, and was widely seen as illegitimate both inside and outside the empire. In particular, before he died Maurice had appealed to King Khusro II, for help, to return the favour Khusro had earlier received in his own fight for the throne. Most of Maurice's family died in the putsch in Constantinople, but it was believed that his eldest son Theodosios had escaped to Persia. Khusro seized on this, and responded to an appeal for help from Narses, the Roman commander in Mesopotamia, who came out for Theodosios.

The result was a slow Persian conquest of the Mesopotamian fortresses, while Phokas instituted a reign of executions in the capital; one of his victims was Narses.

Dara fell in 604, and Edessa in 609, and meanwhile Asia Minor was opened up for invasion by campaigns led by Theodosios (or a pseudo-Theodosios).[13] Khusro's ultimate ambition is suggested by a change he organized in the alliance with the Lakhmid Arabs of the Syrian Desert. Taking a leaf, perhaps, out of the Roman book he deposed and killed al-Numan, the current Lakhmid king, in 602. This, needless to say, angered the Arabs, who gathered a force and eventually defeated a Sassanid army at the Battle of Dhu Qar in 604. This had no obvious effect on the Sassanid arrangements, which involved breaking up the Lakhmid kingdom and in its place organizing four or five Arab regions, strung from the mouth of Tigris-Euphrates eventually round to the Gulf of Aqaba. Each of these was effectively a subject kingdom.

The point here is that this was a comprehensive system based on the concept of Persian control of the whole of the Fertile Crescent, which Khusro had by no means gained when he initiated the change, and did not achieve until several years after the new system was begun. It is possible that he was achieving more than one aim in this. One aim would be to cut down the Lakhmid kingdom, which, like the Ghassanid kingdom on the Roman side, had perhaps grown too powerful and perhaps too independent for Sassanid tastes – a later tradition had it that al-Numan had betrayed Khusro, which sounds like an adaptation of the Roman problem with al-Mundhir. The other aim, if it was intended from the start to be a comprehensive desert-wide system, implies that Khusro from the beginning of the war with Phokas was intent on destroying the Roman Empire and on putting a Sassanid empire in its place.

Having gained control of Mesopotamia, Khusro was able to launch a new strategic move, invading both Syria and Asia Minor along both sides of the Taurus Mountains. Asia Minor was vulnerable once the frontier fortresses had been captured (by Theodosios), in 611, and meanwhile so was Syria. Khusro was so confident of the weakness of Roman defences that he could afford to send armies against both regions. Meanwhile Phokas was challenged by the exarch of Africa, Heraklios, who seized Egypt in 609 and then Cyprus, and finally sent his fleet into the Sea of Marmara; Phokas was murdered in October 610.[14]

By then Antioch and Apameia had both fallen to the Persian army.[15] Then the conquest of Syria stalled, perhaps because the Roman forces in Asia Minor were able to retake some of the lost lands. By now Khusro's policy had turned into a clear intention to conquer. It had been a longstanding ambition of the Sassanid Dynasty, if vague and scarcely realizable, to recreate the ancient Akhaimenid Empire. For the first time the collapse of the Roman Empire now made it seem a reasonable ambition. As the Persian army occupied north Syria from 611 onwards (and Mesopotamia from before that) the possibilities will have become clear. The Persian invasion this time became an occupation, whereas the earlier attacks had been mere raids.

There had been riots – the 'Levantine riots' – in Berytus in 607–608, in Alexandria in 608–610, and in Antioch in 610 – between Christians and Jews and Christians and Christians; one of Phokas' generals, Bonosos, was sent to put the trouble down in the normal Roman brutal fashion, but it was ominous that the trouble was between these communities, for both were, thanks to the prosperity and the growth of population, unusually numerous. At Antioch the (Chalcedonian) patriarch died in the riots and was not replaced for nearly four decades.[16] It was well known that Samaritans had rebelled in Palestine in the last century. The divisions, a combination of theology and class war, which existed between various sets of Christians in Syria and elsewhere were also well known. A pitch by Khusro for local support against the imperial government was almost certain to bring a response, so long as it was clear that the Persians were not about to leave, as before. In 613 Heraklios campaigned into north Syria in an attempt to recover Antioch, and so push the Persians back into Mesopotamia. With a Roman army present in north Syria, any conquests south of Antioch would have to be evacuated.

The Roman army marched as far as Antioch, commanded by the emperor in person, but was there defeated. It was then pursued into Kilikia and defeated again at the mouth of the Kilikian Gates.[17] This was the crucial military event which opened the way for the following Persian successes. The Persians now controlled the communications between Asia Minor and Syria, and with one Persian army operating in Asia Minor, it was no longer possible for Heraklios to send military help into Syria.

Accordingly, the Persian forces in north Syria, under the command of the general, Shahrvaraz, pushed south as soon as the control of Kilikia was assured. The Roman forces steadily retreated, commanded by Heraklios' cousin Niketas. Emesa was taken in 613, and a major battle was fought near the city.[18] It was regarded as a Roman victory, with heavy casualties on both sides, but the Persians were able to continue their advance, taking Damascus in the same year. Palestine was invaded in 614 and another battle had to be fought at Adraa, which resisted, unusually, but was garrisoned by a major Roman force.[19] The two government centres of the Palestinian provinces, Caesarea and Tiberias, were captured. Many of the towns of both Syria and Palestine were able to negotiate their surrender, no doubt paying a ransom for the privilege. Jerusalem, however, resisted and was stormed, with several thousands of dead.[20] The city was looted and the surviving Christian population was taken into exile and the city was burned.

In other words, the Persians treated Jerusalem in exactly the same way as they had treated Antioch and Apameia in the past, and no one should have been surprised, though the Christian sources express the usual outrage. From the Persian point of view, however, the operation was a success; there is no sign of any more trouble in Palestine from the Christians – or the Jews, for that matter – during their occupation. The city was so treated because it had initially surrendered, but the men Shahrvaraz sent to govern it were killed by 'young men of the city' – the semi-militias who supported the chariot teams in the games – so Shahrvaraz clearly thought it merited condign punishment. Niketas retreated to Egypt and attempted to gather funds and soldiers for a counter-attack.

So far the Persians had scarcely bothered to intervene in the religious and societal affairs of Syria. They probably favoured the Monophysites, if anyone, for the imperialist Chalcedonians were definitely hostile, yet the former had not come out in clear support, probably because so far the Persian presence did not seem permanent, and the prospect of a Roman return was strong. After 614, however, this was not so, and in Palestine the situation was rather different. There was a powerful Jewish presence in the region, and a less numerous but equally disaffected Samaritan group. This was one of the reasons the Chalcedonians had been successful in the inter-Christian struggle in this area, whereas in the north of Syria the Monophysites had been able to dispute the control of much of the land with success. In Palestine the Christians needed to remain close to the Roman government as protection.

There had, of course, already been major troubles between Christians and Jews in several cities. In Antioch this had resulted in the death of the Chalcedonian patriarch, blamed in one source on the Jews, and of course, the internal disputes had assisted in the Persian capture of the city, and Jews had been blamed in rumours for having betrayed some places, Jerusalem included, to the invaders.[21] The danger of such disputes in Palestine seems to have convinced many to submit more or less readily to the Persian occupation. The Persian commander Shahrbaraz made his headquarters at Caesarea, the Roman government centre, an indication of intended permanence, and sent officials to secure compliance throughout the land. This is an assumption, but he certainly sent officials to govern Jerusalem when the city eventually surrendered, and a few years later it was possible for Armenian pilgrims to visit Mount Sinai without any problems, which implies a Persian arrangement with the possibly hostile and predatory Bedouin of the Sinai Peninsula.[22]

The Persians, however, certainly acted against the Chalcedonians, who were clearly suspected because they were necessarily imperialist supporters. The monastery of Mar Sabas, the Great Lavra, was sacked, perhaps because the monks resisted, and, it is said, the monks were killed – 'massacred'.[23] This is one instance of what may well have been a fairly widespread hostility developing between Chalcedonians and Persians – after all, the Chalcedonians were the religious party of the imperial authorities, and could be expected to be hostile, even if submissive.

When the Persian forces invaded and conquered Egypt in 617–620, Syria's participation in the war virtually ended. The eventual victory of Heraklios was achieved by campaigns in Armenia and into Babylonia, so that the end for Syria was the evacuation of the Persian forces; the major celebration appears to have been the restoration of the 'True Cross' to Jerusalem, carried ceremonially all the way through Syria in the process. The effects of the episode, which lasted in north Syria for almost two full decades and nearly a decade and a half in Palestine, are difficult to estimate. The only source for such estimation is archaeology, but little has been discerned, in part because of the lack of dating evidence for the period. This is in itself a pointer, since the earlier activity in building suddenly stopped. The building of new churches, and their decoration – the style was dated mosaics at this time – more or less ended. This was probably because the source of finance for such ventures dried up. The absence of the wealthy classes, most of whom seem to have fled, or to have been killed or exiled, would be decisive, as would the effective suppression of the activities of the Chalcedonian Church, and the absence of finance from the imperial government. Similarly the Persian occupation probably effectively suspended overseas trade, and this contributed to the general impoverishment.

There are signs of the upper and middle class evacuation, or at least absence, in the occupation of the large and originally luxurious villas in Apameia and Antioch by squatters, either from the country, or from poorer parts of the cities. The decisive change, however, is that this lower class appropriation of the villas continued after the end of the Persian occupation–that is, those who had fled or been driven out did not return.[24] At Jerusalem the destruction of the former Christian population was followed by the re-imposition by the Persians of the former Roman regulations restricting the Jewish presence in that city, so the city remained largely reduced, even impoverished.[25]

The Persian governing system was simply a continuation of the Roman system, often with the same officials where they had stayed in post.[26] But the original officials must have largely had to be replaced during the long Persian occupation, and it is not clear who took their places. It is probable that the government channels of communication broke down and authority devolved on to the city councils, which were unused by this time to actual government work. Where they existed also, bishops will have assumed authority, as they already had at several places before the Persian conquest. Other Romans, who might well then have suffered the fate of collaborators when the Roman government returned after 630. However things were managed there was obviously much disruption. The Persians' Zoroastrian religion was not imposed, and in fact its practice was kept very quiet and discreet.

The defeat of the Persian forces by Heraklios in his invasion of the Persian kingdom was followed by the collapse of the Sassanid governing system, beginning with the deposition and murder of King Khusro. A series of brief and ineffectual kings and queens followed (including Shahrvaraz, whose reign lasted for six weeks), and meanwhile Heraklios oversaw the evacuation of Sassanid forces from their conquered territory and began a short period of reconstruction. There were many refugees, mainly Christians fleeing from Persia, but some went the other way as well. Within Syria and Mesopotamia there were Christian anti-Jewish outbreaks and riots, notably at Edessa, where the Jews of the city continued to defy the Romans even after the Persian troops had been persuaded to leave.[27] Heraklios attempted to develop a reconciliation among the several Christian sects, without success, and contributed to the confusion by developing his own version, Monotheletism, rejected by all the rest.

The emperor spent much of the time between 629 and 632 in Syria and Mesopotamia. His first headquarters was at Hierapolis/Bambyke, which had graduated from a centre of the worship of Atargatis to a Monophysite town – opposed in both guises to the Greek-speaking Roman Empire.[28] At other times he stayed in Antioch, where he found that the only patriarch was a Monophysite (the Calcedonian patriarch had not yet been replaced), who was cunning enough to agree with the emperor on religious matters in conversation, but to include a sabotaging item in the small print when he was pressed to provide a written confession of faith. When this failed, and the emperor was humiliated by a group of Monophysite bishops, he deprived them of the Great Church of Edessa in punishment.[29]

But Heraklios' most spectacular action was to receive the True Cross from its Persian captivity and return it to Jerusalem. He made this into a spectacular journey through Syria and Palestine, and paid for the restoration of some of the ruined buildings in Jerusalem into the bargain.[30] But when the patriarchal seat had to be refilled – the former patriarch had died in Persian captivity – the elected candidate was a monk called Sophronios, who used his position to criticize imperial policy.[31]

Even as Heraklios was visiting Jerusalem to return the Cross the first raid by a Muslim Arab force had reached the southern part of the Arabian province. It was led by a son-in-law of the Prophet Muhammad, and suffered a defeat at a place called Mu'ta.[32] There is no indication that the Roman authorities understood that this was a different raid from the usual ones by Arabs from the desert, and there is a story that the army was attacked by the local people on its way north. Next year, however, Muhammad himself came north with a force to Tabuk oasis and there established his authority over a region which included the town of Aqaba at the head of the Red Sea, and several dependent towns and villages to north and south.[33] This development cannot have been unknown to the Roman governors in Palestine.

It is probable that the Roman and Sassanid governments had known something of what had been going on in Arabia in the last years, though they had scarcely had time or energy to pay any serious attention to the events. But by 632 Muhammad had succeeded in uniting most of the Arabian Peninsula into a single state, and one which was aggressive and greedy for conquests, as the early raids into the south had suggested. This unification, of course, had involved suppressing the endemic raiding which had kept many of the men of the tribes and clans occupied, but it also required that those raiding energies be directed elsewhere. The direction of expansion was obviously to the north. Arabia had long been in close contact with both of the great empires, as a trading partner above all, but also as a land where there were both Christians and Jews, and plainly the Arabs had been converted to these religions. A substantial element of the Syrian and Iraqi population was Arab, which made both countries prime evangelization territory for the new religion Muhammad had developed. Like every other religion in the region, he was fully prepared to use force to spread the word.

The death of Muhammad in 632 delayed the attempt at conquest only briefly. His successor, the first caliph, Abu Bakr, succeeded in reuniting the Arabian kingdom he had created, and in 634 armies were sent north, one to attack Syria, the other to invade Iraq. The two empires were not prepared for this new crisis, despite the earlier attacks and warnings. The hard-won Roman victory over Persia was expensive in wealth and manpower, and an austerity drive was on, which had involved the demobilization of many of the soldiers.[34]

The Sassanid Empire was, of course, even less prepared, and the Arab army under Khalid ibn al-Walid succeeded in capturing the old Lakhmid centre of al-Hira after a campaign in which several small Sassanid detachments were defeated; al-Hira was surrendered by the Arab elite who seem to have still ruled the city.[35] On both sides of the Syrian Desert there were Arab tribes and clans who were faced with the decision as to who to support, their old ally or their new ethnic brothers. After the destruction of the Lakhmid state by King Khusro, his reorganization of the desert frontier had, of course, been in part designed to cope with attacks such as these new Muslim armies were making, but the Sassanid defeat had brought down Khusro's new system as well as the old one. On the Roman side, there were several Arab groups, some loyal to the empire, others who joined the invaders. The confusion made it even more difficult to cope than usual.

The military reoccupation of the Palestinian and Arabian provinces had scarcely begun. The priority for Heraklios had been to watch events in Persia, which had descended into a confusion of its own, and to attempt to reconcile the various Christian sects. The size of the army at his disposal was much reduced, partly by the losses in the fighting, and partly because his empire had been reduced to little more than Asia Minor, and partly by demobilization to save money. Much of the Balkans had been lost, and the fragments of the empire in the west were virtually independent – when he demanded that troops be sent from Africa to assist in the war against the Muslim armies, he was refused. His journey to Jerusalem was accompanied by a mobile force which ensured that he was not embarrassed by raids or attacks on the way (though the raid to Mu'ta happened at about the same time). Most of these troops will have returned north with him after the delivery of the remains of the cross to the city.[36] The desert forts were perhaps largely ungarrisoned for the moment, though there were certainly some troops at Mu'ta, probably Arabs recently moved there; The Arabs passed through Ma'an without a fight, so that town was clearly without any garrison.

The Muslim attacks into Syria therefore came from a direction which the Romans did not expect, but they also came in a way which led the victims to assume that they were at first not too serious. It would be difficult for Christians who were preoccupied with inter-sect discussions, arguments, and distractions, to conceive that a new and vigorous religion had emerged from the desert of Arabia. Indeed there is some indication that it was assumed at first that the raiders were dissident Jews, for the conflict between Christians and Jews in Syria had now been going on for a generation – at Antioch, Berytos, Alexandria, and Jerusalem – and the latest manifestation had been the Jewish defiance of imperial authority at Edessa.

It was not long, of course, before these misconceptions and military mistakes were corrected, but the early invasion by the Muslims still partook of the nature of raids. No less than four armies, each under a separate commander, were sent into Palestine. One, commanded by Amr ibn al-As, headed for Gaza by way of Aqaba (already in Muslim hands) along the normal trade route from Arabia to the sea. Amr held discussions with the local Roman commander, and then fell into a fight at a village called Dathin. The Muslims were victorious, but the wider results were small, just as was the actual fight.

The other three armies operated east of the Jordan. Yazid ibn Abu Sufyan's force went into the Balka, the plateau between the Wade Zarqa and Wadi Mujib, centred on Philadelphia-Amman; Abu Ubayda ibn al-Jarrah is credited with the capture of Areopolis, Ma'ab, south of Amman, where a Roman force had collected, then rode further north, and is known to have operated in the Golan area east of the Sea of Galilee, which is the area where the Gassanids had their capital-camp, at Jabiya. The area of the third army, that of Shurahbil ibn Hasana, is not known, but the land south of the Wadi Mujib (in present-day southern Jordan) is possible. None of these armies scored any serious military successes, but it is likely that the main aim was diplomatic, as with Amr at Gaza, hoping to recruit among the Arab clans who inhabited the land east of Jordan. It is probable that they succeeded. A force under the governor of Palestina I, Sergius, was driven off, but no towns or cities, apart from Areopolis, were taken.[37]

These were the regions where the invaders would find Arabs already living. The clear intention was to gather local allies. The routes of the invaders were also those of the traditional trading routes from Mecca and southern Arabia into the Mediterranean regions. The people of the places which had surrendered to the Muslims, from Tabuk to Ma'ab, had been granted lenient terms, which eventually were resolved into permission to stay where they were, practice their own religion, and pay a poll tax; these terms also imply permission to leave.

The Roman force defeated at Dathin was a large part of the Roman garrison of Gaza, reinforced from other nearby cities, and the result of the Roman defeat was to allow Amr's forces to raid over much of southern Palestine, supposedly as far as the approaches to Caesarea and Jerusalem. This demonstrated to the Roman government the seriousness of the situation (if the raids east of Jordan had not already done so). An army of a substantial size was gathered, based originally at Emesa, which appears to have been the main Roman military and logistics base. It was put under the command of the military commander at Emesa, an Armenian called Wardan, and the emperor's brother Theodore.[38]

Meanwhile, the Arab forces east of the Jordan collected together to attack the city of Bostra. (The connection of Bostra with earlier Arab forces, particularly the Ghassanids, was probably part of the Arabs' reasoning.) The forces of Abu Ubayda, Yazid, and Shurahbil had focused on the city. They were joined by a small force commanded by Khalid ibn al-Walid, who had been instructed by the caliph, Abu Bakr, to go from Iraq to assist in Syria, after the Syrian commanders had asked for reinforcements. The order resulted in an epic ride across the Syrian Desert, an episode which captivated the chroniclers, but whose route and timing is not clear. Khalid's force emerged into Syria north of Damascus, where he raided several places, including an encampment of the Ghassan tribe which was celebrating Easter at the time. This provides the one firm date in these events – April 634 – with Khalid arriving at Bostra in June.[39]

The Roman army, gathered in Emesa, marched south, perhaps originally to save Bostra, but the city's surrender freed the Arab armies. The arrival of Khalid ibn al-Walid was probably decisive, for he was the ablest of the Arab commanders, with a tradition of victory to his name. The Roman approach, with a large army, compelled the Arabs to join together, so the besiegers at Bostra, plus Khalid's force, moved south to join Amr in southern Palestine.

The Arab forces, perhaps numbering 20,000 men, combined to meet the Romans under Theodore and Wardan, the commander at Emesa. It is probable that the Arabs were more numerous, and were certainly more mobile, being mainly cavalry; the size of the Roman forces is not known, but it was composed mainly of Armenians and Arabs. The battle was bitter, according to the sources, and the Roman forces were defeated. They retreated north and east, but were caught up by the Arabs at Fihl (Pella), across the Jordan, and there they were defeated again. The Romans retreated to take refuge in the city, which is said to have been besieged for four months. This is a fairly slow-moving business. Ajnadayn was fought, it seems, in July 634, but Pella surrendered on terms only in January 635. The Arab pursuit was thus hardly vigorous, presumably because a large part of the Roman army survived both battles. It had clearly retreated along its main line of communication, towards Damascus and its Emesa base. The Pella surrender terms included the right for the Roman army to retreat unmolested; it moved north for Damascus and Emesa.[40]

Both Pella and Skythopolis, west of the river, surrendered to the Arab forces. This is a crucial development. Two cities, Areopolis and Bostra, had been captured already, but the one was small and remote, and the other seems to have been in part taken by surprise. But Pella and Skythopolis were important Greek/Chalcedonian cities, whereas the earliest two had strong Arab connections.[41] The Roman strategy of defence seems to have relied on the fortified cities holding out until they could be relieved, so wearing down the Arab forces and gaining time for the Romans to gather their forces.[42] It was assumed, correctly, that the Arabs were unskilled at siege warfare, which was a Roman specialty – Bostra and Pella both held out for several months. But if the cities were going to surrender at the first appearance of an Arab army, this strategy was bound to fail.

The Roman response to these defeats was for Heraklios, who was at Antioch by now, first to dismiss his brother from command (Wardan had been killed) and then to gather all available troops into a new army, in part from the forces facing Persia. This was sent south to deal with the invaders, and military commanders were appointed for the cities where they did not exist.[43] This was essentially what he had already done, with Theodore's army, but there does not seem to have been any other choice. The Arab army had to be confronted, defeated, and driven out, especially now that it had secured several victories, and cities were falling to it.

The result of the fight at Pella was a surge of advance northwards by the Arab armies. At some point a battle was fought at Marj al-Suffar, somewhere south of Damascus, which seems to have been only a minor affair, but since it was said to be a costly victory for Khalid ibn al-Walid, he was removed from overall command by the new Caliph Umar, and replaced by Abu Ubayda; this is likely to have taken place before the advance on Damascus.[44]

The city was put under siege, which for the Arabs still meant essentially a blockade. Each commander faced one of the city gates, and basically they waited for the city to fall. The resources of the Ghuta were probably fully sufficient to support the Arab army, and to be settled for a time in the lush landscape would be no hardship. A Roman relieving force was defeated at Thanniyet. The city eventually fell in autumn 635 when one of the Arab armies broke through at one of the gates just at the time when the city was negotiating, probably with Khalid, to surrender. The Arab armies met within the city and agreed to treat it as if had surrendered by negotiation, when the city commander (an Arab, Mansur ibn Sarjun) and/or the bishop understood that relief by a Roman army was not on its way.[45]

The Arabs then headed for Emesa, whence the relieving army had come, taking the route through the Barada Gorge and along the Bekaa Valley. An earlier force, perhaps that which had defeated the relieving force at Thanniyet, had gone on ahead, and it is claimed to have captured the city, though this seems unlikely. This force may have used the desert road along the foot of the Antilebanon. Baalbek fell and Emesa was, like Damascus, put under blockade. It fell about the end of 635 or early 636.[46]

By this time the Roman army of response had been gathered. It was basically a part-Armenian and part-Arab force, once again under two commanders, the Armenian Vahan and Theodore Trithurios. The Arab part of the force had been recruited from many of the tribes and clans of the northern desert, including the remnants of the Ghassan and Lakhm tribes who had originally formed the bases of the rival kingdoms. The great army, supposedly 50,000 strong, though that is probably a considerable exaggeration, moved south. The Arabs withdrew from their recent conquests, repeating the tactics which brought them victory at Ajnadayn. They camped in an area of open ground on the Golan Heights east of the Sea of Galilee, at Jabiya, the traditional camping ground of Ghassan, where the former kings had held court. It was probably familiar to the peninsular Arabs from trading visits in the past, but they had also seen it more than once since their invasion began. It was probably the last suitable place for their stand against the approaching Romans, for it had good grazing, was open enough to be a useful place for cavalry warfare; further south it is likely they would be entangled in villages and defended cities, and the land had already been ravaged, so that supplies would be short. In other words this was the decisive battle, and if the Arabs lost here, they would probably be driven out of Syria entirely.

The battle was in the end a three-day affair, but it came at the end of a campaign in the area which had lasted several weeks, and which in turn was at the end of a marching campaign which lasted months. The cavalry of the Arab army was able to confine the Roman army, largely infantry, to a narrow thirsty corner, near the Yarmuk River and finish it off. The Roman forces were under constraint of supplies as soon as they reached the battleground, and in the end they were deserted by some of their Arab allies – the Ghassan under their king – and found their only escape route, a bridge, captured. Their final conduct, where some Roman units panicked and others simply stopped fighting and waited to be killed, has all the marks of a force at the final edge of exhaustion, mental and physical.[47]

The destruction of this army was the end of the last chance for the Romans to hold onto Syria. Heraklios knew it as soon as he was told of the defeat, and he began to pack up to return to Constantinople. 'Farewell to Syria' he remarked, though this was not in fact the end, despite the emperor's pessimism. It was still necessary for the Arab army to gain control over the many cities which were still held by the Roman forces, and this took several more years. Many of the cities were not willing to submit. Yet the Arabs had managed to capture Pella and Damascus and Emesa, and without the possibility of a relieving army, every other city would inevitably and eventually fall.

The Arabs moved north once more, but again without any urgency. Damascus was retaken in December, four months after the battle; Emesa quickly followed, and the latter became the headquarters of Abu Ubayda. He sent forces northwards to attack Chalkis (Qinnesrin), which had been developed in the past decades into a major centre of Roman military power. Heraklios called in the surviving forces from the Mesopotamian garrisons, where they had been watching Persia. An attack on the Jaziran home towns of these Roman troops from Iraq seems to have been the cause of the collapse of this new Roman army. With Chalkis taken, Antioch and Beroea fell, so that the Arabs controlled the central area of north Syria, between the Amanus Mountains and the Euphrates. Heraklios had withdrawn to Edessa, then went further north to Samosata, and finally retired to Constantinople. Next year the Arabs moved across the Euphrates; Edessa fell in 638.[48]

Considerable areas of Syria remained in Roman hands until well after the fall of the northern cities. Much of the coast was untaken, for example. After taking the northern cities, Abu Ubayda turned back to Palestine, even before the threat from Edessa was removed. He laid siege to Jerusalem, which was clearly a lengthy and difficult matter, until the governor, or the citizens, insisted that the city would be surrendered to the caliph in person, not to his commander. So Caliph Umar came north to take the city's surrender, make a ceremonial entry, and order the construction of a new mosque; he had plenty of other tasks to perform as well, such as supervising the division of the booty, and organizing the military commands for the next phase of conquest.[49]

Palestine generally had been subject to ravaging by the early invaders, but after Ajnadayn the region had not been fought over. Now several Arab detachments set out to capture the untaken cities. Gaza fell in 637, not long after Jerusalem, an important capture since the Romans still held Egypt. Other places fell at unknown times. The most obstinate place, apart from Jerusalem, was Caesarea, which held out, assisted, it is presumed, by the Roman fleet until 640 or 641. Shurahbil campaigned in the north of Palestine, taking Tiberias and Acre and Tyre; Amr ibn al-As returned to southern Palestine and cleared up there. Another detachment took Sidon and Berytus. The last place to fall seems to have been Tripolis; an earlier detachment sent from Emesa had taken Laodikeia and the northern coast.[50]

These cities had held out, in large part because they were inhabited by and administered and garrisoned by the imperial government and the Chalcedonian Church. Many of the interior cities, notably Emesa, had quickly surrendered because the Greeks and Chalcedonians had fled before the Muslim advance. There seem to be no notices of the capture of Apameia, similarly already deserted by the wealthy and the Greeks. It was clear, therefore, from early on that the Monophysites were welcoming to the Arabs, but that the Chalcedonians were hostile, and as each of the Greek cities fell, their Greek inhabitants left. Antioch had surrendered, but then later rebelled, and the Greeks left when it was retaken; the same thing happened at Chalkis; the last city to be taken, Tripolis, was evacuated by the Roman fleet; the Chalcedonians evacuated Jerusalem.[51]

It was this which was the definitive change. The Muslims made little or no attempt to convert the Christians and Jews and Samaritans to Islam, at least at first; indeed not converting them was more profitable, since only non-Muslims paid the poll tax. Had the cities retained a numerous Greek/Chalcedonian population, then there would have been a standing fifth column available when and if the Romans made an attempt to recover their lost lands. But without such a population any reconquest would be much more difficult. In the later conquests, one of the Arabs' terms for surrender was that half of the city's houses should be emptied for the Arabs' use; in many cases this had already happened.

But by not making a serious effort to convert the Syrian population to Islam, the Muslims were unconsciously laying out the ground for the later continued and disastrous divisions among the Syrians. What had been originally a division into political units, and then into disputatious Christian sects, became a complex mixture of Christian and Muslim sects and Jewish and Samaritan groups. This was not intended, of course, like every disaster to afflict Syria, but a more attentive conversion effort might have overcome the endemic divisions of Syrian society.

Chapter 16

Top of the World

For a decade and more after the start of the Arab invasions the eventual fate of Syria was unclear. It was only in 638, six years after the beginning of the conquest (eight years, if Muhammad's capture of Tabuk and Aqaba is taken as the beginning) that the second caliph, Umar ibn al-Khattab, travelled to Syria and made some preliminary decisions about governing the conquests.[1]

It has to be said that the new system which Umar devised was neither new nor very systematic, no doubt because it was done in a rush, and without serious consideration of any need for a permanent solution. The population was in effect divided into two: the Muslims, largely for the moment the conquering soldiers, and the rest – and it was the rest who paid the taxes, which were raised in large part at first in order to pay pensions to the soldiers. Such administration as still existed in Syria after the several conquests, battles, and evacuations of the time since AD 600 was continued, though there cannot have been much left in the way of clerks and managers, other than perhaps the bishops. The previous Roman administration had been manned mainly by adherents of the imperial government and the Chalcedonian Church, and most of these men had left with the evacuation of the imperial armies. Local government had always devolved under the Romans on the cities' local councils and their bishops, and this probably continued under the Muslims, as it had with the Persians.

The provincial system, which during the later years of the Roman Empire had included up to a dozen provinces between the Euphrates and Sinai, was reduced to four, and these were *ajnad* (singular *jund*) military commands. Otherwise there was little change: the boundaries of the *ajnad* were more or less those of the Roman system: Filastin was the old Palestina I province, al-Urdunn was the former Palestina II, somewhat enlarged to take in some of Phoenicia and some territory east of the Sea of Galilee; Dimashq (Damascus) was the former Arabia plus most of the two Phoenician provinces; Homs (Emesa) was the rest: Syria I and II, Euphratensis, and the western part of the Jazirah. (When Qinnasrin was made into a new province, it took over Syria I and Euphratensis, leaving Homs inheriting Syria II.) These were movable boundaries, even approximate, since the armies and their commanders were the *ajnad*, not the territory, though they tended to settle down as time passed.[2]

Each of these *ajnad* had an army, or rather *was* an army, and the commander was the governor. The armies were supposed to settle in camps – Jabiya was one of these for a time, but in Syria at least, this did not last long. In Iraq, by contrast, the great camp-cities of Basra and Kufa became the centres of power. On the other hand, some camp-cities were founded in Syria; these were *amsar* (singular *misr*), but none was on the same great scale as the Iraqi cities. One such *misr*, was founded early in the conquest at Ayla (Aqaba), probably before the conquest was complete;[3] a second was at ar-Ramlah, close to Ludd, the Roman Lydda-Diospolis, which seems to have been made the capital of the *jund*[4] – Caesarea, the previous capital, was not captured until about 641, and was always vulnerable to Byzantine sea power. Possibly another *misr* was founded close to Tiberias, the capital of the al-Urdunn *jund*.[5] By putting these camps, which were generally fairly small, next to existing settlements, the *amsar* tended to merge with the older cities. This was, again, in direct contrast to the situation in Iraq, where the great garrison cities were established as completely separate places and were large enough to stay that way. The aim was to have available a large concentrated force, given the stubborn resistance of the Persians to conquest, and of the subject peoples to rebellion. In Syria, the presence of a generally sympathetic Arab population, and of an indifferent Syrian population, made this unnecessary in the end, at least for a time. At the same time the subdivision of Syria was a response to the country's geography, though an over-governor – a viceroy, in effect – was also appointed. Once more this was an obvious response to the need for the commander in the early years of the conquest. All this preliminary organization rapidly hardened into normality.

It should be clear that the Arab conquerors really had little idea of how they were to rule their conquests. The early intention of targeting in the Arabs of Syria and Iraq might suggest indeed that this was the total of the early ambition of the conquest organizers; the resistance of both Byzantine and Sassanid states by their counter-attacks could be said to have compelled the Arabs to go on conquering. The measures arranged by Umar at Jabiya in 638 have all the air of improvisations, designed mainly to provide support for the Arab forces while they stayed alert for attacks or rebellions. The basic problem for the new administration was that the Roman system had required a considerable body of trained manpower, bureaucrats, officers, tax-collectors, and others, which the Arabs did not have, and could not easily produce, hence the reliance on the preceding Roman system, and on the bishops of the cities to produce the tax revenue.

The primitive tax system installed by the conquerors was just as bad. The Arabs, or Muslims, paid no tax, the eventual rationalization being that they did the fighting; in fact, it was because they were the conquerors, and at home in Arabia they had probably paid no tax anyway. The rest of the population was to pay a flat poll tax, which went to 'support' the conquering and occupying armies.[6] This of course, favoured the wealthy, which would tend to bring the upper class, such as were left, to support the Muslim government, though this was probably not something which occurred to the conquerors until later. The old taxes were retained, however, mainly land and property taxes, since, as might be expected, the Arab government proved to be as greedy for money as any other. The tax burden was probably greater than under the Roman system.

The overall effect of the administrative simplification on the remaining Syrian population was therefore probably fairly small. There was no pressure to convert to Islam, which will have been a substantial relief to the Monophysites who had been subject to persecution by the presiding regime. They do not seem to have assisted the invaders, though the Arabs along the desert edge had in some cases become Christian and were recruited to the invading armies, and no doubt they were much more likely to welcome their fellow Arabs than the rest, and were very likely to convert. But the Syrian population had been largely disarmed as a result of Roman imperial policy, so it could not help either the Romans or the Arabs.

As an imperial government, therefore, the early Islamic state left a lot to be desired. Umar appointed over-commanders – viceroys – for the main conquered regions, of which Syria was one. Here Abu Ubayda was succeeded by Yazid ibn Abi Sufyan and then by Yazid's brother Muawiya. They were from a family which, having owned lands near Damascus before the wars, was generally familiar with the local situation.[7] It was also a family which had been foremost in resisting Muhammad at Mecca, a fact their enemies constantly repeated. Yazid died in the plague, a new outbreak of which happened in 638, and Muawiya was left in command, and his governorate was extended to all Syria by Caliph Uthman, his cousin.[8] He established his viceregal capital at Damascus.

The problems of the caliphate began at the very top, where no predictable or efficient system of choosing the caliph himself existed, other than nomination by his predecessor, usually when he was dying. At the level of the governor of the great provinces – what one student of the period has called 'superprovinces', but 'viceroyalties' seems an adequate term – the choice of governor was almost inevitably based on personal relationships or clan connections. These men had the title of *amir* – commander – which was accurate enough, but it emphasized their military role, and so they, equally inevitably, felt that their priority should be their armies, which were their power bases, rather more perhaps than the approval of the caliph. So, for example, none of the *amirs* was in the least inclined to pass on any of tax revenues he collected to the caliph in Medina, but used them to pay the pensions and salaries of his troops.

Furthermore, the *amirs* had a good excuse for paying most attention to their troops, since all of them faced active frontiers. For Syria the main frontier was that facing the Byzantine Empire. On retreating into Anatolia Heraklios had devastated the Kilikian Plain, thus establishing the Taurus Mountains as the Byzantine boundary.[9] The Muslims seem not to have advanced much beyond the Amanus Mountains for a time, so leaving Kilikia as a frontier land – Antioch became one of their frontier command posts. An easier route for an invasion of Anatolia was north along the Euphrates, where Samsat and Melitene were soon captured, so giving the Arabs access to Anatolia north of the Taurus, and not long afterwards the Armenian region more or less fell under distant Muslim control.

The southern frontier with Egypt was much easier to deal with. Amr ibn al-As, the former commander in Palestine, got permission from Caliph Uthman to campaign there, and recruited a reinforcement from the local Arabs and perhaps from the local Palestinians for his invasion. The campaign was surprisingly brief, and within a year or so, Amr had conquered the country and its main city, Alexandria. This eliminated any need for the Syrian governors to bother about their southern frontier.

Making more progress in the north, however, was difficult. The Syrian army was badly damaged by the plague outbreak in 638, and the problems of the succession to the caliphate was another hindrance to further conquests.[10] In the next few years the Jazirah was superficially conquered, by an expedition which simply accepted the submission of the several cities, each of which made a treaty setting out the terms of surrender; only after some time were groups of Bedouin Arabs shifted into the region, which remained strongly Christian.[11]

Muawiya, however, had the possibility of a different strategy. He had only slowly managed to secure control over the Palestinian and Phoenician coastlands and their ancient maritime cities. Several of these cities had resisted so long because they were kept supplied by sea, and Tripolis had been evacuated by Byzantine shipping. The island of Arados held out even longer, until about 649.[12] Once under Muslim control, however, it turned out that the remaining citizens of these cities were quite willing to work for their conquerors. (This had been the case with the Persians as well, who had been able to capture Cyprus in 617, obviously by utilizing the maritime capacity of the Syrian coastal cities.)[13]

The Byzantine command of the sea is evident from the rescue of the Tripolitans in 644, the raid to attempt the recapture of Egyptian Alexandria in 645, and the fact that Arados held out until 649. It was equally evident, as Muawiya's reaction shows, that the only way to make Syria safe was to gain command of the sea for the Arabs. He must have gathered a fleet to gain Arados, but now he summoned more ships from the Syrian coastal communities, and arranged with the governor of Alexandria to send an expedition from Egypt. With these forces Cyprus was raided in 649, presumably this had been the Byzantine forward naval base. The island was raided again next year by Abu'l-A'war ibn Sufyan, governor of al-Urdunn (the province which included the Phoenician coastal cities). According to the source for this the Arabs were amazed at the island's wealth; and the Cypriots were taken by surprise on the first raid. By the second raid a reinforcement had arrived, though the soldiers either fled – the rich are said to have done so first – or were overwhelmed by the Arabs' numbers.[14]

By 655 Muawiya was able to mount a great maritime expedition which met and defeated the main Byzantine fleet, commanded by the Emperor Constans II in person, in the Battle of the Masts, fought on the coast of Lykia. This gave the Syrian Muslims effective command of the sea as far as the entrance to the Aegean. The battle had been a fairly crude affair, from the maritime tactical point of view, probably because neither side had any recent tradition of large-scale war at sea. The result was an application of the Arab raiding by land technique to the sea. The pursuit reached as far as Rhodes.[15]

This was all grist to Muawiya's reputation as an Islamic warrior. He could send raiding forces into Anatolia by land or against the Greek Empire by sea – even aiming to capture Constantinople. This attracted to him the Arabs whose life revolved around raiding and the acquisition of loot: it was an Islamization of their traditional practice.

The northern frontier was however, vulnerable to reverse raids. Heraklios' devastation of Kilikia, leaving an empty land backed by the formidable defences of the Taurus Mountains, made it relatively straightforward for both sides to raid each other, though at the same time the distance involved would give plenty of warning. The first Byzantine attack is reported in 654.[16] And any attempt to refortify the empty land was swiftly stopped by a new raid aimed specifically at the fort. But the jihadis and their Christian counterparts no doubt enjoyed themselves.

The northern frontier of the Muslim Empire with the Byzantine Empire was inactive for a time after the initial conquests. The original conquest of the area had included agreements with the several cities in north Syria – Antioch, Kyrrhos, Beroia (Aleppo), Chalkis (Qinnesrin) and others are all noted[17] – and an agreement with a group of Christians living in the Amanus Mountains at a place called Jarajimah. The agreement was that these people would act as Muslim auxiliaries against the Greeks, in return for which they would pay no tax.[18] This suggests that they were not originally loyal to the Roman Empire, probably for religious reasons, but later the Byzantine government had no quarrel with their beliefs – it is conjectured that they were Jacobites, but were content to accept Constantinople's religious authority. The Greeks called them Mardaites – adapting an Arab term for rebels.[19]

Their privileged position attracted others – bandits, escaped slaves and criminals, in the words of those who disapproved. They soon switched allegiance from the Muslims to the Byzantines, and as their numbers grew they colonized other mountain areas, including the Lebanon.[20] Their position in the mountains was strategically useful for the Byzantines, for they both acted as sources of intelligence and operated as guerillas harassing Arab armies.

The move to Lebanon came in 677, the year after the failure of the first great Muslim attempt to capture Constantinople, and was so successful that Caliph Muawiya, faced with guerillas close to Damascus which his army could not uproot and with losses of the campaign, was reduced to making peace, including paying tribute to secure it.[21] This peace lasted for fifteen years, until the Caliph Abd al-Malik secured a new peace agreement with the Emperor Justinian II, in which it was agreed that the Mardaites would be removed from the Lebanon and probably the Amanus and resettle them inside his borders. Abd al-Malik agreed to pay a large sum of money in exchange, but the Byzantines soon began to rue the bargain. This was condemned, much later, by the chronicler Theophanes on the ground that their removal opened the way for Muslim raids, in which he was quite correct, but his purpose was mainly to denigrate the emperor.[22]

The presence of the Mardaites along the frontier had in effect largely prevented Muslim raids, and had left Kilikia as a frontier land. However, Justinian became involved in Cyprus, which was a joint possession of the two empires, and the Muslims decided he had broken the peace – no doubt they were looking for the opportunity to do so. Raids resumed in 693,[23] and took place almost annually until the next great Muslim attempt on Constantinople began in 716. One of the most significant moves made by the Muslims in this period was to seize and refortify the old city of Mopsuhestia in Kilikia, which meant that they had a forward defence against any reprisal raids by the Byzantines.[24]

The second expedition against Constantinople failed, and was followed by another period of peace, which lasted for about ten years. They resumed under Caliph Hisham in 725, only to be interrupted by the new civil war brought on by the seizure of power by Marwan II and the rebellion of the Abbasids from 744. One of the early measures taken by Caliph al-Mansur in the 750s was to attend to the fortification of the frontier.[25] These places were both defensive posts, and places where new raids could be prepared. But the civil wars had given the Byzantines another respite for a dozen years.

Muawiya held his office of governor of Syria for twenty years, appointed by Caliph Umar and explicitly retained by Uthman. The murder of the latter, however, prevented all external raiding as the empire sank into a civil war for several years – Muawiya made a truce with the Emperor Constans II to keep free of external entanglements for the duration of the war.[26] Out of it all Muawiya emerged as caliph of the whole empire, though this may not have been his aim until the end of the crisis. Apart from his position as one of the three or four most prominent governors, he was also related to the murdered Uthman, and Arab mores demanded that he avenge Uthman's death.

The decisive event of the crisis was the confrontation between Muawiya's 'Syrian' army with that from Iraq led by the Caliph Ali. This is known as the Battle of Siffin, though relatively little actual fighting took place, and that which started ended when Muawiya's men held up pages of the Quran on their spears, to remind the enemy that they should not be fighting fellow Muslims. It seems that Ali's forces, armies from the Iraqi viceroyalty and Arabia, were more numerous than

Muawiya's Syrian army, but that the Syrians were more united. After the shame visited on Ali's army by the enemy's waving pages of the Quran in their faces, Ali's army broke up in disarray.[27]

The precise moment of the disintegration came when Ali accepted the idea of arbitration for solving the disputes. One group separated off because he had submitted a dispute in the matter of religion to earthly compromise, where it should have been left to the judgment of god – that is, of course, reaching a decision with which they could agree. These Kharijites, as they became known, were essentially Bedouin and they returned to their desert homes and, in effect, resumed their pre-Islamic lifestyle of nomadism varied by raiding, though now their raids were refuelled by righteousness, and their victims were usually other Muslims. One of them, not surprisingly, eventually assassinated Ali himself. Muawiya had claimed the caliphal title in the process, and on Ali's death he moved his forces in to take over control of the armies in Iraq.[28]

Syria, perhaps somewhat to the surprise of its inhabitants, had now became the main source of power for the whole Islamic Empire, and Damascus had become the capital of the most powerful state in the world, and one which quickly resumed expanding. This was a land which had been badly damaged in one conquest, and quite supine in the face of another, all in the previous half century. Now it was the land of the most powerful army, and of the ruler of the new empire. The change was surely heady – or it would have been had any real benefit for the Syrians themselves arrived as a result.

The few new towns founded by the Muslims in Syria – Ayla, Anjarr, ar-Ramlah, and others – were no substitutes for the destruction of the major cities, such as Antioch and Apameia, which had happened under the Persians. Neither Antioch nor Apameia ever wholly recovered, nor did Seleukeia-in-Pieria. Indeed, Antioch became a frontier base for the Muslim raids into Anatolia, which provided some military-based continuity;[29] Apameia's site faded, or perhaps it may be said it gradually contracted to the present fortified town of Qalaat al-Mudik, which is no more than the former acropolis of the Selcukid city, as an organized city it had ceased to exist. Other places simply carried on, but without receiving much in the way of new building, other than a few mosques and some churches.

Some regions prospered. Hama, for example, the former Epiphaneia, had not been damaged by the Persians, and had surrendered quickly, so it seems, to the Arabs. The city had built a new Great Church just before the Persian invasion, and this appears to have been converted into a mosque in the eighth century. The archaeology suggests that the wealthy continued to live in their great villas, and the city's market operated as usual.[30] Homs (the former Emesa) may be presumed to have continued to flourish as well, given that it became the capital of the *jund*, though there is little or no evidence either way.

The city that ought to show the influence of the early Islamic years is Damascus, which Muawiya used as his capital. He was governor and caliph for forty years, leaving an indelible mark on the empire. He organized the administration, regularized the taxation system, surveyed the empire to make a register of crown lands, and attempted to develop a consensual scheme of government, recruiting the lords of the Arabian clans and tribes as his counsellors, and not leaning too heavily on the religious authority of his position.[31]

Damascus, nonetheless, acquired a strong Muslim tinge during the Ummayad years, as Muslim notables clustered round the imperial court. Muawiya had a palace just south of the Great Church, and many of his prominent followers and officials settled in the Ghuta, either in villas abandoned by the fleeing Byzantines or in new buildings. The city probably grew in size during this period, for it was now the centre of a great empire and so an attraction for administrators, merchants, and so on, and the cultivated area of the Ghuta also expanded. Caliph Yazid II (720–724) built a new aqueduct to expand the cultivated area, which implies the increased demand for food and so the increased size of the city population. Damascus has been much rebuilt over the years, so little that is primarily Ummayad has survived, but Caliph al-Walid I (705–715) succeeded in taking over the cathedral, where Muawiya had established only a small mosque within the compound.[32]

The same slow Islamization took place in both the cities and the countrysides throughout Syria. Generally the churches were left alone, at least at first, but as the Muslim proportion of the population grew, either by immigration or by conversion, the churches came to be seen as empty; smaller churches often continued in use. A central mosque might be built on a new site, as in Antioch and Jerusalem. But Hama and Damascus, busy cities and soon predominantly Muslim, surrendered their cathedrals.

The threat of Byzantine sea power induced Muawiya to move new settlers into the coastal cities. No doubt the cities were partly empty as a result of the Greek evacuation, when Heraklios withdrew, while Muawiya had also driven 'many of the people' from the cities during his conquest – no doubt some will have returned, though others had surely followed Heraklios' evacuation.[33] The whole region was therefore much less defensible than earlier. Muawiya is said to have moved 'Persians' from some inland places, of which Baalbek, Antioch, and Homs are mentioned, and apparently Basra and Kufa. These Persians could be people left behind when the Persian conquests evaporated, or Persians who had joined the Arabs in the conquest, as several units did, or they could be Christians from Persia, many of whom had moved into the old Roman territories to escape persecution, or possible persecution, at Sassanid hands. They are said to have been settled at Tyre and Acre 'and other places'.[34] Muawiya was thus very careful in his choice of colonists. These people would be either deserters from the Sassanids and so necessarily loyal, or if Christian were either Monophysites or Nestorians, but not Chalcedonians, and would be reasonably reliable as defenders against the Greek Melkite Empire. Arabs were also persuaded to move to the coastal lands on the promise of land, and Muawiya moved artisans to the coast as well. Both Tyre and Acre were refortified.[35]

Once peaceful conditions in the interior were assured the families of the conquerors moved north out of Arabia to join them. They thus reinforced the Arab presence which had begun to grow under the Roman system, but they were now moving into lands which were now less than fully occupied, and into the interiors of the new provices, where before they had lived along the desert margins. The al-Urdunn *jund* seems to have attracted more than the rest: at the battle of Siffin there were five units from that *jund*, whereas none of the others had more than two.[36] Later arrivals went north, into the frontier area of the Jazirah.

There is another reason for this migration out of Arabia. The seventh and eighth centuries in the Middle East were a time of reduced rainfall and increased heat.[37] For Arabia this made life for the nomads increasingly difficult as the pastures failed and wells dried. In Syria the main effect was naturally felt along the margins of the cultivated land. This was the region, a long variable strip of land anything up to 100km wide, stretching from the north at Chalkis (Qinnesrin) to Petra in the south, which had been colonized by Syrians since the early Hellenistic period; it was most substantially occupied during the last Roman centuries and into the earliest Islamic period. It was also the region into which the Arabs had been moving for several centuries.

But there were clearly strains developing even before the Arab conquest. It will have taken steadily increasing amounts of work to win crops in what by then had become an even more agriculturally marginal area. Some parts, such as the Hawran or the Damascus Ghuta, were capable of holding on longer than others, especially with investment from the government in things like Caliph Yazid's aqueduct, and the development of irrigation – as was done by Abd Allah ibn Salih on his estate near Hama, to grow saffron.[38] But southern Jordan, for example, south of Amman, will have failed very early, and this was the area which fell very readily to the Muslim armies – one reason could have been the thin population. The Hawran, however, is an area of higher land which captures more rain than lands to the north and south, and it had areas of very fertile land, so it could have lasted longer. It has, however, been shown that there is considerable activity in the area in the Ummayad period, in contrast with the similar communities of Christian villages near Hama and beyond Apameia in the north. Several villages had the resources to build or to alter buildings; Umm al-Jimal had thirteen churches.[39] The proximity of Damascus, of Bostra, of several smaller cities (in the old Decapolis) and even the powerful Arab presence in the al-Urdunn *jund*, which included part of this territory, all imply the existence of a good market for any surplus produce. But all this ended after 750; most of the Hama area was deserted by the beginning of the ninth century. In the al-Ala hills the settlement history of the area in the eighth century has been described as 'stagnation', which implies a lack of investment, little or no new building, and increasing poverty.[40] Hama and Homs continued in prosperity, but the al-Ala area's 'stagnation' is repeated in the Hawran, and the region to the north, which is open steppe, probably reverted to pasture as farms failed. The Ghuta had its own water supply from the Barada River, fed by the snows of the Lebanon and Antilebanon Mountains, and with Damascus and its requirements it clearly flourished. But the other marginal areas beside the desert faded fairly quickly once the imperial court was removed.

The taxation policies of the imperial government exacerbated the situation. The requirement for a massive income, both to sustain the government and to pay the soldiers, made it necessary for a heavy load of taxes to be heaped on the peasantry. This bore most hardly on the peasantry working the most marginal land. The combination of increasing aridity and heavy taxation drove the peasants from these marginal lands. (In Egypt the symptoms were farmers' strikes, followed by enforcement of return – exactly the same antagonisms that had existed for at least 3000 years.) The abandoned land ceased to be cultivated and reverted to steppe, grazed by animals of the Bedouin. The people who moved went to the better watered lands, perhaps taking over other abandoned marginal lands, perhaps securing a holding for which they paid a rent, perhaps moving into the cities. This can be most easily discerned in the lands east of the Jordan, with the refugees moving into Palestine.[41]

The region of the 'dead cities', north of Apameia, continued under increasing strain through the Ummayad period, with no new building, and some abandonment of collapsed buildings. It would seem that the population was falling slowly. Of course, the markets for the products of the region had failed with the destructions of Antioch and Apameia, and Damascus was probably largely self-sufficient, and anyway much too distant to be supplied economically from the region. To the south the town of Maaret en-Numan appears to have grown, and its 'palaces' were remarked on. It was a strongly Muslim town, whereas the villages east of Hama and north of Apameia remained Christian. It may be that those with money chose to patronize a town noted as being of their own religion – for it may be presumed that most of the wealthy were now predominantly Muslim.[42]

The archaeological evidence is fairly sparse so far, and conclusions are heavily based on surveys rather than excavation, but it seems that there was a certain reduction in the number of occupied sites in these marginal areas in the Ummayad period, with the exception of a few places in the Hawran, though it was not until the succeeding Abbasid period that there was drastic fall in the sites occupied. The reduction in sites was radical when it came, and two immediate causes can be suggested, on top of the more longstanding problems of climate and taxation.

The presence at Damascus of the imperial court obviously imposed a strong demand on the local economy. Food, military supplies and fodder were all required in large quantities; any luxury goods would be in demand as well. Not only that, but the practice of the court, or part of it at least, was to visit one or more of several luxurious 'desert palaces' spread through the desert to the east, north-east and south-east of Damascus. Many of these places were former Roman or Byzantine forts freely adapted, expanded, much decorated, and provided with plentiful supplies of water, organized by elaborate systems, and with agricultural settlements close by.

The precise purposes of these buildings is not agreed: hunting lodges, relaxation, maintaining contact with the desert tribesmen, assisting the Hajj, are some of the modern suggestions; quite probably any or all of these ideas – and others – operated. But which is not often noted is this scale of these enterprises. There are perhaps a dozen of these places in the Syrian Desert, each of which surely cost a fortune to build and maintain. Some were more or less abandoned soon after completion; indeed the biggest, Mshatta, south-east of Amman, was never finished.[43] This was a local version of conspicuous consumption, and these buildings' cost and uselessness were surely one of the reasons the Ummayad dynasty fell from popularity, even within Syria. They are also, along with many other traits, clearly one of the inheritances of the dynasty from the Hellenistic-Roman past.

These were places to which the caliph and/or his family could withdraw; the decoration implies that their stay was devoted to hunting, to pleasure, to bathing, dancing girls, music, and no doubt feasting.[44] The region was part of the pastures of the Arab nomads, who were conspicuous Ummayad allies and supporters, but the attraction of living for a time in such a place may be more that the desert dwelling was part of the lifestyle of the caliphs, an inheritance from the mobile nomadism of the past, as well as being well away from the pressures of governing. It may also be that it became the practice of each caliph to construct his own desert palace – and then when he died it was abandoned.

The Ummayads also built in the cities, notably adapting the Christian Cathedral of Damascus, which had been the temple of Zeus, which had been the temple of Hadad, into the present mosque. In Jerusalem the mosque decreed by the Caliph Umar was an Ummayad building, replacing the reputedly ramshackle early version; a group of substantial buildings close by were of Ummayad date.[45] It was the Ummayads who oversaw the construction of the new town at Anjarr, possibly one of the *amsar*, but it is actually credited to Abbas ibn al-Walid, a soldier and governor of Homs in the early eighth century.[46] This was a place which had traditionally been fortified, the former Gerrha, one of the old Ptolemaic forts, which became an important Ituraean centre, and then a Roman town.

The population of the region was therefore buoyed up for a century or so by the economic stimulus provided by the presence of the imperial court. Wherever it was located, in Damascus, in the field, out in one of the palaces, it had to be supplied, and as the government system became established and elaborated, with a mint, the bureaucracy, the courtiers, these demands would only grow. This provided the incentive for the extra work required to produce in an increasingly arid agricultural region.

For Syria, of course, the presence of the dynasty was a boon in economic terms. The practice of raiding into the Byzantine Empire brought wealth in the form of the looted treasure and saleable slaves into Syria, which is one reason why Antioch made something of a recovery. The existence of a navy stimulated the shipbuilding industry, particularly at Tyre, but also at other Palestinian and Phoenician coastal towns, together with providing employment for sailors and rowers. The country also benefited from its religious associations. Jerusalem was a major pilgrimage destination for both Muslims and Christians, and it was on one of the routes of the Hajj of the Muslim pilgrimage to Mecca.

The north of Syria and the Jazirah were the bases for the main part of the Syrian army. The policies pursued by the caliphs enabled those who chose to indulge in campaigning to do so, either in the frontier raids in Anatolia, or in more distant conquests. The Ummayad caliphs organized, or perhaps more often agreed to, distant expeditions, though not at first involving the Syrian army. During the Ummayad period North Africa was conquered (after an initial defeat) and Spain was invaded and largely conquered, and at the other end of the empire, hard fighting conquered much of central Asia and the Valley of the Indus. The progress of conquest, however, stopped after about 720, and those areas most recently conquered proved to be difficult to hold; numerous defeats occurred between 720 and 750; for Europeans the most significant was the Battle of Tours in 732, but for the empire as a whole the repeated failure to capture Constantinople was more important. One result was that the Syrian army, the largest and most powerful in the empire, had to send out detachments to these distant areas to assist the local Arab armies. Syrians fought in India and central Asia, in North Africa and Spain, in Anatolia and in the Caucusus region. In order to keep Iraq loyal, where the great settlement cities of Basra and Kufa were turbulent and difficult to control, a new *misr* was established between them, at Wasit on the Tigris and manned by a detachment of the Syrian army. And in the second half of the Ummayad period the traditions of victory faded; defeat was more common than victory.[47]

The original Arab forces were now much supplemented by recruits, either from the local Arabs or from the native Syrians, who may or might not have been Muslim converts (*mawali*), and by the immigration of tribes from the Arabian interior. The army which Amr ibn al-As used to conquer Egypt was partly Arab, but was supplemented by at least 4,000 extra men, said to be Greeks and Persians.[48] The later arriving tribes tended to take up lands available to them in the frontier regions, either in north Syria or in the Jazirah. Indeed so many moved into the Jazirah that one of the last Sufyanid caliphs made it into a separate *jund* in about 680. These provided much of the manpower for the Byzantine wars, and those in the Caucasus.

However, it was not just numbers which made this new provincial dispensation necessary. The arrivals came from three different tribes or regions in Arabia. The original dominant group in Syria had been the Quda'a, but they were largely absorbed by the later arriving Yamanis, from southern Arabia. The latter were heavily concentrated in al-Urdunn, though in other areas of the south as well. Later still arrived the Qays, who were settled mainly in the north, along with some of the Mudar tribe; these tended to merge later, just as the Yamanis absorbed others, including the Quda'a, and the Kalb, long settled in Syria. In the Jazirah, however, along with other, much smaller groups, the Mudar groups were almost the only tribe to be settled. The Jazirah province became a Mudari region, and it was this tribal group who gained most renown for their continual raids into Byzantine territory, from both the Jazirah and for Qinnesrin. But the result was essentially two parties, Qays in Qinnesrin and the Jazirah, Yamani in the rest of Syria, where there had originally been several; and the two were by no means on good terms.[49]

These were large armies. It has been calculated that the Syrian army, divided into the four (later five) *ajnad*, may have numbered up to 175,000 men; the Jaziran army may have been about half that.[50] There was a force very much larger than anything the Romans had ever stationed in the region, even during their most difficult wars; again the economic stimulus in Syria of this huge force must have been very great – but only so long as they imported loot; without that, the armies, producing nothing, became burdens. The greater weight attached to the Jazirans was partly because they were from a single *jund*, but also because they were more active, being frontiersmen; on the other hand it was unlikely that the whole Syrian army would be mobilized as a single unit. This is reflected to some extent also in the slow migration of the caliphal centre from Damascus and its region towards the Jazirah, where caliphs settled for lengthy periods at places such as ar-Rusafa or Quinnesrin.

Then in 749 and 750 two blows fell. The first was a major earthquake. There had been several in the previous century; one in 659 caused much damage in the Jericho area, another twenty years later damaged Edessa where the Great Church which Heraklios had handed to the Chalcedonians fell down; another came in 713 supposedly affecting 'all Syria', but centred it seems particularly at Antioch and the coast; it is said to have 'lasted' for three years, which presumably refers to continual aftershocks.[51] These were survived, if with some difficulty, but the earthquake of 749, localized in the Transjordanian area, seems to have been decisive for the region. The city of Bostra was 'swallowed up', according to the source, though enough remained above ground to the reoccupied afterwards, but the site was deserted within another half-century, and Pella, 100km to the west, was similarly severely damaged, as was Gerasa to the south.[52] All this was clearly fixed in local minds as a major destruction – and it certainly affected an unusually large territory – and if Bostra was already in difficulties before the earthquake its subsequent desertion (and that of Gerasa and Pella, and the reduction of Skythopolis to a market town) is hardly surprising. There is some indication also that just at this time some of the villages of the region, such as Umm al-Jimal, were sufficiently damaged to be abandoned.

The other local disaster was of much wider scope. The caliphs of the Ummayad dynasty ruled from 661, when Muawiya secured full control of the empire until 750. In that time the dynasty broke down twice, first in the three years following the death of Muawiya in 680, and then in a civil war which lasted for five years, the second time in the half-dozen years following the death of Caliph Hisham in 743. In the eighty-nine years of the dynasty only three caliphs ruled for more than ten years; the other ten averaged only three years each; and in that time there were two civil wars, the second of which resulted in the near-total wiping out of the imperial family. This was not a stable polity, though it was a rather better record than the first four caliphs (three of whom were murdered). Not only that but it fell into ruin, in a process in which Syria suffered above all.

The last Ummayad caliph, Marwan II (744–750), seized power in a *coup d'etat*, which involved a civil war between elements of the Syrian-Jaziran army, and the murder of several other Ummayads. He had made his reputation as a vigorous and successful commander of the Jazirah army, and used this force as his power base. He was thus identified with the Qays party, and made his main political centre at Harran. This combination made him less than popular in the rest of Syria, and as soon as he went to Harran there was a rebellion in Syria against him. Part of the cause of this was the method he used to gain power, which involved the overthrow of a reigning caliph, and part was the fact that the Kalbi party was already against him. Its section of the army had mutinied even before his coup, and he had sent it home, which was mainly in Palestine, but also in parts of central Syria.[53] It was largely their forces he had defeated on his march south. He had allowed the *ajnad* to choose their own commanders, and the Kalb in Palestine chose the man, Thabit ibn Nu'aym, who had led the mutiny; Marwan let the appointment stand.[54]

The rebellion was more difficult to suppress than his original campaign. He had to besiege or capture or relieve a series of cities: Homs was besieged, Damascus had to be relieved, as had Tiberias. Thabit was commanding the siege there and after being driven off, he had to be defeated again, and this time he was captured and executed. Palmyra was Kalbi territory and submitted on terms. But as soon as the new caliph turned again to head for Iraq a new rising broke out in Syria. Again he had to fight his way city by city from north to south, and this time he had the walls of the cities demolished to prevent further rebellions.[55] A good part of Syria was wrecked.

While he was struggling to establish himself in Syria and then in Iraq, a new rebellion developed in the east. There were large problems in the Islamic Caliphate, which the Ummayads had either neglected or had felt unable to tackle. For Islam almost from the beginning had failed to carry through with its basic promise, an equality of believers. The Arab tribal tradition, the wealth accruing to some of the early commanders, the claimed superiority in class of the first believers, had all contrived to subvert the social message. The Ummayads probably never subscribed to the idea of equality, and after the murder of three of the first four caliphs it is hardly surprising that Muawiya should employ a bodyguard – but this became one of the symbols of inequality, along with wealth and class and tribe.

Then in matters of religion the faithful fell into dispute almost at once, and the future sects were already present in embryo within a generation of Muhammad's death. So the social and religious fabric was divided in several ways: between Sunni and Shi'a and Kharijites; between the several Arabian tribes, which in Syria had now fuelled a civil war; between Arabs and *mawali*, the later converts, usually non-Arabs, who found that accepting the new religion did not bring them its benefits; between rich and poor; and even between various grades of Arabs.

On top of all this social and religious division the Ummayad dynasty was regarded by many as not fit to rule in Islam because its members were not of the family of Muhammad, and it was this which brought the next crisis.[56]

This last issue was also at base the cause of the rift between Sunni and Shi'a (over the fate of the Caliph Ali, murdered by Karijites, but whose sons had died at Ummayad hands in 680), but the causes spread wider than that. Living at Humayma, on the Hajj and trading route (and the Via Traiana Nova/King's Highway) south of Ma'an in southern Jordan, there lived another family which did claim descent from the prophet, and which harboured a long-standing ambition to seize the caliphate. These were the Abbasids, descended from an uncle of Muhammad, and it was two adherents of this family who raised a revolt against Marwan in Khurasan, eastern Iran, in 747.[57]

Their programme including the replacement of the Ummayads by a caliph of Muhammad's family, though no particular person was specified – the absence of specifics was deliberate: the possible candidates were several, and all could keep up their hopes. Socially a more equal treatment of the *mawali* was intended, but above all the revolution represented a drastic change for all those who were discontented, though the precise change they wanted was never specified – again to be precise would obviously alienate some potential supporters.[58] In other words the revolution was to be an ongoing process, once power had been achieved.

Marwan sent armies to contest the Abbasid advance through Iran, and they were defeated. This, of course, signified divine approval to the Abbasid supporters. Marwan gathered his own army from Syria and the Jazirah and marched east, meeting the Abbasids at the River Zab in northern Iraq. He fumbled the battle, and his army, bigger than the Abbasids' by far, was defeated by innovative Abbasid tactics, bad positioning, and Marwan's own panic, which led him to break down a bridge, stranding part of his army on the wrong side of the river. His support in Syria then crumbled, and he fled first west and then south, finding no assistance anywhere; all the cities which he had battered in gaining the caliphate now refused him aid. He was eventually found by an Abbasid patrol in Egypt, and killed.[59]

The Abbasid conquerors, however, were hardly more popular in Syria that Marwan had been. The senior member of the Abbasid family, Ibrahim, had been imprisoned by Marwan, and had died there, a matter which clearly called for revenge. The next senior man, Ibrahim's brother Abu'l Abbas, was proclaimed caliph at Kufa in Iraq, taking the throne name al-Saffah. He carefully appointed members of his own family to command the armies, and it was his uncle, Abd Allah ibn Ali, who chased Marwan and so came to control Syria. Having won the war, he arranged a large dinner party for many of the surviving Ummayads and there had them all murdered as he sat at his meat.[60] The purpose, of course, was to eliminate future 'pretenders', since there was considerable loyalty still to the family in Syria. Abd Allah went on to desecrate the tombs of the Ummayad caliphs, presumably to eliminate centres of memory.[61] This is all very unusual behaviour, liable to alienate rather than please others, but the point was mainly to make it clear that the Ummayad policies were no more, and that a revolution had taken place.

There were still areas of Ummayad armed support, so Abd Allah's ruthlessness may have been justified (though there were still Ummayad family members around). The Syrian armies based in Iraq, at Wasit, held out for some months until the forces surrendered on terms, terms which the caliph partly broke soon after. Another force was in the north from the frontier forces. They were collected at the city of Sumaysat, probably on the great tell there which had defied Marc Antony eight centuries before. The Abbasid forces gathered to form a siege, but it soon became apparent that the Ummayad troops, commanded by Ishaq ibn Muslim al-Uqayli, were mainly interested in making terms. For the Ummayad cause was clearly over, while Abd Allah and that caliph's brother Abu Ja'far were similarly interested in recruiting the army into his own forces – it was, as a frontier army, particularly skilled and experienced. Terms were soon agreed; Ishaq and other commanders were soon rehabilitated.[62]

When the negotiations were completed and this last Ummayad army was incorporated into the Abbasid forces, the Abbasid revolution had succeeded in gaining power. The effect on Syria was profound. The extensive Syrian estates of the Ummayad family were confiscated, as were those of any subordinates who had fought on or had been killed.[63] But the main effect lay in the new absence of the imperial government, now based in Iraq. The brief moment of Syria as an imperial centre was over.

Chapter 17

Decline and Trouble

The condition of Syria after the removal of the Umayyad power and presence may be characterized as resentful. The next century and more was peppered with revolts against the Abbasid regime, thereby constantly reminding that regime of Syria's disloyalty. That regime survived only about the same century or so as the Umayyads before losing control of much of the peripheral regions of the empire. It lasted, in effect, only a little longer than its predecessor, and it failed because of the same faults, disunity, inefficiency and greedy over-taxation – to which it added a disruptive caliphal guard out for its own interests and despite the empire. Syria contributed substantially to that failure.

The removal of the imperial court, the reduction of the Syrian army, the disapproval of the imperial regime, all on top of the climatic deterioration, produced a steady change for the worse in conditions in Syria. By early in the ninth century the 'dead cities' of north Syria had become deserted, the lands east of Jordan were taken over by the Bedouin, who also began to move into the old settled lands west of the river.

The basic problem, of course, was that Syria had lost its imperial purpose. Its northern regions were the bases for warfare against the great Byzantine enemy, which made Qinnesrin and the Jazirah of continuing imperial interest, but the central and southern regions were no longer so necessary or so militant. At the same time the shift of the centre of gravity of the caliphate from Syria to Iraq rendered the Byzantine frontier more distant and perhaps less pressing as a problem. During the Umayyad period raids had been important features of imperial policy, generally only interrupted when a civil war in the caliphate preoccupied Muslim attention.

Twice the Umayyads had made major attempts to capture Constantinople, and each of these had resulted in a peace agreement after the Muslim defeat. So for the Byzantines the lesson was clear: they would be free of raids if there was a Muslim civil war, which was hardly something they could contrive, or if they arranged to defeat a major attack, which was something they learned to do. On the other hand there is no real evidence that the Abbasids were aiming at conquest; their expeditions were raids and no more.

Whatever programme of reforms and renewals the Abbasid family had imagined they could – or might – carry through, it fairly quickly became clear that few were realizable. The need to ensure loyalty in the armies in the period after they secured power meant that those armies had to be paid and commanded by loyalists, above all by members of the family. But, of course, not all those men were loyal. And maintaining a huge army required heavy taxation.

The first Abbasid governor of Syria, Abd Allah ibn Ali, an uncle of the first caliph, had to battle repeatedly in his four years in charge to keep control. The main trouble he faced came, as is only to be expected, from men who wished the Umayyads back. One such problem has been noted already, the pseudo-siege of Ishaq ibn Muslim at Sumaysat, which ended as both sides intended, in the recruitment of Ishaq and his army into Abbasid service. The army had become by this time a salaried professional force, and it was therefore a demand for continued employment which was the basis of the problem at Sumaysat. However, the army also included some who were loyal to the Umayyads more than to their wages, and had clearly been present at Sumaysat in the hopes of restoring the former ruling family. Two of these broke away from the re-employed army and seized nearby forts – this was now the northern frontier – and defied Abd Allah.[1]

Another mixed Umayyad loyalist and army revolt took place in the south. A force in the Hawran commanded by Habib ibn Murra came out in rebellion against Abd Allah soon after his arrival at Damascus, and when he was actually encamped not far away. They were mainly Qays troops, who were soon joined by a force under the governor of Damascus, Uthman ibn Abd-al-Ala ibn Suraqa. This man had been a prominent official in the last decade of Umayyad rule, had switched sides to join the Abbasids, and had been made governor of the province by Abd Allah. He commanded a force in the city which was partly Yamanis from the north and partly Khurasanis brought in by Abd Allah. When he marched against Habib and his men, the Yamanis came out for the Umayyads, and Ibn Suraqa followed them. They returned to Damascus and drove out the Khursanis, but when Abd Allah's own troops arrived, Ibn Suraqa decamped to Beirut with the provincial treasure, and his Qays force, now under Habib, retreated. The Yamanis changed sides again. Habib's original force was defeated, and Ibn Suraqa returned, plus treasure, and was reappointed; the Yamanis were re-employed.[2]

Rather more dangerous than these military mutinies were risings explicitly in favour of an Umayyad return. The armies of Ishaq ibn Muslim and Habib ibn Murra were only using the Umayyad name as a talisman and a threat; but the two small forces in the frontier forts were seriously pro-Umayyad, and there were others similarly clear in their intentions. At Balis on the Euphrates the Qays general, Abu al-Ward, a long-time Umayyad commander, clashed with a Khurasani force which had been stationed nearby, no doubt with the aim of ensuring that this area of known Umayyad loyalists was under control. This did not work, and when Abu al-Ward gathered his men and attacked the Khursanis he was joined by many supporters from the neighbourhood.

More significantly he was also joined by Abu Muhammad al-Sufyani, who arrived from his home at Palmyra, and who was another former Umayyad commander but who also claimed descent from the great Caliph Muawiya. Further, he announced that he was *the* Sufyani, a mythical expected messianic saviour. This combination of military expertise and a messiah was potent. Abd Allah was occupied in the south with the rebellion of Habib ibn Murra, and the first force he sent against Abu Muhammad was defeated. He came north himself with his own army, collected the defeated force and met the advancing Umayyad loyalist army of Abu al-Ward and Abu Muhammad near Homs and this time won. Abu al-Ward died, but Abu Muhammad escaped back to Palmyra. An attempt by a detachment of Abd Allah's army against Palmyra failed, but Abu Muhammad fled to hiding in Arabia.[3]

His nephew Al-Abbas ibn Muhammad al-Sufyani, who had presumably been involved in his uncle's original rising, staged a reprise in Aleppo while the other was still hemmed in at Palmyra, and after Abd Allah had returned to Damscus to deal with Habib. But this time a different army struck at the rising, from the Jazirah, where Abu Ja'far, Abd Allah's own nephew (and brother of the new caliph, Saffah) swiftly arrived to suppress the Aleppine force. It was thus all over, and Abu Ja'far's force was back in the Jazirah, when Abd Allah returned to the north.[4] (The two Abbasids had of course combined to suppress and recruit Ishaq's force, but they were also rivals.)

For a time, therefore, Abd Allah had been beset by simultaneous revolts, all technically in the name of an Umayyad restoration, in the Hawran, on the Euphrates, and on the Byzantine frontier. The removal of Ishaq's army was clearly vital, since if Abu Muhammad had made serious progress in Syria Ishaq may well have joined him, as probably would Habib; Ibn Suraqa would have proclaimed his loyalty, and no doubt other governors would have considered their positions. With all Syria coming out in favour of an Umayyad return, the Abbasid revolution would have stalled badly, and a prolonged civil war was likely, possibly with an Umayyad return.

These revolts were defeated by Abd Allah's classic use of the central position. By controlling Homs and Damascus he was able to keep the various risings – in Aleppo, by the Euphrates, and the Byzantine frontier in the north, and the Hawran in the south – separate and could deal with them one at a time. He ignored the two minor problems in the north for a time, and aimed to use his army – in part Ishaq's experienced frontier army presumably – for a raid into Byzantine territory. But the diehard Umayyad loyalists who had left Ishaq's army gathered and he had to break off the disperse them. They were led by Aban ibn Muawiya, a grandson of the Caliph Hisham, and he and his followers then seized the fort of Kaysum, a little west of Sumaysat. Abd Allah had to besiege the fort, and when he captured Aban he treated him with the cruelty and humiliation he always reserved for true

Umayyads. The other fort was less important, and the force there held out for three years.[5]

The loyalty exhibited towards the Umayyads among the Syrians was clearly less than total. The armies which mutinied had usually done so to ensure their soldiers' continued employment, but also they resented the predominance accorded by the Abbasid commanders to the Khurasani troops which had spearheaded the Abbasid campaign of conquest. The Syrian army, particularly the Qays, had long lorded over all the other Arab armies, and it was this demotion which they did not like.

Abd Allah clearly appreciated this. When his nephew the Caliph al-Saffah died in 754, he used his command of the Syrian army to claim the throne. He had gathered a large force at Doliche (Duluk) in north Syria, with the intention of conducting a raid into Anatolia when he heard of Saffah's death. But he was opposed by Abu Ja'far, his nephew, who also claimed the throne. Abu Ja'far was a more skilled politician, and he could count on the Khurasanis. Abd Allah marched his army towards Iraq, but was held up for over a month at Harran, where the small garrison was loyal to Abu Ja'far. The delay allowed Abu Ja'far to call up the Khursanis, and when the Syrian army discovered that it was to fight them it began to break up.

Abd Allah's army was composed of three groups. The largest was the forces of the Yamanis of the Jazirah and north Syria, but he also had a considerable contingent of Qays troops from southern Syria. These two clearly provided support to the pretender in the hopes of recovering prestige and influence. The real difficulty was that Abd Allah also had a substantial contingent of Khurasani troops, and they proved to be unwilling to fight their fellows in the Abbasid force facing them. When invited to come over, many did; Abd Allah then used the Syrians to massacre the rest. When the battle took place, near Nisibis in the Jazirah, Abd Allah's force was swiftly beaten. He and his brother escaped to Basra, and when found they were kept under house arrest.[6] The defeated army again survived because it was a valuable resource, and was pardoned. On the other hand, it was clearly reduced in both numbers and prestige by its constant failure to impose its will, and it withered away as a political force in the next years. As an army it did not rebel again.

Not surprisingly the turmoil in the caliphate attracted the military attention of the Byzantines. In 752, the year after Abd Allah's first attempt to mount an Anatolian raid had failed, the Emperor Constantine brought an army to the frontier and captured Theodosiopolis, facing Armenia, and Melitene (Malatya) on the Euphrates, which commanded a route connecting Syria and Anatolia. He was presumably hoping to intervene in the fighting between the Muslims in the frontier area, but then he abandoned any such plans, and marched away. Melitene reverted to Muslim control. Constantine took with him people from the region of warfare who chose to move and resettled them in Thrace.[7]

Abd Allah had tried more than once to conduct a raid himself, but again failed, this time because he claimed the throne. His successor as governor in Qinnasrin was Salih ibn Ali, the first member of a family which became prominent in Syria for the next two generations and more. He took an army, said to number 80,000 men, into Anatolia in 756. But he was menaced by the Byzantine army under Constantine, and retired without achieving much; he, like Constantine earlier, collected some locals who had joined him and took them back into Syria.[8]

The new caliph, Abu Ja'far, took the throne name of al-Mansur. He was beset by problems for several years, largely deriving from the promises and assumptions of the revolution. A problem which could be solved relatively easily was that of finance, since he had a large pool of powerless taxpayers to squeeze. One of his early measures was therefore an increase of taxation, specifically directed at the Christian population. Salih ibn Ali had also directed his revolutionary attention at the Christians, exiling the patriarch of Antioch (an appointment in the gift of the Byzantine emperor) and forbidding the display of the cross; church treasuries were confiscated. He also rooted out a group of Zoroastrians who were living in Aleppo and Qinnesrin, and who must have moved there a century and a half earlier during the Persian occupation. This was traditionally regarded as a religion to be tolerated, but it is evident that the Abbasid revolutionaries were more determined to proselytize than their Umayyad predecessors.[9]

The pressure of taxation on the generally compliant Christian population was one of the causes of the next problem for the governors of Syria. In 759 a revolt began in the Lebanese Mountains among the Christian peasantry there, who complained of the burden of taxation. The peasants were Christian, of course, as were most of people of Syria. This was particularly so with those in the more inaccessible regions such as the mountains, who seem to have been relatively untouched by Islam, but some were also descendants of the Mardaites who had moved to the Lebanon nearly a century before. Some had moved to the Byzantine lands in the 690s, but others had stayed in Syria, having made an agreement with the Caliph al-Walid, the terms of which included a continuing exemption from the poll tax.[10] No doubt the new regime would not recognize such an agreement made by the Umayyads, and attempting to collect it from those who felt they were exempt would certainly cause trouble.

But the peasantry were also under pressure from other causes by now. The increasing aridity may not have directly affected the mountaineers, for their hills were the best watered regions of all Syria, but any increase in their population would have an instant effect, since their resources were necessarily few. It may be that it was only the fact of the light taxation they were under which would permit them to survive at all (they had to pay other taxes, such as those on property, of course). The constant disturbances in Syria over the past decade and a half will also have disrupted their markets and impoverished everyone. It will not have helped that their religion seemed to be under threat from the new regime as well.

They emerged from their hills to complain to the sub-governor at Baalbek, and when they received no satisfaction they found a leader in a man called Theodore, who was proclaimed king, and they invaded the Bekaa Valley. They killed any Muslims they met, looted the villages and headed for Baalbek. They were scattered by a force of Muslim cavalry and the survivors took refuge in the mountains. There they were besieged in a mountain fort by forces from both the Bekaa and the coast, until forced to surrender. Theodore and others fled to Byzantine territory.[11] The survivors were not subjected to the poll tax even so, and when an attempt was made by a governor to collect it in the reign of Caliph al-Wathik (842–847) they appealed to the caliph, who agreed that they were exempt.[12]

The rising may best be seen as a symptom of the deterioration of conditions for the peasantry in Syria as a whole. Another aspect of this was the new appearance, at least in any strength, of 'bandits', called 'Zawaqil', for the first time since the late Hellenistic period. They also appear in the same region as at the time of Herod and his sons, in the Hawran and the nearby lands, Batanaea and Leja. They were numerous enough by about AD 800 to become a nuisance which had to be dealt with by the local governor, Ibrahim ibn Muhammad (803–804). He had the sense to recruit two of the larger bands, and sent them to suppress a third – led by a Jew – who had captured the tax revenue caravan of Filastin on its way to either Damascus or Baghdad. The domesticated bands were then used to suppress other, smaller bands.[13] But the appearance of such bands, large enough to be reckoned as small armies, is clearly a symptom of the deterioration of agrarian conditions. That they appeared in the Hawran region is a mark of the marginal conditions in that area, which, with its basalt outcrops and caves, and its small fertile areas, is ideal bandit territory, whereas other areas in the south (east of the Jordan) would cease to the productive much more quickly.

Two or three years after the defeat of Theodore and his Mardaites in 759 al-Mansur finally suppressed the last of those who still expected benefits from the revolution. Then he founded a new city, Baghdad, in celebration, a hugely expensive project which was a clear indication that the Abbasids' revolution of equality had given way to self-aggrandizement, exorbitant display, and luxury.[14] Al-Mansur waited for several more years before setting about what had become one of the main necessary activities of a caliph, raids on the Byzantine Empire. One reason for the delay must have been the need for the empire to recover from the civil warfare of the past twenty years, but another may have been that the man to lead the raid was Salih ibn Ali. He was another of the caliph's uncles, a younger brother of Abd Allah, though he had proved to be loyal in the latter's revolt. Salih had been governor of Egypt, and had sat out the conflict in a pose of studied neutrality when his participation on Abd Allah's side could have given him victory. Salih was then (or maybe earlier) appointed governor of Filastin, where he defeated Abd Allah's governor of Damascus, and later hunted down a recalcitrant at Baalbek. The exact timing of his operations in Filastin is not clear; perhaps he waited until it was clear that Abd Allah was beaten; he also received subsidies from al-Mansur which would have kept him neutral in the decisive moments.[15] After a brief period as governor of Syria after the revolt, he was transferred to Qinnesrin, which was now the headquarters for organizing the Anatolian raids. But the lesson of Abd Allah's revolt was that family members were not necessarily loyal, even though he had been posted to north Syria because he was the caliph's uncle.

It thus seems no accident that the raids were not resumed until Salih died, in 769, though, to be fair, he had been kept busy enough. He is credited by Baladhuri with much of the work of refortifying the frontier; the abandoned land of Kilikia was slowly claimed by the Muslims. Mopsuhestia for a time had been their frontier post, and was several times attacked by Greeks. Al-Mansur ordered it repaired after damage from an earthquake, and soon Adana was reoccupied.[16] Adana, however, if not the others, had to be rebuilt fifty years later, in 809 or 810. The key, however, was Tarsus, which was recognized as such in the reign of the Caliph al-Mahdi (775–785), but not finally built and occupied until late in the reign of al-Rashid, when the governor of Qinnesrin Abd al-Malik ibn Salih sent a substantial garrison to it. This area was largely garrisoned by north Syrians and Khurasanis.[17] The importance of Tarsus was that a strong force there commanded the main route through the Taurus Mountains by way of the Kilikian Gates by either blocking a Byzantine raid or permitting a Muslim one.[18]

The Salihian family, the Banu Salih, also became rich. Salih acquired much of the former property of the Umayyads in Syria and the Jazirah; he even married the widow of the Caliph Marwan II.[19] This of course, assisted in the influence he gained in Syria, while he also to a degree favoured Qays. When he died in 769 he was succeeded in his position and influence by his son Fadl, who was in turn succeded by his brother Abd al-Malik, whose influence at the court of the Caliph al-Rashid rivalled that of the Barmakid family. All this was some consolation to the Syrians, who could assume that the family which held so much property in Syria and the Jazirah could also influence imperial policies; for the Banu Salih, the support of the chiefs of the tribes and the Syrian armies was a source of strength in caliphal politics.

Raids into Anatolia recommenced in 770 and continued almost every year for the next ten. The Caliph al-Mahdi (775– 85) took to commanding them – or at least leading them – himself. His son Harun (the later Caliph al-Rashid) was also involved and developed a taste for it.[20] But these campaigns were really raids, not attempts at conquest such as the Umayyads had made. The object was to gather loot and prisoners – the prisoners were frequently exchanged for captured Muslims, or ransomed.[21] Al-Rashid eventually organized the frontier as a new province, Awasim, from which the raids always set out, and partly in order to keep contact with events on the frontier he developed a new base at Raqqa on the Euphrates.[22] In 806 he led a huge army on a raid, said to number 135,000 men, and in 808 another great force, even larger.[23] But no conquests resulted. The raids had become a sort of ritual, one of the things that a caliph was supposed to do, or at least to organize.

Within Syria the victory of the Abbasids and their revolution had left the chiefs of the tribal factions without patronage except that of the Banu Salih. They competed for what there was by gaining influence with the governors – the repeated presence of members of the Banu Salih in these offices provided some stability – but the local balance could easily be upset by a governor who exhibited partiality. The basic antagonism was, of course, between Qaysites, largely concentrated in the south and centre, and the Yamanis, predominant in Qinnesrin and the Jazirah. The Abbasid victory had been achieved in part by an alliance with the Yamanis, who gained territory and influence in the south, which was resented by the Qaysites.

The factional disputes between Qays and Yamanis were rarely peaceful, and Syria suffered a fairly constant low level of local violence. This included riots in the cities. The governors of Damascus repeatedly faced such problems, and solutions were not helped by the insistence by al-Rashid in particular in moving governors after only short periods in office; the local historian of Damascus comments that urban violence had become normal.[24]

Such a situation could rapidly grow out of hand. In Damascus it did so in 793, when a new governor seemed to favour the Yamani faction. A local notable in the Hawran, Abu al-Haydham, was summoned to Damascus by the governor to discuss a local problem, but he received no satisfaction from the governor, who would not even meet him. Some Qaysite villagers whose homes had been destroyed by Yamanis then appealed to him to intercede for them, but again the governor provided no real satisfaction, which by this time required him to give up supporting the Yamanis. Abu al-Haydham thereupon seized control of the city, which initiated a violent factional conflict that brought in supporters of both sides from Palestine and Homs and the Bekaa, and was only resolved by an imperial expedition from Baghdad led by the Barmakid Ja'far ibn Yahya. The factional root of the problem was not, of course, dealt with, but peace was at least imposed for a while. The city and the Ghuta had suffered serious damage in the fighting, thus reducing the region's wealth still more. It was in part the condition to which the Ghuta had been reduced, and the effects of the search in the Hawran for Abu al-Haydham by the soldiers, which fuelled the rise of the bandits, the *zawaqil*, who had to be dealt with by the later governor, Ibrahim ibn Muhammad.[25]

The reign of al-Rashid was a violent one in Syria, and this continued, inevitably, during the long civil war between his sons, which followed his death and was largely caused by his complicated provisions for the succession. The factionalism continued, in part encouraged by the events of Abu al-Haydham's revolt. Ja'far ibn Yahya's expedition had to attend to a problem in Homs, which was as faction–ridden as Damascus, and another in Palestine and the Balka, in which the monastery of as-Sabas was badly damaged.[26] The civil war which lasted from 810–819 preoccupied all governments, leaving little time to attend to other regions than Iraq. At one point the senior man of the Banu Salih, Abd al-Malik, who had been imprisoned by al-Rashid when he brought down both the Barmakids and the Salihians in 802–803, returned to Syria on behalf of the embattled Caliph al-Amin. The Syrians flocked to join him, an indication of the powerful influence he had in the country, which of course was why he had been imprisoned. But he died soon after arriving and al-Amin's hopes of using Syrians against his enemies died with him.[27]

The long fighting in Iraq meant that many provinces were ignored. Syria virtually fell out of central government control, giving free play to the factions. The open fighting between the brothers Al-Amin and Al-Mamun saw the immediate evaporation of all authority in Syria, and the seizure of power locally by the factions, or by local strong men. Syria, that is, reacted in its usual way where there was no overall authority and broke up into its geographical fragments. Local rulers can be identified at Aleppo, at Qinnesrin, Homs, Damascus, Ramlah, Qurus, and in north Syria; ravaging of the countryside and destruction of villages took place in the Homs area, the Damascus Ghuta, and Palestine.[28]

This was, of course, just the opportunity which surviving Umayyad family members looked to. In Damascus an old man, Abu al-Umaytir, who had lived quietly all his life in the Ghuta – he was said to be about 90 – suddenly emerged in 811 as a caliphal candidate. He maintained his position in the city very precariously for over a year, supported by the Yamanis. Their attacks on Qaysites provoked the usual counter-violence, and the city and the local countryside were once again subject to the violent attentions of the rival forces. Not only did Abu al-Umaytir have to contend with factional opponents, but he found he was briefly displaced by another caliphal claimant, a descendant of the caliph Uthman. The end came when a local Qays notable from the Hawran, Muhammad ibn Salih ibn Bayhas, succeeded in chasing both claimants from the city, and received some recognition from al-Mamun as governor of Syria.[29] He held the position until 823. (Another Umayyad claimant popped up soon after, Said ibn Khalid al-Faddayni, named for his home village in the Hawran, who maintained himself in the country south of Bostra for a few months.)[30] The episode may have been headed by a series of Umayyads, but it was essentially only one more episode in Syrian factionalism.

The north of Syria was fully as factional as Damascus. The region of the Euphrates was subject to blackmail raids by a series of bands, which can be described as *zawaqil*. The most prominent leader was Nasr ibn Shabbath, who managed to gather several of the bands together to attack Raqqa, but every town and city and monastery in the area was subject to their extortions.[31]

In the nature of things these internal fights could accomplish nothing permanent and eventually, once one of the contenders had gained control in Iraq, an expedition would arrive from outside to impose order – not to solve the problem of the factions, again, but mainly to ensure that the taxes were collected and forwarded to the capital. However, the civil war had grievously depleted caliphal resources, and large expeditions were no longer possible. To recover some control in Syria a small expedition was sent under the command of Abd Allah ibn Tahir, the second son of the man who had been more successful than most in securing the throne for Caliph al-Mamun. In 823 he brought a small but efficient army westwards, dealing first with the problem of Nasr ibn Shabbath and his fellow ravagers in the north, partly by conciliating them diplomatically, but in the end by using force on the recalcitrants, including Nasr. He had retreated to the fort at Kaysum near Sumatsat, and Abd Allah's combination of threat and diplomacy brought him to submission. He used the same techniques in Syria and in Egypt. In each case he located the different contending groups, reconciled some and then either persuaded the others to give in or was able, with his own and his new supporters' armies, to crush the irreconcilables.[32]

Again, this was not a solution to the basic problem, but the central government probably did not really care. Syria had never been a major interest of the Abbasids, and its constant factionalism pushed it even further down their list of concerns, while making it ever more unlikely that it would be a credible threat. The appointment in 828 of the caliph's brother Abu Ishaq, the future caliph al-Mu'tasim, as Syrian governor, helped to calm the country by suggesting that Syria would not be wholly ignored by the Abbasid government, and by indicating that Syrians were not to be appointed governors any more; their factionalism now disqualified them, and so put them out of reach of political (and economic) favour. The factions began to fade from that time.

Mu'tasim inherited the caliphate in 833 when Mamun died, and when his nephew al-Abbas failed to challenge him for the position.[33] Mu'tasim had gathered a force of Turkish slave soldiers during his time as Mamun's western viceroy, beginning a process which would eventually destroy the Abbasid caliphate – after the caliphs had done their best to do so first.

The governor of Syria from now on was usually a prominent personage, an Abbasid scion or one of the caliph's Turks, who at first owed all their positions to him. The governor was based in Baghdad, or, when it was built, in the new capital at Samarra. The governor was normally given charge of several provinces: Egypt, Syria and the Jazirah was one normal combination, governed from Iraq from 839 by Ashinas al-Turki. This was intended mainly as a financial arrangement, whereby the revenues of the provinces were forwarded to the governor in Iraq.

The governors appointed their own sub-governors to do the actual ruling for them. This naturally reduced the power of the men on the spot, but it also reduced even further the influence of the Syrians, the chiefs of the tribes. An alternative to a capable Turk was to appoint a child of the royal house, not a development likely to promote efficient provincial government.[34]

The chiefs paid little attention to their inferiors, and the peasantry had suffered along with the townsmen in the various revolts conducted by chiefs for access to power. In 840 another peasant revolt developed, this time in al-Urdunn. The leader, Abu Harb, after attracting a small following, claimed to be the Sufyani, and led his followers, who ultimately numbered 3,000, said to be 'starving and destitute', into ravaging raids into Palestine, looting towns, cities, monasteries, Christians, Samaritans and Muslims alike. It was essentially a class war, with those owning wealth as the targets. The rebels were eventually beaten by a small force sent by the governor which waited until most of the participants had gone home to tend their fields at harvest. It is worth noting that they went into Palestine to do their looting; the lands east of the Jordan were presumably by this time too poor to provide wealth; their rising had begun after the very cold winter and a locust plague; such problems were exactly the sort which would tip a local economy from desperation into starvation. There was also a factional aspect to their campaign, since Abu Harb was supported by some Yamani chiefs, and he headed into Qays and Kalb territory to do his work.[35]

The plots and factional fights and risings did not stop. Indeed, as the central government appeared to become more powerful and centralized, it actually began to lose its grip on the provinces. There was constant trouble in Homs in the 850s and 860s, which brought the attention of an army from Iraq, and another gathered from Damascus and Palestine, but neither was successful in ending the trouble. The basis of the problem seems to have been the tax collection policies of the local governors and their agents, several of whom were driven from the city. The population of the city was mixed, but Muslims, Christian and Jews all joined in the uprising. No doubt the true basic reason was the combination of onerous taxation and the fact that Homs was situated close to the border of the steppe, and would be the first port of call for any farmers who could no longer cope with the dry conditions. In the end the city appealed to the local leader of the Kalb tribe, Utayf ibn Nima al-Kalbi, who came to assist. He allied with another local leader, al-Fusays, who had seized control of Maaret en-Numan and then of Qinnesrin. The Homsis made an attempt to attack Damascus, but were beaten back by the governor's forces. Yet when the imperial government sent another army the people of Homs were able to resist successfully. Utayf fled but was caught and killed. His partner al-Fusays was induced to change sides and was appointed the local governor at Lattakiah. The eventual fate of Homs itself in this confrontation is not known, but probably the city was able to persuade the new governor of its loyalty.

Yet there was more trouble in the city for the next twenty years. Clearly there was something more than mere resentment at the level of taxation behind all of this.[36]

Many of the governors of the Syrian and Jaziran provinces in the period from Mu'tasim's accession onwards were Turks. At Damascus there were half a dozen of these men in succession. They may have been slaves of the caliph, or more probably freedmen, even voluntarily enlisted freedmen. They were neither more nor less competent at the job than any other men, being as keen as others on collecting taxes with sticky fingers. The normal route for men to become governors had always been through the army from the beginning of Arab rule, and the fact that a man was a Turk rather than an Arab (or a central Asian, or a Slav, or a Greek) probably had no effect on his conduct, or on the general animosity with which the local population regarded him.

However, at the centre of the empire the Turkish troops staged a series of coups in the 860s aiming both to retain their privileged position close to the caliph and to secure a caliph who was amenable to their wishes. Three caliphs, beginning with Mutawakkil in 861, were murdered. This was clearly one of the background elements in the problem at Homs and elsewhere in the period, for the constant change in caliphs (six between 861 and 870) reduced central authority over the provinces markedly, as in the civil war of 810–819. Eventually in 877 much of Syria was taken over by the governor of Egypt, Ahmad ibn Tulun, one of the Turkish soldier-governors. This was hardly a new condition for Syria. It had been linked with Egypt several times under the system of governors who had operated from Samarra and never visited their provinces. It was not unknown for a governor of Egypt to intervene in Syria when either he felt it necessary or he could profit by it.

Ahmad ibn Tulun gained permission to increase his forces and had squeezed Egypt to produce substantial treasure. The disorder in Syria gave him the excuse to move in, first into Palestine and then in 877 as far north as the Euphrates. Having done so, he refused to forward the taxation revenues to Samarra, a mark of independence (a large treasure which was spent on buildings and on ludicrous luxury for the rulers). Other parts of the Abbasid Empire had been similarly breaking away since the revolution; Spain, Africa, eastern Iran, but this was the first time a major section of the original Arab Empire had been detached from caliphal rule. It was the decisive break; Islam was never to be united again.

Chapter 18

Invasions

The Arab Empire as constituted in the seventh century AD lasted until the 870s, by which time it had been reduced to Iraq and some additional sections. For Syria the empire lasted for about 240 years, from the original conquest in 638 to the invasion of Ahmad ibn Tulun, which was accomplished by about 878. This period of time was somewhat shorter than the previous episodes of foreign domination, the Late Roman Christian (AD c.300–638) and the Early Roman (63 BC–AD c.300). It was followed by a series of invasions, from Egypt, from Iraq, from Anatolia, and from Europe, which left the country broken into a dozen pieces, all ruled by foreign dynasties.

One of the results of the Islamic conquest had been to make available to the Syrian population the Islamic religion. It had not been received with any enthusiasm. The rate of conversion to Islam had been very slow, and even after over a century of Muslim rule perhaps only 10 per cent were Muslims. Partly this was due to the lack of any pressure to convert. The Muslim dispensation had been to tolerate the old religions, but tax their adherents for the benefit of the Muslims, mainly the soldiers. So one of the main inducements to convert was financial, to escape the poll tax. The old religions, and in Syria that meant Christianity in its several forms, had had a firm enough grip on most people to discourage changing sides. Yet the longer the Muslims ruled invariably there was a gradual shift from one to the other.

It is, of course, impossible to quantify the rate of take-up of the new religion. Without pressure and with so minor an inducement, it was incredibly slow. An essay on the subject has suggested the figure of 10 per cent of the Syrian population, as mentioned, was Muslim by the end of the Umayyad dynasty, but that this had risen to about 50 per cent by the end of Abbasid rule in about 880.[1] However, it is known that large numbers of Christians resisted assimilation all along, and still do. The rate of conversion, therefore, is probably much exaggerated. In the Ottoman census of the 1870s 40 per cent of the Aleppo and Syrian provincial populations remain non-Muslim.[2] The Jewish population of Syria benefited from a toleration which had been unavailable under Byzantine (or earlier under Roman) rule, and Christians found that their internecine conflicts abruptly became much less important, and did not bring official persecution any more – at least until a Muslim fanatic gained power.

The Muslims developed their own internecine disputes. The Abbasid revolution had been accomplished in part by enlisting support from the Alids, those who believed that the caliphate should descend among the heirs of the fourth caliph, Ali. The majority of the Muslims did not agree, and the Alids remained a subterranean and minority movement, occasionally breaking to the surface at times of crisis. Among the Abbasids the Alids were enlisted as supporters twice, only to be discarded once the Abbasids had gained power. Under such pressure and in the light of such betrayals the Alids split into factions.

Their own opportunity came, of course, with the progressive collapse of the Abbasid regime. The Shi'ite faction, as it can now be called, appeared in various places and with various degrees of fanaticism and competence. For Syria, there were probably small groups in existence all through the Abbasid time, but only when the Tulunids seized partial control of Syria were they able to make clear territorial gains, for a time.

The Tulunid rule of Syria was never either complete or all that well-received. It began with a grant from the Abbasid caliph in Baghdad, who was beset by a great slave revolt in southern Iraq. Ahmad ibn Tulun thus gained control as far north as Damascus, and then moved further north to attempt to gain control over the frontier area. He was resisted in arms at Antioch, and was denied Tarsus in Kilikia by the townspeople. The prize was not necessarily the frontier itself, though to gain command there would go some way to prevent interference from the south, but the trade passing through the passes, which he would tax.[3]

A Shi'ite group, the Qaramatiyah, had emerged in the Arabian Desert, in much the same way as the earlier Kharijites. A branch was established at Salamaniya, in the Syrian Desert west of Palmyra, where they controlled the trade route between Kufa and Damascus. This rendered them unpopular in both Iraq and Syria, and with the Tulunids, whose tax revenues suffered. They launched a serious attack on Damascus in 900, beat the Tulunid garrison but failed to take the city. Other attacks damaged Homs and Hama, and reached as far as Baalbek in the Bekaa.[4]

The failure of the Tulunid regime to protect central Syria opened the way for an Abbasid revival. An Abbasid army under Muhammad ibn Sulayman marched round from Iraq, re-established control over the local rulers in the Jazirah, and came south to eliminate the Qaramatiyah, who were defeated in open battle near Hama.[5] A Tulunid army marched north at the same time, and between them these two crushed the Qarmatiyah without difficulty, and then moved on to retake control over Egypt. A large part of the Tulunid army then joined the Abbasids and was sent to Iraq; the Abbasid commander seized the opportunity and marched to Egypt, where the Tulunid regime collapsed at once, attacked by a naval contingent from Tarsus, the Abbasid army, and a contingent from the Hamdanids of north Syria and the Jazirah at the same time.[6]

The restored Abbasid rule depended too much on an able caliph in combination with an able *wazir*, and so did not last long. By 935 another capable provincial governor in Egypt (Muhammad ibn Tughj, the son of the Turkish commander who had defended Damascus in the early 900s) shifted into independence, having gained an honorary title of Ikhshid from the caliph, who perhaps imagined this would keep him loyal. Once again Syria became a victim of these dynasties, though this time the Egyptian control extended no further north than Damascus. In north Syria for a time a man called ibn Ra'iq held power, but not for long.[7]

One of the results of this general instability, building on the frequently indicated dissatisfaction with Abbasid rule expressed in all of Syria during the past century and a half, was that it became clear to Syrians that there was an alternative to the Abbasid system, and that the Abbasid failures in the civil war made such attractions possible. Above all, the country's basic geographical disunity reasserted itself. The Tulunids had never controlled all Syria, having failed to establish control of the northern frontier areas. The Ikhshidids never even attempted to control the territory north of Damascus, which soon fell to a new dynasty out of the Jazirah, the Hamdanids, who had emerged as Abbasid clients in Mosul, and took over Aleppo in 945. No doubt some of the Qaramati remained in Syria after their defeat, though Salamaniya seems to have been destroyed – certainly the number of Shi'ites increased in the tenth century.

The Hamdanids came from an Arab clan, the Banu Taghlib, domiciled in the Jazirah, probably since the original conquest. The first of the family to gain territorial power was made governor of Mosul in 905, as the Abbasid reconquest of the west was beginning, and he joined in that campaign. As Abbasid authority again retreated, the Mosul governor assumed independence and extended his rule westwards, and a cadet member moved west to establish himself as ruler of Aleppo, removing ibn Ra'iq in the process. This was Sayf ad-Dawla Ali, who also took over the rest of north Syria. He clashed with the Ikhshid, but the two men soon agreed to divide Syria between them. Sayf ad-Dawla was allied in seizing Aleppo with another Arab tribe, the Banu Kilab, which was established in the steppe between Aleppo and the Euphrates. This meant that he was disliked by the other local tribes, in particular the Banu Kalb, long-time antagonists to the Abbasids. This produced a Bedouin war, in which many domiciled Arabs were driven into the desert to die and as a result the Banu Kalb had to move south out of the area. The Hamdanids were moderate Shi'ites, who continued to recognize the Sunni Abbasid caliph, presumably as a gesture to stave off hostility. This can only have encouraged the growth of Shi'ism in Syria – the Banu Kalb were Shi'ia, for example, after the Qaramatiyah incursion.[8]

The Hamdanids were also active fighters on the Byzantine frontier, thus reactivating this Muslim pastime after a lengthy break. The signal for this renewed bout of warfare was perhaps the capture of Melitene by the Byzantines in 934.[9]

When Sayf ad-Dawla gained control of Aleppo he built up an armed force, and used it to raid through the mountains. He was only moderately successful, suffering as many defeats as he achieved loot and captives. He also came up against several of the pre-eminent soldiers of Byzantine history: Nikephoros Phocas and John Tzimiskes, who both later became emperors; later, the Emperor Basil II campaigned in Syria.

The failure of Sayf ad-Dawla's *jihad* wars is usually put down to the lack of support he had from the rest of the Muslim regions, but his defeat was really down as much to the military efficiency developed by the Byzantine Empire in the previous century. This cannot have been unknown to him, which suggests he was being merely foolhardy in attacking what was clearly a much stronger power. He deserved his defeat.

But for Syria this was not merely the defeat of an intrusive warlord, for the Byzantine riposte was to conquer a substantial part of north Syria. Sayf ad-Dawla was comprehensively defeated by 965, and four years later the city of Antioch, one of the main centres of the *jihadis*, was captured. Aleppo itself fell later that year, as did Homs, though both were left in the hands of Sayf ad-Dawla; he was compelled to pay tribute. By this agreement the city became a relatively small city state owing allegiance to the Christian emperor, a buffer between the Byzantine conquests and the Muslim powers. The coast from the mouth of the Orontes south as far as the mouth of the Eleutheros became part of the Byzantine Empire, along with Antioch and Kilikia. Sa'd ad-Dawla Sharif, Sayf ad-Dawla's successor, retreated to his Jazirah territories, leaving Aleppo in the hands of a minister.[10]

When the Fatimids from the south attempted to gain control of a weakened Aleppo it was 'protected' by a Byzantine army. The Byzantines do not ever seem to have wished to possess the city themselves, seeing it as more useful as a buffer. Three years later, in 972, the Emperor John Tzimiskes marched his army all the way into Palestine without opposition, calling at Caesarea and Tiberias; he was assisted by the collapse of the Fatimid position in the region.[11]

The conquest of this northern area by Byzantine forces (which included Kilikia) resulted in a decisive change in the population of the conquered area. In each city the population was either deported into Anatolia, or was driven out. This latter fate was that of the Muslims. A new population of Christians, largely from within Syria or Armenia, was invited to replace them. Given that the expelled populations had made their living largely by *jihadi* activities at Byzantine expense, and in the history of Muslim raids into Anatolia over the previous three centuries, it seems a reasonable action, but it began the process of segregating the people of the various faiths into distinct geographical sections. (In Melitene, however, when the same measure had been taken in 934, large numbers of Muslims had instantly become Christians.) This separation, of course, had begun already in Syria as Shi'ites separated themselves off from their Sunni and Christian neighbours for self–protection; the Byzantine action was on an international scale, not a local one.[12]

Southern Syria was meanwhile suffering even more than the north. The Ikhshidid regime was moderately successful in controlling its section of Syria, as far north as Damascus, but was threatened by the enmity of the Fatimid dynasty of North Africa. These were Shi'ites, and during the 960s they found Egypt a fertile field for intrigue. Meanwhile the Qaramatiyah had revived, based at Hasa near Bahrayn, but allied with several of the Bedouin tribes of the desert. Together they raided Iraq repeatedly, sacked and looted Basra, and threatened Baghdad, while the Abbasid army regularly suffered defeat by them. As the Fatimid menace to Egypt grew so did the Qaramati threat to Syria, which they had not raided for several decades. Fatimids and Qaramati did not agree on some aspects of doctrine but were quite prepared to cooperate when they had a common enemy.

The Qaramati could be kept quiet by subsidies – they had developed the habit of attacking the Hajj unless paid to refrain – and were probably receiving subsidies from the Ikhshidids to keep away from southern Syria. In 964, perhaps because no subsidy was forthcoming, perhaps in cooperation with the Fatimid intrigues, they raided Palestine, and sacked Tiberias, the capital of al-Urdunn. In Egypt the Ikhshidid dynasty was failing, with three new *amirs* in eight years, one of them the long-time slave *wazir*. Four years later the Qaramatiyah had an even greater success, capturing both Ramlah, deep inside Palestine, and Damascus; and next year their menace compelled the Ikhshidid governor of Syria to pay tribute to keep them from the same two cities.

That was the year, 969, when the Fatimid armies finally took Egypt, and the year the Emperor Nikephoros Phokas captured Antioch. One of the first results for the Fatimids was a quarrel with the Qaramati, whose activities in Syria now threatened territory the Fatimids regarded as theirs. The Qaramati raided Damascus and Ramlah again in 971, and sent raids into both Syria and Egypt for the next several years. (So when the Emperor John Tzimiskes campaigned as far as Caesarea and Tiberias in 972 he was joining in the ransacking of southern Syria, and had little to fear from any of the various Muslim enemies he might encounter.) At last in 978 the Qaramati were first of all defeated in an invasion of Egypt, and then persuaded to stay home by a subsidy. This annoyed the Bedouin, who had only become nominally Qaramati in order to raid, and the Qaramati movement was sundered and died away.[13]

One of the results of these activities was to finally destroy much of the agricultural activity of the steppe land. The long swathe of territory which had been progressively claimed for arable farming – or at least mixed arable and herding – since the early Hellenistic period, and had been maintained with difficulty until the early Abbasid times, now reverted largely to pastoralism. Of course, this had been in process for a couple of centuries, but the Bedouin raids of the tenth century finally ended the farmers' occupation of these lands. The territory east of Jordan, the Hawran, parts of the Damascus Ghuta, and the lands east of Homs and Hama, and the 'dead cities' region, were all devoid of permanent inhabitants from now on for a millennium.

The Fatimids had, in effect, inherited the lands of the Ikhshidids, and had identified Syria, at least its southern section, as essential to their continued control of Egypt. They were also possessed of an ideology which insisted that they were the rightful rulers of all Islam, which made them a threat to every other Muslim state. They moved to control all Syria, but were faced with opposition from the Bedouin of the desert, by the Byzantines in the north, and by the Hamdanids in Aleppo.

The attacks by the Qaramati on Egypt had been accompanied by a move by Bedouin tribes into Palestine and other parts of Syria. The pattern was that the tribe would establish itself near one of the main cities, but not inside it; the city and the tribe would become a political unit, the former being taxed for the benefit of the latter, a debased version of the system as originally devised by the Arab conquerors in the seventh century. This was difficult to maintain for long, and depended on restraint on both sides, and above all on the two having the same enemies. It was more or less successful at Aleppo, where the Hamdanids and their successors the Mirdasids balanced the demands of the city and the Banu Kilab tribe for a century. In Palestine, however, where the Banu Tayy tried to operate the same system at Ramlah, the city, a smaller place than Aleppo, was soon drained of its wealth and its population. The net result was the conversion of much of southern Palestine to pasture for the Bedouin herds.[14] The tribe had an alliance with the Fatimids, but operated as an independent force even so.

It took some time for the Fatimids, therefore, faced with Qaramatiyah and Bedouin opposition in Palestine, to establish control over them. This left Damascus, their intended main centre in Syria, vulnerable to attack. A garrison of Berber troops proved so undisciplined and unpopular that the citizens rebelled. They were eventually assisted by a force of Turks commanded by Alptekin, who had been expelled from Baghdad. They allied with the citizens, who, as at Aleppo, had organized their own militia in the emergency of the breakdown of government, and expelled the Berbers. Alptekin expanded his control over several of the old Phoenician towns, while also driving the Bedouin from the Ghuta. An attempt from Egypt to suppress this new Syrian state failed, and the Fatimid army was confined to Ashkelon in a siege lasting a year and a half; then a treaty was agreed by which the Fatimids in Palestine were to be confined to Gaza.[15]

In the 970s therefore, there were, for the first time since the early Roman period, a group of independent and semi-independent states in Syria: Aleppo and Damascus being the main ones. There were also the Banu Tayy in south Palestine and, as it seems from later events, Homs was technically Hamdanid but was virtually independent under a governor, as were the smaller towns of Shaizar and Qalaat al-Mudiq (the old Apameia), under local chiefs, apparently Arabs. The emergence of civic militias at Aleppo and Damascus in particular was a new sign that the cities of Syria were once again looking to establish their independence. However they were hardly given a real chance to do so on a firm basis, and it was ominous for anyone looking to this independence of the Syrians, that at both Aleppo and Damascus it had taken outside intervention to achieve it.

The Fatimid ambition insisted on returning repeatedly to attempt to take control of Syria. Alptekin's brief state was defeated in 978, and he himself secured a position in Fatimid service in Egypt. It took longer for the Fatimids to secure control of Damascus itself, partly because the detested Berber troops were used in the expeditions, so provoking strong opposition from the Damascenes. Finally a Turkish commander, Baltakin, who had been there already with Alptekin, gained the city's submission, so long as the local leader, Qassam, remained in effective control; a Berber garrison was thus neutralized. The expedition also led to the suppression of the Banu Tayy in southern Palestine, though not their elimination. All this had caused continuing damage to agriculture, in the Ghuta, the Hawran and Palestine.[16]

The extent of the damage caused by this series of fights and invasions is not altogether clear. No doubt the Banu Tayy caused damage to Ramlah, but some contemporary accounts are complimentary about the city's size, appearance, and prosperity. Al-Muqadasi was a native of Jerusalem, and after travelling widely, he wrote his geography beginning in 985. His description of Ramlah combined his admiration for its fine products and buildings and for its situation in Palestine, with some dislike of its climate and he comments on its difficult water supply and its fleas. Even though he wrote while the depredations of the Banu Tayy were being committed he gives no hint of them. It could be that his notes dated from before the Bedouin invaded, or that the city did not suffer its worst damage until somewhat later; but it is strange that the geographer should ignore the obvious damage already done.[17]

Any independence the Damascenes felt they might have secured as a result of their defiance of the Berbers was only limited, and a more vigorous governor, another Turk, Manjutakin, was soon appointed. He conducted repeated campaigns with the aim of gaining Aleppo, which proved to be beyond his reach, but which did bring under Fatimid control the lands between Damascus and Aleppo, snuffing out any independence they had gained as Hamdanid control weakened. One of the major obstacles to Manjutakin's success at Aleppo was the determined opposition of the city's militia, and when success seemed almost possible, he found himself faced by a Byzantine imperial expedition of rescue led by the Emperor Basil II in person.[18]

The devastation of the Syrian interior as a result of the warfare made it necessary for Manjutakin's force to be supplied from Egypt by sea. The first fleet built was destroyed by a fire, and the second by a storm. It had been sent to supply the Fatimid army which was besieging Tartus, a little to the north of the mouth of the Eleutheros River, and the failure of the supplies made it easy for the Byzantine force under Basil II to relieve the town. But the existence of the naval attempt signals the beginning of recovery for the coastal cities. Ahmad ibn Tulun had already rebuilt the fortifications and constructed a new harbour for the city in the 870s, making it one of the major cities of the coast in the process. (Al-Muqadasi explained that it was his own grandfather Abu Bakr from Jerusalem who was the architect of the harbour.)[19] Tripoli in particular was the Fatimid supply base, and revived quickly under the stimulus.[20]

The coast generally was busy. Tripoli in particular was the port for Damascus, and at one time was garrisoned by Damascene troops. By the eleventh century the whole coast from and the port for Antioch, Suwaydiyah (the successor of Seleukeia) to Gaza had wide connections. The repeated imposition of rule from Egypt from 870 onwards encouraged trade with Alexandria, and with the Byzantine Empire and Sicily and Spain. On the other hand the power of the Byzantines at sea, especially since the reconquest of Crete in 896, provoked defensive measures, of which the creation of the Fatimid navy was obviously one. Gaza, another major port for trade between seaborne goods and those from the Arabian interior, was protected by a beacon system on the coast and a line of fortified towers. The beacons were also used to signal the arrival of a ransom ship: the Byzantines regularly purchased captives from the city. It is clear that, despite the damage caused by the Bedouin in the interior, trade continued, and fuelled the obvious prosperity of the coastlands.[21]

The Fatimid system of government, which attempted to balance several interests – Turks, Berbers, Christians, Egyptians, Syrians – was inherently unstable, and tended to be resolved by the soldiers and by assassination. When there was trouble at the centre, the provinces were abandoned into virtual independence. So Damascus was at least semi-independent, but was also the military base of the dynasty in Syria. Using Berber troops was a guarantee of trouble – Damascus was always hostile to them; the rule of Manjutakin for a decade meant the city was barely under Fatimid influence. On the other hand, the city militia was disliked by the governor, not surprisingly, and he organized a massacre of its leaders in 998.[22] At Tyre, another Berber garrison provoked a city rebellion, led by a sailor, al-Alaqa, though this was put down, despite some Byzantine naval assistance, and the city was sacked.[23] Tripoli was virtually independent under its governor. Apart from Damascus and the Palestinian coastal cities, the Fatimid government really only controlled Tiberias and Jerusalem in the interior. In the north the Byzantine Empire maintained its control over Antioch and Latakiah and the coast as far south as Tartus, but left Aleppo in its autonomy and allowed a faint Fatimid authority in the Orontes Valley.

The Fatimid caliphs were generally able men, and this includes the unusual al-Hakim (996–1021), who came to power after an awkward four years as a minor in 1000, by personally murdering his tutor and regent. He was mentally unbalanced from adolescence and instituted a reign of terror among his soldiers and officials, many of whom he executed or had executed without explanation – though that is not to say he had no reasons. He was all-powerful and as such was able to put into effect a series of eccentric notions, some merely silly, others actively harmful. And yet much of what he did had a distinct shrewdness about it, and he was always careful not to alienate all the parts of his government at the same time. He faced no obvious opposition to these policies – unless of course, his reign of terror successfully picked off those would have objected. For Syria, he was paradoxically more successful than any other of his family except perhaps his son.[24]

One of al-Hakim's measures was to institute a persecution of Christians, which included the destruction of churches, including that of the Holy Sepulchre in Jerusalem. And yet, he also at a different time began a persecution of Sunni Muslims. Within Syria he began with a truce with Basil II, negotiated through the good offices of the patriarch of Jerusalem, which gave him freedom to institute his own policies within Syria without any interference from Constantinople. He supervised the diplomacy which brought Aleppo into his kingdom for a few years, and when he was challenged by the leader of the Banu Tayy in Palestine, who found an Alid pretender and set him up as a rival caliph in Ramlah, he was able to send an efficient Berber army to suppress the threat. In the end he was probably murdered while on a night-time walk through the streets of Cairo, though his body was never found. His sister, the Sitt al-Mulk, seized power in the name of his teenage son, Caliph al-Zahir, leading inevitably to the suspicion that al-Hakim had targeted her for elimination next and that she may well have struck first: by this time the court was surely alert to any signs of trouble approaching.

Why he was able to continue his eccentric and murderous rule for a quarter of a century is not obvious. One reason is that Fatimid doctrine elevated the caliph to a position of absolute power, where opposition was tantamount to apostasy – punished by death in Islamic law. This had a curious side effect, in that al-Hakim came to be regarded by some of his followers – those who survived – as himself divine, actually god. The man who formulated this most convincingly was Muhammad ibn Ismail al-Darazi, though he died in fighting some Turkish soldiers when he attempted a violent rising in his refuge in the Bekaa Valley. But he would not be forgotten. The fact that al-Hakim's body was never discovered powerfully assisted this interpretation of his life.[25]

The fight with the Banu Tayy was yet another chapter in the continuing pressure of the Bedouin on the agricultural area. Perhaps it was the defeat of the Banu Tayy, the succession of a child after al-Hakim's disappearance, and the pressure of the Byzantines in the north – they recovered Aleppo in 1023 – but the three major Bedouin tribes of Syria saw an opportunity to gain control of the whole of the country. It was unfortunate for their plans that at the very moment of their plot they were faced by one of the main political stars of the Fatimid state.

The three Bedouin leaders were Salih ibn Midas of the Banu Kilab, who had recently taken over at Aleppo from the brief Fatimid domination, assisted by a Byzantine force: Sinan ibn Ulyan of the Banu Kalb in central Syria, and Hassan ibn al-Jarrah of the Banu Tayy. Between them they dominated all the Bedouin bands along the desert edge, and their aim was to drive the Fatimids out of Syria altogether.

The opponent who scotched their plan was Anushtakin al-Dizbari, a Turkish slave-soldier in Fatimid employ, who had much experience in administration in Syria, having been governor of Baalbek and Caesarea, and then of all Palestine. He was thus familiar with the leaders of both the Banu Kalb and the Banu Tayy, and had been particularly concerned at the damage the Banu Tayy had done and was doing in Palestine, but when he took serious measures to restrain them, Hassan ibn al-Jarrah got him recalled to Cairo, where, however, he was able to tap his sources of information in Palestine to understand what was going on. The Bedouin tribes had become active once again when the caliph in Cairo was a child and when the Hamdanids were removed from Aleppo. The Banu Kalb raided the Ghuta and blockaded Damascus in 1024, and the Banu Tayy attacked and burnt Ramlah in the next year. Anushtakin was the obvious commander for an expeditionary force which would face the Bedouin joint army when the tri-conspiracy emerged in 1029. He took an army from Egypt, collected local forces in Palestine and met the joint Bedouin army at al-Uqhuwana near the Sea of Galilee, achieving a total victory.[26]

This established Fatimid authority in at least southern Syria for the next decade, especially as Anushtakin was installed as governor of Damascus and Palestine until his death in 1041. He was always a faithful minister of the dynasty, but his local authority was such that he was effectively autonomous – and from 1036 there was a new caliph, yet another child. Anushtakin's ambition was to gain control of Aleppo, which he achieved in 1038, driving out the Mirdasid ruler Thimal, with an army which included Kalb and Tayy contingents; but when Anushtakin died the Fatimid government in Cairo agreed to return Aleppo to Thimal; evidently Aleppo could be dominated by a strong ruler in Damascus, but not by a relatively weak government in Cairo – and such a government could not tolerate a strong ruler in the Syrian province

The Cairo government collapsed into disorder with the murder of the *wazir*, Hasan al-Yazuri in 1058. The Caliph al-Mustansir had succeeded in 1036 at the age of 6 months, and *wazir*s had ruled in his name ever since. This, of course, produced conspiracies, but al-Yazuri had kept his place precariously for eight years. Once he was dead, however – the caliph was apparently unwilling to rule himself, or unable – there was a scramble for power in Cairo, with at least forty *wazir*s succeeding one another in nine years. This period of confusion was followed by a series of low Niles accompanied by famine and plague. The government, without proper direction, with drastically reduced tax revenues, and blamed by the population for the famine, was largely paralysed for years. The result was that Syria was once again neglected and fell into a general disintegration, with the governors of cities becoming effectively independent.[27]

This Egyptian collapse occurred just at the time when a new major enemy had arrived from the east. An invasion of Seljuk Turks from the central Asian steppes had broken into Iran and swiftly moved across to threaten Iraq. In 1055 the Abbasid caliph had no choice but to ask the Turkish leader Tughril to assume protection of himself and his realm – at least the Seljuks were Sunni. Tughril was awarded, or took, the title of sultan. His forces consisted largely of cavalry, some of them well-disciplined, others irregular and travelling with their flocks and their families. For the Fatimids the threat they posed was especially serious since they were Sunni Muslims, and so they were automatically opposed to any Shi'ite state.

Tughril faced, however, a major problem to his west, for the Fatimids and the Byzantine Empire had been at peace with each other since about 1000, a peace which was regularly renewed. It was therefore likely that an attack on one would be regarded as a threat to the other. But both were grievously weakened at the same time, the Fatimids by the chaos and paralysis in Cairo and the Byzantines by internal disputes between factions, a dispute whose main victim was the army and military preparedness.

The caution with which the Seljuk Turks approached the west is indicated by their first move, which was to capture Aleppo, but to leave the Mirdasid ruler Mahmud in office. But this, along with some earlier raids into Anatolia and the capture of some Byzantine posts in Armenia, was enough to bring about a revival of military spirit in Constantinople – though not to revive a spirit of loyalty. A great Byzantine army under the Emperor Romanos IV Diogenes marched west, and was met by a Seljuk army at Manzikert. A combination of ineptitude and treachery resulted in a great Byzantine defeat. After a time, when the magnitude of the Turkish victory began to be understood, large numbers of the Turkish irregulars moved inexorably into Anatolia.[28]

The Sultan Alp Arslan had actually been on his way to invade Syria when the Byzantine army's approach distracted him. Pausing only to release the captured Emperor, in the certain knowledge that this would paralyse any Byzantine response, he marched his army on southwards. As it happened he had been anticipated by another Seljuk force commanded one of his vassals, Atsiz ibn Abaq, who had swept though Syria as far as Palestine with virtually no opposition. He captured and plundered Jerusalem, and ravaged the rest of Palestine; captured Damascus from its Fatimid garrison and in 1076 he tried an invasion of Egypt. By this time the worst of the Egyptian problems were over, and a capable *wazir*, Bedr al-Jamali, had gained control. So Atsiz's invasion failed, either because he was opposed or because he realized he had overestimated his capabilities. The Fatimid garrison of Ashkelon had also held out, and so threatened his communications back to Syria.

Atsiz had in fact constructed a new Syrian state, very like that of Alptakin earlier, but the attack on Egypt had roused an Egyptian response. They recovered Jerusalem from Arzis' earlier conquest, and he returned to the attack. This time he had to blockade the city – it was hardly an active siege – for several months; when the Turks took the city they massacred the Muslim inhabitants. This so alarmed Atsiz that he appealed for help to Tutush, a son of Alp Arslan who had been made ruler of Aleppo by his brother the new Sultan Malikshah. He arrived in time to turn back the Egyptian forces, and his success reduced Atsiz to lord of Damascus. Two years later, in 1079, Tutush seized Damascus, helped by the inhabitants, who had been angered by Atziz's rule. Most of Syria was thus under one rule once more, but again by an invader.[29] Despite a brief return a little later, this was the effective end of Fatimid rule in Syria.

The Fatimid period in Syria was scarcely one of peace and quiet, and one of the results of that was to drive some fundamental changes in the population, not so much in its ethnic make-up as in its religious divisions. One change had taken place even earlier with the acceptance of Shi'ism by some groups, as much a protest at Abbasid rule and a distinguishing mark against neighbours as from conviction. The same reaction, but in the opposite direction, emphasizing their Sunni'ism, had also occurred under Shi'ite Fatimid rule, particularly in Damascus, which proved very resistant to both Shi'ism and the Fatimids. (But Tripoli was reported to be largely Shi'ah.) In the north the Byzantine practice of expelling Muslims from their conquests had created a new block of Christianity of the Orthodox Byzantine type, though they had also welcomed Armenians and Jacobites, who tended to settle in groups.

The death of Muhammad al-Darazi, who had promoted the idea of the Caliph al-Hakim's divinity, left the movement to his disciple Hamza ibn Ali al-Hadi, who preached his message among the hillmen of the southern Bekaa Valley with some success. They were already Shi'ite, and accepted this revision of their beliefs. Later under pressure they retreated into a severe secrecy, which was again a typical Shi'ah reaction. They became called, from their originator, Druzes. Another Shi'ite offshoot, called either Nuzairi or Alawi, whose version of Islam included many elements from the old paganism, which had evidently survived in the hills, had also developed in the Lebanese hills. The pressure they were under, from Sunnis, 'orthodox' Shi'ites and Druzes, led them to migrate from the Lebanese

Mountains to the north into the Bargylus Mountains inland of Lattakiah, which became called the Jebel Nosairi or Jebel Awaliyah.[30]

In the north the ravaging of Armenia by the Seljuks had persuaded some Armenians to move south, and some formed a group of small principalities in the southern Taurus Mountains where they could better defend themselves. They also moved into Kilikia, with Byzantine permission, and into Edessa, where they formed a small kingdom also under distant Byzantine suzerainty.[31]

The geographical divisions of Syria were thus now overlaid by a new division, between groups of different religious persuasions – though these tended over time to coincide. This was, of course, all in addition to the existing Sunni population, and to the Christians, most of whom were Monophysite, though the Greek Orthodox numbers had been boosted by the success of Byzantine conquest in the north. The minorities – though there was for a long time no majority group in the country – tended to huddle together, as did the Alawis in their mountains and the Druzes in the Bekaa, in self-defence. Similarly the Armenians in their mountains were a separate group both by language and by their Monophysite faith. This patchwork effect was to be the mark of Syria for the next 1,000 years, until the present day.

The Turkish rule of Syria became subject to the partible inheritance practiced by the Seljuks in their original homeland, and to their over-extension. They had conquered a huge empire in only a few years, and it inevitably fell apart even more quickly. When Tutush died in 1095, his inheritance was divided between his sons: Ridwan ruled in the north from Aleppo, Duqaq at Damascus. They fought each other. Ridwan established his supremacy but without displacing Duqaq. This permitted the Fatimids, who had maintained a foothold at Ashkelon, to return to Palestine yet again. A forty-day siege of Jerusalem in which the walls were seriously damaged, together with the family feud among the Seljuks, persuaded Ridwan's brothers-in-law Soqman and Ilghazi ibn Ortoq, who governed in the city, to surrender it to Fatimid rule.[32]

The leadership of the Muslim world in the central regions was subject in the 1090s to a whole series of deaths. Sultan Malikshah and his minister Nizam ul-Mulk died within a month of each other in 1092, and Tutush in 1095. In Egypt the *wazir* Badr al-Jamali died in 1094 and was succeeded by his son al-Afdal; the Caliph al-Mustansir died in the same year, but his successor was not his eldest son Nizar, as it should have been by Fatimid succession rules, but al-Mustali, his second son – and Nizar was then murdered, to the consternation and demoralization of the Shi'ites.[33]

Another invasion arrived, this time by way of Anatolia, but from further west. These were a motley group of Crusaders, gathered from various parts of Western Europe, but principally France, intent on 'recovering' Jerusalem for Christian rule. They had originally been asked for by the Byzantine Emperor Alexios I to help cope with the influx of Turks into interior Anatolia after the Battle of Manzikert, and he was naturally horrified by the strange response, and by their strategically unwelcome aim. However, he helped them onwards, and in 1096 they emerged from the Taurus Mountain passes to begin their campaign in Syria.[34]

For a year they besieged Antioch, which was part of Ridwan's kingdom, though it had been part of the Byzantine Empire until a few years earlier. Ridwan was unable to defend or relieve, it effectively, despite gathering support from Soqman and Ilghazi (recently expelled from Jerusalem), and Kerbogha, the Lord of Mosul. A group of Crusaders separated off to take over Edessa, where the Armenians had felt they were under pressure since the collapse of Byzantine protection. By taking the city this group exerted their own pressure on the Seljuks in the Jazirah.[35] After capturing Antioch the main army moved south along the Orontes Valley and then through the Homs Gap to the coast at Tripoli. Intent on Jerusalem above all they did not stop to seize any of the cities along the coast. Eventually they reached their goal, and undertook another major and lengthy siege, which resulted in the capture of the city, and a massacre. It was 1099.[36]

Having conquered a few places, the Crusaders had then to decide what to do with them and how to defend them. Most of those who had taken part and had survived – probably the majority of those who had begun the journey from Europe had died – wished to return to their homes in Western Europe, but considerable numbers intended to stay in the east, and several of the leaders were especially keen on carving out Syrian principalities for themselves. Baldwin of Boulogne had already done so with the County of Edessa, and Antioch was another base, which became a principality for Bohemond of Taranto, a scion of a Norman dynasty from southern Italy. In Palestine there was a certain reluctance to form a secular state in the city in which Christ died, but after Godfrey of Lorraine, the first elected 'Advocate of the Holy Sepulchre', died after a short reign, his brother Baldwin of Edessa, a man of the tougher mind and more practical bent, arrived from Edessa and organized the south as the Kingdom of Jerusalem.[37]

The irruption of the Crusaders had within five years formed three new states in Syria, and they were not yet finished. Further, these were Roman Catholic Christians, who now formed yet another religious group to add to the complex of minorities which made up the Syrian population.

Chapter 19

Western Intrusion

In 1100, when Baldwin of Boulogne, Count of Edessa, became the first king of Jerusalem, his kingdom was still in the process of formation – just as was his former County of Edessa. And the ruler of the only other formed Crusader state, Prince Bohemond of Antioch, had gone off on an expedition to the north and was captured by the Turks.

The first essentials were therefore to expand and then consolidate the states which existed, then to connect the southern kingdom with the states in the north – separated by 200km of hostile country, through which Baldwin had had to fight his way to reach his kingdom. Meanwhile he had to ensure that the principality of Antioch was safeguarded in the absence of its prince. None of this was easy given the headstrong characters of the Crusader leaders, a characteristic which was permanent among many of them, but it was very much assisted by the disunity of their Muslim enemies.

The various journeys by Crusader forces from Antioch south to Jerusalem had clearly revealed this latter condition. Each town had its own chief, some theoretically owing allegiance to a greater lord, but actually virtually independent. The Fatimid control of the south was limited, the Seljuk domination of the north only partial. Not only that but the local lords were quite willing to fight each other if advantage offered, and were quite willing to enlist Crusaders on their side in these fights. The Crusaders quickly appreciated this, and used it for their own purposes.

Godfrey of Bouillon in his few months as lord of Jerusalem had succeeded in expanding his realm quite substantially. Above all he had defeated a large counter-attack from Egypt led by the *wazir* al-Afdal in person. A major battle near Ashkelon resulted in the comprehensive defeat of the Egyptian forces, and the acquisition of a large quantity of loot. The arrival of several Crusader fleets, from southern France, from Italy, and from England had provided much assistance. Godfrey had used the fleets to begin the establishment of his kingdom as a serious economic power by interrupting the seaborne traffic between Syrian ports and Egypt, and by capturing the port of Jaffa.

The major Muslim powers in Syria were still Aleppo under Ridwan, and Damascus under Duqaq, but neither was ready to take on the Crusaders after the early defeats. Tripoli was the centre of a kingdom which dominated the western end of the Homs Gap, controlling several towns from Tortosa in the north to

Byblos and Batrun to the south. The *amir* had had complicated relations with the Crusaders, fighting one force under Raymond of St Gilles, Count of Toulouse, and cultivating good relations with another, notably with Baldwin as he marched south to take up his kingdom. Baldwin was opposed only at one point on this march, by Duqaq at the pass just south of Beirut. After a hard fight he got through. But none of the marches by the Crusaders had resulted in any permanent conquests along the Lebanese coast.

Godfrey's inheritance to his brother was thus a kingdom consisting largely of the Judaean Hills from Hebron in the south to the Sea of Galilee in the north. Galilee in fact had been conquered by Tancred de Hauteville, the nephew of Bohemond, in a brilliant little campaign. But Tancred was as independently minded and as ambitious as Bohemond, and was likely to be as difficult a subject for Baldwin as he had been for Godfrey. Baldwin showed his political sense when he agreed that Tancred should go off to the north to govern Antioch while his Uncle Bohemond was a captive.

In addition to the hill country, the kingdom had ports at Jaffa, acquired during the siege of Jerusalem, and Haifa, further north. Connections with Europe were clearly essential, and Baldwin set about acquiring more of the coast; Arsuf and Caesarea were captured in 1101. These were seen to be all the more necessary when news arrived that a reinforcing force had been destroyed while travelling through Asia Minor. He had deliberately cultivated a reputation for ferocity by permitting a massacre at Caesarea and by ravaging the Muslim villages in the south. Baldwin also had gained a powerful military repute, which stood him in good stead when another inevitable attack came up from Egypt in September 1101.

Al-Afdal did not command the expedition himself this time, and his appointed general, Sa'd ad–Dawla al-Qawasi, operated with care and caution. He advanced as far as Ramlah, but then retired to Ashkelon to collect reinforcements. Then he advanced again to Ramlah, with an army of at least 30,000 men; Baldwin met him with about a twentieth of that – 260 cavalry and 900 infantry. The victory went to the smaller army after a hard fight due to a combination of weight, better arms, professionalism and surprise. A new Egyptian attempt next year had more success and defeated Baldwin's first defence, but he eventually once more destroyed the enemy army, this time at Jaffa.[1] Al-Afdal sent another force next year, but the commander of the army and the commander of the fleet detested each other, and the former would not move north of Ashkelon – likely enough his forces after three defeats were none too keen. The fleet attacked Jaffa, in vain.

One of the more important elements in all this was the regular arrival of fleets from Europe carrying pilgrims and Crusaders, materials and goods to trade. Even as early as the siege of Antioch the arrival of an English fleet was crucial, and at the siege of Jerusalem also. The fortuitous arrival of 200 ships at Jaffa in 1105 enabled Baldwin to produce a big enough army to defeat the third Egyptian attack. Now the arrival of a Genoese fleet allowed him to make a successful attack on Acre. After three weeks the garrison surrendered on terms, by which those who wished could leave the city with their possessions, but the Italians dishonoured the agreement.

The Egyptians made one further major attack soon after Baldwin's capture of Acre. This time al-Afdal sought an alliance with Damascus; Duqaq had died in 1104, and was replaced after some manoeuvrings by the Turkish *atabeg* Toghtekin. A third battle near Ramlah repulsed this invasion, and al-Afdal then did nothing more than send relatively minor raids into southern Palestine, usually in response to Frankish raids.[2] It may be said, therefore, that by 1105 or 1106 the kingdom of Jerusalem was well founded. But this had been achieved at the expense of bitter Muslim enmity, which would not fade away.

The northern Crusader states took rather longer to become firmly founded. The captivity of Bohemond in Turkish hands did not help, and Tancred, his cousin, who took over his principality as regent enjoyed his power and did not work at all hard at getting him free. Tancred expanded the principality by seizing control of Kilikia from the garrisons of the Byzantine Emperor, and by conquering some of the Muslim towns. Bohemond had agreed, when passing through Constantinople, that any lands which had been Byzantine earlier and which the Crusaders captured, would be handed back to Alexios' rule, but he had broken his word, and Tancred was even less willing to surrender any territory he ruled.[3] Further, Tancred was unwelcoming to the survivors of the defeated Crusader army in Asia Minor, above all to Raymond of Toulouse, who had led the first Crusaders to Jerusalem, had vowed to stay in the east, and was a friend of the emperor. Raymond had control of Lattakiah in alliance with the emperor, who had sent in a garrison from Cyprus, and Tancred took him captive until he resigned his claims to Lattakiah to him.[4]

Raymond was a man of his word, unlike Tancred, and he immediately set out southwards, collected his men and his family from Lattakiah and captured the next town south, Jabala, as the base from which to operate. He was aiming to conquer a principality for himself consisting of the Muslim towns along the coast – Tripoli especially – and those inland, using the strategic highway of the Homs Gap to link them; Homs was one of his targets. This was all too clear to the local Muslim rulers, Fakhr al-Mulk abu Ali in Tripoli and Janah ad-Dawla the Lord of Homs (who was the father-in-law of Ridwan, the Lord of Aleppo). They joined together to fight Raymond when it became clear he had only a small army. There followed another of those astonishing Crusader victories, of 300 Crusaders against twenty times their number of Muslims just outside Tripoli. (King Baldwin defeated the Egyptian forces at Jaffa a month later.)

Raymond's victory did not bring him any territory, though it secured his hold on the coast north of Tripoli. He began a close siege of Tripoli, building a castle, Mount Pilgrim, to blockade the city. This siege lasted for six years. During it Raymond died (in 1105) and Tripoli was reduced to a condition of disease-ridden starvation. Raymond's successor was his cousin, William-Jordan, who succeeded in capturing Arqa and defeating another relieving effort mounted by Toghtakin of Damascus, who had taken over Homs. Eventually Tripoli was taken over by an Egyptian force.

Bohemond was released in May 1103, and at once fell into a new crisis. Count Baldwin II of Edessa devised a plan to seize the city of Harran, which was undergoing some internal upheavals. Control of it would significantly assist the defence of his county, which was essentially a Jazirah state, with wide open frontiers to the east, where there were several Muslim-Turkish rulers all too willing to gain prestige by fighting Christians. With Bohemond's help he laid siege to the city in the spring in 1104, but they were attacked by a Turkish force and defeated. Baldwin was captured.[5]

Bohemond and Tancred shored up the defences of Edessa city, defeated an attack, and Tancred took over as regent once again, this time for Edessa. Bohemond had come to the conclusion that it was necessary to go to Europe to persuade more fighters to settle in the east, especially since the Battle of Harran had cost the lives or liberty of almost the whole of the Edessan army. He left, and appointed Tancred as regent in Antioch once again as well.[6] So for a few years Tancred had control of all the northern Crusader territories, and in the process he successfully expanded Antioch significantly – but again he made no effort to get Baldwin of Edessa released. Bohemond never did return, falling into a war with the Emperor Alexios in which he was defeated. Even so Tancred was never more than a regent. Baldwin was eventually released in 1108. At the same time there developed a succession problem in Tripoli which brought King Baldwin north to sort things out. This he did in his usual sensible fashion. The mysterious murder of William-Jordan cleared the way for the recognition of Bertrand, an illegitimate son of Raymond, who came out from France, as count of Tripoli. By now Tripoli was under Egyptian occupation, but was not regularly reprovisioned; in the end the garrison surrendered on terms.[7]

It remained only to clear the route along the coast to connect the northern and southern Crusader states. Tyre held out on its peninsula, but King Baldwin captured Sidon and Beirut in the next year; the road was then open since Tyre on its seaward jutting peninsula could be bypassed. The succession problems of the northern states were largely solved in 1111 and 1112 with the deaths of Bohemond in Italy, of Tancred in Antioch, of Bertrand in Tripoli, and a peaceful succession in both Crusader states. Even before then it could be said with some confidence that the states had become firmly established, and that it would take a major effort of combined Muslim forces to dislodge any of them. The conclave of all the rulers at Tripoli in 1109 had been significant in indicating that they were rather more closely allied than the Muslim states, and the surrender of Tripoli at the same time set the seal on this close relationship. Appeals from one Crusader state to the others were almost invariably answered, at least in these early years.

The warfare and the battles should not, however, blind us to the fact that the geography of Syria had asserted itself with a vengeance. The largest of the new states, Jerusalem, began in the Judaean Hills and spread to the lowlands – just as had the original Hebrew kingdom, and the Maccabean kingdom; the Antioch region in the Amuq Basin had been the base for several kingdoms in the past, going back to the Bronze Age, and more immediately it had been the rival to Aleppo, as it was again; Edessa had been the base of several past kingdoms, always, as in the twelfth century, threatened by other powers from the eastward along the open Jazirah roads; Tripoli was based at the mouth of the Eleutheros, an inheritor of a geopolitical base which was first organized into a local kingdom by Abdi-Ashirta in the fifteenth century BC; inland, apart from Aleppo, the main Muslim power was Damascus, but neither of these found it easy to exert any control over the other Muslim settlements situated between them along the Orontes, such as Hama and Shaizar and Homs. And in the south the Egyptian realm held on to a fortified foothold at Ashkelon, ready when it felt capable, to send another invasion into Palestine, and always able to send mounted raids into southern Palestine.

There now existed, in other words, a traditional contest between states based in much the same regions as had happened in the Bronze Age, the Iron Age, and in the aftermath of the collapse of the Seleukid kingdom – and would recur in the twentieth century. The contest was generally equal when it was fought between the local Syrian states, but this could never be permitted. There were always outsiders who were keen to intervene, usually for their own purposes, and often to the resentment even of those who they came to assist. The complications of the various Islamic sects – Sunni, Shi'ah, Ismaili, and others, including Assassins, now beginning to operate in Syria – was paralleled on the Crusader side by the periodic interference, as the locals saw it, of new Crusaders from Europe, usually with grand ideas of conquest which the locals deprecated for various reasons. Then there were the rulers of Constantinople, Mosul and Egypt, all keen to fish in troubled Syrian waters.

The contest was not, of course, simply one of territories and for lands. Religion was involved as well and the longer the Christian states existed the more the local Muslims became possessed with the emotions of *jihad*, and it was this which finally united them to conquer. But the Christian-Muslim contest was also the contest between two societies organized on differing principles – heredity on the Christian side, for example, was never an overriding Muslim practice, except for rulers. Both were composed of the same mixed populations as had been present when the Crusaders arrived, though many Muslims had been driven out by the Crusaders, or had simply fled, and the Jews, who had been as subject to Crusader massacres as the Muslims, were also hostile. The Syrian Christians had found themselves once more under pressure from fellow Christians to change their beliefs and practices; there is no sign that they enjoyed it any more than their ancestors had; they generally preferred Muslim tolerance, though that was also punctuated by periodic persecutions and massacres.

There were also some new players in the game. Yet another fission had occurred in the Shi'ah, to produce the group called derisively by the Syrian the *hashishiyah*, Europeanized as Assassins. (There is no evidence that they used hashish any more than anyone else in Syria.) They were especially angered at fellow Muslims who did not share their views. Like all fanatics who searched out 'traitors' before attending to their real enemies, they identified their especial enemies in the rulers of Muslim states. Their ideology had been worked out in isolation in Persia, and had been deliberately transferred to Syria because its hills and divisions offered the best opportunity for such niche communities – there were several already, especially of the Shi'ite persuasion.[8]

The Assassins were warily welcomed by the rulers, such as Ridwan of Aleppo and Toghtekin of Damascus, who felt they could use them in their own feuds, but they were disliked by the citizens. So when a compliant ruler died the Assassins tended to be driven out of their base, especially if it was in a city. Their main purpose was in fact to secure for themselves one or more castles, but it was not until the 1130s that they succeeded – Toghtekin gave them the castle of Baniyas, on the border of Damascus and Jerusalem, but when he died, they abandoned it to the Franks, which hardly conduced to their popularity among other Syrian Muslims.[9]

On the Christian side at the same time there emerged a new force, the militant orders of dedicated religious warriors. The Hospitallers were the first to be chartered, in 1113, with the mission of assisting pilgrims both by protecting them from the bandits which infested Palestinian roads and by housing and caring for them. The Templars came next, a few years later. These were, in a sense, the Christian equivalent of the Assassins, both in their fanaticism, and in their semi-independence, which made them as dangerous to their own side as to their enemies, if in different ways. For a group of men whose original purpose was so relatively humble they rapidly developed a most arrogant attitude to everyone else. It was always difficult for any of these orders to accept the validity of any agreement with the infidel; similarly Muslims were often very uncomfortable in the same way.

In such a situation, with divisions and indiscipline and intrigues on both sides, external interference almost constant, and a basic Christian-Muslim divide running geographically from north to south through the country, but also overlapping to both east and west, continual disputes were inevitable. For thirty years the balance lay with the Crusaders. They did not, it is true, expand their territories very much, and then only into desert areas or temporarily, such as in the lands east of the Dead

Sea (Oultrejourdain), but they were normally the aggressors, and this generally restricted the Muslims to a defensive role even when they were victorious.

The usual targets of the Crusaders were, of course, Aleppo and Damascus. An Antiochene army was defeated so heavily by the Aleppan forces in 1119 that 'Field of Blood' was the name the battle was given.[10] Again an attack aimed at taking Aleppo in 1124 resulted in a siege, but the city was not taken. Nor was Damascus in 1129. On the other hand Tyre was captured in 1124, eliminating the last block on the coast road. King Baldwin had expanded his kingdom in the other direction by seizing Ayla (Aqaba) on the Red Sea, and building castles to control the old King's Highway linking Ayla with Damascus. This gave him control of the trade route, and the ability to tax the caravans, and some warning of possible attack from that direction.

The Muslims repeatedly failed in these years to mount a really successful attack. The victory of the Field of Blood did not result in any lasting territorial gains. Their efforts were not helped by Assassin killings, of Mawdud, the *amir* of Mosul, in 1113, for instance. His successor Burzuq attempted an invasion in 1115, but had been told to establish control over Ridwan and Toghtekin first and only then to tackle the Franks. In the event he failed in all these tasks, and died in the battle. On the other hand this was clearly the correct strategic approach, for only a united Muslim attack stood any chance of success. But the lords in occupation in Syria were never going to accept such overwhelming assistance as would tend to their removal.

All this is to say that from very early on, the several powers in Syria, Christian and Muslim, from the Euphrates to Gaza, had established a local balance of power. This included more or less constant warfare on a small scale, with larger wars when crises arose. The death of a Muslim ruler, the minority of a Christian, were such typical problems which often resulted in wars, even battles with thousands of casualties, but few produced any serious territorial changes. The balance tended to tilt to the Christian side because the several states cooperated well; on the Muslim side it was always difficult to achieve a durable alliance, largely because the stronger power was also aiming to eliminate the weaker.

The local Muslim powers in the north were ruled for a time by members of the dynasty of Ortoq, but each man tended to control only one city or region, and rarely did they cooperate well. This began to change in 1127 with the appointment of Imad ad-Din Zengi as the *atabeg* of Mosul. (An *atabeg* was a regent for a child ruler – they usually managed to keep power for themselves, and often the children did not reach adulthood, though the *atabeg*s survived well enough.) After Burzuq was murdered by an Assassin, and his *atabeg* at Aleppo also, Zengi claimed Aleppo, and the citizens were relieved to receive a capable ruler, after misrule by a series of Ortoqid princes since the death of Ridwan. Ridwan's death had been followed by a revolution in which the main victims were the Assassins, whom the citizens actively disliked – no doubt one reason for the murders. The city militia was thus still active and politically significant. The Ortoqid control was originated by Ilghazi of Field of Blood fame, but his family's popularity rapidly declined afterwards.

Zengi was welcomed and immediately secured his Frankish flank by arranging a two-year truce with Count Joscelin of Edessa. In that time he received submissions from the lords of Shaizar and Homs, who were mainly interested in the protection he could provide. Zengi was familiar with Syria, for his father been governor of Aleppo for a time before the Crusaders arrived. He clearly understood the need for wider control than a single city. The agreement with the *amir* of Homs included a joint campaign to capture Hama, which was under the distant control of the *amir* of Damascus, but having captured it Zengi seized it for himself and furthermore made captive the Homs' *amir* as well, though not his city. By this time he had therefore secured control of most of the territory between Mosul and Aleppo, and in Syria from Aleppo to Homs.

Zengi, however, had responsibilities in Iraq and was much distracted by them from Syrian affairs. Homs and Hama and Shaizar drifted from his allegiance and whenever he returned to Syria they tended to return. Zengi's main problem, however, was that he could not trust the *atabegs* of Damascus, descendants of Toghtekin, to remain neutral if he was involved in a Frankish war. At one point he laid siege to Damascus itself, but found it was too well defended – the city militia was fully in agreement with the *atabegs* on the subject of the independence of their city. He managed to defeat King Fulk and capture the castle of Montferrand on the border of his lands with Tripoli's, but to do so he had had to raise a siege of Homs, and he would surely have preferred the city to the castle.

A counter-attack next year by a joint Byzantine and Frank force failed to capture Shaizar, but after they withdrew Zengi was at last able to secure full control of Homs – he had taken Homs as part of the Damascus campaign. There was no guarantee, of course, that he would be able to hold on to the city. In fact, the whole period of his lordship in the west was one of border warfare, with a castle here and a town there changing hands.

In 1144, this all changed. The year before there was a pair of deaths which reduced the crusader defensive power, of the Emperor John Comnenos, who had assumed overlordship of Antioch and Edessa, and of King Fulk of Jerusalem. The hiatus which resulted attracted Zengi, who, on the very day that the next king, Baldwin II, was crowned in Jerusalem, captured the city of Edessa. Prince Raymond of Antioch had quarrelled with both the new emperor, Manuel Comnenos, and Count Joscelin II of Edessa, and Joscelin took his whole army out of the city on an expedition to support an ally. While he was away Zengi laid siege to Edessa with a force large enough to deter Joscelin's intervention, who now had no allies himself. The city fell on Christmas Day.[11]

The result was another great Crusade out of Europe. By the time the expeditions arrived, Zengi was dead, murdered in his bed, and his territories were divided between two of his sons, Sayf ad-Din Ghazi in Mosul and the east, and Nur ad-Din Mahmud at Aleppo and the west. The new Crusaders were persuaded that the best thing to do was to attack Damascus, whose ruler would have much preferred to become a Crusader ally and so defend himself and his city against Nur ad-Din. But to the newly arrived Crusaders, a Muslim was an enemy no matter the local diplomacy. Their attack failed.[12] Count Joscelin and an ally recovered Edessa briefly, but then lost it decisively; soon after, in 1150, Joscelin himself was captured and his widow sold the remaining castles of the county to the Byzantine emperor, John Comnenos. One of the few Crusader states had been extinguished, and the Muslims were recovering a sense of unity.

Baldwin III celebrated his release from the shackles of his formidable mother by attacking and capturing Ashkelon (1153). The Fatimid polity had steadily declined in effectiveness under incompetent caliphs and incompetent *wazir*s, who made things worse by intriguing against, and sometimes fighting each other. It began to look to be a tempting target. Ashkelon had been a Fatimid base from which raids into southern Syria had been made for half a century, so raiding Egypt in return would be a welcome change for the Franks.

On the other hand, the next year Nur ad-Din finally gained his own (and his father's) long-standing aim, the capture of Damascus. An insidious propaganda campaign undermined the authority of the lord of the city, Mujir ad-Din Abaq, who had finally managed to remove the last of the *atabeg*s. After two failed attempts Nur ad-Din's forces were welcomed into the city by the population. The earlier attempts had been foiled in part by an alliance of Damascus and the Franks; now that alliance had frayed, in part by the arrogant behaviour of individual Frankish knights, but also because of the disgust of the Damascenes at seeing their lord paying tribute to the Crusader king. The main reason for the welcome Nur ed-Din received, though, was that he was a *jihadi* warrior who had spent his life fighting the Christian Franks. It was clear to everyone in the region that this change of allegiance by Damascus was crucial.

The spirit of *jihad* had been largely absent in Syria when the Crusaders arrived; division and internecine Islamic warfare, Sunni against Shi'ah, Turks against Arabs, had successfully quashed what had been one of the prime duties of Islamic rulers until a century before. It took time for it to revive. Probably Zengi's conquest of Edessa was the spark which began the revival, but it was the Second Crusade which seems to have convinced the Damascenes that the way of survival against Crusader pressure was Muslim unity. Nur ad-Din's reputation was as a practitioner of *jihad*. He was able to project this idea better than his father because he did not have to concern himself with threats to his position in Syria from other

Islamic powers. From now on the war is carried on as a *jihad* – just as it was in large part on the Christian side, and always had been.[13]

The Crusader states were warrior societies, as much as was Nur ad-Din's kingdom. Power was concentrated in the persons of kings and rulers and their military vassals. But beneath this social layer there were the creators of wealth on which the warrior elites on both sides of the religious divide lived. The Crusader port cities especially housed colonies of Italian merchants, from Genoa, Venice, Pisa, who had often helped to capture those cities. They were less interested in the conquest of more territory than having bases in the eastern Mediterranean through which to tap into the trade of Asia. Beneath the religious hostility this trade continued. Gaza remained the port for incense from south Arabia and Acre, Tyre, Tripoli were all significant trading and manufacturing cities. Antioch to some extent regained its old role as a metropolis in the north. Acre had become the port of trade for Damascus, rather displacing, or perhaps supplementing, Tripoli.

These cities were not particularly large. Jerusalem had a permanent population of perhaps 30,000, who were mainly Christian after successive massacres of Muslims and Jews by the conquerors in 1077 and 1099; it also had a floating population mainly of Christian pilgrims which swelled at times of Christian festivals such as Easter and Christmas. Other cities had also lost much of their Muslim populations, either to massacre or to expulsion. They were replaced by local Christians, by refugees from other parts of Syria, and by immigrants from Europe such as the Italian merchants. Acre developed into the main port for the Jerusalem kingdom, but even it had a population of only perhaps 20,000. Tripoli, as a port, a manufacturing city and a governing centre had many advantages for growth, but probably was no larger than Acre. Tyre is claimed to be the same size as Acre and Jerusalem, but it is a very constricted site.[14]

The Crusader governing elite tended to live in their castles while also maintaining a house in one or more of the cities, mainly Acre or Jerusalem. The construction of several dozen powerful fortresses was probably one of the main sources of income for the working class in Palestine; the other was, as always, agriculture. The Christian population which existed when the land was conquered may have been harassed and driven in and out of its villages, but it always remained the basic population of the country. The Christian peasantry was the bedrock producer, and it soon became obvious that pressure on the country people to conform to Latin Christianity would be counterproductive. A general toleration developed.

The internal collapse of Egypt combined with the expansion of Nur ad-Din's kingdom from Aleppo to Damascus, rendered Egypt a prime target for both sides. The struggle took time. King Amalric (1163–1174) was the driving force on the Crusader side, and had the advantage of relatively easy access to Egypt, now that Ashkelon had been taken. Nur ed-Din had the advantage of being Muslim, but he was at a considerable distance, and was Sunni, whereas the Fatimid government was Shi'ah. Within Egypt, however, the Shi'ites were in a minority; the Fatimids had never seriously proselytized their faith; and the proportion of Christians in the country was still large.

A dispute between two claimants for the post of *wazir* to the child-caliph al-Adid attracted interventions by both King Amalric and Nur ad-Din but with the difference that Amalric went himself while Nur ad-Din sent one of his best commanders, Shirkuh. For six years (1163–1169) they contested for influence in Egypt. Meanwhile Nur ad-Din kept up the pressure on the Syrian frontier. In 1164 he took the opportunity of Amalric's second expedition into Egypt to defeat a major army gathered from all the north at Artah, capturing the rulers of Tripoli and Antioch, the Byzantine governor of Kilikia, and even the titular Count of Edessa. He then proceeded to shave off yet more territory from the Crusader states, capturing part of Antioch's lands, and in particular gaining control of the fortress of Harim, which controlled the main bridge eastwards from Antioch; he also captured Banyas from the kingdom.

At first Shirkuh was overmatched, but he returned in 1167, and again Amalric came to the rescue of the Fatimid *wazir*, though the fight was more difficult this time. Shirkuh was accompanied by his nephew, Salah ad-Din Yusuf (Saladin) on both expeditions, and again on his third, in 1169. These expeditions travelled south from Damascus and past the great castles the Franks had built east of Jordan, and then westwards though the Negev and the Sinai Desert – the Franks controlled the coast road. Shirkuh's third expedition proved to be decisive. Amalric had invaded Egypt for the fourth time but hesitated when he could have stormed and looted Cairo – though this would hardly have given him control of Egypt, nor provided much support for his candidate. Shirkuh arrived as he waited, and Amalric decided the odds were now too great. As he marched back to Palestine, the Caliph al-Adid appointed Shirkuh as his *wazir*, and the defeated *wazir* was hunted down and killed.

There followed a series of deaths which opened the way for Saladin to rise to power. Shirkuh died only two months after his victory, and Saladin moved swiftly to take his place, in what was in effect a *coup d'etat*, to the disgruntlement of some of Shirkuh's officers. His position as the commander of Shirkuh's army led almost without resistance to his appointment as the Fatimid Caliph's *wazir*, and he was then able over the next months to consolidate his hold in Egypt, including defeating the Fatimid army, before Amalric tried once more to gain Egypt, unsuccessfully. The death of the Fatimid caliph followed in 1171, and Saladin at once discarded the Shi'ite regime, and proclaimed the Abbasid caliph at Friday prayers. Three years later, within two months of each other, both Nur ad-Din and Amalric died (1174).

There was no obvious successor to Nur ad-Din, for his son Ismail was still a child; Amalric's successor was his son, Baldwin IV, also a child, but who was infected with leprosy. The way was clearly open for Saladin, using Egyptian resources, to expand into the vacuum in Syria left by Nur ad-Din's death. He had already captured Ayla (Aqaba) to open communications with Syria, and now within months he had secured control of Damascus, where, as a militant Sunni, he was welcome. He was challenged by other members of Nur ad-Din's family, but was able to defeat them; his Syrian realm extended as far north as Maaret en-Numan; the northern part of Nur ad-Din's inheritance, technically under his son al-Salih, was taken over by the lord of Mosul, his cousin, when al-Salih died in 1181.

As Saladin extended his grip over the inland areas of Syria, uniting them once again with the resources of Egypt, the Crusader states sank into controversy. The youth and leprosy of Baldwin IV meant he required a man the Crusaders called a *bailli*, a post which was almost equivalent to a Fatimid *wazir*, and as with Fatimid *wazir*s, it was a position which was likely to go to the strongest and most ruthless. Baldwin's sister Sibylla was his likely heir, and so the man who married her was likely to be the next king and was in the best position to be *bailli*. Intrigue was continuous, divisions deepened, far too many men and organizations had no wish to pay attention to royal policy – this particularly applied to the two great militant orders – and the sickly king's health grew steadily worse.

After some intermittent fighting in the late 1170s, in which the king defeated Saladin's Egyptian army at Mont Gisard, and again in 1179, at Marj Ayun, the king and Saladin made a truce, to last two years. The king's purpose was to relieve his kingdom of pressure while he died and the succession was sorted out. Saladin, however, was more intent on Aleppo, and this time was equally useful to him. In 1183 he finally gained control of the city. It had a considerable population of Shi'ites, so he was not altogether welcome, but he now had control over the entire Crusader frontier. A new truce for four years was agreed in 1185, but too many of the more restless Crusaders detested such a policy. Baldwin IV finally died in 1185, but his successor was his nephew, Baldwin V, who died within a year, still only 9-years-old. Sibylla and her supporters then carried through a coup making herself queen and she appointed her unpopular and barely competent husband, Guy of Lusignan, king. Several prominent lords refused to accept this and left the kingdom. Bad feelings continued.

The contest for the succession was one for the hand of the king's sister, Sibylla but the bad feelings went much deeper. The three Crusader states had drifted apart, and by now Antioch was under Byzantine distant control, and so liable to go its own way. A count of Tripoli had contested the authority of the king of Jerusalem over him fifty years before, and later counts were always liable to insist on their independence – unless under threat, when they demanded help. Within the kingdom, several of the lords were tending to a similar independent point of view, especially as the future king, Sibylla's husband, would be a foreigner. And when the new king arrived, one of the more important lords, Baldwin of Ramlah, left the kingdom to take service in Antioch, unable to bear working with the man. But the king's main problem was to exert control over the military orders of the Templars and Hospitallers. The grand master of the Templars, for example, was captured in 1179, but would not allow himself to be either ransomed or exchanged since he valued himself so highly that he acknowledged no equal. Such a man, in his pride, was well able to disobey his king. The orders had acquired much land, and many castles, and were fully capable of ignoring royal instructions in pursuit of their own interests. The kingdom was, in other words, beginning to break up. And this happened just at the time its Muslim enemy was uniting.

The coup by Queen Sibylla released Reynald of Chatillon, former prince of Antioch by marriage, and now the lord of Kerak in Oultrejourdain by marriage, from any restraint. As prince of Antioch he had angered almost every group in the city, as well as the Byzantine neighbours, by his selfishness and cruelty and greed, and his lack of morality. As lord of Kerak he had raided Aqaba and had committed piracies on the Red Sea. He was notoriously a man liable to break his word, and to ignore general policy for his own profit. The truce arranged in 1185 was still in operation, and most men in the kingdom hoped to renew it, as did Saladin. But Reynald saw from his castle a rich caravan passing by, and he attacked and looted it.

Saladin decided that this was the point at which he could best attack the kingdom. The truce had been broken by a prominent supporter of the new king and queen – thus putting the Crusaders in the wrong and Saladin in the right – the king was known to be a poor soldier, disliked by his subordinates, a considerable proportion of the lords of the kingdom were at odds with him, and the orders were arrogantly disobedient. The tables were thus turned. Amalric had attacked Egypt when it was divided, now it was Saladin's turn to do the same to the kingdom of Jerusalem.

The invasion came in May 1187. Saladin had sent out summonses to all his lands, from Mosul to Egypt, and had gathered an army of at least 30,000 men. By this time Muslim armies were well-trained and disciplined, with a tough centre of Saladin's own Mamluks, the slave soldiers. All this was well known to King Guy, who summoned his own array to Tiberias. (His aim was actually to attack Count Raymond of Tripoli and Galilee, even though a great Muslim army was nearby and Count Raymond had an agreement with Saladin; they were reconciled before the battle.) Guy was manoeuvred into the hills behind the city, and at a field called the Horns of Hattin, the army of the kingdom of Jerusalem was destroyed.[15] For the first time since the First Crusade it was possible for a Muslim army to march where it willed through Palestine.

Saladin showed his quality by concentrating not on Jerusalem, as the Crusaders had done in 1099, but on the cities of the coast. He sent a force at once to secure

Acre, the most important port, then other detachments to gain control of as many of the other ports as possible. By September only Gaza and Tyre survived of the kingdom's coastal fortresses, and in October Jerusalem was occupied. In the interior several of the great castles still held out, but were gradually deduced in the next months.

Control of the coastlands was vital, since Saladin knew full well that the next stage in the war would be the arrival of a relieving force from Europe. By spring 1188, indeed, a fleet from Sicily was already operating along the coast, and deterred him from attacking Tripoli. But the Muslim army was able to capture several of the ports north of Tripoli, including Tortosa and Lattakiah, and then campaign successfully in the Jebel Alawi and into the Principality of Antioch.

The attack Saladin had made on Tyre in late 1187 had failed, and this was crucial for the next stage, since the city now provided the initial base for the Crusader revival. King Guy had been captured at Hattin, but was quickly released, presumably because Saladin expected that his presence in command of the remnant of his kingdom's army would be to his, Saladin's, advantage. To a degree he was right, for Guy was refused entry to Tyre by the man who had taken command there, Conrad of Montferrat. But then, summoning up his resolution, Guy marched his men south and laid siege to Acre. Saladin arrived and laid siege to the besiegers. At sea a fleet from Pisa blockaded the harbour and formed a beachhead close to Guy's position.

The siege lasted almost two years, gradually gathering to it ships and men from all Europe and all the Near East. Famine hurt both the Crusader army and the inhabitants of the city, but Saladin could not break the blockade. In the process Queen Sibylla died and her daughter Isabella was divorced and remarried to Conrad. Guy was thus dethroned, though he did not accept this (and was eventually made king in Cyprus as compensation). The decisive reinforcement at last arrived; first, King Philip II of France, and then King Richard I of England – Richard had conquered Cyprus on the way, which turned out to be a most useful acquisition for the surviving Crusader states. Their arrival in stages finally disheartened the starving garrison, and a surrender on terms was arranged in mid-July.

The king of France went home almost at once, leaving Richard in command. He campaigned along the coast recovering the lost cities as far as Ashkelon, failed to reach Jerusalem, which would have been indefensible without much wider conquests, then made a peace which left the kingdom of Jerusalem holding a long narrow strip of coast. Saladin died a year after the peace. A few years later a German crusade reconquered more of the coast to the north of Tyre, and enabled Tripoli to expand over its own lost coasts. By 1200 the Crusader states once more controlled the entire coast from the mouth of the Eleutheros to Ashkelon.

The kingdom Saladin had created began to break up. He had seventeen sons and two surviving brothers. Most of them received part of his inheritance, a division in which geography reasserted itself with separate kingdoms in Aleppo, Damascus, Homs, Hama, Baalbek and Outrejourdain. The heirs began to quarrel amongst themselves, though without causing serious casualties. The future of the Crusader states was therefore safe for the time being, and they were even able to slowly, piece by piece, expand their territories.

From the Muslim point of view these states were now a nuisance. They attracted Crusades from Europe, which caused wars to break out in Syria, or were diverted to other regions. The Fourth Crusade (1201–1204) was diverted to attack the Byzantine Empire, and the Fifth (1216–1221) attacked Egypt. This last was perhaps a reasonable target since the Egyptian Sultan normally controlled Palestine, but the attack was unsuccessful. Every new Crusade failed to conquer territory, and yet they were damaging.

In 1228 the emperor, Frederick II, who had married the heiress to the kingdom, Isabella II, even persuaded the Sultan al-Kamil of Egypt to cede him Jerusalem. Ten years later another Crusade failed to achieve anything militarily except a defeat at Egyptian hands near Gaza, but some deft diplomacy by Earl Richard of Cornwall recovered territories in the north, including much of Galilee. However none of these gains were really safe and they only took place because of Muslim quarrels. During the 1239 Crusade a raid on a caravan of the lord of Kerak, al-Nasir, provoked him to a counter raid, in which he captured Jerusalem, demolished its meagre fortifications, and then rode away, demonstrating the vulnerability of much of the kingdom. But for both sides this was something which had become steadily more dangerous. It was easier for the Muslims to surrender a town or two to allow the Crusaders such as Frederick II to claim a triumph, but none of the Crusades' gains were strategically vital, and all were vulnerable to a serious Muslim attack, if one could be organized.

Syria had therefore been united for a few years under Saladin (1186–1193), except for the surviving Crusader states, but had then disintegrated once more as he distributed his inheritance among his sons. He did have the consolation of knowing, however, that they were in no danger from his enemies, the Crusaders, who were so weakened that they ceased altogether to wage aggressive war, except when new Crusaders arrived from the west. Eight years of conflict between Saladin's brothers and sons and nephews followed his death until his brother, al-Adil I, emerging supreme in the family as sultan.

Al-Adil ruled from Damascus, with one son as his deputy in Egypt, another son in the Jazirah, a grandson of Shirkuh at Homs, al-Zahir, Saladin's son, at Aleppo, and a cousin at Baalbek. The other heirs had to be content with small lordships, single cities or small regions, so that they were not powerful enough to mount a serious rebellion. Of course, this distribution only worked until al-Adil died, in 1218. The Fifth Crusade, which invaded Egypt shortly afterwards, delayed the quarrel between his successors for a few years, but it broke out in earnest in 1226.

The result of several more years fighting and negotiation was that the Egyptian sultan, al-Kamil, al-Adil's son, secured Damascus and the family supremacy, and his brother al-Ashraf held Aleppo and the Jazirah – several minor princes held the usual cities and regions. The Ayyubite Kingdom was still more or less together, though union was hardly the best description.

Al-Kamil's son Ayyub secured the Sultanate of Egypt from his brother al-Adil II, but spent many years then fighting his uncle, Ismail, who had secured Damascus. In the north the death of al-Ashraf left no serious authority in control. The whole of the Jazirah was ravaged by a band of Khwarizmian Turks who escaped, or fled, from the defeat of their shah by the Mongols. At one point Ayyub called in this band to assist him against Ismail, and they came right through Syria and into Palestine, where they captured and sacked Jerusalem. Then they joined Ayyub in a battle against the joint forces of the kingdoms of Jerusalem, Kerak, Homs, and Damascus, which resulted in the near-annihilation of the army of Jerusalem by the army of Egypt commanded by Rukn ad-Din Baybars at Harbie (La Forbie) near Gaza. Ayyub at last succeeded in gaining control of Damascus soon after and more or less again uniting the Ayyubite inheritance. He also took over, without any serious opposition, those parts of the Jerusalem kingdom he required, principally Jerusalem and the region of the Sea of Galilee. The kingdom was incapable of resisting.

Another Crusade, led by King Louis IX of France arrived, heading straight for Egypt. Sultan Ayyub returned to defend his kingdom, but he died in the midst of the campaign. His son Turanshah was in the Jazirah and took time to arrive, and while the Egyptians waited his mother Shajar al-Durr commanded. But the new sultan was lazy and was soon deposed by the Mamluk Bahri Regiment officers and murdered by Baybars. They then carried through a coup by which their own leader Aibek became sultan. The Crusade was defeated and the French king captured.

The Mamluk coup subtracted Egypt from the Ayyubite Kingdom but did not directly affect Syria for the time being. It took time for the new government to impose itself fully on Egypt. The Mamluks were the logical outcome of the practice of employing Turkish slaves as a bodyguard which had been begun four centuries before by Caliph al-Mutasim, combined with the uncertain and militarized governments of the Islamic lands. The Egyptian Mamluks were, however, all of one people, the Qipchaks, and all purchased at more or less the same time, soon after the destruction of the Qipchak Kingdom of the steppes of Europe by the Mongols in 1222. There were so many Qipchak boys for sale after this that the price fell and Sultan Ayyub bought them up in large numbers. They were trained as highly professional soldiers, but developed a much stronger *esprit de corps* than usual among such regiments because of their common origin.

Such a force was not new in the Islamic world, of course, and Turkish Mamluks had been around for four centuries, constantly involved in politics, and Saladin's military successes were in large part due to the fact that he could keep his Mamluks in the field for much longer than other forces, which were not professional and expected to be able to go home in times of peace, or inactive warfare. By contrast the Mamluks lived in barracks, and were always on call. They were also much better trained than most Islamic troops, and were really the only soldiers on the Arab side who could fight the western knights on anything like equal terms – which is why they were so important, of course.[16]

In Syria the Ayyubid ruler of Aleppo, al-Nasir Yusuf, quickly gained control of Damascus, but was defeated when he invaded Egypt. The two regimes' teams bickered with each other for several years until the Caliph al-Mustasim in Baghdad brokered an uneasy peace and was conscious of the looming presence and approach of the new great power, the Mongol Khanate. In 1258 the Khan Hulegu captured and sacked Baghdad, and the Abbasid caliph died in the process. Almost every ruler in Syria had contacted the Mongol ruler and had offered submission, though some changed their minds – al-Nasir Yusuf of Aleppo swung to and fro with the political wind, leaving him extremely vulnerable to accusations of bad faith.

In Egypt the new sultan, Aibek, married Shajar al-Durr, and co-opted her younger son by Ayyub as a co-sultan. He succeeded in defending Egypt against the attack by al-Nasir Yusuf, but only because a Mamluk regiment in al-Nasir's service changed sides. But one of his own regiments, the Bahriyya, commanded by Rukn ad-Din Baybars, deserted to take service with al-Nasir. Only after Aibak was killed at Shajar's instigation and she was murdered in return, and Aibek's son was deposed by Saif ad-Din Qutuz, did the Bahriyya return to Egyptian service.

The Mongol advance struck Syria in 1259. The invasion had been well-prepared diplomatically, and the smaller Syrian powers either took the Mongol side or stood neutral. Approaching through the Jazirah and capturing its cities with ease, Hulegu's army reached Aleppo in January. Al-Nasir Yusuf was in Damascus where he gathered an army and was joined by forces from Hama and Kerak. At Aleppo the city was taken but al-Nasir's garrison refused to surrender the citadel. There was dissension in his army at Damascus and when some deserted it was out of the question to march to Aleppo. Probably it would have been too late anyway, for the Mongols had taken no more than six days to break into the city, where they massacred the Muslims and spared the Christians.

The Armenian king of Kilikia and Prince Bohemond VI of Antioch came to the Mongol camp and rendered their submission, and were both rewarded with concessions of territory. Al-Nasir Yusuf fled to Egypt on receiving the news of the capture of Aleppo and the Mongols under Hulegu's commander, Kitbuqa, took Damascus without resistance, sending detachments south through Palestine to occupy Nablus and Gaza. It is clear that they had an accurate understanding of the politics and political geography of the country. The Franks of the Jerusalem Kingdom had been divided in their responses, between those who wanted to render submission like Prince Bohemond of Antioch, and another group, a rash few, who wanted to fight, despite the odds. That is, the Crusaders remained true to their past, divided as ever. The first Frankish raid was by Julian, lord of Sidon and the castle of Beaufort on Mount Hermon, who sent a raid into the Bekaa, which defeated a small Mongol force. Kitbuqa replied with a larger force which took and badly damaged Sidon town. The lord of Beirut and the Templars also tried a raid into Galilee and it was destroyed.

Hulegu sent an embassy to Egypt demanding submission; Sultan Qutuz had the ambassador killed as his reply. This of course meant war. But thousands of miles away in Mongolia the Great Khan Mongke died, and Hulegu, Mongke's brother, had to take most of his army away from Syria to involve himself in the succession struggle. The war was therefore between the full strength of the Mamluks and a reduced Mongol army, under Kitbuqa, and the Mamluks could afford to go on to the offensive. Qutuz first defeated the small Mongol force which he found at Gaza, then marched up the coast making friendly contact with the Franks at Acre, who supplied provisions but would not join the fighting. The Mongol force came south from Damascus, where a rising of the Muslims had to be suppressed and Kitbuqa had to leave a strengthened garrison. The two armies met in battle near the Sea of Galilee, not far from the Horns of Hattin, at a place called Ain Jalut. The Mongols were deceived into charging by a feigned retreat of part of the Mamluk force, then surrounded, and slowly destroyed; Kitbuqa was captured, insulted his captors and was then executed.

Without opposition the Mamluk army now marched north as far as the Euphrates. Ayyubite princes were confirmed in office at Homs and Hama, and the Mongols were driven from Aleppo. A weak Mongol attempt to recover the city was defeated. And suddenly Syria was once again united under Egyptian suzerainty, as it had been in effect under Saladin. But this new government was scarcely very friendly or comfortable: on the journey back to Egypt the commander of the Bahriyya Regiment, Rukd ad-Din Baybars, who had already murdered one sultan, murdered Qutuz with a sword thrust into his back. Baybars became the next sultan.

Chapter 20

Destruction and Neglect

The relations between Mamluks and Mongols never improved after their initial collisions. Having seized power, Baybars' first task was to extend his control over all Syria, but he was pre-empted by a second Mongol invasion. The governors of Aleppo (a man who had been chosen locally to replace an unpopular appointee of Qutuz') and Damascus were not inclined to obey the upstart sultan and acted independently. Other quasi- or actually independent areas of Syria included Hama and Homs under Ayyubid rulers, and Kerak, under an Ayyubid prince, the three Crusader states, and a variety of regions never inclined to obey any central power.

The Mongols had retained the ability to cross the Euphrates, probably at al-Bira (Birejik, the former Seleukeia Zeugma). An army of several thousands of soldiers, commanded by Baydar, an officer of Kitbuqa's, headed for Aleppo. The new governor and his soldiers, formerly Ayyubite Mamluks perhaps learning from the previous year, left the city to the invaders and moved south. On the way they were joined by al-Mansur of Hama and his troops, and, near Homs, by the king of Homs, a descendant of Shirkuh, with his forces. They faced the Mongols just north of Homs, at a place identified as near the grave of Khalid ibn al-Walid, the Arab conqueror. Outnumbered four-to-one, the Ayyubite Mamluk army defeated the Mongols.[1]

So the victory at Ain Jalut was no accident. The disciplined, well-armed, and professional Mamluks were again more than a match for the lighter armed Mongols. The Mongol army largely survived, and retreated eastwards to Salamiyya, then went north to Aleppo, where the population was pushed out, some massacred, and then herded back in. In effect, despite their defeat, the Mongol army had recovered control of north Syria. The former governor did not return; he and his supporters headed south to Egypt.

The Franks tried to take advantage of all these events with an expedition as far as the Golan, but this was defeated by a Mamluk detachment. Baybars was approached more than once by various Frankish leaders hoping to negotiate a truce, but he would not do so. The Franks could not, in any case, control their own people, when the Templars and Hospitallers steadily gained more strength and independence; they were rich from their holdings in Europe and could afford to buy up lordships when the lords went broke.

With Damascus in his hands, Baybars was in a commanding position in Syria, but the country was littered with other states – the three Frankish states, at least four Ayyubid kingdoms, Aleppo, the Assassins in their Nosairi castles, a small state in the Amanus Mountains around the castle of Sahyun (Saone). The Armenian Kingdom controlled Kilikia. After two centuries of constant warfare these were all well-fortified with castles and walled cities, none of which were easy for any contemporary army to capture, and being involved in a siege often brought relieving forces into action.

The Mongols had largely withdrawn northwards, eventually leaving north Syria and the Jazirah shattered and uncontrolled. Several of the cities – Edessa, Raqqa – were ruined and almost depopulated; others had fallen under the rule of a local strongman. In effect, the region was a chaotic no man's land.

Over the next twenty years Baybars and his successors constructed a new state in Syria, which in union with Egypt, lasted six centuries, an achievement quite comparable with the construction of the Roman Empire. However, in order to do so, Baybars and his most capable successor Qalawun had to adopt the methods of the Mongols by wreaking extensive and permanent destruction.

Baybars' situation in the 1260s was, to be sure, extremely difficult. His major enemy was the Mongols, who repeatedly raided into north Syria, and were always liable to mount a major invasion. Experience had shown that Sunni Muslim states in Syria would normally oppose such attacks, but not invariably. Experience also showed that any other state in Syria, Christian, Frank, Shi'ite, Armenian, would probably join such an invasion if it was directed at Baybars and his new Mamluk state. This would be even more certain once Baybars had located a surviving member of the Abbasid family and had him 'elected' as caliph in the Sunni interest; the Caliph al-Mustansir was even sent in command of an armed expedition on the assumption that he would attract support, and in the hope that he would recover Iraq from Mongol control.

Strategically Baybars was pinned between the Mongols to the north and east, and the Crusader states on the west. In 1261 he moved north to secure Aleppo and al-Bira, and turned his destructive power on the lands of the principality of Antioch. Prince Bohemond VI had joined the Mongol invasion and had even ridden with Kitbuqa through Damascus when the city capitulated. He was still, along with King Hethoum of Armenian Kilikia, allied with the Mongols, and was therefore a good target. No doubt Baybars was prepared for a Mongol force to arrive to rescue their ally, but in fact he had plenty of time to ravage Antiochene lands, though he made no attempt to besiege or capture the city or any of the forts.[2] He could not afford to become locked into a siege with the possibility of a Mongol force arriving to relieve it.

This tactic was repeated in the next years, steadily weakening Antioch. In a very similar way small Mamluk expeditions were sent eastwards, into the Jazirah, into

Kurdistan, into Iraq, hopefully to gain control of most or all of these lands, but above all with the aim of keeping the Mongols busy and at a distance, out of Syria. And all the time Baybars chipped away at the independent sections of Syria, using whatever means or methods came to hand. For example he lured the lord of Kerak, the Ayyubid prince, al-Mugith Umar, to a meeting at Mount Tabor, where he was removing the Benedictine monks from the monastery. Al-Mugith was arrested, tried by a packed court and imprisoned in Egypt, after which his two castles, at Kerak and Shawbak, and his principality, were taken over as part of the Mamluk sultanate. This secured the great route to Mecca, the King's Highway.[3]

Control of north Syria was the real area of concern, threatened by both a Mongol attack and by the alliance of Bohemond VI of Antioch and Hethoum of Armenian Kilikia. These two raided into Syria in 1262 and the year after, perhaps as a reply to Baybars' raid into Antioch, but possibly aiming at the conquest of some castles; they were defeated in the first attack and deterred by the presence of a Mamluk force in the second. On the first occasion the raid may have been of Mongol inspiration to distract Baybars. A major Mongol effort was being organized by the Ilkhan Hulegu to attack his fellow Khan Berke of the Golden Horde. Baybars mobilized when he heard of the Mongol gathering, fearing an invasion of Syria. The Armenian raid could have been a means of preventing him from interfering in the Mongol civil war.

That war died down at the end of 1264, and next year a major Mongol effort was made to capture the fortress of al-Bira on the Euphrates. Again Baybars reacted decisively, and the garrison held out well until reinforcements arrived, whereupon the Mongol force retreated, abandoning its siege machines (or fled, depending on the source, Mamluk or Mongol).[4] It was understood that the Franks of the kingdom of Acre were in communication with the Mongols, and Baybars – though he never needed such an excuse – took the opportunity of his full army being present to deal serious blows at them. News had arrived that Ilkhan Hulegu had died in mid 1265, so it was unlikely that any new Mongol attack could be organised for some time. There was thus an opening for a Frankish war, which would necessitate attacks on fortified cities and castles. This was an uncertain proceeding, as the Mongols had just discovered at al-Bira, and Baybars would need some time to gain his object.

He arrived unexpectedly before Caesarea late in February, where the town fell at once, and the citadel a week later. The inhabitants were dismissed and allowed to leave, but the town and its citadel were destroyed. Haifa below Mount Carmel, just to the north, and just across the bay from Acre, was next attacked. Again the place was destroyed, and this time, those who had not fled at his approach were massacred. Baybars next attacked the great coastal fortress of Athlit, and burned the village at the castle gate, but the garrison of the castle itself resisted successfully. He turned back south to attack Arsuf, where the Templars gave in on the promise of freedom but were then killed. Arsuf was then razed.[5]

The practice of destroying the Crusader fortifications had been one of Saladin's methods. He had applied it mainly to inland castles and towers. At the capture of Acre one of his commanders had recommended its destruction, but he had refused, only to have the Crusaders eventually retake it.[6] The creeping Christian recovery of much of the coast and of areas of the interior after his death had allowed many places he had reduced to be refortified. Baybars in this campaign therefore had to redo much of Saladin's work. He turned on Acre after finishing at Arsuf, but found that the city had been reinforced from Cyprus (and later more troops arrived from France). This made it, in his view, too strong to be attacked with any hope of success in the relatively short time he had available. But the arrival of reinforcement by sea from such distances can only have made him more determined to clear the coast of such threatening cities, which could be so easily made bases for reconquest. On the other hand, this campaign had taken about ten weeks; the Crusader places were vulnerable, after all, and Mamluk siege techniques, relying mainly on the deployment of stone-throwing mangonels to break open the walls, but also on discharges of Greek fire, had proved most successful.

Next year Baybars made another threat at Acre but again decided it was too strong to be attacked, then he turned inland, besieged and took the Templar castle at Safad and then the nearby castle at Toron. This gave him control of Galilee, and pushed the Frankish boundary westwards. Safad was repaired and designated the governing centre of Galilee.[7]

In the knowledge that the new Ilkhan, Abagha, was embroiled in a war with Khan Berke of the Golden Horde, Baybars was able to attend to the north-west frontier. A passing raid on Antiochene territory brought him to the Beylan Pass through – or rather over – the Amanus Mountains. An Armenian blocking force at the pass was defeated, and in the fight a brother and a son of King Hethoum were killed and his heir, Leon, was captured. The Mamluk army then descended into Kilikia, capturing several cities including Sis, the royal city, and raided throughout the kingdom as far west as Tarsus, looting and destroying, killing several thousands of people, and taking 40,000 captives away when they retired. This was quite enough for Hethoum. He spent the next year negotiating peace with Baybars, who required the handing over of six forts on the frontier and the rescue of a friend, Sunqur al-Ashqar, from Mongol captivity in exchange for Leon.[8]

The two small areas in the Nosairi Mountains under the control of the Assassins and Muzaffar al-Din Uthman were now being steadily squeezed. The Assassins, of course, were Ismaili Shi'ites, and, apart from their practice of assassinating perceived enemies, they represented an awkward island of Shi'ah rule in a now predominantly Sunni kingdom. But their original fanaticism had faded into blackmail, and they received 'tribute' from several monarchs and paid tribute themselves to the Templars and Hospitallers to prevent attacks on their fortresses. Baybars began by taxing these tribute payments, and then prohibited the payments to the Hospitallers – which the Assassins then diverted to him. Thus established his supremacy and by 1270 he was able to insist on the replacement of a recalcitrant Assassin amir by a more pliable man. The little Principality of Uthman, the two castles of Sahyun and Balatunus, was also first reduced to accepting his overall suzerainty. Finally between 1271 and 1273 the castles of both of these were seized by either a *coup de main* or a longer blockade. Baybars thus rounded out his control of interior Syria without having to fight other Muslims, and so without the creation of recrimination or of martyrs.[9] Baybars may have recruited some of the Assassins to do their work for him, but they were dangerous instruments, and if he did so, he soon abandoned the idea. But their people lived on as non-lethal Ismailis in a fairly compact area east of their former castles.

Indefatigably Baybars set his army to attack Antioch on his return from ravaging Kilikia, but his generals were lethargic, and no longer greedy enough for loot to press the attack. Baybars demobilized his forces for the season. Next year he ravaged the land around Acre, and the year after, 1268, he set out to make further Frankish conquests. In March he captured Jaffa, whose defences had been neglected, despite the recent conquests of other Crusader cities; after destroying the town he went on to attack the great castle of Beaufort, high on its hill. Ten days' bombardment sufficed. The men were enslaved, the women and children released, just for a change – the dependents increased the burden on the Crusader cities, and they were deprived of any men of fighting age. As at Safad, the castle was repaired and strengthened and well-garrisoned.

The army marched north, menaced Tripoli, and passed Tortosa and Lattakiah without stopping. Its target was Antioch, the greatest and wealthiest city of the Frankish east. The main part of the army began the siege of the city, while one detachment was sent to seize St Symeon, the port of the city, to stop reinforcements and provisions coming in, and another to block any attempt to bring in a relief from Kilikia. These precautions were scarcely needed. But Antioch did not have an adequate garrison to defend its long circuit of walls, so within only four days a breach had been made and the Mamluk army poured in. The people were either killed or enslaved, including several thousands who had taken refuge in the citadel. Every soldier acquired a slave, and there were many more to glut the market; a huge quantity of loot was collected and distributed.

The Principality of Antioch was destroyed as a state. Prince Bohemond was also Count of Tripoli but he had been quite unable to assist in the defence of his main city. It was his and his father's policy to rely on their alliance with the Mongols to protect them from Mamluk attack, and yet it had not done so some since the Mongol defeat at Homs in 1260. The fate of Armenian Kilikia had been a clear warning, but Bohemond did not change course – though it is, it must be said, difficult to see what else he could have done other than become subject to Baybars. Several of the castles in the principality were at once abandoned; only

Qusair, under a Frank who was friendly to the Muslims, and the town of Lattakiah remained of the original state.[10]

The border war across the Euphrates continued. Mongol forces were able to reach as far west as the neighbourhood of Aleppo; Mamluk raids reached in the other direction as far as Ras al-Ayn, at the headwaters of the Khabour River, and a Mamluk garrison held Qarqisiyah and al-Rahba at the junction of the Khabour and the Euphrates. One raid reached and captured Harran; afterwards the Mongols evacuated the city and burned it – yet another ruined city. Twice more Mongol armies of considerable strength laid siege to al-Bira, but on the first occasion in 1272 they were defeated by Baybars' relieving army, which crossed the Euphrates under fire and fought its way ashore against heavy opposition; in the second attempt the Mongol force, which was half composed of Mongols and half of Christians from Armenia and Georgia, broke up amid mutual suspicions of betrayal before really settling into the siege. Baybars meanwhile sent another destructive invasion into Kilikia, where it wreaked great damage and met virtually no opposition.[11]

The result in Kilikia was not total destruction but certainly much damage was caused, many lives were lost, and several cities destroyed.[12] Exactly how much destruction took place is not certain in all these ventures, both there and in Syria and the Jazirah. Sis, the Armenian royal city, is said to have been destroyed in the first Mamluk invasion in 1266, but there was enough of the city nine years later to merit another sack and another 'destruction'. By this time urban populations no doubt knew well enough to flee from their city in advance of its capture, and the Mamluks deliberately evacuated cities which were in danger of being captured. The citizens would be able to return and rebuild after the raiders had gone; on the other hand, there will have been plenty of casualties, much wealth was destroyed, or removed, and much work was needed to repair the damage. Aleppo, for example, was reportedly captured, looted, destroyed, abandoned, reoccupied, according to the sources, but a large number of buildings in the city survive from before all these events. It would seem that 'destroyed' is invariably an exaggeration.[13] In the end, of course, raids repeated often enough would compel abandonment. And on the Syrian coast, the Mamluks were not just raiding, they were conquering and systematically dismantling the cities and castles; any attempt to return to their destroyed homes by refugees would produce only killing.

In 1277 Baybars mounted a full-scale invasion of the Sultanate of Rum, in central Anatolia, a Seljuk kingdom subjected by the Mongols. This was the outcome of a complex series of diplomatic contracts and intrigues. Rum was a subject ally of the Ilkhanate (like Antioch and Kilikia) and so an enemy of the Mamluks – and a Rumi army had participated in the siege of al-Bira. The Mamluk army fought its way through the mountains, defeating a major Mongol army on the way, and Baybars reached the Rumi capital at Qaysariyah (Caesarea); he had left the Aleppo army to guard the Euphrates, and sure enough an attack came and was brushed off.

The expedition was able to stay at Qaysariyah for no more than five days. The absence of the whole Mamluk army at such a distance from Egypt and Syria was clearly very tempting to its enemies – Baybars would never have risked such a campaign if Antioch and Kilikia had not been conquered first. But it demonstrated the power of the Mamluk state, while at the same time demonstrating the geographical limitations of its military reach.[14]

Baybars died in 1277, a month after returning to Damascus, and was succeeded by a confused two years. His son al-Said Berke Khan became sultan, but meddled with the military system he had inherited, replacing comrades of his father's with men he hoped would be loyal to him personally. This did not work and he was deposed by his father's most senior commander, al-Mansur Qalawun al-Afri, who then did much the same but with more subtlety; he was assisted in gaining support by a rebellion led by Baybars' rescued friend Sunqur al-Ashqar, who had been appointed governor of Damascus. When defeated, Sunqur fled to the desert, whence he wrote to the Ilkhan Abagha, pointing out the disturbed condition of the Mamluk state. Then he returned to Syria and went to live in his castle of Sahyun. Whether or not he needed the nudge, Abagha organized an invasion. Berke Khan had been exiled to Kerak and began collecting supporters, but suddenly died, conveniently for Qalawun. That is, Qalawun was faced with a very similar situation to that of Baybars in his first years, and used the same methods to overcome it.[15]

The Mongol forces came from at least three directions, from Armenia in the north, through the Jazirah from the east, and through Kilikia from the west – all regions which Mamluks had invaded in the past decade. However, once they realized that Sunqur had no army of his own and was comfortably ensconced in his castle, the invasion faltered. They did raid as far as Aleppo; the city had been abandoned and was looted. Then they retreated. Sultan Qalawun had not left Egypt during this, but a large part of his forces had been in Syria preparing to meet any further Mongol penetration.[16] Next spring, however, Qalawun brought the full Mamluk army out of Egypt and marched it north; he was clearly expecting an attack – both he and Baybars operated a highly effective espionage system and a pigeon post which jointly kept them informed of distant events even while they were in Egypt. On the way he made lengthy truces with the Franks of Acre and with Bohemond VII of Tripoli, so clearing his coastal flank. A Mongol envoy had in fact offered an alliance with the Franks of Acre, but was apparently turned down.[17]

Qalawun had to put down a conspiracy in his army, having been alerted by informants in Acre. He then consoled two other internal enemies: Sunqur was allotted his own principality around his castle at Sahyun, and Baybars' son al-Masud Khadir was given autonomy at Kerak.[18] But these and earlier disturbances provide adequate reasons for Abagha's new invasion. He must have expected to be fighting a much less united state than the one he finally met. When the invasion came in October (1281), there was a dispute in the army over where to meet it, which almost broke up the army. And Qalawun lost the argument.

The Mongol army, said to number 80,000 men (though this is probably a considerable exaggeration) moved south from eastern Anatolia along the Euphrates Valley into north Syria – the reverse march of Baybars four years before. The region had been evacuated, the pastures burned, and the army's progress southwards was slow. The Mamluk army had been gathered at Damascus for several months and moved forward to Homs to meet the attack. It was outnumbered, but was in position on its chosen battleground for three days before the Mongols arrived – they had been marching for weeks, and also all night before the battle. In all but numbers the Mamluks were better prepared – they had a central and clear command, where the Mongol commanders were several, they were better disciplined and trained, their equipment was better, and they were fighting for both their homes and their lives.

The battle was between mainly cavalry-archer forces, and the Mongols made the classic and decisive mistake of concentrating extra weight on their right wing, which charged successfully and scattered the Mamluk left wing, then followed the fugitives instead of turning on the Mamluk centre and right as they should have done. The Mamluk centre and right held firm, then counter-attacked, winning their battle before the Mongol right woke up and returned. And then the Mamluks improved on their battlefield victory by a relentless pursuit as far as the Euphrates. The Mongol army was destroyed.[19]

This was the signal for the Mamluks to begin the final elimination of the Crusader states, but it was a matter which took time, even though there was no danger of a Mongol intervention – though there was a constant likelihood that troops would arrive from the west. The cities were well established and well-integrated into the local economy, and their capture and destruction would be very disruptive; on the other hand Baybars had shown that even that largest and strongest of the cities were vulnerable if resolutely attacked. The end of the possibility of Mongol support for the Crusaders – refused already anyway – or of any Mongol distraction, meant that it was now possible for the Mamluks to concentrate fully on the Crusaders, and no doubt it was a congenial task. These campaigns were much assisted by the constant infighting and bickering within the small Crusader enclaves which were all that was left. Neither the Templars nor the Hospitallers were responsive to their technical royal lords, and would rarely cooperate; the lord of Jubail instigated a civil war in the County of Tripoli; Venetians and Genoese and Pisans fought with each other; succession disputes preoccupied rulers in Acre, Cyprus, and Tripoli.

Qalawun began his campaign in April 1285 with a well-prepared assault on the Hospitaller castle of Marqab, near Lattakiah. Technically this was part of the County of Tripoli but the count had neither the strength nor perhaps the inclination to intervene, after the Hospitallers had so often refused to obey him. And anyway this was one of the strongest fortresses in the Latin lands. But the castle fell after a month.[20] Two years later Lattakiah, damaged by an earthquake, fell to an opportunistic attack.[21] In the same year Qalawun was able to clear the way to the coast by the Homs Gap by suppressing Sunqur's principality at Sahyun.

The continuing disputes in Tripoli persuaded the Venetians to request that Qalawun intervene, though they must have known that this was an invitation to conquest – but the Genoese had virtual control of the port, and a Muslim takeover might well benefit the Venetians. The request allowed him to disregard the truce of 1281, and to mount a major attack. The city received reinforcements from Cyprus and Acre, but in the midst of the siege the Venetians and the Genoese both deserted; the Mamluk assault came at the same time and the city fell. A general massacre of men ensued, with women and children enslaved. The city was demolished to prevent it being used as a new base by the Latins. The fall of the city was followed by the unresisting capture of Nephin and Batrun to the south; the lord of Jubail, who had been one of those involved in the internal troubles in Tripoli, submitted rapidly, and was permitted to stay in office for another decade. Another Crusader state had been extinguished.[22]

The reaction in Acre was to ask for a new truce, which Qalawun granted; in Western Europe the Pope preached a new crusade, but most people were busy, or no longer interested. A band of northern Italians did set out, and landed at Acre but they proved to be a disastrous reinforcement. They were noisy, drunken, and spoiling for a fight – but the only people they could find to attack were Muslims inside the city who had come to market their produce. In a riot the Italians murdered any Muslims they could find. Qalawun denounced the truce.

Qalawun began preparations to attack, instancing the riot as his reason for breaking the truce. But he died before the attack could begin. His successor was his son al-Ashraf Khalil, who quickly nipped the inevitable plot in the bud. But he did not abandon the expedition, though it was delayed until the spring of 1291. Then he brought the full strength of the Mamluk kingdom to bear, with forces from Egypt, from Damascus, and from Hama, and a great mangonel brought from Krak des Chevaliers. The delay allowed the city to receive reinforcements from Europe and Cyprus, but these were never enough; as at Antioch there were never enough soldiers to properly man the walls.

The city held out for six weeks, but the walls were battered to destruction. On 18 May the Mamluks forced an entry, and this was followed by the usual sickening scenes of massacre, enslavement, and panicking refugees. The Templars' tower on the end of the peninsula held out for ten more days, but then collapsed during a mass assault, burying attackers and defenders together. Al-Ashraf, determined like his father and Baybars never to have to repeat such a fight, or to accept the continuing threat to his flank in case of another Mongol war, burned the buildings of the city, dismantled the towers and castles; the partly destroyed wall was left to fall down.[23]

Al-Ashraf followed his triumph by clearing out the rest of the Crusaders. Tyre fell at once, despite its inherent military strength, Sidon fell after a short fight; at Beirut, when it was clear that an attack was coming the garrison fled to Cyprus; the monasteries on Mount Carmel were sacked and the monks killed; at Athlit the Templar garrison evacuated the castle; at Tortosa the same. Then the sultan's men systematically destroyed all coastal forts, castles, towns, orchards, crops and villages, driving the peasants away from the coast into the interior. Nothing was left which might assist an invader from the sea, neither supplies nor shelter.[24]

Between them Baybars and Qalawun were the founders of the new state, the Mamluk Sultanate – though it was based on its Ayyubid predecessor and it was Baybars who had done the real work. He was an extraordinary combination of highly competent soldier, innovative administrator and cunning diplomat. His main achievement was to unify Syria and attach it firmly to Egypt, so that the new state was strong enough above all militarily, to fight its formidable Mongol enemy. But his ruthlessness – his necessary ruthlessness, he would have insisted – left a wrecked Syria, an expensive army to be maintained, and a general system built on slave soldiers bound to serve individual commanders (amirs) who thus had the power to create trouble. It was a system built for his own use, and only occasional successors could operate it successfully. Together with destroyed Syria, it was a system which promoted instability at the centre and was avid for the resources of the rest of the population – a recipe for impoverishment, where a sultan with real concern for his people would have eased the burden to allow recovery. Baybars built a state capable of beating the Mongols, which was his primary purpose, a great achievement in itself, but then it froze in position, unable to relax, when if it was really to survive relaxation was necessary.

Al-Ashraf himself only survived for two more years before he was murdered. The Mamluk government then became a constant series of plots and murders and depositions, exactly the sort of condition which attracted enemy attention. The intrigues centred on al-Nasir Muhammad, Qalawun's son, who was enthroned three times (and deposed twice). Meanwhile a competent Ilkhan, Ghazan, had revived and improved the Mongol army, partly on Mamluk lines. The intrigues along the frontier which had been a feature of Baybars' reign also revived. Ghazan had converted to Islam, a political gesture aiming to secure support from his subject peoples, but this also entailed religious conflict. One group of Mongols, Oirats, several thousand strong, fled to the Mamluk Sultanate for refuge. They were planted along the Palestinian coast, on the devastated lands, as a protective force.[25]

Ghazan, however, was intent on an invasion, particularly in the light of the governmental confusion in Cairo. The governor of Damascus, Qipchaq, (a Mongol captured in Baybars' Rumi campaign) was on the wrong side of a new coup in 1298 and fled to Ghazan, who in turn was feeling threatened in Anatolia and the Jazirah. He invaded Syria in December 1299, aiming for Damascus. The Mamluk forces were not ready, and were delayed on the march north by a rebellion of the Oirats in Palestine, but they did reach the battle area north of Homs in time to fight.

The battle this time was a Mongol victory, and it was followed by the occupation of Damascus and by Mongol raids throughout the south as far as Gaza. But it was also followed by continued Mamluk and local resistance. Garrisons held out in castles and towns – even in Damascus the citadel was not taken. And to the north most of the cities had been bypassed on the rapid Mongol move to Damascus. So while Ghazan's army had adopted some of the methods of the Mamluk army, the Mamluks in their defeat were fighting in the way of the Crusaders, holding out in former Crusader castles. Ghazan withdrew on news of a revolt in Persia, but he must have been glad to escape. Syria was not to be conquered at one blow if the Mamluk army survived, and certainly not by the undisciplined Mongols.[26]

Ghazan tried again next year, but atrocious weather kept the two armies apart. He mounted a third invasion in 1303, reached again as far south as Damascus, but was then caught by the Mamluks at Marj en-Suffar, south of Damascus, where the Mongol army was thoroughly defeated. The retreating soldiers were harassed by the peasantry on their flight, but in the Bekaa Valley it was the Mamluks who were attacked, by the Druzes. This was a region of Shi'ite minorities who had been attacked after the capture of Tripoli and again after the conquest of Acre, and who had fought back with some success. The men of this area were also regarded, with justice, as some of the best infantry soldiers in Syria, and were recruited into the Mamluk armies. No doubt their military training was also useful against their employers.[27]

The invasion of 1303 was the final Mongol effort. The Ilkhanate broke up thirty years later. One result was that the Mamluk forces, without a serious enemy to keep them alert, became less efficient, for their only enemies were internal dissidents, like the Lebanese mountaineers, and the men of the northern frontier, or Egyptian Bedouin. After 1310 for the first time since the death of Qalawun in 1290 a sultan, al-Nasir Muhammad, kept his throne for a long period, and ruled competently. For a full generation he was in power and the kingdom had a certain peace.

Syria had been terribly battered during the previous century. The only way Saladin, his successors, and the Mamluks had been able to ensure that they were not subjected to a successful western invasion had been to deny the invaders any possible base and all possible supplies. Every castle and city on the coast had been destroyed; those castles which were left standing were several miles from the sea so that a good warning of an attack would be received. The only city left near the coast was Tripoli, but the ruins were abandoned and the new city was five miles inland; at Beirut the cathedral was converted to a mosque which implies a continued Muslim occupation, but the fort and the walls had been brought down. It is a mark of the success of this policy that no Crusader invasions arrived, despite the available base in Cyprus and continual western command of the sea.

The effect on the Syrians was, of course, equally damaging. Without ports for their goods the export trade was much reduced. The numbers of people killed and enslaved is uncountable but must have been a substantial percentage of the pre-Saladin population. Moreover the massacres by the Mamluks had been often of town dwellers, and so merchants, shopkeepers, artisans, and with the towns gone these wealth creators were not replaced. The Mamluk taxation system did nothing to reduce the economic pressures on the surviving peasantry. There is evidence of a flight from the land to the towns and cities to escape such taxation (and to escape the Mongols). The rural population was replaced by incoming Bedouins, some of whom settled to agriculture, and others remained as nomads, but they all retained their tribal organization, which dealt with the Mamluk authorities as a unit. The Mamluks regarded them as allies, and they often fought as military auxiliaries – but they were not easily taxable. Indeed, the nomad confederacies of the desert were bribed by huge payments to refrain from interfering with the trade caravans and the Hajj. The age-long mercantile expertise of Syria was severely damaged.

The internal dynastic disputes of the Mamluks were mainly confined to coup and counter-coup in Cairo, but these could easily spill over into Syria. Al-Nasir Muhammad had been exiled to Kerak in 1308, after his second deposition, but used the castle as a base from which to mount a return to power, first winning over most of the Syrian governors, who were not partisans of the man who had displaced him; the only man he could not persuade, the Damascus governor, was removed, and then all the Syrian governors joined al-Nasir on an expedition to Egypt. This was al-Nasir's definitive re-establishment on the throne: he ruled for the next thirty years.

It was then necessary for al-Nasir to eliminate his assistants. Through death or deposition and arrest he was able to replace all the Syrian governors in the next years with his own men. Two of them fled to the Mongols and tried to invade Syria in 1313, but without success. From then on al-Nasir's own Mamluks occupied these governing positions, and he was safe.

One of the new governors was Taqriz al-Husami, installed as governor of Damascus, and eventually given responsibilities for virtually all Syria. For three decades Taqriz made a success of his post, and was remembered as a good governor even by the Syrians he taxed (though al-Nasir had him killed in the end). At the end of the fourteenth century, however, Damascus was the centre of a bitter civil war and suffered considerable damage. In 1400–1402 Syria and Damascus were damaged again by the armies of Timur Lenk. Syria in other words had little or no chance to recover from the earlier devastation.

Then in the mid-fourteenth century came the Black Death. Plague outbreaks began in 1348 and were repeated on average every seven years or so for the next century and a half. Syria did not suffer quite so badly as Egypt whose dense and closely packed population was peculiarly susceptible (on average suffering an outbreak every four years), but then Syria received the plague at an even lower level of economic activity, and in both countries it was endemic for centuries, as Napoleon's army discovered; in Aleppo in the eighteenth century there were outbreaks every ten years on average, and this is probably typical of other regions, though it was obviously more a city disease than one in the countryside.[28]

In a brief economic survey covering the last part of the Mamluk Sultanate, virtually the only Syrian product to enter international trade was raw cotton, which was grown in many areas. This had developed in the Crusader period, as had some silk production in the Aleppo region. But Syrian manufacturing was so reduced that Syria was importing cotton cloth from Europe while exporting the raw material in the opposite direction.[29]

Only Damascus and Aleppo could be counted as major cities once the Mongol and Crusader threats had been removed. Aleppo had suffered more extremely than Damascus and took longer to recover from its troubles. Damascus on the other hand, functioned as an alternative Mamluk capital to Cairo, and was prosperous as a governing centre; it was endowed with new buildings and a large well paid garrison. But Aleppo began to recover in the later fourteenth century, and Damascus suffered in its turn in the civil warfare attendant on the succession disputes of the later fourteenth century and Timur Lenk's invasion, and the subsequent concentration of the government in Egypt brought an end to that source of wealth. Aleppo was better placed as a trading entrepôt and grew to overtake Damascus before the Ottoman conquest. But elsewhere the urban population was small and less than productive.[30]

The economic impoverishment and reduction in the population is probably the basic explanation for the unusual success of the Ottoman conquest in 1516–1517, but by that time the whole Mamluk system had declined in effectiveness. The succession to al-Nasir Muhammad (died 1340) had been another chaotic series of murders and depositions until a new series of sultans, from the Circassian regiments, seized power with al-Zahir Barquq in 1382. Their rule was no improvement and featured the same difficulties, with long dynastic disputes in the 1420s and 1460s.

Control of the nomadic fringes in both Egypt and Syria was poor, revenues from the depopulated and impoverished land was much reduced, and the numbers of Mamluks – the soldiers – were also much less. The rigorous system of training fell into disuse, though individual Mamluks were always highly competent fighters. In the fifteenth century the northern frontier became steadily more problematic. At issue was control or domination of a group of buffer states which separated the Mamluk Kingdom from the Ottoman Sultanate in Anatolia and whoever controlled Armenia and the Jazirah. A conflict in the 1460s and 1470s resulted in a Mamluk strategic defeat by the Ottomans, but an Ottoman dynastic dispute then prevented any further activity – the Mamluks, significantly, were much less aggressive. An open war between 1485 and 1491 which was fought on the frontier left both powers drained, but the frontier unchanged.[31]

The sultan in this period was Qa'itbay, who ruled from 1468–1496, but the usual scramble for power followed his death. By 1501 a new sultan had emerged, Qansuh al-Ghawri, who had ideas for modernizing the Mamluk army, and even tried to promote economic development, though he was opposed by most of the Mamluks. He made serious attempts to import the use of gunpowder weapons, which had been largely responsible for Ottoman successes. He even supervised the casting of cannons personally. The Mamluks were not unfamiliar with gunpowder weaponry, as is to be expected of a military caste. But the gunpowder weapons of the fifteenth century were little improvement on Mamluk traditional weapons, and at the same time Mamluk tradition and training was unable to assimilate the changes needed.[32] Also, the financial strain of these changes was imposed on a treasury which was much reduced from its opulent past, and a naval threat from the Portuguese in the Indian Ocean had to be countered as well – for the tax on trade was now one of the main sources of finance.

A new threat was the sudden emergence of a new Iranian power, the Safavid Kingdom. This was more than just a political menace, for the founder, Shah Ismail, was a militant Shi'ite, and the Sunni Mamluks had plenty of Shi'ite groups within their borders who might well welcome the arrival of a Shi'ite invader. So now there were two serious powers in the north. The Ottoman Empire was equally menaced, also having substantial Shi'ite groups inside its borders. It must have seemed fortunate that the other two fell to fighting each other in 1514. The Ottoman Sultan Salim I was successful in his first campaign, defeating Ismail in a great battle at Chaldiran, but in the process he also seized control of much of the borderlands disputed with the Mamluks, particularly the Principality of Albistan, and so he seemed to pose a newly serious threat to the Mamluk Kingdom.

Sultan Qansuh al-Ghawri came north to Aleppo and gathered his army there, much annoying the Aleppines because of his troops' bad behaviour. He probably only did this as a precaution, for Salim had already encroached on his area earlier, but to Salim this looked more like a threat to his flank if he marched against the Safavid state. Salim changed his plans and attacked the Mamluks first.

The armies met at Marj Dabiq, north of Aleppo in August 1516. It was the meeting of an experienced and modern Ottoman gunpowder army with an antiquated and weakened Mamluk force. Not only that but the Mamluk left wing, commanded by Kha'ir Bey, the governor of Aleppo, fled at the start by prearrangement with Salim – and Sultan Qansuh collapsed and died during the battle. So not only was the Mamluk army outfought, and riddled with treachery, but the Mamluk state was, in effect, beheaded.[33]

At Aleppo the fugitives found themselves shut out of the city by the citizens. Their bad behaviour before the battle thus earned its reward; they were allowed neither shelter nor food, neither water nor clothing nor medical care, and many were killed by the citizens. The survivors fled on further south, as far as Damascus, which was marginally more accommodating. Even the garrison of Aleppo citadel fled, leaving the whole treasury of the state there, enough to finance several future Ottoman wars. It was, of course, the proceeds of Mamluk taxation, far more than was needed, but governments always 'need' more, and medieval governments tended to be hoarders. When Salim's forces reached Damascus the city also opened its gates to him and welcomed Ottoman rule.

Salim hesitated about attacking Egypt, but was persuaded when a new sultan was enthroned at Cairo, so threatening an attempt to recover Syria. He therefore sent his army to finish off the Mamluk state. The traitorous ex-governor of Aleppo, Kha'ir Bay, was rewarded with the viceroyalty of Egypt. After a brief period of hunting down surviving Mamluks, Salim proclaimed an amnesty, and they came out of hiding to be reassembled into an Ottoman regiment. Salim needed trained soldiers to control and defend his conquests so he continued to employ Mamluk armies as garrisons in both Egypt and Syria. But inevitably this proved unsatisfactory, for they could not easily accept their subordination and demotion. After Salim's death in 1520, and the succession of the untried Ottoman Sultan Suleiman (later, described as 'the Magnificent), the Syrian Mamluks, under the governor, Jan-Birdi al-Gazali, former Mamluk governor of Hama, were brought to rebel. Al-Gazali proclaimed himself sultan, but Aleppo refused to join him. He expected Kha'ir Bay to bring Egypt to join him, but this did not happen. He laid siege to Aleppo and this pinned him down, so that the Ottoman army from Anatolia could pass through the Taurus and relieve the siege. His forces were pushed south to Damascus, and there defeated. The Syrian Mamluks were thus finished, and much of Damascus was destroyed by the janissaries. (The Egyptian Mamluks fought next year in Suleiman's siege of Rhodes.)[34]

The Mamluk administration of Syria had been based essentially on the preceding Ayyubite kingdoms, modified as conquests were made. The two main governorships were Aleppo and Damascus, with lesser provinces governed from Safad and Kerak in the south, Tripoli (the new city) on the Phoenician coast, and Hama; Gaza seems to have been governed from Egypt. But Damascus governed most of Palestine, and as far north as Homs and Beirut; Aleppo therefore governed from Homs northwards. These divisions were more or less maintained by the Ottomans, but the overall supremacy of the two cities was institutionalized: they became *vilayets*, and their territories were divided into subordinate *sanjaks*, seven for Aleppo and ten for Damascus. Later Tripoli was made a third *vilayet*, taking *sanjaks* from the other two.

One of the reasons for this change – Sidon was later also made a *vilayet* – was the complication of the Lebanese communities. These included the Ismailis, the Druzes, and the Maronite Christians as well as Sunnis. Their leaders met Salim as a joint delegation at Damascus in 1516 and secured confirmation of the autonomy they had enjoyed under the Mamluks from him. This made the Mountain a clear excepted region, but also, since the basis of the autonomous region was religion, and so a threat to the Sunnis, surrounding that region with *vilayets*, whose governors had more armed power than mere *sanjaks*, was clearly a sensible imperial precaution.

The Ottoman conquest, in keeping with its swift occurrence, made little or no difference to Syrian life. The whole country had been declining in economic activity and population since the beginning of the deliberate destruction of the Muslim reconquest, and the policies of the Mamluks and the Ottomans did nothing to resist that decline. The elimination of towns and cities was not complete, of course, but it was widespread enough to stunt any economic revival for several centuries. About the only serious international trade was that in eastern goods, mainly from India, which reached Syria by way of the Persian Gulf. The Syrian entrepôt for this trade was Aleppo, but the goods went right through to Europe by way of Alexandretta, shipped in European ships and handled by European factors in the city. They were high value, low bulk goods, even when they were rolls of silk, and so little in the way of local employment resulted. The other main city, Damascus, seems to have relied mainly on the Hajj as its source of economic activity. (The Hajj was a major trading expedition as well as a pilgrimage, and another source of spices and eastern goods.) Jerusalem was a consuming city, somewhat underpopulated, which pilgrims visited, and where religious inhabitants lived on charity, mainly from outside. These cities produced little other than what was needed for the existence of their own populations. The only traded product remained raw cotton, exported through the slightly revived ports of Jaffa, Beirut, and Tripoli.

The taxation system of both Mamluk and Ottoman regimes was one of tax-farming, with little or no official supervision, in which the only profiteers were the tax farmers. The Ottoman governors achieved their posts by purchase, and their immediate aim was to recover their investment. They changed with extreme rapidity at Aleppo, presumably because it was reckoned a profitable post; the average in the eighteenth century was one governor a year; in other places, however, governors lasted much longer. Everything the Ottoman government did seemed to be designed to suppress initiative and extract wealth for the benefit of a few individuals and Constantinople.[35]

This is the point at which the autonomy of the Lebanese religious minorities becomes significant. They were subject to neither the governors nor the tax farmers, but directly to the sultan, to whom, when he insisted, they paid a tax. There was, of course, considerable scope for evasion and underpayment. This was one of the bases for local wealth which in turn supported the positions of the leaders of those communities.

The leaders were locally hereditary chiefs and at various times one or other of these dynasties emerged to local power often with some imperial approval, at least for a time. This was always no more than temporary, since those minor chiefs subject to their power were resentful, while the sultan in Constantinople feared any local power broker as a likely rebel. For the Syrian governors this local (and belligerent) area was the more awkward, since the main lines of communication between Egypt and Palestine to the south and Constantinople ran either along the coast, or through the Bekaa Valley, so any caravan therefore required strong protection.

A series of brief local supremacies followed one another from the late Mamluk period to the eighteenth century: the Assafs of north Lebanon, the Sayfas of Tripoli, the Ma'ns of the Druze region, the Shihabs from the Bekaa. The most notable individual was Fakhr ed-Din II of the Ma'n who dominated the whole region in the early seventeenth century. But he became so powerful locally as to pose a threat to the sultan's expedition against Persia in 1633, and he was suppressed.[36]

This pattern of local dynastic power also appeared in Palestine, where several Bedouin groups have been traced as dominating particular areas for various periods. The Qansuhs dominated the region south of Damascus throughout the sixteenth century; the fall of Fakhr ed-Din to the north allowed the governor of Damascus to assert more control over them. In the Bekaa after the fall of Fakhr ed-Din other local dynasties emerged. In northern Palestine the Turanbays were dominant for a time. All these families had their origins in the late Mamluk period, emphasizing both the obvious slackening of Mamluk control and the lack of change brought by the Ottomans.[37]

It is scarcely possible in the Mamluk and Ottoman periods to compile a history of Syria. Politically, events passed the country by; economically and socially it was stagnant and declining under constant misrule and neglect. The Mamluks did pay some attention to it, because it was their route from Egypt, their more valuable base, to the dangerous northern frontier; the Ottomans controlled all the neighbouring lands, Anatolia, the Jazirah, Iraq, Egypt, even Cyprus and the sea, and so they left Syria in a position of neglect, even more than had the Mamluks.

The Lebanese autonomous groups can be discussed, with their minor dynasties, and those of other regions, and the few cities can be described in a sociological way; the Hajj passed through annually, bringing a rhythm of brief weeks of prosperity separated by longer periods of depression to Damascus. Christian pilgrims visited in small numbers. But it was all fairly static, or at most just slow-moving, with little movement except at the local level. It is characteristic of the Ottoman conservatism and negligence that communications between Egypt and Constantinople were by land through Syria, rather than by sea, quicker and easier, another inheritance from the Mamluk period. Only in the nineteenth century, beginning with Napoleon's intrusion, and after six centuries of general neglect, did events occur to bring Syria to the attention of the sultan in Constantinople and the rest of the world.

Chapter 21

Slow Recovery: More interventions

When General Bonaparte marched his French army from Egypt along the Sinai coast road he followed the route of perhaps a dozen other aspirant conquerors: Tuthmosis IV, Rameses II, Ptolemy I and VI, Kleopatra VII, Ahmed ibn Tulun, Ikhshidid armies, Fatimid armies, Saladin, Baybars, Qalawun, and others; and he faced a series of obstacles, just as they had. He had to fight at el-Arish, at Gaza, and at Acre; he had to fend off relieving forces at the Jordan and from the Samarian hills, whose cavalry was successful in also fending off his raids. And he, like several of his predecessors, was defeated in the end. It helped that British warships under the ingenious Commodore Sir Sidney Smith were at hand to assist the defence, but most of the fighting and dying was done by the local people.[1]

His expedition also reveals that some changes had taken place in Palestine fairly recently. The Ottoman governing system had been particularly slack in the eighteenth century, and it was possible for local notables to gather official positions, usually with Ottoman permission if not actual encouragement. Acre had been rebuilt by a line of such men, and its modern fortifications, originally designed to resist who-knows-what enemies, had been strong enough to defeat the French.

The commander in Acre was Ahmad al-Jazzar, a fierce old man, none too popular with the Ottoman government, but useful as it turned out. Al-Jazzar was the latest of the long series of locally autonomous rulers scattered through Syria, going back to late Mamluk times. He had inherited much of his power and position from his predecessor Zahir al-Umar, who had begun with control of Tiberias and Safad and had expanded over a period of forty years (1730–1775) to build a principality covering northern Palestine and southern Phoenicia from Sidon to Jaffa, and inland as far as the Upper Jordan. It was he who had begun the refortifying of Acre. He was alternately allied with and at odds with his neighbours and the sultan in Constantinople, but his main significance is that he made serious efforts to develop his small semi-state, encouraging immigration and agricultural development, though to offset this, he insisted on monopolizing trade, a regressive action, and of course he imposed a heavy taxation. He rebuilt Acre into a fortified port, channelling the trade of his principality through the town. In the end it took an expedition from Egypt followed by an imperial naval expedition to bring him down (in 1775).

After a few years Zahir's power was replicated by Ahmad al-Jazzar, another adventurer, reputedly a Bosnian, adept at seizing his opportunities. He began with control of Beirut, expanded by securing an appointment as governor of Sidon, which included Acre, and so developed a principality which was much the same in size and organization as that of Zahir. It was this which, in alliance with the small but useful British naval squadron, succeeded in defeating General Bonaparte and his forces.

Al-Jazzar had to fight his neighbours, particularly in the Nablus area – these had also fought against the French successfully – to form local alliances, and to intrigue with and bribe the sultan's government to keep his power. He was made governor of Damascus for brief periods, and he was still fighting when he died in 1804. Power at Acre was then seized by one of al-Jazzar's soldiers, Ismail, who was then besieged by the forces of the governors of Aleppo and Damascus and those of Suleiman, another of al-Jazzar's men. He was finally defeated by Suleiman after the governors had left, and Suleiman was then appointed to al-Jazzar's old post of governor of Sidon. He extended his original principality to add control of the coast from Lattakiah to Gaza, and inland as far as the line of the Jordan; he was allied with Bashir II of the Druze principality in the Lebanon, and twice he was also made governor of Damascus.

On Suleiman's death in 1819 he was succeeded by Abdallah Pasha, the son of one of Suleiman's officials, an adolescent who was manoeuvred into the post by intrigue and bribery at Constantinople in the normal Ottoman way. The minister who conducted the necessary negotiations was Suleiman's finance minister, Haim Fahri, who as a Jew was not eligible for the governorship. Once he had put Abdallah in place, Fahri was unceremoniously killed.[2]

It will be seen that the political practices of these men – Zahir, al-Jazzar, Suleiman, Abdallah, and Haim Fahri – were very much those which can be seen in previous Islamic polities. The only legitimacy flowed from the activities and military power of these men, who also required the approval of the sultan, whose power over distant provinces was very limited in the face of obdurate local governors. It has to be said that the behaviour of the armies these men recruited and commanded was somewhat worse than those of the Muslim reconquerors six centuries before, though in both cases massacre seems to have been the favoured tactical method. The governing methods of the rulers also tended towards the instant execution of dissidents, monopolization of trade for their own benefit, and the imposition of heavy taxation. Of course, better methods had not yet been developed in the Ottoman Empire, so they were merely adopting the methods and practices they had seen in operation in their earlier careers, which were usually violent and various.

Palestine, therefore, was a region which was bidding fair to become the base for one of the successor states of the Ottoman Empire when it should collapse finally.

Others included Egypt, still, or again, under Mamluk rule, the North African pirate states, Mosul, controlled by the Jalili family since 1726, possibly Iraq which was governed by one man for over twenty years, Albania, and other areas. These were all ruled by governors technically appointed by the sultan, but were actually virtually independent. In Syria, besides the Acre-Sidon principality, Bashir II of the Lebanese Mountains was autonomous, and the governorship of Damascus was frequently held by a member of the local Azm family. The authority of the central government was clearly fading away.

Then came Bonaparte's expedition to Egypt. In Palestine his presence had seemed to enhance the local power of al-Jazzar, which was transmitted to his successors. This regime was, however, unstable. Each man who gained control did so only when he had fought off several competitors, and when he had gained some mark of approval from Constantinople, even then he had to fight to retain his position. None of the lords of Acre could be considered legitimate rulers: all of them had in fact stolen or usurped their positions, and the process of succession to their power was messy in the extreme.

In Egypt the matter was rather different. Bonaparte and the French had ruled the country for three years, and in the process had severely reduced the numbers of the Mamluks, who had long revived from their defeat by Salim I, but had never recovered a clear and permanent control of Egypt. A British and Ottoman expedition had gained control from the French, and when the British left, in 1803, there was a four-sided conflict between two sets of soldiers and two lots of Mamluks for control, with the population suffering ever increasing hardship and oppression. The eventual winner, by cunning and guile rather than by threats and violence, but still fully in the Ottoman style, was Muhammad Ali, originally from Albania, who first emerged as commander of the Albanian troops, then eliminated his competitors one by one – just as was simultaneously happening at Acre. He was made governor by the sultan after two years of riots by soldiers (unpaid) and by citizens, and after several officially appointed governors had failed to enforce their authority. He was first chosen by popular acclamation, in May 1805, and this was ratified by an imperial appointment in August. His rise was, of course, individual, but by no means different in essentials from other usurping governors in the empire.[3]

It took Muhammad Ali several years before he could be sure that he was firmly in control in Egypt, but his method of government was generally much the same as that produced by al-Jazzar and company in Acre, and indeed he might well have taken lessons from the men of Acre: arbitrary executions (and the occasional massacre), an essentially military rule, personal enrichment, heavy taxation, and an economic policy aimed at monopolizing in his own hands the profits of trade. Nevertheless there was some room, once internal peace was assured, for economic development.

Muhammad Ali remained in control in Egypt until 1849, a long reign which helped to stabilize the country and the regime.[4] This did not happen in Syria, where there were repeated disturbances, both internal and external. At Aleppo, for example, the city had not fallen under the control of a single ruler partly because of the rapid turnover of governors, and partly because two parties existed in the city who disputed with each other. One was the janissary garrison, which had evolved from a foreign and well-disciplined force into a locally recruited one, which ran extortion rackets when it was not paid; the other was the Ashraf, technically an association of the descendants of the family of the Prophet, but which in Aleppo had become a political faction competing, often violently, with the janissaries. Both factions were therefore local; they were largely eliminated after 1800, however, the Ashraf by a treacherous massacre by the janissaries (and a popular rising against an extortionate Ashraf governor) and then the janissaries when their leaders were murdered at a meeting with an unusually determined governor, Jalal ad-Din. This brought the city under more direct government influence, though hardly under its full control. Damascus did not have such an exciting time, where the governorship was often awarded to one of the men of Acre, Zahir, al-Jazzar or Abdallah, for a year or two. They generally chose to exercise their powers from a distance; in 1831 a citizens' uprising drove out a governor who was more than usually extortionate. The contrast between the situation in the great cities and the local powers on the coast is striking.

The external threats to Syria in the early nineteenth century came from Arabia and Egypt. Arabia had produced a new sect, the Wahhabis, who in 1803 captured Mecca, thereby interfering with the Hajj, which the sultan regarded as one of his primary responsibilities. They had already raided Karbala in Iraq, and in 1805 they captured Medina. They were in fact only the latest manifestation of the movement of Bedouin tribes out of central Arabia towards the north. This had been particularly pressing throughout the eighteenth century, and by the end of that century new tribes had taken over the pastures of the Hawran, where they clashed with the Druze settlers, and had taken over also the pastures about Palmyra. Others had penetrated further north into the lands east of Aleppo, and into the Jazirah. Virtually the whole Jazirah was now nomad territory.

Sultan Salim III (1789–1807) had directed Muhammad Ali of Egypt to attack the Wahhabis as early as 1806. It was part of the responsibilities of the governor of Egypt to supervise the Hajj in Arabia (just as it was that of the governor of Damascus to do so in Syria) and its interruption reflected very badly on the reputation of the sultan. Muhammad Ali ignored this and repeated demands from Sultan Mahmud II (1808–1839) until he was ready. Then in 1811 he solved his main internal problem by murdering a group of Mamluks who had come to a meeting with him in Cairo (sixty-four men in all – this action was copied at Aleppo a few years later) and then sent his son Tussun to fight the Wahhabis. The war took some years to conclude, ultimately by a six-month siege of the Wahhabi capital conducted by another son of Muhammad Ali, Ibrahim, who was a more than capable soldier. In Syria this undoubtedly relieved the pressure of the nomads somewhat, but their occupation of formerly cultivated lands had now become too much to accept.

Muhammad Ali was an empire-builder of the type of Baybars. An expedition conquered Sudan, and he held on to the Hejaz and part of Yemen after defeating the Wahhabis. In the process he developed an efficient army and a new navy, and gained control of trade in the Red Sea and access to the resources of Nubia, which were mainly gold and slaves. But he ran up against both the lord of Acre and the sultan. In 1830 he quarrelled with Abdallah of Acre and sent his son and his army and navy to the attack. Perhaps to his surprise – for such inter-governor fights were by no means unusual – he was then designated a rebel by the sultan. Ibrahim was able to conquer Acre, though it took six months, and then to defeat successive Ottoman forces, at Homs, in the Amanus Mountains, and then in central Anatolia – he penetrated just about as far as his predecessor Baybars. At that the western powers imposed a halt. Ibrahim withdrew to Syria but Muhammad Ali had by his son's victories reconstituted the Mamluk Kingdom as far as the Taurus Mountains.

One of the factors in Muhammad Ali's determination to conquer Syria had been the action of the sultan in 1831 in directing the governor of Aleppo to attack the governor of Iraq. Like Egypt, Iraq had a force of Mamluks who were a disruptive element in the provincial government. There was also a janissary regiment, which, like that suppressed at Aleppo, was by this time mainly locally recruited. In the face of resistance by these forces the sultan found it impossible to impose his authority either through or in spite of the governor. From 1816, however, a governor, Da'ud Pasha, gained and kept control, and in 1826 the janissaries were dissolved and reconstituted as a regular Ottoman force. But this meant they were under the control of Da'ud Pasha, which gave him altogether too much local strength for the sultan's taste.

In 1831, therefore, the governor of Aleppo, Ali Rida, was given an army and sent to suppress Iraq's near-independence. Assisted by the soldiers and the Mamluks, he succeeded; the surviving Mamluks were disposed of in the same way that Muhammad Ali had used. Three years later Mosul, ruled by the Jalili family for over a century, was brought under more direct central control as well.

For Muhammad Ali this carried a clear lesson. Any too-independent local governor was in danger of being suppressed by force. After the suppression of Da'ud Pasha, Muhammad Ali was the most likely next target, especially as he seemed to be expanding his territory into Palestine at the expense of Abdallah of Acre, whose city he was besieging at the same time that Ali Rida was conquering in Iraq. If so, taking the offensive would make sense, so the campaign in Palestine developed after the capture of the city and after his designation as a rebel by the sultan, into a direct trial of strength with the sultan. But occupying Syria was not enough; Muhammad Ali required a legal basis for his rule, and all he could get in 1833 was a concession that Syria was his for his lifetime – just as any other governor might get.

Ibrahim remained in Syria as his father's viceroy. Unfortunately for his subjects he also brought with him some of the less popular practices of his Egyptian rule – forced labour, military conscription, and heavy taxation – one of the reasons for the war had been that Abdallah in Acre had given refuge to Egyptians who had fled from Muhammad Ali's military and civilian conscription. The Egyptian regime also imposed the state monopoly trade system, which had existed already under the Ottomans (and Abdallah), but in this case it was more rigorously enforced. These various measures progressively alienated whatever local support the Egyptians may have originally had. Revolts against the imposition of heavy taxation happened as early as 1834. In the Hawran a plan to replace the Druzes who had moved into the area in the previous generation with Egyptian fellahin produced a revolt, hardly surprisingly. So Ibrahim found it increasingly difficult to control his viceroyalty, though an Ottoman attempt at reconquest in 1839 resulted in another Egyptian victory, at Nezib north of Aleppo.

Muhammad Ali was now seen by some of the European powers – not France – as a menace. Britain and Austria sent a joint naval force to operate along the Syrian coast. In 1840, first Beirut and then Acre were captured from the sea; inland, Ottoman and British agents stirred up rebellion; by the end of 1840 Ibrahim had withdrawn his forces to Egypt, and his father signed a treaty next year which gave him the hereditary governorship of Egypt; Syria and the Hejaz reverted to Ottoman control. He may well have regarded the outcome as a victory, since he had clearly gained a larger legitimacy of rule in Egypt.

The effects of the brief Egyptian rule were not all bad. The presence of the large Egyptian army – up to 80,000 men – in Syria, particularly in the north, meant a new and stimulating market for local produce. Ibrahim insisted that food be sold to the army at a government-set low rate, but anything surplus to that was saleable in the local market, or could be exported. The government price may have been low, but it was a certain sale. In the Aleppo area Ibrahim encouraged the resettlement of the recently abandoned lands, first by controlling the incursions of the nomads, then by arranging finance and supplies for the settlers. During the few years he was in control in the north he oversaw the resettlement of over 100 villages in this area. Some of these were still partly occupied before his measures, but a fair number had been wholly deserted. They occupied the land south of Aleppo and east of the city as far as the Euphrates.

Ibrahim's motive was perhaps mainly the wish to have a more dependable source of food for his army, but he also invested some of his own money in the project. It was clearly his will which was driving the process, so when he pulled out, and his army left, the project partly collapsed. The nomads returned with their extortion and wrecking, and the peasants largely left or were driven out. The lesson was not lost on the more perceptive Ottoman officials, however, and, particularly near Aleppo there were local efforts to resume the resettlement process. This began, as it had with Ibrahim, when a governor of Aleppo, Uthman Pasha, campaigned to reduce the nomads' depredations; at the same time he organized the provision of supplies for the peasant settlers. But it took a full generation for settlement east of Aleppo to recover to the extent it had reached in Ibrahim's time; on the other hand, this new expansion was more securely founded, in that it did not depend to anywhere near the same extent on a government market or government handouts.[5]

Ibrahim's measures of control and development in other parts were much less acceptable than his work in the north. He had begun by imposing a less unpalatable regime than the squabbling local governors, and by establishing toleration of religious groups, which occasioned several days of celebration in Jerusalem, but his taxes and the monopolies were increasingly resented. It was the hillmen who objected first. The Nablus region, home of the people who had held off Bonaparte's Frenchmen, rebelled in 1834, and their example was followed by the Shi'ite Malawati in southern Lebanon, and the Alawis in the Jebel Alawiah. These risings were relatively small-scale and were quickly suppressed. But the rising of the Druzes in the Hawran – where the hill country was becoming called the Jebel Druze – proved more difficult to end. It was probably only the fact that the amir Bashir II had a credible autonomy in the Mountain that prevented a rising there as well, for the moment.

Ibrahim, like the lords of Acre before him, had to deal with Bashir II, amir of the Lebanon. He was a distant descendant of the Ma'an family of the seventeenth century, and of the Shihab family which had taken over their position when the Ma'an line died out. Bashir I had been elected as amir of the Mountain by the assembled chiefs in 1697, and was confirmed as regent for his nephew, after some hesitation, by the sultan. Bashir II gained power in 1789, also as a result of election by the chiefs of the various sects and villages and regions.

The Lebanese were a mixture of Maronite Christians, Druzes, and Sunni Muslims, occupying the Lebanese Mountains and dominating the Phoenician coast and the Bekaa Valley to either side. They were divided also into factions, but the whole country was dominated by a set of interconnected chiefly families, the Shihabs as precarious overlords, the Abu'l-Lama and the Janbalats, who were Druzes, the Khawazin who were Maronite Christians, and others. These had support from the peasantry of their regions, but only to a degree, and more than one amir was overthrown, or at least had his power reduced, by a peasant revolt.

Bashir II was reduced to the status of a puppet of al-Jazzar almost as soon as he was installed as amir, but he survived. He was never secure, however, and in 1821 he fled for refuge to the Hawran after a revolt of the peasantry in protest at his heavy taxes. Next year he had fled again, this time to Muhammad Ali, after a fight with the governor of Damascus, who was backed by the sultan. This made him a client of sorts of the Egyptian ruler, and this was particularly useful when Ibrahim campaigned northward in 1832. This meant, of course, that when the Ottomans returned in 1840, Bashir had to flee once more. One of the crucial events in the Ottoman recovery was a revolt by the Maronites whom Ibrahim had armed to use them against the Druzes in the Hawran, and who now were supposed to surrender their weapons. They assumed, probably rightly, that if they did so they would be subjected to the same heavy taxation as others in Syria, from which they had been largely exempt. Their rebellion was joined by the Druzes and the Muslims, both angry at both Bashir and Ibrahim; Bashir took refuge with the British ships and went into exile in Malta.

He and Ibrahim left a situation in Lebanon which soon degenerated into a civil war. It was not, of course, entirely their fault, but their activities had certainly helped to enflame it. The larger background included the growing influence of the Maronite Christians over the whole Mountain. They had been migrating south into the Druze lands for a century and a half, changing the area into one of mixed communities. They were richer, more numerous, and better educated than the Druzes. Meanwhile Druzes had been also migrating, past Mount Hermon into the Hawran, where they occupied some deserted villages and reinforced the population of others – rather as Ibrahim's work in the Aleppo region had done. The participation of Maronites in fighting the Druzes in the Hawran had not endeared them to fellow Druzes on the Mountain.

The Maronite Church had gradually edged into communion with Rome, and this had become part of the basis for French interest in their welfare. In reply the British had dabbled in the Druze interest, with little success other than to undermine French and Maronite supremacy, and in Palestine had constituted themselves protectors of the Jews. At the same time the British had been of particular assistance to the Ottomans in driving Ibrahim back to Egypt. Then between them, the British and the Ottomans attempted to restore the old Shihabi regime, with the appointment of Bashir III, a cousin of Bashir II, as amir. However, despite his participation in the Lebanese rising against his cousin and Ibrahim, Bashir III failed entirely to establish his authority. He had some support from the Maronites, but none from the Druzes, whose chiefs had been losing authority under Bashir II, and felt they now had an opportunity to recover lost ground. Within a year Bashir was facing a siege by the Druze chiefs, and was soon formally deposed by the sultan.

There were plenty of outside interventions in the subsequent crisis, by the British and the French, to start with; more distantly the Russians claimed a 'protectorate' over the Greek Orthodox Christians in the whole empire, which eventually led to the Crimean War – and in a sense this could be seen as an outgrowth of the

Lebanese crisis. The sultan in Constantinople saw in the civil conflict in Lebanon the possibility of imposing his own control more tightly. The Ottoman policy since the beginning of the century, and above all since the proclamation of the 'Tanzimat' reforms in 1839, was to regain control over the government system and the provinces. This had been difficult, hampered by such awkwardnesses as the Wahhabis, Ibrahim in Syria, and the autonomy of the Lebanon. The alternating encouragement and interference from the Europeans had hardly been helpful either. But progress was being made. The janissaries, a powerful obstructive force unwilling to give up its privileges, had been eliminated in the only way possible with an armed group, by defeat and massacre, Iraq had been recovered from its nearly-independent governors, and now Syria had been retaken from the Egyptian rebels. Select importations from European practice had been made: to train a new army, develop a new fleet, produce schools and colleges to train more efficient bureaucrats and diplomats and administrators and provincial governors. By 1840 sufficient progress was made to make the autonomy of the Lebanon stand out as an obstacle and an anomaly.

A variety of attempts were made to impose a specifically Ottoman system in place of the Shihabi regime; the '*dual qaimaqamate*' of lieutenant-governors (*qaim maqam*) for the Druze and Maronite countries, with the boundary between them running along the Beirut–Damascus road; then the addition of a *majlis* (consultative council) to assist them. All this was under the authority of the governor in Beirut. None of these expedients – which emerged essentially from the Ottoman mindset which tended to think in terms of religious groups, or millets – was much liked, but it seemed to work for a time.

Among the Maronites of the north, the supremacy of the Khawazim family had bred increasing resentment among the peasantry. They rose in anger under the leadership of Taniyus Shahin, a blacksmith. They drove out the lords, redistributed their estates, and set up a peasants' republic. They were supported either distantly or openly by both the governor in Beirut, to whom the lords had been a major obstacle, and by the Maronite hierarchy, which had a new patriarch who detested the Khawazim. The success of this rising inspired the Druzes to the south, but their object was not so much the lords and landlords as the Christians who were living in what many Druzes considered to be their land. Their rising was actually led by the local Druze lords as a means of recovering the authority which had been eroded by Bashir II and Bashir III and by the governors. (The Shihab family had originally been Druze, and had the title 'Prince of the Druzes', but had converted to Maronite Christianity, thus leaving themselves open to the accusation of apostasy by the Druzes and the Muslims. In their antipathy towards the Christians the Druzes were joined by the Sunni Muslims, who resented the steady emancipation of the Christians and the consequent reduction in their own authority and privileges).

Once again the fighting quickly developed into massacres of Christians, by the Druzes and Muslims, and spread to Damascus, where the Christian quarter was sacked and looted and destroyed, with its inhabitants murdered, if they did not escape. The Maronites of the peasants' republic did not interfere, the governor of Beirut covertly encouraged the killings, and the Muslim authorities generally either did not intervene or helped the killing along.

But the time had passed when this was behaviour which the outside world would ignore, and it gave a perfect excuse for them to intervene under cover of 'rescuing' their Christian co-religionists, though the real purpose was political. Britain and France had recently been allied with the sultan in a war, and had no wish to lessen their influence, and both saw the anti-Christian risings as useful material for an intervention. France sent forces to suppress the risings, but the British worked with the Ottoman authorities to limit French involvement. Neither was overly concerned about the welfare of the locals. Between them the three governments imposed a new regime on Lebanon, which by this time was a devastated ruin: an administrator who must be a Catholic Christian (*mutassarif*), would be appointed by the sultan; a local council composed of twelve men from the six religious groups in the country was formed, to act as advisors, and to operate as tax collectors. The feudal privileges were abolished, thereby quieting some of the fears and resentments of the peasantry. From the title of the administrator, the regime became called the Mutasarrifiyya.

The result of the civil war and rebellions and massacres had therefore been that the Christians of Lebanon had emerged as the group which was now dominant. The new regime operated more or less successfully for half a century. Yet it had not healed the antipathies left by the fighting, the Druzes continued to be resentful, and the Ottoman state was not pleased at having had to admit foreign intervention – and therefore possible future foreign interferences – over an internal problem.[6]

The peace which fell on Lebanon was largely replicated in the rest of Syria. A new provincial system was imposed, but the real improvement was in the quality of the governors. Economically a considerable development now began to take place. On the desert fringes the reclamation of the farmlands became a steady progress in both the north, and in the central area, about Hama. There was a steady market in industrializing Europe for the raw materials, notably cotton and silk, produced in the country. Above all the population grew, thanks to the better government and the better food, though better hygiene was not a local priority.

It was after the resolution of the Lebanese crisis that there began an inflow of peoples from outside. So far as can be discerned that had scarcely happened on more than a very small scale since the early Mamluk period. The expulsions of the Crusaders and the arrival of the Turcomans had been in the thirteenth century; since then there had been no obvious immigration, except for a few Turks who were officials, and janissaries who evidently settled in Damascus and Aleppo, though after a time their replacements were recruited locally. From the mid-nineteenth century, however, small groups began to arrive from a variety of countries and for a variety of reasons, though largely, since this was the 'Holy Land' to three religions, most arrivals were for religious reasons; at the same time Syrians began leaving.

There had always been the transient pilgrims, particularly Christians, who visited Jerusalem and Bethlehem and other sites. Some of these died in the country on their journeys, a few stayed on, but most returned to their home countries. Economically they were probably of little significance. But the numbers of these pilgrims grew with the improved transportation systems of the later nineteenth century and in particular with the development of steamships. But it is the permanent residents who are the more important. After 1850 a fair number of Protestant 'missionaries' arrived with the aim of converting either Muslims to Christianity or various local Christian groups to Protestantism; they had little success.

There was also a fairly steady immigration of Jews from Europe, notably from Russia, where pogroms were all too common. They headed mainly for Palestine, of course, and the Jewish population of Jerusalem grew from about 4,000 in the 1830s to about 13,000 in the 1870s and to 45,000 in 1914; other centres where they settled included Safad, Tiberias, and Jaffa. Very few settled outside such cities, or in the rural areas.

Russian hostility had been one of the sources of Jewish immigration, and it was also the source of emigration from the Caucasus region, when the Chechens and Circassians – Muslims – were conquered by the Russian army after bitter resistance in the 1860s. Many of the inhabitants of the mountains fled and others were deliberately expelled; they were received and resettled by the Ottoman authorities. There had been other such arrivals from recent Christian conquests already – Algerian refugees from the French, who settled in Galilee and Damascus, Bosnians who escaped the Serbs or the Austrians, and went to Caesarea, Cretan Muslims who went to Tripoli and Damascus. The Ottoman sultan was also the caliph of the Sunni Muslims, and it was seen as his duty to receive those fleeing Christian persecution. The Caucasian refugees were partly settled in the Balkans, but mainly they were sent to Syria, where their settlements were scattered from the Khabour Valley to the Transjordanian lands.

These people had a hard time, moving from their hills to the deserts, and mountains to lowlands. They were also in many cases placed on the desert margins as a means of reclaiming the cultivable lands. Several villages of them were placed between Hama and Homs, more of them in and close to the Golan Heights east of the Sea of Galilee, and still more east of the Dead Sea. One of the places revived by their arrival was Amman.

It was while these inward movements were taking place that emigration by Syrians began. Egypt was the earliest destination, where skilled labourers were needed by the new government, but by the 1880s North and South America had become the favourites. In this therefore the Syrians and in particular those from Lebanon were participating in the same migration as other peoples of the Mediterranean. In the United States it was noted that Syrian migrants were more highly qualified than other groups.

There was a constant movement within Syria from the country to the cities, something which, as in Europe, had been happening for centuries, but which in the nineteenth century gathered pace. This was partly the attraction of city life, and the possibility of employment, and partly the growth of the population, which in the rural areas meant smaller plots of land, or mainly seasonal work, or unemployment. Some of this movement could be absorbed by the desert margin reclamation, but more by the towns and cities. Damascus and Aleppo doubled in population between 1800 and 1914, though the earlier figures are uncertain. Other places grew much faster but from a lower base. The most explosive growth was probably by Beirut, which grew from a small town of a few thousand to 150,000 by 1914. Generally it was the older cities – Hama, Homs, Tripoli, Lattakiah – which grew. The rate of expansion in the Palestinian towns was slower, but all began from a lower base than those of the north and centre; only Jerusalem was really sizeable by 1914.[7]

All this development was accompanied by a general expansion of agriculture and specialization into cash crops, and the establishment of a fairly small industrial section. Tobacco was a new crop, and olives were expanded, though the basic crops of wheat and cotton remained the most widespread. The traditional handcraft industries expanded with the growth of population but they also faced competition from European machine-made goods. Efforts were made to improve internal communications, but roads and steamships and railways required much start-up capital, and while such resources were certainly available in Syria it was difficult to mobilize them until these minor industries and systems had been proved to be profitable.

External capital chose to focus on transport links with a reasonable possibility of profit. So the first road to be improved was that between Beirut and Damascus, and the first railway was between Jaffa to Jerusalem for the tourist and pilgrimage traffic from Europe. There were of course, age-old tracks all through the country, and the introduction of wheeled carts, perhaps by the Circassians, supplemented the transport of goods by the normal donkeys, mules, and camels.

By 1914 there were railway lines from Aleppo to Amman and to the coast at Tripoli, Beirut and Acre as well as Haifa, and with an extension as far as Medina for the Hajj traffic; the Berlin-Baghdad line had passed the Euphrates, though it took until late 1917 to connect the Syrian lines with those of Anatolia through the Taurus and Amanus Mountains. Ports for larger ships had been developed at Beirut and Jaffa, but these were expensive projects.[8] Elsewhere a mixture of old and new methods was required. At Gaza, for example, which exported goods to fill 'twenty-five large ships' and many smaller ones in 1905, the port was still undeveloped and goods had to be lightered from shore to ship. Clearly the development of the area had well preceded the improvement of the port, and this is to be expected, but it did not make marketing foods easy. The city of Gaza itself had grown from about 2,000 inhabitants in 1840 to about 40,000 in 1900, a rate of growth implying much local development and the establishment of a considerable amount of industry.[9]

In 1878 the Sultan Abdul Hamid II had dispensed with the parliament which had been recently introduced and reverted to the autocratic government which was more usual in the Islamic world. He did continue with the reforms, developing a reasonably efficient administration and encouraging economic improvements. He was overthrown in 1908, though the replacement government, the Committee of Union and Progress, was unable to win the wars which the empire's neighbours wished on it and territories in the Balkans and Africa were lost. By 1914 the Ottoman Empire consisted of just two large sections: the basically Turkish Anatolia and the mainly Arab or Arabic lands of Syria and Iraq. And in Syria there had developed a general dislike of Turkish rule, especially since the Committee was largely composed of Turkish nationalists, who even thought of compelling the Arabs to use the Turkish language. Not surprisingly a small group in Syria had emerged whom we can call Arab Nationalists.[10]

Within that empire, Syria was half of the Arab half. It had a population of less than five million, was basically agricultural, and produced few goods that anyone outside Syria needed or wanted. It was, however, beginning at last to recover from the long centuries of destruction and neglect which had followed the defeat of the Crusader states, but it was in no condition to cope with another Great War. But this was what it was now forced to do.

Chapter 22

Consequences of the Great War (AD 1914–2011)

In the twentieth century the history of Syria becomes very busy and crowded, and the literature on it is overwhelming. In this chapter, however, no attempt will be made to go into full detail on the events since 1914 – not that this has been done in the rest of the book – since that would clearly overburden and overbalance the account, and impose on the events of the twentieth century with much greater significance than the rest of Syria's eventful history, which would be wrong. As in the rest of this account the main purpose is to reveal the patterns of the country's past – and the twentieth century certainly does that.

For four years a British army based in Egypt fought its way into and then north through Syria. Provoked by a Turkish invasion of Sinai, which forced the closure of the Suez Canal, the British laboriously drove the Turks back to Gaza, where the Turks blocked any further advance for a year. By this time the British attacks at Gallipoli and in Iraq had both been defeated, and the Ottoman Empire was more or less still intact, rather to everyone's surprise. By this time also the British and their allies had agreed on how they were to divide up the empire once they had won the war. It was, of course, necessary to conquer territory in order to take control of it at the peace; and after two defeats British pride was at stake. In the wider context of the World War, however, as opposed to the ambitions of the Allies, the invasion of Syria was probably unnecessary.

Why the British in particular should have bothered with Syria is not at all clear. It provided no strategic advantage, it contained no useful resources (unlike the oil of Iraq), and the invasion attracted the attention of only a relatively small Turkish force, so as a diversion it cost more than it gained. The only discernible reasons were to do with the imperialist grasp for more territory, and to prevent France from claiming the whole. Of course, the whole war was an imperialist adventure for every country involved, and the British army in Syria was an imperial force, including contingents from much of the empire; but the invasion of Syria happened largely because a British army faced a Turkish army, and so they had to fight.

The campaign took the same route as all the other invaders of Syria from Egypt, along the road paralleling the north coast of Sinai, though in order to support the British army, the old road was supplemented by a railway and a water pipeline. This led the army to el-Arish and Rafa, and then to Gaza, at all of which battles were fought, as usual. The faltering grip of the early British commanders was largely to blame for the two defeats at Gaza in early 1917; the imposition of a new commander, General Sir Edmund Allenby, who had learned his craft in both South Africa and France, and enjoyed getting out among the troops – conditions all lacking in his predecessors – brought order and intelligence to the conduct of operations. The third battle of Gaza was a fight which spread over 50km of front, and took two weeks, and even then much of the Turkish army escaped destruction. But the British captured Jerusalem by the end of the year, which had been their early aim, and provided a useful propaganda and morale booster.[1]

There was little likelihood that the Turks would be able to recover lost ground, but the collapse of Russia released new Turkish forces from their Russian front, while it also compelled the British to transfer much of their Palestinian army to France. This delayed further conquests in Syria until reinforcements had been brought in, mainly from India, so from mid-1918 Allenby commanded an army which was even more a British imperial force. A second great battle in September, near Jaffa, but which the British arrogantly named 'Armageddon', as though it marked the end of the world, finally broke open the Palestine front. Within a month British and Australian and Indian and Arab cavalry rode all the way to Aleppo, but there they met a Turkish force strong enough to stop them. By this time also, the whole British army was infected with malaria, and whole regiments were falling sick more or less simultaneously. The armistice therefore came just in time to avoid a Turkish counter-attack which might well have driven the advanced British forces back into central Syria.[2]

To the campaign in Palestine a minor contingent of French troops was attached, and an even smaller unit of Italians, so making it theoretically an Allied force. There was also a minor campaign by an Arab army led by Prince Faisal, the son of the Sharif Husayn of Mecca, who had come out in rebellion against the Ottoman Empire after complex negotiations with devious British officials in Egypt. This force fought its way slowly north along the line of the Hejaz Railway, raiding the Turkish garrisons, but this 'desert campaign' was of little consequence. The British, therefore, did by far the greater part of the fighting. They had recruited these allies, to whom a variety of contradictory promises had been made, though the immediate military rewards were meagre. Further, these promises overlapped, so British intentions, French demands, and Arab hopes could not all be satisfied in full. On the other hand, all involved surely understood that any promises made before the end of the war, and any expectations indulged by the participants, were no more than provisional, and the war had to be won first. As it happened, the armistice agreed with the Ottoman Empire blocked the Allied advance before all Syria had been conquered, and the Turkish determination not to accept the Allied peace terms meant that a large region in the north, fully half of the old *vilayet* of Aleppo, remained in Turkish hands. The French had occupied the area lightly for a time, but were then chivvied out by Turkish actions, by a combination of local hostility, Turkish forces, and Turkish irregular fighters. This was in effect the first partition of Syria, between the north which remained part of Turkey, and the rest.[3]

The British and French divided the rest (and so this was the second partition). By doing so they largely shut out the Arabs, and the French were awarded the largest section, geographically, though in fact the division was essentially done according to British requirements. The French had hoped for all the northern area, which the Turks' hold on had reduced, and at one time for Palestine as well. The British wanted only Palestine, to which they attached the land east of the Jordan Valley, and which they named Transjordan. This was awarded to Abdallah, another of Sharif Husayn's sons (a third partition). The French consoled themselves with having gained the greater part of Syria, including the predominant cities of Aleppo, Damascus, and Beirut, but this was essentially only what the British did not require – and they had to accept that Mosul, another of their ambitions, where there was oil, would go to Iraq.

All of this was done without bothering much about the wishes of the Syrians, or even enquiring about those wishes. The Syrians' treatment by the Turks during the war had been as if they were an enemy country, which of course in the end was correct. The overall commander of the Turkish forces for much of the war had been Jamal Pasha, technically Minister of Marine in the Ottoman government, but actually one of the senior men in the Committee of Union and Progress. He employed the usual Ottoman methods in squeezing as much revenue as possible, as much in the way of requisitioned goods, and as many conscripts as possible from Syria, reducing the country, whose overseas trade was blocked by the Allied control of the sea, to universal poverty. Famine even affected such rich agricultural areas as the Lebanese region and the Damascus Ghuta. Jamal Pasha did not forget his revolutionary aims, however, and early in the war he took an opportunity to abolish the Mutasarrifate in Lebanon; he also shot a group of Syrians who were overt Arab Nationalists, thereby, of course, enhancing their cause; by 1918 Syria was desperately anti-Ottoman and anti-Turkish, and hungry for freedom.

There were two competing groups in Syria who had hoped to use the Allied victory to gain power. One was, of course, the Hashemite family of the Sharif Husayn, who had certainly contributed something to the military campaign – and a good deal more than France or Italy. Husayn became king of the Hijaz by self-proclamation in 1916, and he had ambitions to add Syria and Iraq to his kingdom. His family certainly gained kingships in Transjordan and in Iraq as a result of his policy, though neither was free of Allied control. But the real prize was Syria, and Damascus and Aleppo were the main targets of their soldiers in the desert campaign. In both cities the Arab army had a plausible claim to have been the first to enter. This was a less than useful claim politically, for no one else paid any attention to such a claim, and anyway the Arab forces were swiftly superseded in control in the cities by non-Arab troops, who were more willing to avoid looting and to be able to ensure order and the protection of the population.[4] Also the desert Arabs, with their arrogant assumptions of superiority, propensity to loot, and liability to resort all too quickly to violence, were thoroughly unpopular with the urban Arab populations.[5]

Their competitors were native Syrians who had no more wish to be subject to an occupation by desert Arabs than by Turks – and even less by the British and French. The few Arab Nationalists who had existed before 1914 had mainly been executed at Jamal Pasha's orders, but they had already spread the word amongst much of the rest of the population. The idea had been adopted as much to reject any foreign occupation as to practice a loyalty to some sort of Arabism. That is, in Syria Arab Nationalism was essentially a Syrian Nationalism, and it looked to all Syria to become a single state, from the Taurus to Sinai. This was also, plus Iraq, what Sharif Husayn had thought he was promised, to add to his Arabian kingdom, though his agreement with the British contained plenty of ambiguities, and, of course, conditions had changed by 1919.[6]

The British also had agreements with their other Allies, though only that with the French applied to Syria-Iraq. They had drawn various versions of their preferred division of these countries, but the main outlines had been clear from the start: Palestine and most of Iraq to the British; Syria and Lebanon to the French. Not that either considered the agreement binding, and both had been embarrassed by the publication of the agreements by the Russian revolutionaries in early 1918. This exerted pressure on them against the idea of formal annexation.

These complications produced much intrigue and argument during the negotiations at the peace conference in Paris in 1919. And then, even after the treaties had been negotiated between the Allies, Turkey refused to agree, so technically the Turkish War went on until 1923. The conclusions of the conference were hardly helped by the United States' intervention against the idea of annexations – though the United States was never a party to the Middle Eastern war. But the idea that the conquered lands could become wards of the new League of Nations – 'mandates' – provided enough cover for the British and French to take over their chosen parts of Syria, since no one in Europe really believed that the Syrians could rule themselves, nor that the Arabs could rule them. A brief attempt in Damascus in 1920 to create a Syrian kingdom with Faisal as king was quashed by the French, who in effect had to conquer their mandate before they could rule it. They defeated the Damascus militia in battle at Maysaloum in 1920, and then had to put down 'rebellions' in the Jebel Alawiyah and in the Aleppo region.

The policies pursued by the British in Palestine and the French in Lebanon and north Syria contributed very largely to the increased dislike felt by the Syrians for their occupiers. In Palestine the British permitted a much higher level of immigration by European Jews than had happened before 1914. This was backed up by considerable financial resources and had developed a particular ideology,

Zionism, which presumed that, since the Jews had originated in Palestine, land was still theirs in some way. Zionists also claimed that Palestine was an 'empty' land, and that it was therefore available. They took such phrases as 'Promised Land' out of context and applied them to themselves; 'a land without people for a people without land' was another, though it had nothing to do with Jews or their spurious claims.[7] Not that all Jews were Zionists, but that ideology developed powerfully among the Jews of Europe as they went through the trauma of Nazi Europe. Those Jews who lived in Palestine, however, were overwhelmingly Zionist.

In Lebanon and north Syria the French had adopted the old Ottoman practice of seeing the Syrian population as a set of religious groups – Sunni, Shi'ite, various Christian sects, various Muslim sects. They took as their starting point the Maronite Christian supremacy in the Mutasarrifate and extended it by redrawing the internal boundaries in accordance with Maronite ambitions: thus the new Lebanon was extended to include the cities of the coast (including Beirut), Tripoli, the Bekaa Valley, and the western slopes of Antilebanon Mountains. This brought under Franco-Maronite rule large numbers of non-Christians. This was now called the 'State of Greater Lebanon' – 'Grand Liban'. Another partition.

The French plan was to subdivide their mandate lands into several sections which would develop their own identities, thus making the whole the easier to control. Lebanon was the first to be organized. Aleppo and Damascus necessarily formed two more of these sections. They included most of the country, and were populated largely by Sunni Muslims. Two concentrated minorities, the Alawis in their mountains, which the French now called the Jebel Alawiyah, and the Druzes in the Hawran – the 'Jebel Druze' – were separated off as two other 'states'; the north-east corner, inhabited largely by Bedouin nomad tribes, was made into the Jazirah state. More partitions. The ultimate intention, at least originally, was that these should each have their own administration, each with a Syrian as figurehead president, but actually administered by French officials. Within a few years the French government decided it could not afford to pay so many administrators – and it had discovered that Syria was by no means a wealthy or populous country and needed to be subsidized from French finances. Also the Syrians were annoyed to have their country so cavalierly carved up. In 1925, a large-scale rebellion by the Druzes of the Hawran broke out and set off sympathetic detonations elsewhere in Syria. It took substantial reinforcements of French troops to 'restore order'; the Hawran was not finally subdued until 1927.[8]

During the Great War the Turks had carried out repeated massacres of Armenians, assuming they were in rebellion, or at least sympathetic towards the Allies. Syria had received considerable numbers of refugees fleeing from this, perhaps 150,000 or more of them; many of them settled in and about Beirut. This reinforced the Armenian minority in Syria, but made their numbers now large enough to be noticed; in Beirut they were numerous enough to found their own schools and a university; often they were favoured for jobs by the French, to inevitable local resentment.⁹ In 1917 the British government, for curious wartime reasons, had announced that it regarded Palestine as the 'national home' for the Jewish people. This was meant to be an essentially meaningless concept, but it probably encouraged the continuing migration of Jews from Europe to Palestine. Furthermore, some pre-1914 experiments in settling in the rural areas were taken up; the financial backing for Zionism permitted the purchase of land on which such settlements were made. (It is curious that the money came from wealthy men, capitalists and entrepreneurs, whereas many of the settlements were socialist or communist in political inspiration.)

These immigrations were, until the 1920s, relatively small in numbers of people, and the Armenian source had largely dried up; the source of Jewish migration was, however, very large. One other attempted invasion was by Wahhabi Arabs out of the Arabian Desert into Transjordan. In Arabia they, led by Abdul Aziz ibn Saud, were fighting King Husayn of the Hijaz, and raids against his son Abdallah's lands were clearly regarded as part of the same war. A great raid in 1924 was driven off by the Royal Air Force's aircraft and armoured cars, and when Ibn Saud finally conquered Hejaz from Husayn's son Ali in 1925 the British came to an agreement with him, drawing a boundary between the two kingdoms. This upset the regular migration cycle of the Banu Sakhr, who occupied the land south of Amman and migrated annually to and from the Wadi Sirhan; the boundary cut them off from the grazing in the wadi. The agreement was later modified to allow the tribe to resume its regular movements, but it was an indication of the problems which the new regime imposed on the inhabitants. However, this episode did prevent further raids and blocked another immigration, and perhaps a new invasion.¹⁰

The Arab population of Palestine had been apprehensive from the start about British policy. They, like the other Syrians, had looked to some sort of independence after the war, preferably as part of a united Syria. This did not arrive. The British installed a version of their well tried colonial regime. The British, however, also produced excuses for doing so, which suggested a certain guiltiness of conscience. They claimed that they required to control Palestine as a forward defence for the Suez Canal, then that they needed to guard the oil pipeline which was built to transport oil from Iraq to the terminal at Haifa, then that they were needed to control the country when Jews and Arabs began killing and fighting each other. That is, just as French policy switched about at the behest of politics and finance in France, so British reasons for staying on in Palestine changed with the altering conditions there. Both were in fact acting as they did in the hope that they might stay longer. But the successive changes and excuses make it clear that both surely understood that this permanent occupation was not possible.

Neither of the two 'mandatory powers' were at all successful in governing their section of Syria. The Druze rebellion in the French area was echoed a decade later by the Arab uprising in Palestine, though the immediate causes were different. The immigration of Jews from Europe had continued at a modest pace in the 1920s, but it increased greatly from 1933 onwards. The Arab population also grew by natural increase, but the Jewish immigration was very visible, and was decreasing the Arab numerical predominance; above all the Jews were heavily concentrated in one area, the coastal plain from Jaffa northwards. Elsewhere, apart from a strong Jewish presence in Jerusalem, the Arabs still predominated heavily.

In Lebanon, by contrast with the rest of French Syria, a constitution had been agreed with the French in 1926, despite protests from other areas at this clearly deliberate French aim of consolidating the partition of Syria and at the extension of the Lebanese boundary to include a large section of land principally inhabited by Muslims – Sunni, Shi'ite, Druze – who were thus placed under a governing system biased towards the Christians. The French, however, also retained powers of interference, which were vague and therefore threatening. Like the Mutasarrifiyya, the constitution allowed for twelve 'senators', and the complex make-up of the republic in terms of religious groups was held to require from the start that a difficult balance be kept between the representatives of the various sects within the government. In 1926 the first Cabinet included two Maronites, and one each from the Sunni, Shi'ite, Druze, Greek Catholic and Greek Orthodox sects; later Cabinets had only three or four members, since there was really very little work for the ministers to do.

The constitution continued to be fiddled with, and then it was suspended by the governor for a year and a half. All the time the underlying conflict was between the sects, with much discontent voiced by the various Muslim groups. The Maronites tended to head the government, but it was the French governor who pulled the strings. The French thus found that they had to stay in control, if from a certain distance, in order to prevent the Lebanese fighting each other – or so they decided. This was a similar situation, and a similar solution, to that of the Jews and Arabs in Palestine.

The British canvassed plans to 'solve' the 'Palestine problem', but without much conviction. Whatever plan the Arabs would accept, the Jews rejected. This gave the British the excuse they sought to evade any League of Nations pressure to comply with the mandate intention to move the country towards independence, not that there was much of that pressure. In Iraq they had done so by 1930, in a formal sense, though defence and foreign affairs remained under British control, and a British garrison remained. In Syria a similar arrangement eventually emerged. There had been constant arguments between the French governor and garrison and the aspirant Syrians, usually over a prospective constitution. One was eventually imposed by the French in 1930, but the next stage was a treaty to replace the mandate, and thus make progress towards real independence, and this was even more difficult to achieve, largely through French reluctance.

The rival suggestions for a constitution not being agreed, in 1936, with the Syrian Chamber of Deputies suspended by the governor, the Syrian leaders announced a National Pact; riots and street battles followed, and then a general strike which lasted for fifty days. This finally brought the French governor to the stage of serious negotiations, but these were conducted in Paris, on the French side without any haste and with manifest insincerity, and without conceding anything to Syrian demands. However, the end of the right-wing Sarraut government after the 1936 elections and its replacement by the left-wing Popular Front government of Leon Blum, rescued the process, though the Syrians had to be satisfied with a version of the Anglo-Iraqi agreement by which defence and foreign matters remained with the French. The effect of this was felt in Syria in the next few years, as Turkey exerted pressure on the French to gain control of the Sanjak of Alexandretta, or Hatay, as the Turks called it. This was populated by the usual mixture of ethnic groups, but in this case including a large number of Turks. The French, concerned to avoid making another enemy as the threat from Germany grew, gradually caved in to the Turkish government, and by 1939 it had pulled out of the Hatay and Turkey had annexed it. Syrian protests as this further amputation of 'Syrian territory' had no effect. When the annexation took place, several thousands of Armenians fled for refuge in Syria, and most of the Arabs also moved out to the more congenial Syrian homeland.

By 1936, therefore, Palestine was the one part of the former Ottoman lands not to have a treaty providing at least for formal independence and looking towards eventual full independence; and there was no prospect of one so long as the British insisted that both Jews and Arabs must agree. It is no surprise therefore that there followed an uprising by the Arabs, though this was only partly aimed at independence and was directed as much against Jewish immigration. The intermittent fighting went on until 1939, when it died away without resolution.

By this time, of course, the whole Middle East was involved in the crisis which was Hitler's War, whose approach had already affected affairs in French Syria and British Palestine. The fighting when it began approached the Syrian region steadily, first in the western Mediterranean, then in the Egyptian desert, and finally reaching Syria itself. One result of the war was an increased demand for goods produced in Syria and therefore an increase in local prosperity. Another, however, was an increase in Anglo-French hostility. The alliance between these two formed in 1939 was broken by the French acceptance of the German armistice in June 1940, but in the long run it is this brief alliance which is the anomaly. The two countries had been in a state of subdued competition and near-hostility ever since the peace of 1919. Both had intrigued to undermine the other in their Middle Eastern territories – the British had allowed Druze rebels to take refuge in Transjordan after their rebellion, for instance – so that the fighting which developed between the imperial powers in 1940–1942 was hardly unexpected. It began with the British bombardment of the French battleships at Mers el-Kebir in Algeria, and continued at various places around the world, from Canada to the Pacific islands. One of those places was Syria.[11]

In Syria the local governors cleaved to the Vichy regime of collaboration with Nazi Germany. In Iraq the halfway independence of the 1930 treaty was resented, while the monarchy was seen as British stooge – and anyway was represented in 1941 by a child, King Faisal II. A coup by some soldiers was organized, and was then contested by a rapid British response from the sea and from Transjordan; the plotters asked for German assistance, but it came far too late and far too weakly, and so was useless when it arrived. But to reach northern Iraq, the German aircraft had staged through Syria, and this provided the British with a pretext for attacking the French there; another was that the Vichy authorities in Syria sent arms to the rebels in Iraq; there were plenty of reasons for the British invasion of Syria which followed.

By energetically switching forces between Egypt, Iraq and Palestine, the British commander, Field Marshal Archibald Wavell, succeeded first in suppressing the Iraq revolt, and then in concentrating his forces against Syria, which was invaded from the south into Lebanon and towards Damascus, and from the east through the Jazirah and Palmyra, and menaced by sea. A five-week war sufficed to eliminate the Vichy regime. In its place was installed a Free French (Gaullist) governor, but he was supervised by a British military presence; furthermore, the British had insisted that by the end of Hitler's War Syria and Lebanon must become fully independent states. This would put paid to the constant bickering along the northern boundaries of Palestine and Transjordan.

The outbreak of Hitler's War had the effect in Palestine of damping down still further the remnants of the Arab uprising, since Britain could now impose an even larger garrison on the country. In their reactions to the war, however, the Arabs and the Jews not surprisingly differed. Perhaps lulled by the progressive independence of Syria, Lebanon (a fully independent state by 1943), Iraq, and Egypt into believing that Palestinian independence was inevitable, the Arabs paid little attention other than to prosper. The Jews, on the other hand, chose to exploit the war for their own belligerent purposes. Both men and women were encouraged to join the British forces with the aim of gaining military training and experience, and eventually the British agreed to the formation of a specifically Jewish Brigade (as they had in the previous Great War). Jewish immigration largely stopped, though illegal migrants, fleeing from the pervasive anti-Semitism in Europe, did enter to some extent, with some tragedies as immigrant ships sank.

The aim of the Zionists was to have available the trained manpower to constitute an army after the war ended. But, of course, if one has an army it tends to be used. The political intention of the Zionists had shifted from bringing Jews to Palestine into making Palestine a Jewish country, and ultimately a Jewish state.

In such a state there would be no room for Arabs – just as there was no room for Armenians and Arabs in the Turkish Hatay. In the background, of course, was the understandable desperation induced by the increasing knowledge of Nazi extermination policies in Europe. Given the general unwillingness of the other countries to accept refugees Palestine seemed the only possible destination for the Jews of Europe. This was not to the liking of either the Arabs or the British, but the pressure on the latter became too strong, and an uprising by the Jews in Palestine after the war added to the weight. The army they had trained was turned on the British, then on the Arabs.

In French Syria the British insisted that the French stick to their wartime agreement to institute complete independence. The French did not go with any good grace, at one point bombarding the Syrian Parliament building to intimidate the Syrian government. So the British were in the awkward position of insisting on independence for the two northern sections of Syria – Lebanon and the Syrian Republic – while also awarding independence to a third section, Transjordan – and yet apparently clinging on to Palestine where neither the Jews nor the Arabs wanted them.

Despite their acquired military expertise, the Jews were always unable to fight the British directly, so they resorted to terrorist methods – assassinations, murders, atrocities, bombs, thefts of weapons – and generally failed to provoke the violent response they hoped for. But in Britain things were changing. The Labour government of Clement Attlee which came to power in 1945 was not committed to maintaining the empire, and decided to evacuate India in 1947. Then the appalling winter of 1947–1948 brought the country into dire straits, and the decision was made to leave Palestine also. After all, without India the need to control the Middle East was much diminished. It was thought that the Suez Canal should be held, but neither the Nile Valley nor Palestine were any longer required – and leaving them would certainly greatly reduce Britain's immediate problems. The mandate system performed its final act when the British announced that they would hand their mandate for Palestine back to the United Nations, which scarcely knew what to do with it; in the end the United Nations gave up, just as the British had. As in Lebanon and north Syria with France, it was events in Britain, and policies decided there, which proved decisive.[12]

There followed a perfect demonstration of the validity of the British contention that they had been 'holding the ring' to keep Jews and Arabs from killing each other, for that is exactly what they immediately did. In addition, there followed the realization of all the Arabs' fears. The military expertise (and often the service in the British forces) proved more than adequate for the Jews of this new state of Israel to defeat the untried and numerically smaller armies of the surrounding Arab states. Only the British-trained Arab Legion of Jordan, which had actually seen action, was militarily successful. But the victorious Israelis then put into operation their strange claim that they should possess all Palestine, and they used their terror-methods to force tens of thousands of Palestinians out of their homes and into refugee camps. (This spontaneous flight was the normal reaction of civilians when war approached; what was not normal was that the Israelis prevented the refugees from returning to their homes when the fighting stopped.) As a result the people who had possessed just 6 per cent of Palestinian land in 1946 came to control 80 per cent in 1949. Seven hundred thousand Palestinians were driven out.[13]

Since then the dominating issue in the Middle East has been Arab anger at Israeli deeds and policy. As usual in the twentieth century outside countries did not refrain from intervening. Until 1956 the British retained a presence or an influence in Egypt and Jordan, but the two Great Powers of the post-1950 world, the United States and the Soviet Union, found the region a choice area for their intrigues and their proxy wars. Israel soon became aligned with the United States, and received more aid and many weapons. This provided Soviet Russia with the whole of the Arab Middle East for its own clients, who were happy enough to receive gifts of weapons; neither Great Power proved able to exert any real control over its clients, nor did their rival ideologies have much effect. Wars in 1956, 1967 and 1974 demonstrated that Israel was capable of defending itself, but it also took the opportunity to seize more territory.

It was not alone in this. Two areas of Palestine had survived Jewish conquest in the original 'War of Independence' as the Israelis inaccurately called it, in 1948–1949. Each was taken under the control of an Arab neighbour, Gaza by Egypt, the 'West Bank' by Transjordan, which had renamed itself Jordan in 1949. (The 'West Bank' is in fact the ancient area of the Judaean and Samarian Hills, but these names cannot be used by Arabs since they are the names used by Israel, and to Israel they imply that they ought to be Jewish territory.)

The political condition of the new Syrian Republic was particularly unstable. Its small army was beaten by Israel in the 1948–1949 war, after which the officers blamed the politicians and the politicians blamed the army, both correctly, but neither set was willing to cooperate to make improvements. With at least the knowledge and probably the encouragement of a United States agent, the head of the army, Colonel Husni Zaim, arrested the elected president, Shukri al-Quwatli, and sent him into exile, then installed himself as president. From now on stability escaped Syria for a generation.

Zaim's power lasted for four months before he was arrested and shot by a group of annoyed officers. His replacement, another colonel, also lasted only four months. The third colonel to seize power, Adib Shishakli, chose to operate through civilian front men. The soldiers certainly had a valid complaint about the politicians since the army which had been sent to fight Israel was no more than 7,000 strong, yet it had gained and kept control of some small sections of Palestine, even while being unable to help the Palestinians. The colonels all set about increasing the size of the army, to 43,000 by 1951. This was a large force for a country of the size and limited resources of Syria, particularly as this enlargement was accompanied by costly mechanization.

This effect in Syria was one of the results of the Israeli expansion over most of Palestine. In Jordan King Abdallah annexed the West Bank, but this was hardly popular with the inhabitants, one of whom stabbed the king to death in the mosque in 1951; his successor Talal was deposed; his grandson Husayn took power in 1952. Egypt went through an even more drastic upheaval in 1952–1953, when the monarchy was abolished; the result was another military dictatorship. All these events were, of course, only in part a consequence of military defeat, having much more profound internal causes, but the humiliation of their armies necessarily brought a similar humiliation to the political leaders.

None of the four states of Syria was really politically stable. Jordan was the only monarchy, a condition which helped its internal stability, but its population, especially after 1967, included large numbers of Palestinian refugees both from the 1948–1949 war and from the 1967 Israeli conquest of the West Bank. The ruling elite of the kingdom was from the original population, largely of Bedouin origin. The two groups did not meld for a long time, if ever. But the Palestinians were better educated and more skilled with modern methods and became one of the economic mainstays of the state. The kingdom was disrupted more than once by the tensions these matters caused. One of the results was that King Husayn was as keen as Egypt to conclude a peace agreement, so that he could concentrate on his kingdom's internal matters; but Jordan remained overshadowed by militant Israel.

The Syrian Republic was as subject to upheaval as the rest of its neighbours. The Shishakli regime was finally replaced in 1954 by a restored parliament, which elected Shukri al-Quwatli as president once more. But under the cloak of the successive colonels in the previous five years there had developed a group of political parties who had learned that parliament would not be sympathetic towards them. Quwatli led the original independence party, the National Bloc, but by the 1950s other parties had emerged, either as new parties or as breakaways from the Bloc. The most significant for the future was the Baath, which adopted a socialist programme, but it refused to assist the new regime by joining it, despite a fairly strong representation in the new parliament.

Lebanon by contrast was the apparent success story in the region during the 1950s, but the prosperity which developed, based above all on trading relations with all and sundry – the 'Merchants' Republic' – hid the underlying instability. The Maronite regime was based on keeping down several of the 'minorities' – though every group was a minority – and this became steadily more irksome to them, especially as the economic rewards of the economic system were maldistributed, leaving the 'minorities' with much less than they craved. The regime was in effect a continuation into independence of the French colonial regime, but it did not have the French army at its back. The system broke down briefly into a civil war in 1958, but this was quickly damped down with the help of United States' power, though the warning was not heeded, and the basic instability continued.

The most stable of the four states was seemingly Israel. However, considerable internal strains also existed, as hundreds of thousands of Jewish immigrants arrived. Many came from Muslim states – Syria, Iraq, Yemen, North Africa – where Israel's militancy and its treatment of Arabs turned local hostility onto long-term Jewish minorities. Absorbing the large numbers who arrived was difficult, and new settlements were placed close to the country's boundaries. The forced evacuation of the Palestinians left much land available.[14] At the same time the country was obsessed by the perception – a perfectly correct perception – that its neighbours were invariably hostile. It became Israel's policy to pre-empt any apparent attack being prepared by its own attack, and this only increased neighbourly hostility.

But Israel's policies were inflexible and triumphalist as a result of its military victory, and this only prevented peace. There were negotiations with King Abdallah as early as 1949, and it would have been possible to have concluded a peace as early as late 1949 with Syria, but Israel's demands were too much for Colonel Zaim, and the moment passed. Having had their advances rejected, the Arab states had no choice but to arm themselves; thus Israel's paranoia was increased.

In 1956 President Nasser of Egypt nationalized the Suez Canal and Israel then joined Britain and France in an attack (the 'Suez affair'). Each of the three partners had a different purpose in mind, so it is not surprising that the coalition fell apart almost at once, in the midst of the fighting. Israel came off best, seizing substantial military equipment from the Egyptian army and effectively eliminating Egypt as an active enemy for several years. This was also the effective end of British and French influence in the Middle East.

The Syrian Republic's political instability continued. The Suez War did not involve it despite the republic having a military pact with Egypt, but two years later the two countries entered a political union, forming the United Arab Republic. This, however, only lasted three years, collapsing under the increasingly bad conduct of arrogant Egyptian officials in Syria; Syria had found itself once again occupied, not a partner in a union. A military coup in Damascus extinguished the union with little resistance. Another coup in 1963 brought the Baath Party to power in partnership with the army, though this was followed by Baathist infiltration of the army command posts. The men involved were very largely from the Muslim minorities – Alawis, Ismailis, Druzes – at the expense of the majority Sunnis.[15] There followed a Baathist coup in 1966, putting Salah Jadid in power, but with Hafiz al-Assad as his military colleague. Assad directed the minority takeover of the army, while Jadid aimed to gather civilian support. These two also had different views on policy, and their differences gradually split the Baath Party.

The defeat of the army in the 1967 war with Israel halted Assad's progress, and left the republic shorn of the Golan Heights, from which it had been intermittently shelling northern Israel for years. Given the defeat, the loss of this territory was hardly surprising, but it gave subsequent Syrian governments a complaint with which to rally patriotic sentiment in their own favour – something for which they did not use the Turkish Hatay. Assad eventually seized power for himself in a new military coup in 1970. His colleague Jadid was consigned to everlasting imprisonment.

Meanwhile the Sunni reaction to rule by the minorities in both Syria and Lebanon was developing. One aspect in the Syrian Republic was the increasing importance of another political party, the Muslim Brotherhood, which emphasized the Islamic – Sunni – foundation of Arab society, but was especially socially conservative – that is, reactionary. In 1964, with a Baath-army government introducing socialist measures, the Muslim Brothers provoked a riot in Hama, a notably conservative city; the army replied by shelling the mosque at the centre of the uprising, whence the muezzin had systematically roused the population to violence. The Muslim Brotherhood was not, however, very popular generally, though it tended to be the focus for opposition in the absence of any other effective opponents of the Baath. It did represent, however, the emergence of a more coherent Sunni reaction against domination by the minorities.

The disruption of the Arab union had not stopped Egypt and Syria fighting Israel together in 1967, though their coordination was minimal. In 1973 they did better, but still ultimately failed, and Israeli armies ended the fighting by threatening both Cairo and Damascus. For both countries this was a clear message. Egypt eventually, after a long series of intermittent battles along the line of the Suez Canal, made peace, and achieved an Israeli withdrawal to the old borders, and gave up control of Gaza. Syria also came to an agreement, but an armistice, not a peace, since Israel insisted on holding on to the Golan area, and indeed in 1981 announced that it had annexed that territory.

But the biggest side effect was felt in Lebanon, which had scarcely been involved in any of the wars, but had been the recipient of large numbers of Palestinian refugees. They were largely concentrated in camps, particularly near Beirut and Tripoli, which it was in the interest of all involved to maintain. Apart from this indigestible mass of people, their presence threatened to upset the awkward religious balances of Lebanese politics, since they were almost entirely Sunnis and so could increase the weight of the Lebanese Sunnis were they to be incorporated in the national system. They were also fairly well-armed, and the camps were well organized politically by the Palestine Liberation Organization, which thereby gained local influence. But in 1975 Lebanon had collapsed into a hideous parody of a civil war, in which it was difficult for anyone to detect any real purpose or political intention in any of the parties, with the result that the fighting simply went on. In the process Beirut was reduced to ruins.[16]

Both Syria and Israel intervened in this tangle, as did the United States, briefly. Syria took over the eastern half of the country, which just happened to be that region which Syrians in 1920 had seen the French transfer to the old Mutasarrifate, so manufacturing their 'Grand Liban', and which Syrians had always wanted returned. This at least stifled the fighting in that area. Israel invaded the southern part in 1982, moving along the coast and deliberately targeting the Palestinian camps near Beirut. They recruited local militias and then watched while the militias conducted massacres in the camps. The two interveners fought each other in the air over Beirut, the Syrians being defeated, but it was the Israelis who withdrew and the Syrians who kept control of half the country for another twenty years.

Israel had, of course, brought on itself the vicious and continuing enmity of the Palestinians. The refugees of 1949 were joined by more in 1967, and the failure of the Arab states persuaded many Palestinians that guerrilla war was the only option left – thus using the same tactics against Israel that the Jews had used against the British. At the same time Israel, fuelled by the old Zionist claim to both rule and possess all Palestine, began planting 'settlements' in Palestinian territories. This was, of course, imperialism, and the 'settlers' were, and are, colonizers of the most militant, fanatical and ruthless sort. The Israeli behaviour was clearly designed to intimidate, and even to drive out still more Palestinians. They were eventually contested by an uprising – 'intifada' – which had no real long term effect, though the few small Jewish settlements in the Gaza area were eventually withdrawn. Gaza then fell under the control of a Sunni Muslim dictatorship, Hamas (originally encouraged by Israel in order to undermine Fatah, the successor to the Palestine Liberation Organization). This region, effectively a city state, with an overcrowded and desperate population, proved to be the most willing to challenge Israeli military domination, and Israel reacted regularly by siege and bombardment, after which the ruins were rebuilt by someone else's money. There was no sign that the Gazans were willing to give in – but then they were given no alternative. Israeli policy had driven them to extremes and was itself unable to change.

Within Israel itself the imperialist urge was built on eliminating all the bases of the preceding Arab presence. The surviving Arabs were in effect confined to their villages and parts of the towns, which were not maintained well, and they were treated very much as second-class citizens. The Arab villages which had been abandoned were seized, allocated to Jewish families, and renamed. The old Arab names were purposely forgotten. Jewish archaeologists excavated old sites of the Roman and earlier periods, and claimed to recognize sites named in the Old Testament of the Bible, which were therefore claimed to 'prove' biblical accounts of historical events. (It is a truism in archaeology that one finds what one looks for.) Only a few non-Israeli archaeologists continued to work on the remains of the later periods, of which the Mamluks have left considerable evidence of their presence. Minor Jewish military activities, such as the Maccabean wars and the futile defence of the Masada fortress against Rome, or the disaster (to the Jews) of the Second Revolt against Rome (AD 132–135), were sought out and interpreted either as victories or as glorious sacrifices.[17]

The mass Jewish immigration after 1949 was thus a much more thoroughgoing matter than any previous similar movement of peoples into Syria, and more akin to the genocidal conquest of the North American natives than any earlier event in Syrian history. The roots of this rather excessive policy were clearly in the fears of an Arab return; if traces of the Arab past in Palestine could be removed, then perhaps the prospects of an Arab return could be obviated.

A further effect on Israeli society has been the general militarization of that society, where everyone is given military training, and the steady rightward trend of politics has been clear for forty years. The propensity to have generals or former guerilla commanders as Prime Ministers has been all too obvious, and renders Israeli politics only a version of that practiced by its neighbours.

The dictatorship of Hafiz al-Assad in the Syrian Republic was technically Baath Party rule, and considerable efforts were made to improve conditions in the Syrian Republic. The process was socialist, building subsidized houses for the poor, overmanning uneconomic factories to provide employment, erecting high tariff barriers to 'protect' local industries, and a universal secret police, whose presence was as ubiquitous and ugly as was the Israeli occupation of the Palestinian West Bank. The regime may have been Baathist in ideology, but it was military in fact, and its reaction to opposition was to apply violence. In 1982, in the most notorious case, another rising in Hama pitted local Islamists against the secular army. The army won, but only by a heavy bombardment of the city, which was much more damaging than the earlier fighting. Thus the Baathist-army regime survived, though it was clear that its rule was precarious.[18]

The Lebanese fighting died down in the 1990s, assisted by the continuing Syrian occupation of much of the east. The fighting had, however, shifted the internal power balance, and had brought about the emergence of an armed Shi'ite group under Syrian auspices, Hezbollah, which adopted a militantly anti-Israeli posture as a means of gaining local credibility. Israel attempted to suppress it by an attack in 2000, which largely failed, at least according to Hezbollah – though one result was that it did cease most of its attacks on Israel. Its main purpose was to gain power in Lebanon, after all, but it was successfully resisted by the other Lebanese groups. The assassination of a Lebanese politician in 2004 led to a combined push by Lebanese groups and outsiders to remove the Syrian occupiers of the eastern half of the country, which was largely successful, and which thereby reduced Hezbollah's influence.

By this time Hafiz al-Assad was dead, and had been succeeded by his son Bashir, who had been practicing as a dentist in London. He found that the Baathist-army establishment was immovable, and soon accommodated himself to it. There seems little doubt that he had little real power, and he certainly demonstrated little political sense. Any hopes for an amelioration of conditions or a change in foreign policy faded quite quickly.

Conclusion: The Patterns and The Prospect

The condition of Syria has been one of continuous disturbance and upheaval since before the Great War, but since 1919 this has been a particularly acute problem, a mixture of religious conflict, political upheaval and repression, violence, ruined cities, massacres, and wars. In other words, it has reverted to the normal condition which has always existed when the Syrians are left to their own devices. It is only when an outside power – Egypt and the Hittites, Assyrians, Macedonians, Romans, Mamluks, Ottomans – establishes a grip on the land that a semblance of peace descends on it. And too often achieving that peace costs a great deal, with wrecked cities, massacred populations, devastation of the countryside, and continuing oppression.

Syrians on their own fight each other. This has been the case whenever they were independent of outside control – in the Bronze Age, in the Iron Age, after the collapse of the Seleukid Kingdom, in the Crusader Period – and now in the twentieth and twenty-first centuries AD. The basic problem, and perhaps the major cause of the violence, remains the country's geography. Palestine is the largest section which is an obvious geographic unit, but even that is split into the lowlands and the highlands, and is separated from the lands to the east by the Great Rift Valley; Damascus and Aleppo, or their predecessors, are perpetual rivals, and are separated by a considerable distance, while several other cities in the present Syrian Republic regularly assert themselves against domination from elsewhere; Lebanon's vertical geography has been a constant element from the emergence of Byblos as a cedar-exporting port for Egypt until the Syrian occupation of the interior – a strong set of independently minded coastal cities, mountains with obdurate populations, the Bekaa Valley. To the east the Syrian/Arabian Desert has been repeatedly a source of migrants, a factor of such importance that the immigrants have several times imposed their version of the Semitic language on the rest of the population – Amorite, Aramaic, Arabic. This is a change which has not occurred with other migrants, though their languages – Greek, Latin, French, English, Hebrew – have had some temporary effect. Of course, holding on to one's conquered language is a very effective way of resisting an intruder or a conqueror – so the Palestinian Arabs go on speaking Arabic, forcing Israelis to learn and use their language. (One is reminded of the long English resistance to the use of Norman French, a resistance ultimately successful.)

When the Syrian Republic collapsed into civil war in 2011 it did so along geographical lines, just as Lebanon had in 1975. Aleppo and Damascus took opposing sides, the Jebel Alawiyah opposed Aleppo, the Hawran opposed Damascus, and so on; the hill people of the Antilebanon opposed Damascus as well, and were themselves opposed by the Hezbollah from the Bekaa Valley. The result has been extensive destruction, particularly of the provincial towns, Hama (again), Homs, Aleppo, parts of Damascus.

The same argument can be made concerning Palestine. The most obdurate opposition to Israel from within the country comes from the people of Gaza and the Judaean Hills. This, if the Israelis would pay serious attention to the history of the land, repeats a condition which had happened at least three times in the past, perhaps four. The most obvious is in the Crusader Period. The initial conquest by the Crusaders consisted of Jerusalem and the Judaean Hills, to which the highland area of Galilee was soon added. From there they fanned out to conquer the lowlands, which took a lot longer. Jaffa was captured very quickly, but Tyre not for a quarter of a century, and Ashkelon not for half a century (and Jaffa was the first port taken by the Maccabees from the hills – both conquerors were aiming at the resources which could only reach them by sea). Later Saladin conquered the hills before moving into the lowlands, and when the Third Crusade campaigned to recover the territory of the kingdom of Jerusalem, it proved to be impossible for the Crusaders to fight their way up into the hills, and they had to be content to recover no more than the lowlands; the highlands remained under Muslim control, and the eventual result was the Muslim conquest of all Palestine.

This pattern is of course familiar to Israelis from their Jewish predecessors, who have done the same on two earlier occasions. The Maccabees, like the Crusaders, began by controlling the highlands; they never succeeded in conquering the lowlands except briefly and never wholly, but the highland areas remained Jewish territory for much longer. Earlier, Judah had held out longer than any other Syrian kingdom against the Assyrian conquest; it eventually fell to the Babylonians, though only over a century after the rest of Syria; in the same way it took the Roman Empire repeated wars and two centuries to finally destroy Jewish power in the hills. But the episode the Israelis know best would be the original Hebrew infiltration of the highlands from the desert. Once they were established and organized, the Philistines, with their modern armaments and weapons, were unable to dislodge them – though the Hebrews were never able to conquer much of the lowlands. (This is always assuming that the story of the early Hebrew kings is true, and that the Philistine wars actually happened, of course.) There was an even earlier episode when Egyptian control over the hill country during the Bronze Age was constantly under challenge from the inhabitants – the Labayu episode, for example.

This historical pattern is so frequent that it is obvious that it is in Israeli interest to concentrate on maintaining control of the hill country. Yet it has proved to be especially difficult to do so. They have sliced up the region with roads and settlements, forts and confiscations, and walled it in with a concrete barrier – which is a confession of defeat, of course. They are no longer able to drive out the Arab inhabitants – 1949 cannot be repeated. So it is highly unlikely that they will ever predominate numerically, though they can certainly keep the Arabs in a constant state of subjection and poverty for the short term. Similarly, and even more obviously, with Gaza. This city has been the fortress guarding the route between Egypt and Palestine for as long as it has existed; it is now (as the events of 2014 showed, and other bombardments earlier) unconquerable by Israel, which can batter it into ruins, but its people survive, embittered and increasingly hostile and obdurate – for they have nowhere to go. The Gazans in Gaza are as intractable a problem for the Israelis as their fellow Palestinians in the Lebanese refugee camps.

A consideration of the history of Israeli relations with its neighbours makes it clear that the state's expansion has now largely ceased, that its military policy has reached an impasse, and that unless its foreign policy changes its superiority even in military matters will soon begin to decline. Since 1973 Israel has failed in all its wars except in causing destruction. Neither in Syria nor Lebanon, nor in Gaza, has it been able to extend its control into new territory. The Hezbollah survived an Israeli invasion and battering, the Gazans have survived more than one long-distance air and artillery barrage; in effect both communities have metaphorically thumbed their noses at Israel from within their destroyed towns and homes. Egypt and Jordan have withdrawn from participation other than in a mediating role. The Jewish settlements on the West Bank are becoming steadily more difficult to establish. Zionism as an imperialist policy has just about run its course.

The impossibility of Israel expanding any further is demonstrated by the bankruptcy of its policy, but also by the historical considerations, conquest of the hills has been achieved from the lowlands only once, by the Roman Empire in AD 66–70 (and perhaps in AD 132–135) – but this was a power able to marshal the resources, military and economic, of the whole of the Mediterranean Basin; its victory was, as Agrippa II pointed out when the Jews of Jerusalem seemed set on rebellion, as inevitable as anything in human affairs. (The British imperial army in 1917–1918 succeeded in doing so, but in this case the Arab inhabitants were largely neutral, and the British invaders were fighting the Ottoman army, almost as alien as themselves.) Modern Israel does not have the disproportionate power to do the same; in fact, the conquest of the lowlands – present-day Israel – by the highlanders is historically much more likely in the long run. The conclusion must be that Israel should make peace while it is still in control, and not wait for its defeat – for any power basing itself solely on its military prowess always suffers defeat.

The geography of Syria has also been at the basis of the fragmentation of religious belief in that country. The mountainous areas have been the refuges for minorities and dissidents since the time of the Roman Empire, just as they have been the refuges for political dissidents in all empires. The Alawis, the Druzes, the Maronites, the Ismailis, have all flourished and survived because they remained in their mountain refuges, just as the Jews survived in the Judaean Hills in the Hellenistic (and earlier) periods. The Lebanese Mountains were the refuge for pagans when the Christianized Roman Empire began persecuting them, then the refuge for Christians in the face of Muslim authority, and then the refuge for Maronites and Druzes against the Fatimids and the Mamluks and the Ottomans. By grouping themselves together these 'communities' were able to survive, though they frequently began by violently attempting to secure better land or to forcibly convert others. Usually their attempts were defeated, and they retreated into their hills, or hunkered down in a particular region and kept quiet – the Ismailis in the Homs Gap, for example, after their mountain refuge around Masyaf was conquered. These are another source of division, of course.

None of this is news, of course, to those who study such matters. But it is worth emphasizing in the Syrian context, where the study of the serious history of the country has led too many historians to limit their researches to a particular period, or a particular region or state. The Mamluk and Ottoman periods have drawn their researchers, but they tend not to connect with the preceding Crusader Period, or the succeeding twentieth century. Similarly the Hellenistic Period is scarcely considered in the context of the preceding Assyrian-Babylonian-Persian Period of poverty and destruction. There are good reasons for this division, of course, in the considerable stretches of time involved in each period (rarely less than three centuries), in the differing and multiple languages needed for each sector – English, French and Arabic for post-1914, plus Hebrew later, but Arabic and Turkish for the Ottoman Period, Medieval Latin and French, Arabic, Greek, Syriac, and perhaps Coptic and Turkish for the Crusader Period, and so on. The discontinuity of the seventh century AD, between the Christian Byzantine Period and the succeeding Muslim Ummayad Period is especially sharp historiographically.

It is therefore clear that the default situation in Syria is either control from outside, a condition which is all too likely to be imposed after a destructive conquest, or division and warfare if the country is left to itself. This has been the pattern for at least 5,000 years, and the last century had not done anything to change it.

It is also clear that no single Syrian state ever had, or has, the resources to unify the country from within. In fact it seems unlikely that any Syrian state had ever seriously tried to do so, though some may have wished to do so. Resistance from other Syrians was always enough to prevent such a conquest. It is certainly possible for one state to conquer a neighbour, but usually the resistance is strong enough to wear down the conqueror's strength, and the conquered population is then sufficiently restive to force the victor to expend much of its strength in maintaining its control – the British and French problems in holding down the populations of their mandated territories, and the Israeli dilemma in holding the West Bank and Gaza are classic cases.

It follows that the Israeli–Zionist ambition to recreate the 'Empire of David' is unlikely ever to be realized – not to mention that the original never existed. In the same way the ambition of the Sunni population, or perhaps of the Syrian Republic, to unite the whole land into a 'Greater Syria' is impossible to achieve.[1] For a start, a new Muslim conquest of all Syria is not conceivable, and international intervention would always prevent any serious progress towards such a goal, since it would probably require extensive massacres; and similarly an Israeli conquest of Jordan, the Syrian Republic, and Lebanon is equally impossible. Note also that 'Greater Syria', besides aiming to include Palestine, would need to wrest a substantial area from Turkey to be achieved – again not a serious proposition. (It may be noted, however, that the Israeli ambition and the Syrian are in effect mirror images of a united Syria.)

The latest manifestation of such an aim is the current (2015) appearance of the 'Islamic State', which is pretending to revive the Caliphate of all Muslims on the basis of the short term success of a few thousand brutal killers. As soon as the project began it ran into opposition from Shi'ites, from Turks, from Kurds (the latter two both fellow Sunnis) and fairly quickly from outsiders as well. Within a month or two it had ceased to expand and had begun to face defeat; it is hanging on largely thanks to its inherent ferocity and destructiveness, and the divisions amongst its enemies. Fairly quickly it became clear that the leaders of the regime were enjoying the fruits of their conquest and leaving the actual fighting to their dupes. It is unlikely to last very long.

And yet the revival of Sunni militancy in a less obnoxious form is the only possible social basis for any attempt at achieving Syrian unity by conquest. The Sunnis are the basic population of most of the Syrian Republic, of the Palestinian Arabs, of the people of the Bekaa Valley, and of those living along much of the coast of Lebanon, of the Turkish part of north Syria, of Jordan. If any single ethnic–religious group in Syria could unite the country it is the Sunnis. But, again, even stating the issue in this way makes it clear that it is a non–starter. The widespread disgust at the brutality and bloodlust and non–Islamic behaviour of the 'Islamic State' extends to the vast majority of the Sunnis as well as everyone else. Unification of Syria by any single group from inside the country is politically, militarily, and socially out of the question.

So, for the future, only two options remain: either the several states and communities will continue to fight each other for the foreseeable future, with rebellions and uprisings a regular occurrence, or they will find some way to live with each other – and that will mean mutual tolerance of the minorities by the majorities and acceptance of their status by the minorities. Past cases in which independent Syrians of different beliefs have coexisted for lengthy periods suggest that they can do so, and there are elements in Islamic theology and political practice which can form the basis for such toleration. So it is quite possible that a disunited Syria will continue for another two or three centuries, amid regular wars and disturbances. But such a condition also invites outside interference. The United States and the Russian Republic were as busy in Syria in 2014 as the British and French and then the Soviet Union and the United States were in the twentieth century. And such interference is not going to stop. Outside interference has always in the past led on to outside conquest, and usually to massive destruction; it is quite likely that sooner or later this will recur. Syria is, after all, surrounded by greater states, all united – Egypt, Iran, Turkey – and all of these have been the origins of invasions and conquests of Syria in the past.

The more difficult option would be for the many Syrian communities to resolve to tolerate each other. This may well be beginning to happen. Israel and Jordan have existed without fighting each other for over half a century. Egypt and Israel have cooperated several times in helping to end fighting in Gaza. Syria and Turkey may not like each other, and Syrians still resent the loss of Hatay in 1939, but neither shows any willingness to escalate the dispute into active hostility – one can call this toleration. The Syrian rebellions which began in 2011 are the opposite of toleration, though that is at the basis of the wishes of many of the rebel groups, and the misgovernment which the Syrian Republic has suffered since 1914, at the hands of Turks, French, British, their own rulers, the Baath and the army, and the two Assad dictators, has made such a rebellion surprising only in that it took so long to happen. In the same way the various conflicts within Lebanon are the result of misgovernment and oppression going back to Ottoman times. Neither of these countries shows any willingness to even think seriously about toleration.

The future for the Syrian region is therefore likely to be more of the same: internal intrigue, rebellions, wars, and outside interference. Every state now existing has perpetrated massacres which have set up visceral hatreds amongst the survivors; every state oppresses part of its own population. And every state is ruled by an elite of sorts which can only be dislodged by violence. There seems little hope that this condition will ever change.

Notes and References

Introduction

1. Peter M. M. G. Akkermans and Glenn M. Schwartz, *The Archaeology of Syria* (Cambridge, 2003) and Trevor Bryce, *Ancient Syria* (Oxford, 2014) though to be accurate they both stray over their borders when necessary.
2. Boundaries within this region have also served, for shorter or longer periods, the Hellenistic kings, the Crusaders and the Mamluks.

Chapter 1

1. The culture was first defined by D. A. C. Garrod, 'A New Mesolithic Industry: The Natuf of Palestine', *Journal of the Royal Anthropological Institute* 61 (1932) pp. 157–266; O. Bar-Yosef and F. R. Valla (eds.), *The Natufian Culture in the Levant* (Ann Arbor, MI 1991) has a series of essays bringing the subject up to that time; for Palestine see also Francois Valla, 'The First Settled Societies, - Natuf (12,500–10,200 BP)', in Thomas E, Levy (ed.), *The Archaeology of Society in the Holy Land* (London, 2003).
2. For modern Syria see Akkermans and Schwartz, ch. 2.
3. A. J. Legge and P. A. Rowley-Conwy, 'Gazelle Killing in Stone Age Syria', *Scientific American* 272 (1987) pp. 76–83; A. M. T. Moore, et al. *Village on the Euphrates: From Foraging to Farming at Abu Hureyra* (Oxford, 2000).
4. Akkermans and Schwatz, pp. 133–139, and reference there.
5. D. Stordeur, 'New Discoveries in Architecture and Symbolism at Jerf el Ahmar (Syria) (1997–1999) in *Neo-Lithics* 1 (2000) pp. 1–4.
6. Y. Nishiaki, *Lithic Technology of Neolithic Syria* BAR S 840 (Oxford, 2000).
7. H. T. Wright, 'Prestate Political Formations', in W. Sanders et al. (eds.), *On the Evolution of Complex Societies: Essays in Honor of Harry Hooijer* (Malibu CA, 1992) pp. 41–77; G. Stein and M. S. Rothman (eds.), *Chiefdoms in Early States in the Near East: The Organizational Dynamics of Complexity* (Madison WI, 1994).
8. Three preliminary reports on the excavations by A. Tsuneki et al. are in the *Bulletin of the Ancient Orient Museum* (1997–1999) pp. 18–120.
9. O. Bar-Yosef, 'Earliest Food Producers–Pre-Pottery Neolithic (8000–5500)', in Levy (ed.), *Archaeology* pp. 190–201.
10. H. de Contenson, *Ramad: site néolithique en Damascène (Syrie) aux VIIIe et VIIe millenaires avant l'ére chretienne* (Beirut, 2000).
11. Akkermans and Schwartz, p. 60.
12. See Chapter 3.
13. Paolo Matthiae, *Ebla, an Empire Rediscovered*, (trans.) Christopher Holme (London, 1980) pp.186–189.
14. C. J. Moor, 'The Semitic Pantheon of Ugarit', *Ugarit Forschungen* 2 (1970) pp. 185–228.
15. For example, Wolfram von Soden, *The Ancient Orient, an Introduction to the Study of the Ancient Near East* (trans.) Donald G. Schley (Grand Rapids MI, 1994) pp. 18–24.

Chapter 2

1. Akkermans and Schwartz, pp. 154–159; E. F Henrickson and I. Thuesen (eds.), *Upon this Foundation: the Ubaid Reconsidered* (Copenhagen, 1989).

2. Summarized in Levy (ed.) *Archaeology* in an article by Avi Gopher, 'Early Pottery-Bearing Groups in Israel–the Pottery Neolithic Period' pp. 205–225.
3. B. Rothenberg, *Timna: Valley of the Biblical Copper Mines* (London, 1972).
4. T. E. Levy and S. Shalev, 'Prehistoric Metalworking in the Southern Levant: Archaeometallurgical and Social Perspectives', *World Archaeology* 20 (1989) pp. 353–372.
5. Toby A. H. Wilkinson, *Early Dynastic Egypt* (London, 1999) pp. 224–225; the issue was originally discussed by Henri Francfort, *The Birth of Civilisation in the Near East* (London, 1951).
6. Guillermo Alzage, *The Uruk World System, the Dynamics of Expansion of Early Mesopotamian Civilisation* 2nd ed. (Chicago, 2005).
7. E. Strommenger, *Habuba Kabira, eine Stadt vor 5000 Jahren* (Mainz, 1980).
8. G. Van Driel and C. van Driel-Murray, 'Jebel Aruda, the 1982 Season of Excavation, Interim Report', *Akkadica* 33 (1983) pp. 1–26.
9. Akkermans and Schwartz, pp. 197–203.
10. Wilkinson, *Early Dynastic Egypt* p. 43.

Chapter 3

1. C. I. Woolley and R. Barnett, *Carchemish* III (London, 1953).
2. M. Danti and R, Zettler, 'The Evolution of the Tell es-Sweyhat (Syria) Settlement System in the Third Millennium BC', in M. Fortin and O. Aurenche (eds.) *Espace naturel, espace habite en Syrie du Nord (10e - 2e millenaires av. J.C.)* (Lyons, 1998) pp. 209–228.
3. G, Buccellati et al. 'Tell Ziyada: The First Three Seasons of Excavation', *Bulletin of the Canadian Society for Mesopotamian Studies* 21 (1991) pp. 17–40.
4. Lisa Cooper, *Early Urbanism on the Syrian Euphrates* (New York, 2006).
5. This is based on Cooper, *Early Urbanism*, table 3.1, pp. 49–52, though her figures are on the conservative side.
6. Akkermans and Schwartz, pp. 229–230.
7. Briefly discussed by Ram Gophna, in Levy (ed.) *Archaeology* pp. 277–279.
8. Michael C. Astour, 'An Outline of the History of Ebla (Part 1)', in Cyrus H. Gordon (ed.), *Eblaitica* 3 (Winona Lake IN, 1992) pp. 3–82, and 19–26.
9. An issue much discussed in the early years of the study of the city and its archives; for some sensible remarks, G. Buccellati, 'Ebla and the Amorites', in ibid. 83–104.
10. Cooper, *Early Urbanism*, ch. 7; the hunt for 'places of worship' has been continuous since the first spade was sunk in an excavation on the region; all too often such places have been found because they were being looked for.
11. Ram Gophna, 'Early Bronze Age Canaan: some Spatial and Demographic Observations', in Levy (ed.) *Archaeology* pp. 269–276 (though his maths is inaccurate).
12. Astour, 'Outline' pp. 26–51.
13. William G. Dever, 'Social Structure in the Early Bronze IV Period in Palestine', in Levy (ed.) *Archaeology* pp. 182–296.
14. Michael C. Astour, 'An Outline of the History of Ebla (Part II)', in Cyrus H. Gordon (ed.) *Eblaitica* 4 (Winona Lake IN, 2002) pp. 68–73 and 76–80.
15. Ibid. 101–125.
16. Ibid. 164–171 – 'wave of destruction' is Astour's phrase.
17. See note 11.
18. Akkermans and Schwartz, pp. 288 290.
19. Buccellati, 'Ebla' (note 10).

Chapter 4

1. Bryce, *Ancient Syria* pp. 18–22; Klengel, *Syria* pp. 41–80.
2. Toby Wilkinson, *The Rise and Fall of Ancient Egypt* (London, 2010) pp. 118–122.
3. Gernot Wilhelm, 'The Kingdom of Mittani', in J. M. Sasson (ed.), *Civilisations of the Ancient Near East* vol. 2 (New York, 1995) pp. 1243–1254.

4. Klengel, *Syria* pp. 51–64.
5. Stephen Quirke, 'Frontier or Border? The Northeast Delta in Middle Kingdom Texts' in *The Archaeology, Geography, and History of the Egyptian Delta in Pharaonic Times* (Oxford, 1989) pp. 261–275.
6. Y. Aharoni, *The Land of the Bible, a Historical Geography* 2nd ed. (trans.) A. E. Rainey (London, 1979) pp. 144–147.
7. Fernand Bisson de la Roque et al. *Le Tresor de Tod* (Cairo, 1953); Ezra Marcus, 'Amenemhet II and the Sea, Maritime Aspects of the Bit Rahina (Memphis) Inscription', *Aegypten und Levante* 7 (2007) pp. 137–190.
8. James G. MacQueen, *Babylon* (London, 1964) pp. 52–53; Joan Oates, *Babylon* (London, 1986) p. 65; Georges Roux, *Ancient Iraq* (London, 1964) p. 182.
9. Quoted in Bryce, *Ancient Syria* p. 22.
10. Roux, *Ancient Iraq*.
11. David Ilan, 'The dawn of Internationalism - the Middle Bronze Age', in Levy (ed.) *Archaeology* pp. 297–319; Fiona Richards, *The Anra Scarab, an Archaeological and Historical Approach*, British Archaeological Reports, international series, S-919 (Oxford, 2001) pp. 16–21.
12. F. Braemer et al. reports on excavations 1992–1994, *Syria* p. 70 and 73, 1992 and 1996.
13. Genesis 14; Aharoni, *Land of the Bible* pp. 140–142; Akkermans and Schwartz, pp. 319–320.
14. H. H. von der Osten, *Svenska Syrienexpedition I: Die Grabunh von Tell es-Salihiyeh* (Lund, 1956); Wayne C. Pitard, *Ancient Damascus* (Winona Lake, 1987) pp. 37–38.
15. Akkermans and Schwartz, pp. 318–319; Ross Burns, *Damascus, a History* (London, 2005) p. 3.
16. On the name, see Pitard, *Ancient Damascus* pp. 10–12, 39–48.
17. Bonnie Magniess-Gardener, 'The Middle Bronze Age of Transjordan', in E. D. Oren (ed.), *The Hyksos, New Historical and Archaeological Perspectives* (Philadelphia, 1997) pp. 303–321.
18. Wilkinson, *Rise and Fall* pp. 164–167.
19. Manetho, *Aegyptiaca* frag. 42.
20. See the essays in Oren (ed.), *Hyksos*; A. Spalinger, 'Some notes on the Chariot Arm of Egypt in the Early Eighteenth Dynasty', in P. Kousoulis and K. Magliveras, *Moving Across Borders* (Leuven, 2007) pp. 119–137.
21. Trevor Bryce, *The Kingdom of the Hittites* (Oxford, 1998) pp. 64–75.
22. Ibid. 76–84, 88–89.
23. Ibid. 89–96; the origin of this is 'The Bilingual Testament of Hattusili I, included in Mark W. Chavalas, *The Ancient Near East*, Historical Sources in Translation (Oxford, 2006) no 106.

Chapter 5

1. A. Spalinger, 'Some Notes on the Chariot Arm of Egypt in the Early Eighteenth Dynasty', in P. Koulouris and K. Magliveras, *Moving Across Borders* (Leuven, 2000) pp. 119–137.
2. Wilkinson, *Rise and Fall* pp. 167–172; the essays in Oren (ed.), *Hyksos*, provide many sidelights on Hyksos history.
3. Wilkinson, *Rise and Fall* pp. 172–175.
4. Eliezer D. Oren, 'The "Kingdom of Sharuhen" and the Hyksos Kingdom', in Oren (ed.) *Hyksos* pp. 253–284.
5. Patrick E. McGovern and Garman Harbottle, '"Hyksos" Trade Connections between Tell el-Daba'a (Avaris) and the Levant: a Neutron Activation Study of the Canaanite Jar', and William G. Dever, 'Settlement Patterns and Chronology of Palestine in the Middle Bronze Age', both in Oren (ed.) *Hyksos* pp. 141–158 and 285–302.
6. Dever (previous note); David Ilan, 'The Dawn of Internationalism–the Middle Bronze Age' in Levy (ed.) *Archaeology* pp. 277–315.
7. W. F. Albright, *The Proto-Sinaitic Inscriptions and their Decipherment* (Cambridge MA, 1966); R. Gans, *The Genesis of the Alphabet and its Development in the Second Millennium BC* (Wiesbaden, 1988).
8. Wilkinson, *Rise and Fall* pp. 176–178.
9. Ibid. 183–191.

10. Bryce, *Hittites* pp. 102–105; Klengel, *Syria* p. 82; MacQueen, *Babylon*.
11. Bryce, *Hittites* pp. 108–111.
12. Paolo Matthiae, *Ebla, An Empire Rediscovered* (London, 1981); Akkermans and Schwartz p. 326.
13. Bryce, *Hittites*, ch. 5.
14. For the genealogy, see Aidan Dobson and Dyan Hilton, *The Complete Royal Families of Ancient Egypt* (London, 2004) pp. 122–141.
15. Akkermans and Schwatz pp. 346–348.
16. Ilan (note 6).
17. Wilkinson, *Rise and Fall* pp. 202–205.
18. Ibid. 206–208; Betsy M. Bryan, 'The Egyptian Perspective on Mittani', in Raymond Cohen and Raymond Westbrook (eds.), *Amarna Diplomacy* (Baltimore, 2000) pp. 71–84; Donald B. Redford, 'A Gate Inscription from Karnak and Egyptian Involvement in Western Asia during the Early Eighteenth Dynasty', *Journal of the American Oriental Society* 99 (1979) pp. 270–287.
19. Gernot Wilhelm, 'The Kingdom of Mittani in Second Millennium Upper Mesopotamia', in J. M. Sasson (ed.) *Civilisations of the Ancient Near East* (New York, 1995) vol 2 pp. 1243–1254; Michael Astour, 'Mittani', in Donald B. Redford, *The Oxford Encyclopedia of Ancient Egypt* (New York, 2001) vol. 2 pp. 422–424.
20. S. Smith, *The Statue of Idrimi* (London, 1949); Sir Leonard Woolley, *A Forgotten Kingdom* (Harmondsworth, 1953) pp. 117–126; Bryce, *Ancient Syria* pp. 33–36; Amanda H. Podany, *Brotherhood of Kings* (Oxford, 2010) pp. 135–138.
21. Chavalas, *Ancient Near East* no 89.
22. Redford (note 18).
23. Detailed on Kamose's victory stele at Karnak, and translated in Donald Redford 'Textual Sources for the Hyksos Period', in Oren (ed.) *Hyksos* pp. 1–44, and 14–15.
24. Leon Marfoe, Kamid el-Loz, *Settlement History of the Biqa' up to the Iron Age* (Bonn, 1998) referring to Patricia Bikai, *Tyre, Report of an Excavation* PhD dissertation (Beirut, 1976).
25. Margarite Yon, *Ugarit*.
26. James M. Weinstein, 'The Egyptian Empire in Palestine: a Reassessment', *Bulletin of the American Schools of Oriental Research* 24 (1982) pp. 1–28; these expeditions are not mentioned in Catherine H. Roehrig (ed.) *Hatshepsut: from Queen to Pharaoh* (New Haven, 2003).
27. Donald B. Redford, *The Wars in Syria and Palestine of Thutmose III* (Leiden, 2003) provides a full array of sources and an interpretation.
28. The campaign is described in all Egyptian histories besides Redford's book: Wilkinson, *Rise and Fall* pp. 215–218; Klengel, *Syria* p. 91; Grimal, *Ancient Egypt* pp. 213–214, are examples.
29. Redford, *Wars in Syria* pp. 210–216.
30. Ibid. 217–219; Klengel, *Syria* pp. 92–94.
31. Klengel, *Syria* p. 94; Redford, *Wars in Syria* pp. 220–228.
32. Wilkinson, *Rise and Fall* pp. 218–219.
33. Pitard, *Ancient Damascus* pp. 53–56.
34. Redford, *Wars in Syria* pp. 229–237.
35. Ibid. 238–240.
36. Klengel, *Syria* pp. 95–96; Marfoe, *Kamid el-Loz* pp. 166–170, notes the drastic depopulation of the Bekaa in the Late Bronze Age, with an estimated drop of population by 80 per cent; for once it seems likely that enemy activity can be assumed to be the direct cause.
37. Klengel, *Syria* p. 96.
38. Betsy Bryan, *The Reign of Thutmose IV* (Baltimore, 1991).

Chapter 6
1. Bryce, *Hittites* pp. 151–152.
2. Wilkinson, *Rise and Fall* pp. 244–248; Amanda H. Podany, *Brotherhood of Kings* (Oxford, 2010) pp. 191–198.
3. Aharoni, *Land of the Bible* 172; Bill Manley, *The Penguin Atlas of Ancient Egypt* (London, 1996) pp. 80–81.

4. William L. Moran (ed and trans.) *The Amarna Letters* (Baltimore, 1992) contains most of the letters; some are published in almost any collection of documents of the period.
5. Moran, *Amarna Letters* pp. 101–103.
6. Bryce, *Hittites* pp. 158–167.
7. Ibid. 169–171.
8. Ibid. 177–178.
9. Moran, *Amarna Letters* has at least forty-four letters concerning Abdi-Ashirta's conduct; Bryce, *Ancient Syria* pp. 46–54; Klengel, *Syria* pp. 161–166.
10. Moran, *Amarna Letters* has thirteen letters concerning Labayu; Aharoni, *Land of the Bible* p. 175.
11. Bryce, *Hittites* pp. 174–177, *Ancient Syria* p. 43.
12. Wilkinson, *Rise and Fall* pp. 288–292.
13. Klengel, *Syria* pp. 154–155, 158–159.
14. William J. Murnane, *The Road to Kadesh, a Historical Interpretation of the Battle Reliefs of King Sety I at Karnak* (Chicago, 1985) pp. 55–64; Aharoni, *Land of the Bible* pp. 176–179.
15. Aharoni, *Land of the Bible* p. 179.
16. Murnane, *Road to Kadesh* pp. 65–91.
17. Ibid. 91–100.
18. Bryce, *Ancient Syria* pp. 72–73.
19. K. A. Kitchen, *Pharaoh Triumphant* (Warminster, 1982) pp. 50–632; Marc van de Mierop, *The Eastern Mediterranean in the Age of Remesses II* (Oxford, 2007) pp. 36–40; Wilkinson, *Rise and Fall* pp. 301–307; Bryce, *Hittites* pp. 255–261, *Ancient Syria* pp. 72–76.
20. Bryce, *Hittites* pp. 261–262.
21. Kitchen, *Pharaoh Triumphant* pp. 67–68.
22. Ibid. 68–70.
23. Bryce, *Hittites* pp. 284–291.
24. Kitchen, *Pharaoh Triumphant* p. 74.
25. Ibid. 74–81; Klengel, *Syria* pp. 118–120; Bryce, *Hittites* pp. 304–309.

Chapter 7

1. Quoted in, amongst others, Aharoni, *Land of the Bible* p. 184.
2. K. A. Kitchen, 'The King list of Ugarit', *Ugarit Forschungen* 9 (1977) pp. 134–142.
3. James M. Weinstein, 'The Egyptian empire in Palestine: a Reassessment', *BASOR* 241 (1981) pp. 1–28.
4. Wilkinson, *Rise and Fall* pp. 323–327.
5. Bryce, *Hittites* pp. 364–366.
6. Numerous studies have been made of these events: N. K. Sanders, *The Sea Peoples* (2nd ed) (London, 1985), is probably still the best; Eric Cline, *1177, the Year Civilization Collapsed* (London, 2014), is the latest; for the Hittites see Bryce, *Hittites* pp. 367–379, for Egypt's fight, see Wilkinson, *Rise and Fall* pp. 327–332.
7. Ras Shamra tablets, 18.147 and 20.18; cf. M. C. Astour 'New Evidence on the Last Days of Ugarit', *American Journal of Archaeology* 69 (1965) pp. 253–258; Bryce, *Ancient Syria* pp. 90–91.
8. Cline, *1177* discusses the various possibilities.
9. Akkermans and Schwartz p. 340.
10. Bryce, *Ancient Syria* p. 93; Klengel, *Syria* pp. 182–184.
11. For this section and the paragraphs which follow see the detailed summary by Lawrence A. Stager, 'The Impact of the Sea Peoples in Canaan (1185–1050 BC)', in Levy (ed.) *Archaeology* pp. 332–348.
12. J. D. Hawkins, 'The Inscription from the Aleppo Temple', *Anatolian Studies* 61 (2011) pp. 35–54; Bryce, *Ancient Syria* pp. 111–112.
13. Akkermans and Schwartz p. 369.
14. A. K. Grayson, *Assyrian Royal Inscriptions* vol II p. 22.
15. Klengel, *Syria* pp. 184–186.

16. Pitard, *Damascus* pp. 81–89 (though this is based largely on biblical sources, on which issue see my comments later in the chapter.)

17. This is a controversial area, much mixed in with nationalistic and religious attitudes and beliefs. I tend towards accepting the arguments of the so-called 'Copenhagen school'. For a useful discussion of the controversy see Amy Dockser Marcus, *Rewriting the Bible, how Archaeology is Reshaping History* (London, 2000), which has references to the main items in the argument.

18. Pitard, *Damascus* used the biblical source, 89–93; that source is II Samuel 8.3–8 and 10.1–19, repeated at I Chronicles 18.3–8 and 19.1–19.

19. I. Finkelstein, 'The Great Transformation, the 'Conquest' of the Highlands Frontiers and the Rise of the Territorial States' in Levy (ed.) *Archaeology* pp. 349–365.

20. See the discussions in Marcus, *Rewriting the Bible* and Israel Finkelstein and Neil Asher Silberman, *David and Solomon* (New York, 2006).

21. Chavalas, *Ancient Near East* pp. 311–316.

22. Ibid. 305–307; but see Niels Peter Lemche, *The Israelites in History and Tradition* (London, 1998) pp. 36–44, for a trenchant criticism of the translation, the reconstruction, and even the discovery of the stone.

23. Josephus, *Contra Apionem* 1.119; this is, of course, a very late source, but he gives his own sources and may be accepted, if with some reservations.

24. Ibid. 1.175.

25. Josephus, *AJ*, 8.324.

26. Klengel, *Syria* p. 204.

27. Aharoni, *Land of the Bible* pp. 323–330; Wilkinson, *Rise and Fall* pp. 385–396; Israel Finkelstein and Niel Asher Silberman, *David and Solomon* (New York, 2006) pp. 71–81.

28. The city has often been inserted, on the argument that it should have been attacked, and I Kings 14.25–26 claims he looted the temple there: a circular argument.

Chapter 8

1. James G. MacQueen, *Babylon* (London, 1964) p. 117.

2. Bryce, *Neo-Hittite Kingdoms* pp. 163–165.

3. *RIMA* 2.43.

4. A. K. Grayson, *Assyrian Royal Chronicles* (Wiesbaden, 1976) 2.46–61.

5. MacQueen, *Babylon* pp. 117–118.

6. *RIMA* 2. 214–219.

7. *RIMA* 2.293–293.

8. Shigeo Yamada, *The Construction of the Assyrian Empire* (London, 2000) is the most detailed discussion of Shalmaneser's campaigns, pp. 77–107, for the first campaign; Bryce, *Ancient Syria* pp. 119–120.

9. Yamada, 95–98.

10. Ibid. 108–120.

11. Ibid. 120–129.

12. Ibid. 130–143.

13. Ibid. 143–163; Bryce, *Neo-Hittite Kingdoms* pp. 225–230.

14. Yamada, 163–164; Bryce, *Neo-Hittite Kingdoms* pp. 230–231.

15. Yamada, 166–169.

16. Ibid. 170–177.

17. Ibid. 180–183.

18. Yamada, 185–195; Bryce, *Neo-Hittite Kingdoms* pp. 237–238; Pitard, *Ancient Damascus* pp. 132–148.

19. Bryce, *Neo-Hittite Kingdoms* pp. 238–239.

20. Yamada, appendix A.

21. H. W. F. Saggs, *The Might that was Assyria* (London, 1984) pp. 77–78.

22. *RIMA*, 3.204–205.

23. *RIMA*, 3.209–213; Bryce, *Neo-Hittite Kingdoms* p. 247.

24. Bryce, *Neo-Hittite Kingdoms* pp. 249–250.
25. Pitard, *Ancient Damascus* pp. 160–167.
26. Bryce, *Neo-Hittite Kingdoms* p. 252.
27. Saggs pp. 82–84.
28. *RIMA*, 3.204–205.
29. Bryce, *Neo-Hittite Kingdoms* p. 256.
30. Ibid. 255–256.
31. Ibid.

Chapter 9

 1. H. W. F. Saggs, *The Might that was Assyria* (London, 1986) pp. 83–84.
 2. Saggs, *Might* pp. 85–86.
 3. H. Tadmor (ed.), *The Inscriptions of Tiglath-Pileser III, King of Assyria* (Jerusalem, 2007) nos 100–101, 124–125, 132–133.
 4. Paul Bentley Kern, *Ancient Siege Warfare* (Bloomington IN, 1999) pp. 42–58.
 5. Tadmor (ed.), *Inscriptions* no. 168.
 6. Bryce, *Neo-Hittite* pp. 173–174, 261.
 7. Tadmor (ed.), *Inscriptions* nos 102–103
 8. Tadmor (ed.), *Inscriptions* nos 56–57.
 9. Tadmor (ed.), *Inscriptions* nos 62–63; Bryce, *Neo-Hittite* p. 265.
10. T. J. Wiseman, *Iraq* 13 (1951) p. 21.
11. H. J. Katzenstein, *The History of Tyre* (Jerusalem, 1973) pp. 211–214.
12. 2 Kings, 15.23–26.
13. 2 Kings, 15.29–30; D. Winton Thomas (ed.), *Documents from Old Testament Times* (London, 1958) p. 55.
14. Thomas (ed.), *Documents* p. 55; Ephraim Stern, *Archaeology and the Land of the Bible* vol II (New York, 2001) pp. 104–105.
15. 2 Chronicles 28.18–19.
16. Pitard, *Ancient Damascus* pp. 186–189; Bryce, *Ancient Syria* pp. 133–134.
17. 2 Kings 15.30; Thomas (ed.), *Documents* p.55.
18. Stern, *Archaeology* p. 104.
19. Thomas (ed.), *Documents* p. 55.
20. 2 Kings, 17. 3–5.
21. Saggs, *Might* p. 92.
22. Bustenay Oded, *Mass Deportations and Deportees in the Neo Assyrian Empire* (Wiesbaden, 1979) includes a list of deportations in his appendix (116–135).
23. Bryce, *Neo-Hittite* 275 276.
24. K. A. Kitchen, *The Third Intermediate Period in Egypt* 2nd ed. (Warminster, 1966), paras 335–336; Stern, *Archaeology* pp. 105–106.
25. Bryce, *Neo-Hittite* pp. 280–281.
26. Ibid. 285–286; Oded, *Mass Deportations*, appendix.
27. 2 Kings 18.8–35; Kitchen, *Third Intermediate Period* para 346; Katzenstein, *Tyre* pp. 246–251; Stern, *Archaeology* p. 106.
28. W. G. Dever, 'Social Structure in Palestine in the Iron II Period on the eve of Destruction', in Levy (ed.), *Archaeology* pp. 416–431, with a map on 419.
29. 1 Chronicles 5.26.
30. Katzenstein, *Tyre* p. 256.
31. Oded, *Mass Deportation* appendix.

Chapter 10

 1. Wilkinson, 410–415.
 2. J. MacQueen, *Babylon* (London, 1964) pp. 134–139.
 3. Chavalas, 411–415.

4. *ANET* 293a.
5. Stern, *Archaeology* pp. 60–62; Katzenstein p. 293.
6. Stern, *Archaeology* pp. 228–235; Josiah's death is recorded at 2 Kings 23.29 and 2 Chronicles 35.20–22.
7. Stern, *Archaeology* 237–238 (Ammon), 259–260 (Moab), 268–273 (Edom).
8. Extracts from the *Babylonian Chronicle* are in Chavalas, 415–418, and Thomas 75–83.
9. 2 Kings 24.17.
10. 2 Kings 25.22–23.
11. Stern, *Archaeology* pp. 327–331.
12. Katzenstein pp. 328–336.
13. Herodotus 2.159 and 4.42.
14. Thomas pp. 87–88.
15. Katzenstein pp. 340–341.
16. Wilkinson pp. 416–417.
17. 2 Kings 25.22–26; E. Unger, *Babylon* 2nd ed. (Berlin, 1970) partly translated in Chavalas, 387–388.
18. J. Blenkinsopp, *David Remembered, Kingship and National Identity in Ancient Israel* (Grand Rapids MI, 2013).
19. Chavalas 418–419.
20. Stern, *Archaeology* p. 359; Akkermans and Schwartz p. 389.
21. Stern, *Archaeology* p. 348.
22. J. M. Cook, *The Persian Empire* (London, 1983) ch 8.
23. Argued by M. Sartre, 'La Syrie sous la domination achemeniede', in C. R. Dentzer and W. Orthmann (eds.), *Archeologie et histoire de la Syrie* vol. 2 (Saarbruck, 1989) pp. 9–18.
24. Ebla: Akkermans and Schwartz pp. 390–391 (and fig. 11.19); Lachish: Stern, *Archaeology* pp. 466–468 (and fig III.16); Sidon and Belesys; Cook, *Persian Empire* p. 174.
25. Stern, *Archaeology* pp. 514–522; Akkermans and Schwartz pp. 386–388.
26. Diodoros 26.41; J. Elayi, 'Tripoli (Liban) a l'epoque perse', *Transeuphratene* 2 (1990) pp. 59–72.
27. Akkermans and Schwartz p. 389; E. Stern, 'New Evidence on the Administrative Division of Palestine in the Persian period', in H. Sancisi-Weerdenburg and A. Kuhrt, *Achaimenid History IV, Centre and Periphery* (Leiden, 1990) pp. 221–226.
28. Chavalas, 420.
29. Ezra 1.8–11, 5.13–16.
30. P. Briant, *From Cyrus to Alexander a History of the Persian Empire* (Winona Lake IN, 2002) pp. 45–49.
31. L. Cagni, 'Considerations sur les testes babyloniennes de Neirab pres de Alep', *Transeuphratene* 2 (1990) pp. 169–185;
32. 2 King 16.6; *ANET* 284–285.
33. Ezra 5.3, 5.17, 6.6–12.
34. Stern, *Archaeology* pp. 393–400, 434–436.
35. Stern, *Archaeology*.
36. E. Stern, 'Between Persians and Greeks: Trade, Administration and Warfare in the Persian and Hellenistic Periods (539–63 BCE)' in Levy (ed.), *Archaeology* p. 432 - 445.
37. Stern, *Archaeology* book 3.
38. Briant, *Cyrus to Alexander* pp. 507–510.
39. Xenophon, *Anabasis*, 1.4.4–18.
40. North Syria: Sidon: Amrit: M. Dunand and N. Saliby, *Le Temple d'Amrith dans le peree d'Aradus* (Paris, 1985); Tyre: Arrian, *Anabasis* Bambyke: Arrian, *Anabasis* Mout Gerizim: Sarepta: J. B. Pritchard, \repta, 4 vol (Beirut, 1988–1989).
41. Wilkinson 428–429; Briant, *Cyrus to Alexander* p. 525, 573–577.
42. Briant, *Cyrus to Alexander* pp. 577–578; Cook, *Persian Empire* pp. 168–169.
43. Briant, *Cyrus to Alexander* p. 589.
44. Wilkinson pp. 429–430.
45. See note 39.

46. Stern, *Archaeology*, 358; Briant, *Cyrus to Alexander* pp. 651–652.
47. Diodoros 16.48.7–48.2, 15.42.1–43.4; Briant, *Cyrus to Alexander* pp. 653–655.
48. Diodoros 15.92.2–93.6; Wilkinson pp. 432–434; Briant, *Cyrus to Alexander* pp. 663–665.
49. Diodoros 16.40.3–5.
50. Cook, *Persian Empire* p. 223; Briant, *Cyrus to Alexander* pp. 683–685; Stern, *Archaeology* pp. 359–360.
51. Arrian, *Anabasis* 2.14; Curtius Rufus 4.1.7–14; Diodoros 17.39.1–2.
52. Arrian, *Anabasis*, 11.13–24; Curtius Rufus 4.41.18; Diodoros 17.43–45.
53. Arrian, *Anabasis*, 2.20.4; Curtius Rufus 4.2.24; Polyainos 4.3.4.
54. Arrian, *Anabasis*, 2.25; Curtius Rufus 4.6.8–29; Diodoros 17.48.7–49.1.
55. Arrian, *Anabasis*, 3.6.1; Curtius Rufus 4.8.10.
56. H. Seyrig, 'Le monnayage de Hierapolis de Syrie a l'epoque d'Alexandre', *Revue Numismatique* 11 (1971) pp. 11–21.

Chapter 11

1. The catafalque was supposed to go from Babylon to Macedon; but it was at Damascus when Ptolemy seized it; Diodoros 18.28.2–6.
2. Diodoros 18.38.2–5.
3. Arrian, *FGrH* 156, F 9, 34–38.
4. Diodoros 18.43.1–2.
5. Diodoros 18.63.6, 73.1–2.
6. This follows from the action of Antigonos in driving Ptolemy's forces out the next year: Diodoros 19.57.1 and 58.1.
7. Diodoros 19.59.2.
8. Diodoros 19.80.3–85.3.
9. Diodoros 20.73.1–76.6.
10. Diodoros 19.94.1–98.1.
11. J. D. Grainger, *The Cities of Seleukid Syria* (Oxford, 1990) pp. 39–47.
12. P. R. S. Moorey, *Cemeteries of the First Millenium BC at Deve Huyuk, near Carchemish*, BAR 187 (Oxford, 1980).
13. The city existed in 306 (Diodoros 20.47); there is no record of its actual foundation.
14. Diodoros 20.113.1–2.
15. Diodoros 21.1.5.
16. Plutarch, *Demetrios* 32.
17. Eusebius, *Chronographia* 2.119.
18. I dealt in detail with this in my book, *The Cities of Seleukid Syria* (Oxford, 1990) to which I may refer any who need more information.
19. Grainger, *Cities* pp. 70–71, map 6(D).
20. Ibid. 74–75, map 9(A); Johannes Malalas 8.201.
21. Grainger, *Cities* pp. 72–74, map 6(B).
22. Ibid. 84–85, map 6(C).
23. Aelian, *On the Nature of Animals* 12.2; G. Goossens, *Hierapolis de Syrie*.
24. The site of Thapsakos is unclear; I believe it to have been at Zeugma; others place it at various places up to 100km south of Zeugma. But it seems to me obvious that Seleukos would have used the traditional crossing place for his bridge, for this was where all the roads lead. The confusion and inaccuracy of the Wikipedia entry on 'Thapsacus' gives a good idea of the difficulties.
25. J. Sauvaget, *Alep* 2 vols (Paris, 1941).
26. Johannes Malalas 8.203; Strabo 16.2.10.
27. Seleukeia: Polybios 5.61.1; Kyrrhos: Polybios 5.50.7; this latter figure is of a regiment, who were of course citizens.
28. Johannes Malalas 8.201.
29. Appian, *Syrian Wars* 57.
30. Ibid.; Pliny *NH* 6.119, says Alexander was the founder; Tacitus, *Annals* 6.41.

31. Tacitus, *Annals* 6.41.
32. Appian, *Syrian Wars* 57; cf. G.M. Cohen, *Hellenistic Settlements in Syria* (California) 2005, pp. 71–76.
33. Karrhai: Diodoros 19.9.1; Ichnai: Isidorw of Charax 1.
34. This is inference only; Ptolemy 5.14.10, places it south of Zeugma; Appian, *Syrian Wars* 17; Pliny *NH* 5.87.
35. G. Clarke, *Jebel Khalid on the Euphrates* (Sydney, 2002); Amphipolis: Appian, *Syrian Wars* 57.
36. Appian, *Syrian Wars* 57.
37. Diodoros 33.41; Appian, *Syrian Wars* 57; the pre-Hellenistic name was Sizara.
38. Polybios 5.45.7.
39. R. M. Bradfield, *Seleuco-Belos* (Burford, 2002).
40. G. G. Aperghis, *The Seleukid Royal Economy* (Cambridge 2004).
41. H. Hauben, 'Philokles, king of the Sidonians and General the Ptolemies', *Studia Phoenicia* 5 pp. 13–27.
42. H. Seyrig, 'Aradus et sa peree sous les rois seleucides', *Syria* 28 (1951) pp. 206–227.
43. J. D. Grainger, *Seleukos Nikator* (London, 1990) pp. 196–199, based on an obscure comment in an inscription from Ilion (*OGIS* 219 = Austin 162).
44. J. D. Grainger, *The Syrian Wars* (Leiden, 2010) pp. 81–87.
45. Ibid. ch 7.
46. Chalkis: Strabo 16.2.10; Dion: Josephus *AJ* 14.47; Pella: R. H. Smith, *Pella of the Decapolis* 2 vols (Wooster, 1973 and 1989).
47. Josephus *AJ* 13.357.
48. Stephanus of Byzantion, *sv* 'Hellas'.
49. Curtius Rufus 4.8.9; Eusebius, *Chronographia* 197.
50. C. H. Kraeling (ed.), *Gerasa, City of the Decapolis* (New Haven CN, 1938).
51. Pliny, *NH* 5.75; Strabo 16.2.25; *Letter of Aristeas* 115.
52. Arrian, *Anabasis* 2.26–27; Diodoros 20.73.3–74.1; Martin A. Meyer, *History of the City of Gaza* (New York, 1907; reprinted 1966) pp. 46–47.
53. Polybios 5.70.3–5.
54. Stephanus of Byzantion *sv* 'Philadelphia 3'; Strabo 16.2.34.

Chapter 12
1. D. Gera, 'Ptolemy son of Thraseas and the Fifth Syrian War', *Ancient Society* 18 (1987) pp. 63–73.
2. Polybios 9.27 5; Grainger, *Syrian Wars*, ch 13.
3. Polybios 30.25.1–26.9.
4. E. Schurer, *The History of the Jewish People in the Time of Jesus Christ* vol. 1 revised ed. (Edinburgh, 1973) pp. 125–137.
5. O. Morkholm, *Antiochus IV of Syria* (Copenhagen, 1966) pp. 116–117.
6. Schurer 1.137–164; M. Hengel, *Judaism and Hellenism* 2 vols (London, 1974).
7. Schurer 1.164–173.
8. Ibid.
9. I Maccabees 7.10.
10. Schurer 1.178–180.
11. Grainger, *Syrian Wars* pp. 343–350.
12. Glanville Downey, *A History of Antioch in Syria* (Princeton NJ, 1961) pp. 121–122.
13. Josephus AJ 13.138–141.
14. Schurer 1.189–199.
15. Grainger, *Hellenistic Phoenicia* pp. 123–133.
16. I Maccabees 10.84.
17. G. Bowersock, *Roman Arabia* (Cambridge MA, 1983) pp. 18–19.
18. Josephus *AJ* 12.230–233.
19. Josephus *AJ* 12.319; I Maccabees 5.6–17.

20. Josephus *AJ* 13.275–281.
21. Josephus *AJ* 13.276–280; J. D. Grainger, *Wars of the Maccabees* (Barnsley, 2012) ch. 9.
22. Grainger, *Syrian Wars* ch. 18; see, for the sources, E. van't Dack et al. *The Judean-Syrian-Egyptian Conflict of 103–101 BC. A Multilingual Dossier concerning the 'War of Scepters'*, (Brussels, 1989).
23. Diodoros 34/35.15–16; Grainger, *Hellenistic Phoenicia* pp. 135–138.
24. *Chronicle of Edessa* 2.
25. Diodoros 31.19a; R. A. Sullivan, 'The Dynasty of Commagene' *ANRW* 2/8 (Berlin, 1977) pp. 732–798.
26. E. A. Myers, *The Ituraeans and the Roman Near East* (Cambridge, 2010).
27. C. Chad, *Les Dynastes d'Emese* (Beyrouth, 1972).
28. Pliny *NH* 5.81 –89.
29. Austin 222.
30. Josephus *AJ* 13.14.3; Athenaios 4.153 B–C (from Poseidonios); Strabo 14.2.7.
31. Grainger, *Wars of the Maccabees*, chs. 13 and 14; G. M. Cohen, *The Hellenistic Settlements in Syria, the Red Sea and North Africa* (California, 2006) pp. 242–243.
32. Grainger, *Wars of the Maccabees*, ch. 9.
33. Josephus AJ 14.14.3.
34. Justin 40.1.4; Appian, *Syrian Wars* 48; Josephus *AJ* 13.16.4; Grainger, *Cities of Seleukid Syria* pp. 175–177.
35. Polybios 31.2.9–11; Appian, *Syrian Wars* 46.
36. Josephus *AJ* 12.10.6; I Maccabees 11.16–21.
37. Plutarch, *Pompeius* 39.3.
38. Josephus *AJ* 14.38–40; Strabo 16.2.16.
39. Strabo 16.2.10.
40. Josephus *AJ* 14.39.
41. Ibid 14.56–81.
42. Apameia: Dio 47.27.2–5; Appian, *BC* 3.77; Josephus *AJ* 14.11.1; Laodikeia: Appian *BC* 3.71, 4.60–62; Dio 47.29–30.
43. Plutarch, *Antony* 34; Dio 47.20–22.
44. Grainger, *Wars of the Maccabees* ch. 19.
45. Schurer 1.287–330; biographies of Herod can be all too lurid; two relatively clear examples are Michael Grant, *Herod the Great* (New York, 1971) and Peter Richardson, *Herod, King of the Jews and Friend of the Romans* (Columbus SC, 1966).
46. Dio 51.2.2–3.
47. Pliny *NH*.
48. For the governors see Schurer 1, and E. Dabrowa, *The Governors of Roman Syria from Augustus to Septimius Severus* (Bonn, 1998).
49. R. D. Sullivan, 'Papyri reflecting the Eastern Dynastic Network', *ANRW* 11.8 (Berlin, 1977) pp. 908–989.
50. Josephus *AJ* 19.338–341.
51. Josephus *AJ* 17.206–323; Schurer 1.330–335.
52. Josephus *AJ* 17.342–343; Schurer 1.354–357.
53. J. D. Grainger, *The Cities of Seleukid Syria* (Oxford, 1990) maps 3 and 4.
54. Dio 48.24.2.
55. E. Will, *Les Palmyreenes, la Venise des Sables* (Paris, 1992); J. Teixidor, *Un Port Romain du Desert: Palmyre* (Paris, 1984).
56. Schurer 1.357–398 and 455–470.
57. E. Mary Smallwood, *The Jews under Roman Rule* (Leiden, 1976) pp. 357–358.
58. Josephus *BJ* 3.68.
59. Josephus *BJ* 2.344–401; the speech is clearly a composition by Josephus, but Agrippa undoubtedly made one in this sense.
60. M. Sartre, *The Middle East under Rome* (Cambridge MA, 2005) p. 77.
61. Josephus *AJ* 18.53; Tacitus, *Annals* 2.56.4.

62. Sartre, *Middle East* pp. 74–76.
63. Schurer 1.471–483.
64. Josephus *BJ* 3.68.
65. Bowersock, *Roman Arabia* pp. 76–83.

Chapter 13
1. James D. Anderson, 'The Impact of Rome on the Periphery: the Case of Palestina–Roman period (63 BCE–324 CE)', in Levy (ed.) *Archaeology* 446–469.
2. L. Marfoe, *Kamid el Loz, 14, Settlement History of the Biqa up to the Iron Age* (Bonn, 1998).
3. J. D. Grainger, *The Seleukid Cities of Syria* (Oxford, 1990) pp. 116–117.
4. Ibid. 117–119.
5. Diodoros 19.94; Strabo 16.4 21 and 26; Robert G. Hoyland, *Arabia and the Arabs* (London, 2001) pp. 70–77.
6. Peter Richardson, *Herod, King of the Jews and Friend of the Romans* (Columbia SC, 1996) ch. 8.
7. Duane W. Roller, *The Building Program of Herod the Great* (California, 1998) pp. 133–144 and 209–212.
8. Ibid. 239–240.
9. Ibid. 244–245; John F. Wilson, *Caesarea Philippi, Banias, the Lost City of Pan* (London, 2004) ch. 2.
10. Ibid. 241–242.
11. Benjamin Isaac, *The Limits of Empire, the Roman Army in the East* rev. ed. (Oxford, 1993) pp. 361–363.
12. Glanville Downey, *A History of Antioch in Syria* (Princeton, 1961).
13. Fergus Millar, *The Roman Near East 31 BC–AD 337* (Cambridge MA, 1993) pp. 527–528.
14. Josephus, *AJ* 17.287.
15. Linda Jones Hall, *Roman Berytus, Beirut in late Antiquity* (London, 2004).
16. G. Goossens, *Hierapolis de Syrie* (Louvain, 1943).
17. Roller, *Building Program* pp. 176–178.
18. Arthur Segal, *From Function to Monument, Urban Landscapes in Roman Palestine, Syria, and Provincia Arabia* (Oxford, 1997) ch. 1.
19. Ross Burns, *Damascus, a History* (London, 2005) pp. 61–68.
20. Schurer, 1.534–558; Shimon Applebaum, *Prolegomena to the Study of the Second Jewish Revolt (AD 132–135)* BAR S 7 (Oxford, 1976).
21. Anderson (note 1).
22. L. J. F. Keppie, 'Legions in the East from Augustus to Trajan', in Philip Freeman and David Kennedy (eds.), *The Defence of the Roman and Byzantine East* BAR S 297, vol. 2, pp. 411–429.
23. Barbara Levick, *Vespasian* (London 1994) ch 4.
24. J. D. Grainger, *Nerva and the Imperial Succession Crisis of 96–98* (London, 2003) pp. 92–94.
25. F. A. Lepper, *Trajan's Parthian War* (Oxford, 1948); Julian Bennett, *Trajan, Optimus Princeps* (London, 1997) ch 13.
26. For this concept see Keith Hopkins, 'Taxes and Trade in the Roman Empire (200 VV–AD 400', *Journal of Romans Studies* 70 (1980) pp. 101–125; for Syria specifically seen Nigel Pollard, *Soldiers, Cities, and Civilians in Roman Syria* (Ann Arbor MI, 2000), ch. 5.
27. The main study of this region is by Georges Tchalenko, *Villages Antiques de la Syrie du Nord*, 3 vols (Paris, 1953–1958); for a useful account, with full references to more recent studies see Warwick Ball, *Rome in the East* (London, 2000) pp. 207–233.
28. Ian Holder, *The Auxilia from Augustus to Trajan* BAR S 70 (Oxford, 1980) app. III.
29. Ibid. 209.
30. J. Fitz, *Les Syriens à Intercisa*, Latomus 122, 1972.
31. Steven K. Ross, *Roman Edessa* (London, 2001) pp. 46–56.
32. General accounts of the Roman frontier are in Graham Webster, *The Roman Imperial Army* (London, 1969); David J. Breeze, *The Frontiers of Imperial Rome* (Barnsley, 2011); E. Dabrowa, 'The Frontier in Syria in the First Century AD', in Freeman and Kennedy (note 20).

33. Antony Birley, *The African Emperor Septimius Severus* (London, 1988); Barbara Levick, *Julia Domna* (London, 2007).
34. H. Halfmann, 'Die Senatoren aus dem ostlichen Teil des Imperium Romanum bus zur Ende des 2 Jh. n. Chr.', *Hypomnemata* 58 (Gottingen, 1979).
35. *Scriptores Historia Augustae* (*SHA*) Marcus Aurelius 20.6–7.
36. *SHA*, Verus, 8.2–3; Dio 71.2.4; Ammianus Marcellinus 23.6.24.
37. Downey, *Antioch* pp. 226–227.
38. Juvenal.
39. *SHA*, Avidius Cassius; R. Syme, 'Avidius Cassius, His Rank, Age and Quality', *Bonner Historia Augusta Colloquium 1984/1985* (1987); M. L. Astarita, *Avidio Cassio* (1983).
40. Millar, *Roman Near East* pp. 308–309.
41. Ian Hodder, *Auxilia* BAR.
42. Tacitus, *Histories* 3.24.3.
43. M. P. Speidel, *The Religion of Iuppitur Dolichenus in the Roman Army* (Leiden, 1978).
44. Acts 11.26.
45. Tacitus, *Annals* 3.24.25.
46. Johannes Malalas 276.10.11.
47. M. Sartre, *The Middle East under Rome* (Cambridge MA, 2005) pp. 347–348.
48. Ibid.
49. The sources are collected and translated in M. A. Dodgeon and S. N. C. Lieu, *The Roman Eastern Frontier and the Persian Wars* (London, 1991) ch. 3.
50. J. C. Balty, 'Apamee (1986), Nouvelles donnees sur l'armees romaines d'Orient et les raides sassanides du milieu du IIIe siecle', *Comptes Rendus de l'Academie des inscriptions et belles lettres* (1987) pp. 229–231.
51. H. R. Baldus, 'Uranius Antoninus, a Roman Emperor, from Palmyra's Neighbouring City and his Image', *Annales Archaeolgiques Arabes Syriennes* 42 (1996) pp. 371–377.
52. Millar, *Roman Near East* p. 163; Zosimus 1.32.2; H. G. Pflaum, 'La fortification de la Ville d'Adraha d'Arabie (253–260 et 274–275) d'après les inscriptions recemment decouvertes', *Syria* 29 (1952).
53. Millar, *Roman Near East* p. 165; Warwick Ball, *Roman in the East* p. 77; David Potter, *Prophecy and History in the Crisis of the Roman Empire, a Historical Commentary on the Thirteenth Sybilline Oracle* (Oxford, 1991) app. 4.
54. Dodgeon and Lieu pp. 57–67.
55. Millar, *Roman Near East* pp. 167–169.
56. Dodgeon and Lieu pp. 80–85.
57. *SHA*, Claudius 11.1–2; Probus 9.5; Zosimus 1.44.1–2.
58. *SHA*, Aurelian 22.1–2.28.5; Zaosimus 1.50.2–1.56.2.
59. *SHA*, Aurelian, 31.1–10; Zosimus 1.59.1–61.1.
60. R. Stoneman, *Palmyra and its Empire: Zenobia's Revolt against Rome* (London, 1992); P. Southern, *The Empress Zenobia: Palmyra's Rebel Queen* (London, 2008); a recent account is in Bryce, *Ancient Syria* pp. 275–318; for a corrective against romantic distortion, see Millar, *Roman Near East* pp. 159–173 and 319–336.

Chapter 14

1. For Diocletian's new system, see A. H. M. Jones, *The Later Roman Empire* 2 vols (Oxford, 1964) ch. 2; *The New Empire of Diocletian and Constantine*; another account is in Stephen Williams, *Diocletian and the Roman Recovery* (London, 1985); any history of the empire has a substantial discussion of his work.
2. Jones, *Later Roman Empire* pp. 42–47.
3. The main documents are collected in J. Stevenson, *A New Eusebius* rev. ed. by W. H. C. Frend (London, 1987) docs 237–247 and 273.
4. G. Downey, *A History of Antioch in Syria* (Princeton, 1961) pp. 242–250.

5. Linda Jones Hall, *Roman Berytus, Beirut in Late Antiquity* (London, 2004) pp. 129–194, and John Francis Wilson, *Caesarea Philippi, Banias the Lost City of Pan* (London, 2004) pp. 85–113, for two examples of the transition from paganism.

6. Aurelius Victor, *de Caesaribus*, 39; Eutropius 9.24–25; the treaty is translated and discussed by Beate Dignas and Engelbert Winter, *Rome and Persia in Late Antiquity* (Cambridge, 2007) pp. 122–130.

7. Map in David Kennedy and Derrick Riley, *Rome's Desert Frontier from the Air* (London, 1990) p. 259.

8. P. K. Hitti, *History of the Arabs* 7th ed. (London, 1960).

9. G. W. Bowersock, *Roman Arabia* (Cambridge MA, 1982) pp. 133–137.

10. Ibid. 138–142.

11. Dignas and Winter pp. 32–34.

12. Georges Tchalenko, *Villages Antiques de la Syrie du Nord* 3 vols (Paris 1953–1958); the reinterpretation by G. Tate, *Les Campagnes de la Syrie du Nord, IIe au VIIe siecles* (Paris, 1992) tends to reduce commercial activity and enhance equality; it is evident that rival French ideologies are at work here. For the Hawran see J.-M. Dentzer, *Hauran I–V* (Paris, 1985); several articles on the settlement east of the Jordan are in G. R. D. King and Averil Camerion (eds.), *The Byzantine and Early Islamic Near East, II, Land and Settlement Patterns* (Princeton NJ, 1994).

13. Michael Decker, 'Food for an Empire: Wine and Oil Production in North Syria', in Sean Kingsley and Michael Decker, *Economy and Exchange in the East Mediterranean during Late Antiquity* (Oxford, 2001) pp. 69–86.

14. Theodoret, *Historia Philotheos*, summarized by Peter Brown, 'The Holy Man in Late Antiquity, *Journal of Roman Studies* 61 (1971) pp. 80–101.

15. Linda Jones Hall, 'The Case of Late Antique Berytus: Urban Wealth and Rural Exchange–a different Economic Dynamic', in Thomas S. Brown and John W. Eadie (eds.), *Urban Centers and Rural Contexts in Late Antiquity* (East Lansing MI, 2001) pp. 63–76.

16. Sean A. Kingsley, 'The Economic Impact of the Palestinian Wine Trade in Late Antiquity', in Kingsley and Decker (eds.) *Economy and Exchange* pp. 44–68.

17. Kevin Butcher, *Roman Syria and the Near East* (London, 2003) pp/ 173–174.

18. Hill, 'Late Antique Berytus'.

19. Georges Tchalenko, *Village Antiques de la Syrie du Nord* 3 vols (Paris, 1953–1958).

20. Theotoret, *Historia Philotheos*, 18; Frank R. Trombley, *Hellenic Religion and Christianization* (Leiden, 2001) 2.159–161.

21. Theodoret, *Historia Ecclesiasticae*, 5.21; Trombley, *Hellenic Religion* 1.126–126.

22. John of Ephesos, *Historia Eccles* 3.27.

23. C. H. Kraeling, *Gerasa, City of the Decapolis* (New Haven CT, 1938).

24. Trombley, *Hellenic Religion* 1.188–243.

25. Wilson, *Caesarea Philippi* pp. 103–107.

26. A. Voobus, *A History of Asceticism in Syria* 2 vols (Louvain, 1958–1960); W. H. C. Frend, *The Rise of the Monophysite Movement* (Cambridge, 1972) pp. 88–91; Joseph Patrich, 'Church, State and the Transformation of Palestine–the Byzantine Period, (324–640 CE)', in Levy (ed.) *Archaeology* pp. 470–487, at 487.

27. Downey, *Antioch in Syria* pp. 342–345.

28. Trombley, *Hellenic Religion* 1.112–115.

29. E. D. Hunt, *Holy Land Pilgrimage in the Later Roman Empire, AD 312–460* (Oxford, 1982) pp. 28–50.

30. Joseph Patrich, 'Urban Space in Caesarea Maritima, Israel', in Burns and Eadie (eds,) *Urban Centers* pp. 77–110.

31. R. Dussaud, *La Penetration des Arabes en Syria avant Islam* (Paris, 1955); see also the essays in King and Cameron (note 11); Greg Fisher, *Between Empires* (Oxford, 2011) ch. 2.

32. Procopius, *Persian Wars*, 1.7.1–9.25.

33. L. M. Whitby, 'Procopius' Descriptions of Dara (*Buildings* II.1–3)' in Philip Freeman and David Kennedy (eds.), *The Defence of the Roman and Byzantine East* BAR S 297 (Oxford, 1986) pp. 785–796.

34. Procopius, *Persian Wars*, 1.22.1–19; G. Greatrex, *Rome and Persia at War, 502–532* (Leeds, 1998) pp. 213–221.
35. Procopius, *Persian Wars*, 1.17.40 –41 and 45–48.
36. R. P. Casey, 'Justinian, the limitanei, and Arab-Byzantine relations in the sixth century', *Journal of Roman Archaeology* 9 (1996) pp. 214–222.
37. Downey, *Antioch in Syria* pp. 533–543.
38. Procopius, *Persian Wars*, 2.3.1–6 and 14.1–2.
39. Downey, *Antioch in Syria* pp. 521–523, 528, 533.
40. Procopius, *Buildings*, 2.10.2–25; cf. Downey, *Antioch in Syria* pp. 546–553.
41. H. Kennedy, 'Justinianic plague in Syria and the archaeological evidence', in L. K. Little (ed.) *Plague and the end of Antiquity: the Pandemic of 541–750* (Cambridge, 2007) pp. 87–98; William Rosen, *Justinian's Flea, Plague, Empire and the Birth of Europe* (London, 2008).
42. Downey, *Antioch in Syria* p. 558.
43. Frend, *Rise of the Monophysite Movement* ch. 7.

Chapter 15
1. G. W. Bowersock, *The Throne of Adulis, Red Sea Wars on the Eve of Islam* (Oxford, 2013) for one astonishing episode.
2. Evagrius, *Church History* 5.10; John of Ephesos, *Church History* 6.6; Clive Foss, 'Syria in Transition, AD 550–750, an Archaeological Approach', *Dumbarton Oaks Papers* 51 (1997) pp. 189–269.
3. John of Ephesos, 3.42–43; Foss, 'Syria in Transition', p. 238 and 252.
4. Theophylact 7.1.1- 4.6, Evagrius, 6.4–7 and 9.
5. Evagrius, 6.14–15.
6. Theophylact 4.1–2, 4.13.24; Evagrius, 6.19; Dignas and Winter pp. 42–43.
7. Foss, 'Syria in Transition', pp. 200–204.
8. Michael G. Morony, '"For Whom does the Writer Write?" The First Bubonic Plague Pandemic according to Syriac Sources', and Hugh W. Kennedy, 'Justinianic Plague in Syria and the Archaeological Evidence', in Lester K. Little, *Plague and the End of Antiquity, the Pandemic of 541–750* (Cambridge, 2007) pp. 59–86 and 87–95.
9. Procopius, *Wars*, 2.11.1; Khusro bathed in the Mediterranean as a gesture of victory; at Apameia he held a chariot race in the hippodrome.
10. Foss, 'Syria in Transition', pp. 199–200, 217–226.
11. Ibid. 211–217.
12. W. H. C. Frend, *The Rise of the Monophysite Movement* (Cambridge, 1979) pp. 283–288.
13. Al-Tabari 5.338–39 and 359–370; James Howard-Johnson, *Witnesses to a World Crisis* (Oxford, 2010) pp. 438–439.
14. W. E. Kaegi, *Heraclius, Emperor of Byzantium* (Cambridge, 2003) pp. 45–51.
15. Theophanes, *Chronicle* '6102'; Downey, *Antioch in Syria* p. 575.
16. *Chronichon Paschale* pp. 699–700; Downey, *Antioch in Syria* pp. 572–574; Kaegi, *Heraclius* p. 58.
17. Sebeos, *History* pp. 114–115; Kaegi, *Heraclius* pp. 75–77.
18. Kaegi, *Heraclius* p. 78.
19. *Quran, sura* 30.1–3.
20. Sebeos, *History* pp. 115–116; Alfred J. Butler, *The Arab Conquest of Egypt* 2nd ed. (Oxford, 1978) pp. 54–68; Michael J. Moroney, 'Syria under the Persians, 610–629 AD', *Bilad as-Sham Proceedings* 1 (Amman, 1983) pp. 87–95; Robert Schick, *The Christian Communities of Palestine from Byzantine to Muslim Rule* (Princeton NJ, 1993).
21. Kaegi, *Heraclius* pp. 79–80.
22. Sebeos, *History* p. 119; cf. a note on this in the Historical Commentary, p. 210.
23. A. N. Stratos, *Byzantium in the Seventh Century* vol. 1 (Amsterdam, 1968) p. 108.
24. Foss, 'Syria in Transition' pp. 225–232.
25. Moroney, 'Syria'.
26. Ibid.

27. Kaegi, *Heraclius* pp. 203–204.
28. G. Goossens, *Hierapolis de Syrie* (Louvain, 1943) pp. 174–180.
29. Kaegi, *Heraclius* p. 214.
30. Ibid. 205–208.
31. Ibid. 209.
32. Theophanes, *Chronographia* '6123'; al-Waqidi, 755–757; F. McG. Donner, *The Early Islamic Conquests* (Princeton NJ, 1981) pp. 105–110; W. E. Kaegi, *Byzantium and the Early Islamic Conquests* (Cambridge, 1992) pp. 71–74, 79–83.
33. Al-Waqidi, 1015–1018; al-Baladhuri, 92–94; Donner, *Conquests* p. 107; Kaegi, *Byzantium* p. 80; P. K. Hitti, *The History of Syria* (London, 1951) makes more of this than others do.
34. Kaegi, *Heraclius* pp. 221–222.
35. Donner, *Conquests* pp. 179–180.
36. Kaegi, *Byzantium* p. 75.
37. Donner, *Conquests* pp. 112–119; Kaegi, *Byzantium* pp. 83–97.
38. Kaegi, *Byzantium* pp. 98–99.
39. Donner, *Conquests* pp. 119–124.
40. Ibid. 129–136.
41. Pella: Ali Zeyadieh, 'Settlement Patterns: an Archaeological Perspective; Case Studies from Northern Palestine and Jordan, in G. R. D. King and Averil Cameron, *The Byzantine and Early Islamic Near East II, Land Use and Settlement Patterns* (Princeton NJ, 1994) pp. 117–132 and 121–122; Skythopolis: Yoram Tsafrir and Gideon Foerster, 'From Skythopolis to Baysan– Changing Concepts of Urbanism' in ibid. 95–115.
42. Kaegi, *Byzantium* pp. 100–104.
43. Ibid. 105–108.
44. Donner, *Conquests* pp. 130–131; not mentioned by Kaegi, *Byzantium*.
45. Ross Burns, *Damascus, a History* (London, 2000) pp. 98–100; Donner, *Conquests* p. 131.
46. Donner, *Conquests* p. 132.
47. Accounts of the battle are numerous: Burns, *Damascus* pp. 100–103 is reasonably clear; all accounts vary in detail and interpretation.
48. Donner, *Conquests* pp. 148–151.
49. Ibid. 151–152.
50. Ibid. 152–154.
51. Downey, *Antioch in Syria* does not accept this rebellion.

Chapter 16
1. Baladhuri 139.
2. Baladhuri 131–132; Tabari 1.2524–2425.
3. Donald Whitcomb, 'The *misr* of Ayla: settlement at al-Aqaba in the early Islamic period', in G. R. D. King and Averil Cameron, *The Byzantine and Early Islamic Near East*, II, *Land Use and Settlement Patterns* (Princeton NJ, 1994) pp. 155–170.
4. Baladhuri 143; Alan Walmesley, *Early Islamic Syria, an Archaeological Assessment* (London, 2007) pp. 74–75.
5. This is only a possibility, but Tiberias had become the capital of al-Urdunn.
6. G. L. Hawting, *The First Dynasty of Islam* 2nd ed. (London, 2000) p. 37; Hugh Kennedy, *The Prophet and the Age of the Caliphate* (Harlow, 1986) pp. 68–69.
7. Baladhuri 128.
8. S. Humphreys, *Muawiya ibn Abi Sufyan, from Arabia to Empire* (Oxford, 2006).
9. Baladhuri 163–164; Tabari 1.2396.
10. F. McG Donner, *The Early Islamic Conquests*; Michael W. Dols, *The Black Death in the Middle East* (Princeton NJ, 1979) pp. 21–25.
11. Chase E. Robinson, *Empire and Elites after the Muslim Conquest* (Cambridge, 2000) ch. 2 for the Jazirah cities.

12. Andrew Palmer, *The Sixth Century in the West Syrian Chronicles* (Liverpool, 1993) 58 (Chronicle of Zuqnin) 177 (Dionysios).
13. Theophanes, *Chronicle* 344; Geoffrey Greatrex and Samuel N. C. Lieu, *The Roman Eastern Frontier and the Persian Wars* vol. II (London, 2002) pp. 195–196.
14. Palmer (ed.), *West Syrian Chronicles* 58 (Chronicle of Zuqnin) 173–174, 176 (Dionysios); Baladhuri 152–153; Theophanes, *Chronicle* 343–344.
15. Palmer (ed.), *West Syrian Chronicles*, 179–180 (Dionysios); Theophanes, *Chronicle* 345–346.
16. Theophanes, *Chronicle* 345.
17. Baladhuri 144–149.
18. Ibid 159.
19. A. J. Toynbee, *Constantine Porphyrogenitus and his World* (Oxford, 1973) p. 82.
20. Theophanes, *Chronicle* 355.
21. Ibid. 363.
22. Ibid 366.
23. Ibid 372, Baladhuri 165.
24. Ibid. 363–365.
25. Baladhuri 163, 166.
26. Theophanes, *Chronicle* 347.
27. Hugh Kennedy, *The Armies of the Caliphs* (London, 2001) p. 8.
28. G. R. Hawting, *The First Dynasty of Islam* (London, 2000) pp. 27–31.
29. Hugh Kennedy, 'Antioch from Byzantium to Islam and back again', in John Rich (ed.), *The City in Late Antiquity* (London, 1992) pp. 181–198; Clive Foss, 'Syria in Transition, AD 550–750: an Archaeological Approach', *Dumbarton Oaks Papers* 51 (1997) pp. 189–268, 190–197.
30. Foss, 'Syria in Transition', pp. 230–232.
31. Clive Foss, 'Muawiya's State', in John Haldon, *Money, Power and Politics in Early Islamic Syria* (Farnham, Surrey, 2010) pp. 75–96.
32. Ross Burns, *Damascus, a History* (London, 2005) and *Monuments of Syria* (London, 1999) pp. 79–85, for a description of the mosque.
33. Baladhuri 117, 126.
34. Ibid. 117–118.
35. Ibid.
36. Hugh Kennedy, *The Armies of the Caliphs* (London, 2002) pp. 8–11.
37. H. H. Lamb, *Climate History and the Future* (Princeton NJ, 1985) pp. 426–428.
38. P. M. Cobb, *White Banners, Contention in Abbasid Syria* (Albany NY, 2001) p. 30.
39. Foss, 'Syria in Transition', 234.
40. Ibid. 245–258.
41. E. Ashtor, *A Social and Economic History of the Near East in the Middle Ages* (London, 1976) ch. 2; Donald Whitcomb, 'Islam and the Social–Cultural Transition of Palestine–Early Islamic Period (638–1099 CE)', in Levy (ed.) *Archaeology* pp. 488–501; Walmesley, *Early Islamic Syria* pp. 107–112.
42. Baladhuri 131; Foss, 'Syria in Transition', p. 236.
43. Walmesley, *Early Islamic Syria* pp. 99–104.
44. Garth Fowden, *Qusayr Amra, Art and the Ummayad Elite in Late Antique Syria* (California, 2004).
45. M. Ben-Tov, *In the Shadow of the Temple* (Jerusalem, 1985).
46. Alastair Northedge, 'Archaeology and New Urban Settlement in Early Islamic Syria and Iraq', in King and Cameron (eds.), pp. 231–268; Anjarr is discussed on pp. 233–235.
47. A convenient list of defeats is in K. Y. Blankinship, *The End of the Jihad State* (Albany NY, 1994) table 4 pp. 233–235, though it is restricted to the years 725–742.
48. Kennedy, *Armies* 4 and 5.
49. Blankinship, *End* pp. 47–57.
50. Ibid. 49–50, 54.

51. Palmer (ed.), *West Syrian Chronicles* pp. 30–31 (Maronite Chronicle), 40 (Chronicle of Zuqnin) 46 (Chronicle 'of Disasters'), and 80 (Two Chronicles).
52. Foss, 'Syria in Transition', pp. 244–245, 257.
53. Hawting, *First Dynasty* pp. 96–97; M. A. Shaban, *Islamic History, a New Interpretation* vol. 1 (Cambridge, 1971) pp. 160–161.
54. Hawting, *First Dynasty* pp. 97–98.
55. Ibid 97–99.
56. Hugh Kennedy, *The Early Abbasid Caliphae* (Beckenham, 1981) pp. 38–40.
57. Hawting, *First Dynasty* pp. 109–112; Kennedy, *Early Abbasid* pp. 41–41; Shaban, pp. 180–182.
58. Kennedy, *Early Abbasid* ch. 2.
59. Hawting, *First Dynasty* pp. 117–118; Kennedy, *Early Abbasid* pp. 44–48; Kennedy, *Armies* pp. 50–51.
60. Tabari (ed. Goeje) 2.51; Kennedy, *Early Abbasid* p. 48.
61. Tabari (ed. Goeje) 3.56–58.
62. Kennedy, *The Prophet* p. 129.
63. Ibid. 129–130.

Chapter 17

1. Paul M. Cobb, *White Banners, Contention in Abbasid Syria, 750–880* (Albany NY, 2001) p. 49.
2. Ibid. 76–78.
3. Tabari 3.52–53; W. Madeley, 'The Sufyani between Tradition and History', *Studies in Islam* 68 (1984) pp. 5–51; Cobb, *White Banners* pp. 46–48.
4. Cobb, *White Banners* pp. 48–50.
5. Ibid. 49.
6. Jacob Lassner, *The Shaping of Abbasid Rule* (Princeton NJ, 1980) pp. 19–38; Hugh Kennedy, *The Early Abbasid Caliphate* (London, 1981) pp. 58–61.
7. Theophanes, *Chronicle* 427, 429.
8. Ibid. 430.
9. Ibid.
10. Baladhuri 161.
11. Ibid 162; Theophanes, *Chronicle* 431; Cobb, *White Banners* pp. 112–115.
12. Baladhuri 162.
13. Cobb, *White Banners* pp. 119–120; David Ayalon, 'The Military Reforms of Caliph al-Mutasim: their Background and Consequences', in his *Islam and the Abode of War* (Aldershot, 1994) pp. 14–20.
14. A useful account of the planning and building of Baghdad is in Hugh Kennedy, *The Court of the Caliphs* (London, 2004) pp. 132–145.
15. Kennedy, *Early Abbasid Caliphate* 59; Cobb, *White Banners* p. 27.
16. Baladhuri 165–169.
17. Ibid. 169–170.
18. E.g. Theophanes, *Chronicle* 467.
19. Kennedy, *Early Abbasid Caliphate* pp. 74–75.
20. Theophanes, *Chronicle* 444–45; there were raids annually from 770 to 776 and from 778 to 782; Byzantine raids in reply took place in 778 and 781.
21. A. J. Toynbee, *Constantine Porphyrogenitus and his World* (Oxford, 1973), gives a list of prisoner exchanges on 390–393.
22. Kennedy, *Early Abbasid Caliphate* pp. 130–131.
23. Theophanes, *Chronicle* 482–483; Tabari 3.709–711.
24. Cobb, *White Banners* pp. 104–105, quoting the Damascene historian al-Asakir.
25. Cobb, *White Banners* pp. 82–88.
26. Ibid. 91.
27. Kennedy, *Early Abbasid Caliphate* pp. 74–75.
28. Cobb, *White Banners* pp. 93–95.

29. Ibid. 56–62.
30. Ibid 63.
31. Ibid 94.
32. Hugh Kennedy, *The Prophet and the Age of the Caliphate* (London, 1986) pp. 155–156.
33. Cobb, *White Banners* pp. 34–36.
34. Ibid. 36; Kennedy, *Prophet* pp. 166–168.
35. Cobb, *White Banners* pp. 116–118.
36. Ibid. 99–101.

Chapter 18

1. Richard W. Bulliet, *Conversion to Islam in the Medieval Period, an Essay in Quantitative History* (Cambridge MA, 1979) ch. 9.
2. Kemal H. Karpat, *Ottoman Population 1830–1914, Demographic and Social Characteristics* (Madison WI, 1985) table I.6, p. 117.
3. Shaban, *Islamic History* 2.109–112; Hitti, *Syria* 2.537–539.
4. Hitti, *Syria* 2.109–112; Hugh Kennedy, *The Prophet and the Age of the Caliphates* (London, 1980) pp. 287–292.
5. Tabari 3.2232–2242.
6. Shaban, *Islamic History* 2.133.
7. Hitti, *Syria* 561–563.
8. Kennedy, *Prophet* pp. 275–277.
9. Theophanes Continuatus, *Chronographia* 176; Stephen Runciman, *The Emperor Romanos Lecapenus and his Reign* (Cambridge, 1929) pp. 141–142.
10. M. Canard, *Histoire de la dynastie des Hamdanides de Jazira et de Syrie* (Paris, 1953).
11. A. A. Vasiliev, *A History of the Byzantine Empire* (Madison WI, 1964 pp. 309–310.
12. Kennedy, *Prophet* pp. 280–281; Runciman, *Romanos* p. 142.
13. Kennedy, *Prophet* pp. 291–292, 327.
14. Ibid. 325–326.
15. Ibid. 323–325.
16. Ibid. 326.
17. Muqadasi 140, in LeStrange 303–306.
18. Hitti, *Syria* 2.555.
19. Muqadasi 162–163 in LeStrange 323–329.
20. Nasr-i-Khusraw 6, in LeStrange 348–350.
21. Muqadasi 174 in LeStrange 442; Kennedy, *Prophet* p. 328; Martin A. Meyer, *History of the City of Gaza* (New York, 1907) p. 78; G. D. Goitein, *A Mediterranean Society* (California, 1967) especially pp. 212–213.
22. Burns, *Damascus* p. 138.
23. Ibn al-Qalanisi 50–51; Hitti, *Syria* 580; Kennedy, *Prophet* pp. 330–331.
24. Kennedy, *Prophet* pp. 331–37.
25. Various accounts of al-Darazi are in Hitti, *Syria* 584, Kennedy, *Prophet* pp. 336–337, and J. J. Saunders, *A History of Medieval Islam* (London, 1972) p. 138.
26. Hitti, *Syria* 581; Kennedy, *Prophet* pp. 339–341.
27. P. K. Hitti, *A History of the Arabs* (London, 1963) p. 622; a more graphic account is in John Bagot Glubb, *The Course of Empire* (London, 1965) p. 216.
28. Vasiliev, *History* 1.355–257; Michael Angold, *The Byzantine Empire 1025–1204* (Harlow, 1997) pp. 44–48; Speros Vryonis, *The Decline of Medieval Hellenism in Asia Minor and the Process on Islamization from the Eleventh through the Fifteenth Century* (California, 1971) pp. 70–113.
29. Hitti, *Syria* 573–575; Steven Runciman, *A History of the Crusades* vol. 1 (Cambridge, 1951) pp. 75–76.
30. Hitti, *Syria* 585–587.
31. Vryonis, *Decline* pp. 108–110; T. R. S. Boase, T. R. S. Boase, *The Cilician Kingdom of Armenia* (1978).

32. Runciman, *Crusades*, 1.265–267; Carole Hillenbrand, *The Crusades, Islamic Perspectives* (Edinburgh, 1999) pp. 43–47.
33. Hillenbrand, *Crusades* p. 33.
34. Runciman, *Crusades*, 1.142–194; Jonathan Harris, *Byzantium and the Crusades* (London, 2003) pp. 53–63.
35. Runciman, *Crusades*, 1.213–249; Glubb, *Course of Empire* pp. 243–263.
36. Runciman, *Crusades*, 1.279–288.
37. Ibid. 292, 305 and 325–326.

Chapter 19

References

The main source for this chapter has been Stephen Runciman, *A History of the Crusades*, 3 vols, (Cambridge, 1951–1954), which is both detailed and well sourced; a more recent account is Malcolm Barber, *The Crusader States*, (New Haven, 2012), but this only covers the first century, to 1193. On the Muslim side, are P. M. Holt, *The Age of the Crusades*, (London, 1986), and Paul M. Cobb, *The Race for Paradise, an Islamic History of the Crusades*, (Oxford, 2014); Carole Hillenbrand, *The Crusades: Islamic Perspectives*, (Edinburgh, 1999) is less a history than a series of essays; also Bernard Lewis, *The Assassins*, (London, 1967). Also for background see *The Oxford History of the Crusades*, (Oxford, 1999, illustrated version 1995), and Kenneth M. Setton (general editor), vol. I, *A History of the Crusades*; Marshal W. Baldwin (ed.), vol II, *The First Hundred Years*, and Robert Lee Wolff and Harry W. Hazard (eds.), *The Later Crusades*, (Wisconsin, 1969). Islamic sources are available in translation in Francesco Gabrieli (ed.), *Arab Historians of the Crusades*, (London, 1969), and Philip K. Hitti (trans.), *An Arab-Syrian Gentleman and Warrior in the period of the Crusades, Memoirs of Usamah ibn-Munqidh*, (Princeton NJ, 1929).

Saladin has been the subject of much study. The most detailed biography is Malcolm Cameron Lyons and D. E. P. Jackson, *Saladin*, (Cambridge, 1982), with Andrew S. Ehrenkreutz, *Saladin*, (Albany NY, 1972) as an alternative, but less detailed, account. The century following the Third Crusade is considered in Runciman's third volume, but has proved less interesting to historians. A brief account linking both sides is P. M. Holt, *The Crusader States and their Neighbours*, (Harlow, 2004). The Ayyubite Kingom after 1193 is studied in Stephen Humphreys, *From Saladin to the Mongols*, and the early Mamluk Sultanate is in Reuven Amitai-Preiss, *Mongols and Mamluks, the Mamluk Ilkhanid War 1260–1281*, (Cambridge, 1995). See also Jonathan Riley-Smith, *The Atlas of the Crusades*, (London, 1990).

1. Runciman, *Crusades* 2.74–80; R. C. Smail, *Crusading Warfare 1097 - 1193* (Cambridge, 1956) pp. 175–177.
2. Runciman, *Crusades* 2.89–90.
3. Anna Comnena, *Alexiad* 319–323, 340–341; *Gesta Francorum* 6–7, 11–12; J. H. and L. L. Hill, 'The Convention of Alexios Comnenos and Raymond of Saint Gilles', *American Historical Review* 58 (1953) pp. 323–327.
4. Runciman, *Crusades* 2.30–34.
5. Ibid 2.40–43; Smail, *Warfare* pp. 177–178.
6. Runciman, *Crusades* 2.43–47.
7. Ibid. 2.66–69.
8. Bernard Lewis, *The Assassins* (London, 1967).
9. Ibid. 105–108; John Francis Wilson, *Caesarea Philippi, Banias, the Lost City of Pan* (London, 2004) pp. 130–135.
10. Smail, *Warfare* pp. 179–180.
11. Runciman, *Crusades*, 2.235 0 237; Cobb, *Paradise* pp. 134–135.
12. Runciman, *Crusades*, 2.280–285.
13. Carole Hillenbrand, *The Crusades: Islamic Perspectives* (Edinburgh, 1999) pp. 108–117; Cobb, *Paradise* pp. 143–145.

14. Adrian J. Boas, *Crusader Archaeology* (London, 1999), ch. 2; the population figures are from Benvenisti, *The Crusaders in the Holy Land* (Jerusalem, 1970), and are always unreliable and inaccurate – guesswork only.
15. Smail, *Warfare* pp. 189–197.
16. James Waterson, *The Knights of Islam* (London, 2007) for recent survey.

Chapter 20
1. Reuven Amitai-Preiss, *Mongols and Mamluks, the Mamluk-Ilkhanid War, 1260–1281* (Cambridge, 1995) pp. 50–53.
2. Ibid. 54.
3. P. M. Holt, *The Age of the Crusades* (London, 1986) pp. 94–95.
4. Amitai-Priess, *Mongols and Mamluks* pp. 111–114.
5. Steven Runciman, *A History of the Crusades* (London) 3.318–319.
6. For a table giving a list of castles, towers, towns, cities, dates of building and destruction see Ronnie Ellenblum, *Crusader Castles and Modern Histories* (Cambridge, 2007) pp. 305–317.
7. Runciman, *Crusades*, 3.321–322.
8. Amitai-Priess, *Mongols and Mamluks* pp. 116–119; Runciman, *Crusades*, 3.322–323.
9. Amitai-Priess, *Mongols and Mamluks* p. 55; Bernard Lewis, *The Assassins* (London, 1967) pp. 121–123.
10. Amitai-Priess, *Mongols and Mamluks* p. 123; Runciman, *Crusades*, 3.324–327.
11. Amitai-Priess, *Mongols and Mamluks* pp. 122–131.
12. Ibid. 133–136.
13. For Aleppo's building history see Yassar Tabbaa, *Constructions of Power and Piety in Medieval Aleppo* (Pennsylvania, 1997).
14. Claude Cahen, *The Formation of Turkey*, (Harlow, 2001) pp. 200–207.
15. Amitai-Priess, *Mongols and Mamluks* pp. 179–183; Holt, *Age of the Crusades* pp. 99–102.
16. Amitai-Priess, *Mongols and Mamluks* pp. 183–185.
17. Ibid. 185–186.
18. Ibid. 186–187.
19. Ibid. 187–201; Runciman, *Crusades*, 3.391–392.
20. Francisco Gabrieli, *Arab Historians of the Crusades* (London, 1969) pp. 334–338 (Tashrif); Runciman, *Crusades*, 3.395.
21. Runciman, *Crusades*, 3.403.
22. Gabrieli, *Arab Historians* pp. 342–343 (Abul-Fida and Maqrizi); the complicated preliminaries to the conquest are discussed in Robert Irwin 'The Mamluk Conquest of the county of Tripoli', republished in Robert Irwin, *Mamluks and Crusaders* (Farnham, 2010) no III.
23. Gabrieli, *Arab Historians* pp. 344–350 (Abu l-Fida and Abu l-Mahasin).
24. Runciman, *Crusades*, 3.421–423.
25. Holt, *Age of the Crusades* p. 108.
26. Ibid. 110–111.
27. P. K. Hitti, *History of Syria* (London, 1951) 2.632–634.
28. Michael W. Dols, *The Black Death in the Middle East* (Princeton NJ, 1979) appendix 1, pp. 305–314; Abraham Marcus, *The Middle East on the Eve of Modernity* (New York, 1989) pp. 256–258; David Ayalon, 'The Plague and its Effects on the Mamluk Army', *Studies on the Mamluks of Egypt* (London, 1977),no. V.
29. Robert Irwin, 'Egypt, Syria and their Trading Partners, 1450–1550', *Mamluks and Crusaders* no IV.
30. Ira M. Lapidus, *Muslim Cities in the Later Middle Ages* 2nd ed. (Cambridge, 1984), ch. 1.
31. Carl F. Petry, *Twilight of Majesty* (Seattle, 1993) pp. 88–109.
32. Robert Irwin, 'Gunpowder and Firearms in the Mamluk Sultanate Reconsidered', *Mamluks and Crusaders*, no XX.
33. Petry, *Twilight* pp. 199–229.
34. Andre Clot, *Suleiman the Magnificent* (London, 2005) pp. 31–33.

35. For Aleppo, see Marcus, *Middle East on the Eve*; for Damascus Karl K. Barbir, *Ottoman Rule in Damascus, 1708–1758* (Princeton NJ, 1990).
36. Hitti, *Syria*, 2.678–696; P. M. Holt, *Egypt and the Fertile Crescent 1516–1922* (London, 1966) pp. 112–123.
37. Abdul-Rahim Abu-Husayn, *Provincial Leaderships in Syria, 1575–1650* (Beirut, 1985).

Chapter 21

References

The major accounts on which this chapter are based include P. M. Holt, *Egypt and the Fertile Crescent, 1516–1922* (London, 1966); Roger Owen, *The Middle East in the World Economy, 1800–1914* (London, 1981); and Charles Issawi, *The Fertile Crescent, 1800–1914* (London, 1988); this last is a documentary collection, but also includes detailed introductions to each section.

1. Nathan Schur, *Napoleon in the Holy Land* (London, 1999).
2. Thomas Philipp, *Acre, the Rise and Fall of a Palestinian City, 1730–1831* (New York, 2001).
3. Several biographies by al-Jabarti show conditions at this time: see Jane Hathaway (ed.) *Al-Jabarti's History of Egypt* (Princeton, 2009) part III; for a French perspective see Ronald T. Ridley, *Napoleon's Proconsul in Egypt, the Life and Times of Bernadino Drovetti* (London (n.d.))
4. Afaf Lutfi al-Sayyid Marsot, *Egypt in the Reign of Muhammad Ali* (Cambridge, 1984).
5. Norman Lewis, *Nomads and Settlers in Syria and Jordan, 1800–1980* (Cambridge, 1984).
6. Leila Rarazi Fawaz, *An Occasion for War, Civil Conflict in Lebanon and Damascus in 1860* (California, 1994); Kamal Salibi, *A House of Many Mansions* (London, 1988); William Harris, *Lebanon, a History 600–2011* (Oxford, 2012).
7. For Palestine see Gudrun Kramer, *A History of Palestine* (Princeton NJ, 2006) ch. 6.
8. For Palestinian transport see Ruth Kark, 'Transportation in Nineteenth Century Palestine: Reintroduction of the Wheel', in Ruth Kark (ed.), *The Land that became Israel, Studies in Historical Geography* (New Haven, 1990) pp. 57–76.
9. Martin A. Meyer, *History of the City of Gaza* (New York, 1907) pp. 107–108.
10. C. Ernest Dawn, *From Ottomanism to Arabism, Essays in the Origins of Arab Nationalism* (Urbana IL, 1973).

Chapter 22

References

The Mandate Period is well covered for Syria and Lebanon by Stephen Longrigg, *Syria and Lebanon under French Mandate* (Oxford, 1958) and Philip S. Khoury, *Syria and the French Mandate* (Princeton, 1987). For Palestine two other books, A. J. Sherman, *Mandate Days, British Lives in Palestine 1918–1948* (London, 1997) and Naomi Shepherd, *Ploughing Sand, British Rule in Palestine 1917–1946* (London, 1999), cover major aspects; for an overview of British policy, rather dated by now, see Elizabeth Monroe, *Britain's Moment in the Middle East, 1914–1956* (London, 1954); for a particular aspect of British policy which had been the subject of conflicting interpretations see Martin Bunton, *Colonial Land Policies in Palestine 1917–1936* (Oxford, 2007).

For the period after 1949 there are numerous books: for Lebanon, Tabitha Petran, *The Struggle over Lebanon* (New York, 1987), and the later chapters of William Harris, *Lebanon in History* (Oxford, 2012). For Syria, Derek Hopwood, *Syria 1945–1986, Politics and Society* (London, 1988); Tabitha Petran, *Syria, a Modern History* (London, 1972) and John McHugo, *Syria from Great War to Civil War* (London, 2014).

1. John D. Grainger, *The Battle for Palestine* (Woodbridge, 2006).
2. John D. Grainger, *The Battle for Syria* (Woodbridge, 2013); the Turkish threat at the end of the fighting is normally ignored in British accounts, but it was all too real.
3. Longrigg, *Syria and Lebanon* pp. 118–120.

4. Elie Kadourie, 'The Capture of Damascus, 1 October 1920', in *The Chatham House Version and other Middle Eastern Studies* 2nd ed. (New England, 1984).

5. The Arab army's campaign is well known from the work of T. E. Lawrence, of course, but it was really only a minor element: T. E. Lawrence, *Revolt in the Desert* (London, 1927), is somewhat less unreliable than *The Seven Pillars of Wisdom* (London, 1935).

6. James E. Gelvin, *Divided Loyalties, Nationalism and Mass Politics in Syria at the Close of Empire* (California, 2005).

7. Discussed by Gudrun Kramer, *A History of Palestine from the Ottoman Conquest to the Founding of the State of Israel* (Princeton NJ, 2008) pp. 165–168.

8. Michael Provence, *The Great Syrian Revolt, and the Rise of Arab Nationalism* (Austin TX, 2005).

9. Philip Mansel, *Levant* (London, 2010) p. 321.

10. Norman Lewis, *Nomads and Settlers in Syria and Jordan 1800–1980* pp. 131–133; Joseph Kostiner, 'Britain and the Northern Frontier of the Saudi State, 1922–1925', in Uriel Dann (ed.), *The Great Powers in the Middle East, 1919–1939* (New York, 1988).

11. John D. Grainger, *Traditional Enemies, Britain's war with Vichy France, 1940–1942* (Barnsley, 2013); the Syrian section is on pages 80–112.

12. William Roger Louis, *The End of the Palestine Mandate* (Austin TX, 1986).

13. Kramer, *History of Palestine* pp. 317–319.

14. Shalom Reichman, 'Partition and Transfer: Crystallization of the Settlement Map of Israel Following the War of Independence, 1948–1950', in Ruth Kark (ed.), *The Land that Became Israel* (Jerusalem, 1990) pp. 320–330, especially the map on page 329.

15. Nikolaos van Dam, *The Struggle for Power in Syria* (London, 1979).

16. Tabitha Petran, *The Struggle over Lebanon* (New York, 1987); Kamil Salibi, *A House of Many Mansions, the History of Lebanon Reconsidered* (London, 2003); Mansel, *Levant*, ch. 17.

17. Meron Benvenisti, *Sacred Landscape, the Buried History of the Holy Land since 1948* (California, 2000).

18. Raphael Lefevre, *Ashes of Hama, the Muslim Brotherhood in Syria* (London, 2013) especially pp. 109–115.

Conclusion

1. Daniel Pipes, *Greater Syria, the History of an Ambition* (New York, 1990); this is also the basis of Philip Hitti's *History of Syria, including Lebanon and Palestine* (Oxford, 1951), and Tabitha Petran, *The Modern History of Syria* (London, 1972), who calls it 'Natural Syria'.

Index